CD-ROM Software,
Dataware, and Hardware

DATABASE SEARCHING SERIES

Edited by Carol Tenopir

CD-ROM SOFTWARE, DATAWARE, AND HARDWARE

Evaluation, Selection, and Installation

Péter Jacsó
University of Hawaii

No. 4 in the Database Searching Series
Carol Tenopir, Series Editor

1992
Libraries Unlimited, Inc.
Englewood, Colorado

Copyright © 1992 Libraries Unlimited, Inc.
All Rights Reserved
Printed in the United States of America

LIBRARIES UNLIMITED, INC.
P.O. Box 3988
Englewood, CO 80155-3988

Library of Congress Cataloging-in-Publication Data

Jacsó, Péter.
    CD-ROM software, dataware, and hardware : evaluation, selection, and installation / Péter Jacsó.
        xv, 256 p. 22x28 cm. -- (Database searching series ; no. 4)
        Includes bibliographical references and index.
        ISBN 0-87287-907-0
        1. Optical disks--Library applications. 2. Libraries--Automation.
    3. CD-ROM. I. Title. II. Series.
    Z681.3.067J33   1991
    025.3'0285--dc20   91-30705
                                                                          CIP

To my wife for the past wonderful 20 years

CONTENTS

ACKNOWLEDGMENTS

This book is the result of a series of classes and workshops I have taught over the past three years at the library schools of Columbia University, Rosary College, and the University of Hawaii and at various conferences. The material is based on research I did at the University of Hawaii.

However, I would not have been able to come to the United States to teach had I not received extensive support for work, research, and regular conference attendances abroad from my managers throughout many years in my native Hungary. I am grateful to three people who had the greatest impact on my career: Matók Gyuri, Rudolf Laci, and Szőnyi Kati.

Many of the faculty members of the School of Library and Information Studies (Wally Grant, Jerry Lundeen, Larry Osborne) and librarians of the Hamilton Library (Martha Chantiny, David Coleman, Ralph Neufang) of the University of Hawaii gave valuable assistance in installing and testing CD-ROM products.

Students in my classes and workshops, too many to list here, provided helpful feedback, views, and opinions. General comments about users' perceptions of certain features of CD-ROM databases are distilled from information gained from hundreds of student assignments and term papers, from class discussions, and from individual conferences with students. I am also grateful to students of Carol Tenopir, who prepared the index for the book in her class on abstracting and indexing. Librarians at the Kailua Public Library are thanked for their valuable and friendly service.

This book could have not been written without the encouragement and extraordinary support of Carol Tenopir. My academic advisor in a research project related to CD-ROM, Tenopir reviewed and commented on much of this work and other publications of mine. She has been as professional, collegial, and demanding in her capacity as editor as she is in her teaching and writing. I am, however, solely responsible for any errors that may remain, and the opinions and views expressed are mine.

Finally, the ultimate thanks go to my wife, Tiszai Judit (a.k.a. Csucsusa), who has made this and many other projects not only possible but also worthwhile. She produced many of the analyses and illustrations in this book, acting very much as a coauthor. She has been a companion, and a wonderful one at that. This book is dedicated to her for having been the source of so much joy and inspiration over the past 20 years.

INTRODUCTION

Compact-Disk — Read-Only-Memory (CD-ROM) technology and applications have come of age in the early 1990s. The question nowadays is not whether or when to utilize CD-ROM products, but which ones to buy. In a fairly rare move, database producers made libraries a primary target market for a new computer product. Librarians embraced the new information distribution medium with great enthusiasm, fostering and evangelizing its use. Computer magazines and computer professionals discussed CD-ROM technology less than library journals and librarians.

Given the nearly 600 megabyte capacity of compact disks (CDs) to store the equivalent of more than 200,000 pages or 1 million catalog cards and the ability of CDs to provide access to that much information in a versatile way at a relatively low cost, it is understandable that CD-ROM products were love at first sight.

THE CASE FOR EVALUATION

The honeymoon period, however, is over. Practicing and potential users of CD-ROM products should take a closer look at what they are buying or licensing. An ever-increasing number of CD-ROM products are available, irrespective of the type of information needed. Even those who have one or more CD-ROM databases already may reconsider their choices, because CD-ROM use-agreements usually are not of the "till-death-do-us-part" nature but rather are short-term commitments in the form of subscriptions.

Moreover, switching from one CD-ROM abstracting/indexing (A/I) database subscription to another does not have the same negative consequence as switching printed A/I journal subscriptions. If a subscriber had the printed form of *Library and Information Science Abstracts* (*LISA*) from 1986 and then switched to *Library Literature* (*LIBLIT*) in 1989, subscriber and patrons would have to become familiar with two tools. In the CD-ROM versions of most A/I publications there is significant retrospective coverage, typically five to ten years, even for a new subscriber.

The evaluation, comparison, and selection of CD-ROM databases will become increasingly important with the growing number of publications available on CD-ROM. Informed choosing applies both to the initial decision to acquire such a publication and to the subsequent decision to renew or replace. Having used, seen, and heard about dozens of other CD-ROM databases, librarians will develop their own wish lists of features that they would like to see available in CD-ROM databases.

EVALUATION METHODOLOGY AND CRITERIA

This book is an attempt to systematically review the most characteristic features of CD-ROM databases and the computer facilities required to use them. It is meant to help the librarian in the evaluation, comparison, selection, installation, and operation of CD-ROM products. It does not directly discuss the pros and cons of CD-ROM applications or their underlying technology.

Most CD-ROM databases represent a different incarnation of long-existing printed, microfiche, microfilm, and online publications. Making the information available in a new medium usually does not improve the content of the publication; its scope, coverage, authenticity, comprehensiveness; or the quality of the data. Therefore, many criteria used to evaluate traditional forms of publications apply to CD-ROM databases.

However, the software components of CD-ROM databases not only make the data more accessible but also help you in exploring the overall quality of the databases and in checking and verifying the completeness, accuracy, consistency, and currency of information.

While this applies also to online databases, in the CD-ROM environment, you, the users, are not under the pressure of online connect time and other usage charges. Nor is the free testing period as restricted as with the online databases, where you are limited to 30 or 60 minutes of free sampling and testing, if that much, and only when the database is introduced. Many CD-ROM publishers make their products available for a 30- to 60-day test period without charge. With CD-ROM, you have many more opportunities to explore databases.

You may not have the time, resources, or interest to evaluate a database by all the criteria discussed in this book. However, these criteria will be helpful in creating questions to ask of database publishers, practicing users, or hardware manufacturers or in suggesting what to look for in product reviews. As a user, you do not have to apply all the tests in this book to select the product most appropriate for you. Consulting sources to find answers can often be an equally good substitute.

In addition, not all of the criteria discussed here may be relevant to you. Some of them apply, for example, only to bibliographic databases; others, only to directories. In these cases the discussion is presented accordingly. The importance of many criteria depends on the environment in which the CD-ROM product will be used, i.e., whether the end-users are professional librarians, library patrons, grade-school students, majors in a discipline, the general public, or researchers.

The vehicle for the evaluation is a score sheet, similar to those illustrated in appendixes 1, 2, 3, 4, and 5 at the end of this book. You will customize the score sheet first by adding your own criteria and deleting those without relevance. Then you will assign a weight to each of the criteria on a scale of 1 to 10 to indicate how important a criterion is for you. As you proceed with the evaluation you will assign a grade (again, on a scale of 1 to 10) to indicate how satisfied you are with that criterion. The product of the weight and the grade gives the score, and the total of the scores will provide a quantitative measure that you may use to compare alternatives. These score sheets may be useful as a checklist even if you evaluate only a single product.

EVALUATION EXAMPLES

The evaluation criteria and methods are explained and illustrated throughout the book. CD-ROM databases (software and dataware) most often used for illustrations and examples are those whose subjects and contents are familiar to most librarians or that are widely used. Various indexes of general interest periodicals; abstracting/indexing journals of library and information science; and directories of serials, books, and library professionals are the most often used examples. The software packages most often used for examples come from H. W. Wilson Company, SilverPlatter, Dialog, University Microfilm International, Knowledge Access, OCLC, Online Computer Systems, Inc., and EBSCO. Titles of packages and databases have been telescoped according to popular usage. For example, Grolier Electronic Encyclopedia is referred to as Grolier Encyclopedia and Compton's Multi-Media Encyclopedia as Compton's Encyclopedia.

The emphasis is on bibliographic, abstracting/indexing, and directory/referral databases. While the first category of databases is purely textual, the last two include both textual and numeric data. Full-text databases and multimedia products that include text, graphics, audio, animation, or full-motion video are occasionally mentioned. Purely numeric, audio, or image databases are not discussed. Examples of comparisons and evaluations should be considered as such and not as an endorsement of any product.

A CAVEAT

The features of CD-ROM databases keep changing and improving. The version you use may have new options and/or may have corrected errors, failings, or shortcomings reported here, and prices may have fallen or increased. CD-ROM products change extremely quickly. What is true about a product today may not be completely valid tomorrow.

It would have been a disservice to readers if only hypothetical or unidentified examples were used, so real products are evaluated throughout. A CD-ROM publisher may have solved some problems and improved the product in the meantime, so the user should keep this in mind when reading evaluations presented here. In your evaluation you will examine the most current version of each database.

1

CD-ROM PRODUCTS AND PRODUCERS

CD-ROM databases are the result of a series of complex technical and intellectual processes. The technicalities may not be of interest to those of you who evaluate and select CD-ROM databases, but you should be familiar with the intellectual and technical components of a product to fully understand the possible alternatives.

Many different organizations are involved in the CD-ROM industry. You may come into contact with only one of them, possibly a company that publishes the CD-ROM database and sells you a complete CD-ROM application package. The package may include the CD-ROM database, the CD-ROM drive, and the personal computer hardware and systems software needed to use the database. Or the company may be an independent dealer who offers you a lock, stock, and barrel option. This approach, like packaged tours, may be very convenient, but is not necessarily cost effective. If you are familiar with the components and requirements of CD-ROM applications, you may make much better choices by selecting the ones most appropriate to you.

The distinction between the hardware and the database components is obvious. To use a CD-ROM database, you need a CD-ROM reader. There are different generations of CD-ROM drives with differing speeds, sizes, and levels of convenience. More than a dozen companies manufacture CD-ROM drives.

It may be less obvious that the CD-ROM databases themselves have two components: the software and the data component. These are inseparably bundled in the CD-ROM databases offered for purchase or license. Despite the integration of software and data, the distinction is important for two reasons.

First, even now several databases are offered that have the same data component but a different software component. The bibliographic datafile produced by the Public Affairs Information Service, Inc. (PAIS), is available in two different packages, one with the software produced by Online Computer Systems, Inc. (OCSI) and another with the software produced by SilverPlatter, Inc. (SPIRS). The datafiles of the Educational Resources Information Center (ERIC), the Library of Congress (LC-MARC), the National Library of Medicine (MEDLINE), the National Agriculture Library (AGRICOLA), and the Government Printing Office (GPO) are available on CD-ROM with three to eight different software programs. In these databases, however, the data components differ slightly in the time period coverage, document type coverage, and access points.

Second, it is very likely that in the near future the alternative will exist to make just the data available on CD-ROM, allowing users to choose whichever CD-ROM retrieval software they prefer. This means that the data on CD-ROM will be software independent. Other CD-ROM standards have been accepted very successfully, so this standard will probably be adopted by all the major database publishers. The draft of the standard, known as the CD-ROM Read-Only Data Exchange (CD-RDx), has been distributed for adoption to U.S. government agencies, and many independent datafile producers and software developers are already studying the implementation issues.[1,2]

Knowing the strengths and the weaknesses of the software and data components helps you to choose the most appropriate software and the most appropriate data for the information needs of your library. To fully explore alternatives, you need to understand the process behind the scenes; learn who the protagonists are in the CD-ROM industry and familiarize yourself with the terminology. Apart from the manufacturers of CD-ROM readers and the independent distributors and value-added resellers of CD-ROM products (who will be described in chapter 7), the following must be distinguished:

1. datafiles and their producers

2. software packages and their producers

3. CD-ROM databases and their publishers

DATAFILES AND THEIR PRODUCERS

Datafiles originate from a source (the file producer or information provider) that selects, collects, organizes, and records information about books, articles, companies, people, products, and so on. The file producer arranges the data in some structure and usually adds information to enhance the value of the data gathered.

The datafile may be purely textual (such as bibliographic datafiles), textual-numeric (such as a product directory), or purely numeric (such as census files). It may include graphics, still and moving images, and sound, with or without text (such as encyclopedic datafiles). The datafile may be a collection of the original documents (such as full-text files).

A datafile may be produced jointly by two or more organizations. CANCERLIT is produced by the National Institute of Health, the National Cancer Institute, and the International Cancer Research Data Bank; AGRICOLA is produced by the U.S. Department of Agriculture and the National Agricultural Library.

To facilitate the further processing of a datafile, it is saved in some computer-readable format, for example, on disk or tape. This file may be processed by the producer or an independent company to print a directory, an abstracting/indexing journal, or a book. Additionally or alternatively, it may be used to create a database on magnetic disk or on CD-ROM.

Some datafile producers may publish the database themselves; others may make arrangements with independent companies to license the datafile, and they in turn create the database and:

1. make it available on a large computer that may be accessed from terminals in online mode. Access may be limited to terminals within an organization or may be available from anywhere in the world through telecommunication networks.

2. publish and distribute it on CD-ROM, which is then made available locally from one or more personal computers.

In either case, a set of special programs is used to create the database (database creation software) and to retrieve information from the database by searching it and displaying the results (retrieval software).

CD-ROM SOFTWARE PACKAGES
AND THEIR PRODUCERS

Making a database from a datafile requires a set of programs to restructure the data elements, to create various indexes, and occasionally to select parts of the datafile by some criteria. After processing, the datafile becomes software dependent. To emphasize the dependence of the data on the software, in this book it will be called *dataware* whenever this distinction is necessary. Dataware created by one software program cannot be used (i.e., searched) by another software program.

Those who search the database do not have to know about the dataware creation software. Still, it has an important impact on how one may use the database. The dataware creation software determines which data elements are searchable, how the indexes are created, how the data is segmented, how much space is needed for the database, whether a large database requires one or more disks, and so on. The retrieval software and the dataware creation software together determine what and how you can search and display and how long these operations take (i.e., what is the response time to a query).

A database is the integration of the (retrieval) software and the dataware. This is obvious in the online world, where the software packages of DIALOG, BRS, or DATASTAR serve to users the various databases, such as Magazine Index, Dissertation Abstracts, Sociological Abstracts, Compendex, or Books in Print.

In the CD-ROM world this integration of software and dataware may not be so obvious. A library may have the CD-ROM versions of Magazine Index, Dissertation Abstracts, Sociological Abstracts, Compendex, and Books in Print, which implicitly means that Infotrac, ProQuest, SPIRS, OnDisc, and Bowker-CD software packages are being used. The exceptions are multi-publisher databases.

If you want the CD-ROM version of INSPEC you have no choice, as it comes only in one version on CD-ROM that uses the ProQuest software of University Microfilm International. If you want to create a database from the INSPEC datafile you may subscribe to it on magnetic tape and use a software package such as STAIRS, DOBIS-LIBIS, NOTIS, or the Micro-CDS/ISIS software to set up a database. You may not, however, subscribe to the INSPEC datafile on CD-ROM by itself. Only the INSPEC database is available, as defined by the ProQuest software.

If you want the CD-ROM version of the ERIC datafile, you have three choices (OCLC, SilverPlatter, and Dialog publish databases from the ERIC datafile), but you cannot have it with, for example, the ProQuest software. Neither the CD-ROM dataware nor the software is yet available separately.

The term *CD-ROM software* in this book refers to the retrieval software unless otherwise indicated. It is also often called search software, retrieval engine, or search engine in various publications.

Another category of CD-ROM software is the so-called systems software, which is independent of the individual applications but without which you cannot use most CD-ROM products. This is the CD-ROM Extension (MSCDEX) software, and it is discussed in chapter 6. Another type of systems software that you may need to be aware of is CD-ROM network software, which allows two or more personal computers to use the same CD-ROM database. This also is discussed in chapter 6.

The software may be produced by the same company that is the file producer, by the publisher of the database, or by an independent company (a third party). Some CD-ROM software producers (also known as software developers) work behind the scenes and grant license for the use of their program to one or more CD-ROM publishers. Digital Library Systems is such a company. Its superb software is used with the Disclosure dataware and with all the CD-ROM products published by Dialog. Another such company is Fulcrum, whose software is used in databases published by EBSCO. Starting in 1992 UMI will use Fulcrum's software with all its databases.

Others are much more prominently involved in the CD-ROM business. Online Computer Systems, Inc. (OCSI), for example, not only developed and adapted the software for PAIS, for all the Bowker products, and for the Grolier Encyclopedia, but also keeps a high profile in CD-ROM hardware and network software development.

Most software producers focus on IBM and compatible personal computers. Some companies develop software for use on the Macintosh (Aries Systems of Knowledge Finder, for example), but only a few producers develop software for both. SilverPlatter is one of the few that produce both Macintosh and PC versions of the software: MacSPIRS and SPIRS, respectively.

Sometimes the software does not have its own name, or the name is not widely used in any documentation. In such situations we use the name of the dataware or the name of the publisher hyphenated with the letters *CD*, i.e., Compton-CD or EBSCO-CD software. The same applies when a software package is used with databases of different publishers and the software has no readily recognized name: we call such software Bowker-CD or Grolier-CD. If a datafile is published with more than one software package, a qualifier is used when necessary, such as OCS-PAIS or SPIRS-PAIS. This is the shorthand equivalent of the longer description, such as the SilverPlatter version of PAIS or the version of PAIS that uses the software developed by OCSI. It is possible that the same software has its own name when used with databases of one publisher, but not with the other. An example is the software produced by Digital Library Systems that is used by both Dialog and Disclosure, Inc. We use Dialog OnDisc and Disclosure-CD in such a situation.

DATABASE PUBLISHERS

Those who integrate dataware and software and provide user documentation and user support are the database publishers. The database publisher may be the file producer and also the software producer; it is also common that the database publisher, the file producer, and the software producer are three different organizations. (See figure 1.1.) Sometimes the database publisher is also the software producer but not the file producer. Some variations are illustrated by figure 1.2 and explained below.

The National Library of Medicine is the producer of the MEDLINE datafile. MEDLINE is licensed—among many others—by Dialog, SilverPlatter, and EBSCO. SilverPlatter is the producer of the SPIRS software and is the publisher of the SPIRS-MEDLINE database; it does not produce any datafile itself. EBSCO is just the publisher of this database, as both the datafile and the software (Fulcrum Technology's FulText) are licensed. On the other hand, EBSCO is the file producer and database publisher of Magazine Article Summaries and The Serials Directory. Dialog is merely a database publisher, as it does not produce but licenses the datafiles and the software. This same software is licensed by Disclosure, Inc., which is the datafile producer and database publisher of Compact Disclosure.

The H. W. Wilson Company is the producer of the Wilsondisc CD-ROM software, the publisher of 18 CD-ROM databases, and the producer of 16 CD-ROM datafiles. The datafiles of two databases published by H. W. Wilson—the MLA International Bibliography and the Religion Indexes—are produced by the Modern Language Association of America and the American Theological Library Association, respectively.

Neither the software nor the datafile licensed by a publisher is necessarily exclusive. As mentioned earlier, the software produced by Digital Library Systems is used not only with the databases published by Dialog, but also with those whose publisher is Disclosure. Similarly, the CD-ROM software of OCSI is used with the PAIS database whose datafile is produced by Public

Dataware producer	Software producer	Search software	Publisher	Database
Am. Theological Libr. Assoc.	H.W. Wilson	Wilsondisc	H.W. Wilson	Religion Index
H.W. Wilson	H.W. Wilson	Wilsondisc	H.W Wilson	Education Index
Disclosure Inc.	Digital Library System	Compact Disclosure	Disclosure Inc.	Compact Disclosure
USDE	Digital Library System	OnDisc	Dialog	ERIC
USDE	SilverPlatter	SPIRS	SilverPlatter	ERIC
USDE	OCLC	CD450	OCLC	ERIC
LC	OCLC	CD450	OCLC	Education Library
Grolier	Online Computer Systems, Inc.	no name	Grolier	Electronic Encyclopedia
Bowker	Online Computer Systems, Inc.	Bowker Plus	Bowker	Books in Print Plus
Public Affairs Inf. Service	Online Computer Systems, Inc.	no name	Public Affairs Inf. Service	PAIS
Public Affairs Inf. Service	SPIRS	SPIRS	SilverPlatter	PAIS
EBSCO	Fulcrum Technology	Ful/Text	EBSCO	Serials Directory
NLM	Fulcrum Technology	Ful/Text	EBSCO	MEDLINE

Fig. 1.1. Contributors to databases.

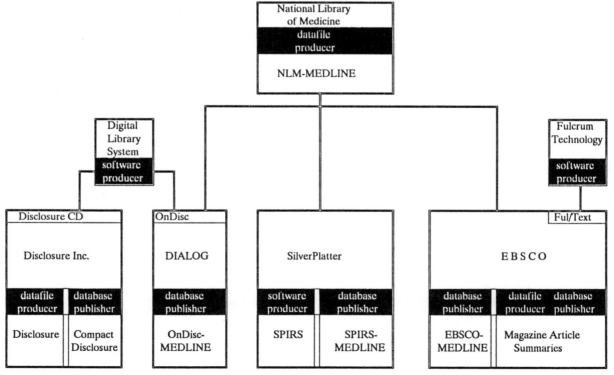

Fig. 1.2. Datafile producers, software producers, database publishers.

Public Affairs Information Service, Inc., and also with all of the datafiles produced by Bowker, including Books in Print Plus, SciTech Reference Plus, Ulrich's Plus, and Variety Video Directory Plus databases.

Datafile licenses typically are granted to a single database publisher, unless the datafile producer decides to publish the datafile itself. For example, Sociofile is SilverPlatter; Library Literature is Wilson. Proprietary datafiles are usually published in a single version, with one software. A unique exception is the PAIS datafile, which has been available with the software of OCSI for several years and (since April 1991) is published simultaneously with the SPIRS software.

The exceptions to exclusivity are datafiles in the public domain, such as those of the Library of Congress, the Government Printing Office, the National Technical Information Services, the Educational Resources Information Center, or the National Library of Medicine. These are published by several database publishers and are called multi-publisher databases.

For example, several versions of ERIC are available, such as SPIRS-ERIC, CD450-ERIC, or OnDisc-ERIC. In multi-publisher databases, the dataware component can be different not only in terms of the structuring of the data, but also in content. The ERIC or NTIS dataware is also different content-wise in the OCLC, SilverPlatter, and DIALOG versions of the database. On the other hand, the same datafile is available in SPIRS-PAIS and OCSI-PAIS.

Sometimes many database publishers use the same datafile, but one or two make modifications that significantly affect the quality of the dataware. Both MARCIVE and Auto-graphics clean up the GPO datafile, while six other publishers use it as received. Further examples are mentioned whenever relevant in chapter 3.

The dataware component of multi-publisher databases may differ significantly in terms of retrospectivity, source coverage, and language coverage. In some cases the database publisher may decide to publish two versions of the same datafile. This is the case with the MEDLINE datafile as published by EBSCO and DIALOG. Both publishers have a full database and a subset database from the MEDLINE datafile. Figure 1.3 shows the features of some of the MEDLINE dataware, not considering the software differences.

Publisher	Database	From	Complete set	Clinical journals only	Core journals only	English journals only	IBM	Mac
Aries	KnowledgeFinder MEDLINE	10 years back	Y					Y
BRS	Colleague MEDLINE	1976				Y	Y	
CD Plus	CD Plus Medline	1966	Y				Y	
CSA	Cambridge MEDLINE	1976	Y				Y	
DIALOG	OnDisc MEDLINE	1984	Y				Y	
	MEDLINE Clinical Collection	1984		Y			Y	
Digital Diagnostics	Bibliomed	1985			Y	Y	Y	
EBSCO	Core MEDLINE	3 years back					Y	
	Comprehensive MEDLINE	1966	Y				Y	
SilverPlatter	SPIRS MEDLINE	1966	Y				Y	
	MacSPIRS MEDLINE	1966	Y					Y

Fig. 1.3. Some MEDLINE dataware.

The database publisher may decide to selectively process the datafile, but this is the exception and has relevance (at least for comparison purposes) only in the case of multi-publisher databases. You may regret that the PsycLIT database does not include conference proceedings, which are available in the original datafile, but you do not have a choice as it is exclusively available on CD-ROM from SilverPlatter.

Uncommon as it may be yet, it may happen that a database publisher (who is also the datafile producer) changes to another software and re-publishes the database. Grolier started with the KnowledgeSet software, then two years later changed to the OCSI software. Gale Research, Inc., introduced its Encyclopedia of Associations database with the KAware software of Knowledge Access International in 1988, but then let SilverPlatter publish it exclusively with the SPIRS software beginning in 1991. Information Sources, Inc. took the opposite course of action with its software CD product. They started out with the SPIRS software and changed to the KAware software in 1991.

Publishers may also drop databases with little or no notice. H. W. Wilson dropped the GPO dataware in 1990; Microsoft introduced Bookshelf with much fanfare in 1987 and did not update it for at least four years. By 1991 its 1987 World Almanac and Book of Facts is a tad outdated, but because it is often bundled for free with CD-ROM players, it managed to remain on the best-seller list even though the far less touted Reference Library database incorporates more current editions of similar reference publications at a better list price (figure 1.4).

REFERENCE LIBRARY	MICROSOFT BOOKSHELF
Webster's Thesaurus	Roget's II Electronic Thesaurus
Webster's New World Dictionary of Quotable Definitions	Bartlett's Familiar Quotations
Webster's New World Dictionary	American Heritage Dictionary
Dictionary of 20th Century History	-
Guide to Concise Writing	Houghton Mifflin Usage Alert
National Directory of Addresses and Phone Numbers	US Zip Code Directory
Legal and Corporate Forms for the Smaller Business	Forms and Letters
-	Business information Sources
-	Chicago Manual of Style
-	Houghton Mifflin Spelling Verifier

Fig. 1.4. Reference Library versus Bookshelf.

REFERENCES

1. Neil Shapiro and Elias Diamantopolis. "CD-ROM Disc Interchangeability: Beyond ISO 9660." *DISC Magazine* premier issue (Fall 1990): 40-43.

2. Linda Helgerson. "Universal Operability: The Technical Solution." *DISC Magazine* premier issue (Fall 1990): 36-39.

2

CD-ROM SOFTWARE EVALUATION

The evaluation of the software component of a CD-ROM database includes assessment of the user interface, the basic and advanced search facilities, the capabilities of the system to manage the temporary and long-term storage of queries and query results, and the output facilities available.

The software evaluation criteria apply to most of the databases, though to differing extents. Features like positional and proximity operations are essential in lengthy records of full-text databases and to a lesser extent in large abstracting databases, but are dispensable in indexing databases that add nothing but one or two index terms to the bibliographic citation. Some software criteria are of interest only to the experienced searcher, not to the casual user of the database who would not care to learn the use of advanced features even if they are available.

You have to differentiate in the evaluation between search features that make retrieval quick and easy for the novice and those that allow the librarian or the expert user to make precise searches and produce high quality output. Those who want to find and print a few citations approach the database with different expectations than those who have to compile comprehensive bibliographies. The weighting of the criteria helps to make this distinction.

Software should always be evaluated with a view to the database it will be used with. Actually, the dataware component has priority: you choose an information source primarily by its subject content, but you do not ignore how easily you can find the information, and that depends mostly on the software. To put it very simply, the dataware evaluation tells what you can find and the software evaluation tells how you can find and present the information in the database. The software and the dataware, however, are integrated, and their chemistry may make a database good or bad. The software and the dataware must be considered together.

Software features are discussed first because many of the techniques used to analyze the database and explore its content and quality require familiarity with the facilities of the software. The availability of software makes many of the traditional evaluation steps easy and offers new evaluation possibilities. You always have been expected to check the currency of the abstract/indexing service (the time gap between the publication date of the original document and the availability of its abstracting/indexing record) or whether the mandatory data elements are consistently present in the records. This required tedious samplings and calculations, and your samples may not have been representative. In many CD-ROM databases such analyses are very easy to do, and even if they take time it is not your time, but that of the computer.

The software part of a database consists of several components. When the software is written it is usually broken down into modules by major functions. This is done mostly to split the jobs of designing, writing, testing, and maintaining the software among developers. This functional split may be transparent to a searcher, but it comes in handy when evaluating the software. The major modules of the software include the following:

1. interface functions
2. search functions
3. set and query management functions
4. output functions

INTERFACES

The user interface is that part of the CD-ROM software through which users give their instructions to the system and the system displays results, messages, and explanations. Much research has been done about the human factors of information retrieval and human-machine communications in general. Apart from the thousands of articles and conference papers on the subject, an excellent series of monographs on human/computer interaction is published by Ablex Publishing Corporation. Two volumes may be of particular interest for those who would like to learn more about user interfaces.[1,2] Though these books are meant primarily for developers and are not related to CD-ROM applications, the principles discussed can be used as criteria in evaluating the user interface of CD-ROM databases.

The evaluation of the interface is probably the most subjective part of the CD-ROM software evaluation process because much depends on look and feel, individual preferences, and similar non-tangible issues. Also, much depends on the previous experience of the user. For example, those who used the LEXIS and NEXIS online services will easily learn the ProQuest software, which uses a similar interface and command language.

Regarding the search and output capabilities of a software package, most of the evaluation criteria may be answered by yes or no or by specifying a number, such as whether field-specific index browsing is available or how many terms may be used in a query. Questions related to the interface require descriptive answers and are often matters of taste. The following criteria can be used for the comparison of user interfaces:

- types of interface
- levels of interface
- styles of interface
- help and tutorial facilities
- ease of use
- ergonomic issues

Types of Interface

The user may give instructions either by entering the appropriate command with correct syntax, by selecting an option or a series of options from a menu, or by filling out a form. These are known as command-driven, menu-driven, and template-driven interfaces (respectively) and are illustrated in figures 2.1, below, and 2.2-2.3, page 10. *Template-driven interface* is not a widely used term; this style is sometimes referred to as form fill-in. Many consider it a variation or part of the menu-driven interface. (The use of function keys and icons to represent commands has to do with the style of the interface.)

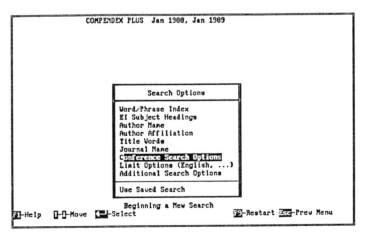

Fig. 2.1. Menu-driven interface.

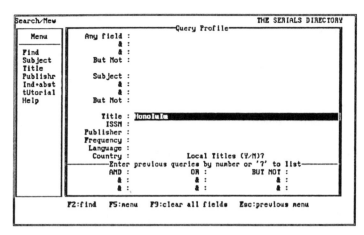

Fig. 2.2. Template-driven interface.

Fig. 2.3. Command-driven interface.

Just as it is easier for most tourists abroad to recognize the name of a food or a drink and point to it on a menu than it is to correctly recall and pronounce the name of a food in another language, it is easier for casual users of a CD-ROM system to choose options from menus than to remember the exact details and punctuation of commands.

The menu-driven system guides the user through the paths of selecting and searching terms and displays results, but it may be too slow for routine activities. This is the same problem faced by users of automatic teller machines (ATMs). First-time and infrequent users appreciate the step-wise approach, but being prompted and coached at every step of a withdrawal transaction may slow down and annoy other users. You will, however, appreciate the menu-driven mode again when doing a transaction new to you. Similarly, the menu approach may make you impatient when you perform simple subject searches, but you will appreciate the prompting again when you do something more complex, such as a date limitation, and you are advised that the date format is dd-mm-yy.

Templates (fill-in forms) also provide guidance for users and save them the inconvenience of having to recall what data elements with which prefix (tag) can be searched. Template-driven systems present the criteria by which the database may be searched, and you fill in the form with a request by entering terms in the appropriate blanks, or cells.

As with most of the other features, the best solution is when the system allows you to choose the approach you prefer in a given situation. Not only do different users have different preferences, but also the same user may wish to use the command-driven mode for quick subject searches and the menu-driven mode for more complex searches. When language codes, country codes, document-type abbreviations, or field identifiers may be needed, selecting the appropriate codes from a list is much easier than looking them up in printed documentation. If you do not know whether PY (publication year), YP (year of publication), or PD (publication date) is the correct field identifier for publication data or whether the value is entered in the form of yyyy, yyyymm, yy, yymm, yy-mm, mm-yy, or one of a dozen other possible formats (where y stands for the year and m for the month), you certainly appreciate the menu-driven approach of Bluefish as illustrated in figure 2.4.

Only a few CD-ROM software packages offer more than one type of interfaces. Dialog OnDisc, Compact Cambridge, and Wilsondisc are among the few that feature multiple interfaces. But whereas OnDisc offers identical features in menu and command modes and Compact Cambridge provides nearly identical facilities, in Wilsondisc the menu- and template-driven modes are much more limited than the command mode (Wilsonline). For example, you may use compound terms in "OR" relationship, limit a search to a given time period, or define a print format only in the command mode.

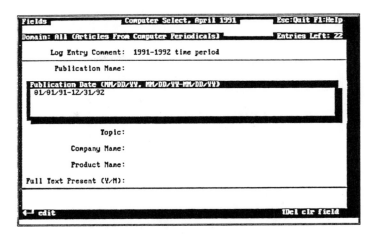

Fig. 2.4. Prompt for number format in Bluefish.

Levels of Interface

Some CD-ROM systems compensate for the lack of the two types of interfaces by offering different levels of menu-driven interfaces. The OCSI and EBSCO software offer novice and expert modes that differ in the extent of prompting, hand-holding, searchability, and functionality.

Menu systems differ significantly among CD-ROM products. Some packages provide menus throughout the complete process, as in the Dialog OnDisc databases. Others provide menus only at the very beginning, then "abandon" the user for the rest of the search, and provide menus again when printing/displaying the results. The latter approach is used by SilverPlatter and UMI. The difference is demonstrated in figures 2.5 and 2.6, pages 12 and 13, which show a search for abstracted articles published in English-language clinical journals about toxoplasmosis in humans.

OnDisc provides an option list for each step. In SPIRS you are left on your own at the very beginning, and though you could invoke some help in the process, it is far less convenient than the automatic prompting by OnDisc. Furthermore, in SPIRS you cannot limit the search to clinical journals.

To display or print an item in bibliographic citation format, OnDisc presents a list of options, but in SPIRS you have to know the code name "citn" for this format, as illustrated by figures 2.7 and 2.8, pages 14 and 15. There are many other differences which will be discussed in this chapter. Most of them can be traced back to the lack of some retrieval features, but many are due to different approaches as how to give an instruction to the software, i.e., by selecting from an option list or by typing the command with its parameters.

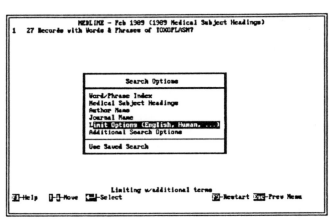

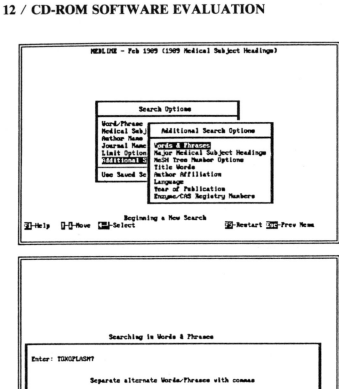

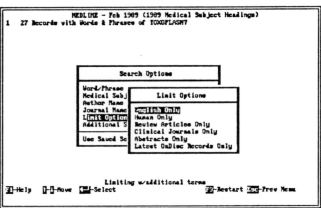

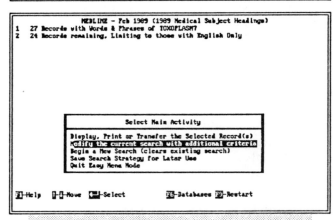

[similar limit screens - not shown here]

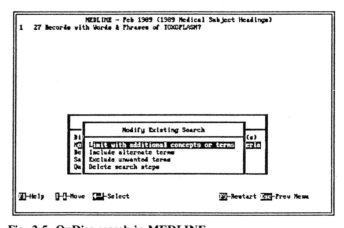

Fig. 2.5. OnDisc search in MEDLINE.

```
┌──────────────────────────────────────────────────────┐
│ SilverPlatter 1.6      MEDLINE (R) (1/91 - 2/91)    Esc=Commands F1=Help │
│                                                        │
│  No.    Records      Request                           │
│                                                        │
│                                                        │
│                                                        │
│                                                        │
│ Find:  Toxoplasm*                                      │
└──────────────────────────────────────────────────────┘
```

```
┌──────────────────────────────────────────────────────┐
│ SilverPlatter 1.6      MEDLINE (R) (1/91 - 2/91)    Esc=Commands F1=Help │
│                                                        │
│  No.    Records      Request                           │
│  #1:         75      TOXOPLASM*                         │
│                                                        │
│                                                        │
│ Find:                                                  │
└──────────────────────────────────────────────────────┘
```

```
┌──────────────────────────────────────────────────────┐
│ SilverPlatter 1.6      MEDLINE (R) (1/91 - 2/91)    Esc=Commands F1=Help │
│                                                        │
│  No.    Records      Request                           │
│  #1:         75      TOXOPLASM*                         │
│                                                        │
│ Find:  and la=english                                  │
└──────────────────────────────────────────────────────┘
```

```
┌──────────────────────────────────────────────────────┐
│ SilverPlatter 1.6      MEDLINE (R) (1/91 - 2/91)    Esc=Commands F1=Help │
│                                                        │
│  No.    Records      Request                           │
│  #1:         75      TOXOPLASM*                         │
│  #2:      41902      LA=ENGLISH                         │
│  #3:         54      #1 AND LA=ENGLISH                  │
│                                                        │
│ Find:                                                  │
└──────────────────────────────────────────────────────┘
```

```
┌──────────────────────────────────────────────────────┐
│ SilverPlatter 1.6      MEDLINE (R) (1/91 - 2/91)    Esc=Commands F1=Help │
│                                                        │
│  No.    Records      Request                           │
│  #1:         75      TOXOPLASM*                         │
│  #2:      41902      LA=ENGLISH                         │
│  #3:         54      #1 AND LA=ENGLISH                  │
│                                                        │
│ Find:  and human in mesh                               │
└──────────────────────────────────────────────────────┘
```

```
┌──────────────────────────────────────────────────────┐
│ SilverPlatter 1.6      MEDLINE (R) (1/91 - 2/91)    Esc=Commands F1=Help │
│                                                        │
│  No.    Records      Request                           │
│  #1:         75      TOXOPLASM*                         │
│  #2:      41902      LA=ENGLISH                         │
│  #3:         54      #1 AND LA=ENGLISH                  │
│  #4:      38949      HUMAN                              │
│  #5:         41      #3 and (HUMAN in MESH)             │
│ Find:                                                  │
└──────────────────────────────────────────────────────┘
```

```
┌──────────────────────────────────────────────────────┐
│ SilverPlatter 1.6      MEDLINE (R) (1/91 - 2/91)    Esc=Commands F1=Help │
│                                                        │
│  No.    Records      Request                           │
│  #1:         75      TOXOPLASM*                         │
│  #2:      41902      LA=ENGLISH                         │
│  #3:         54      #1 AND LA=ENGLISH                  │
│  #4:      38949      HUMAN                              │
│  #5:         41      #3 and (HUMAN in MESH)             │
│ Find:  and case report in mesh                         │
└──────────────────────────────────────────────────────┘
```

```
┌──────────────────────────────────────────────────────┐
│ SilverPlatter 1.6      MEDLINE (R) (1/91 - 2/91)    Esc=Commands F1=Help │
│                                                        │
│  No.    Records      Request                           │
│  #1:         75      TOXOPLASM*                         │
│  #2:      41902      LA=ENGLISH                         │
│  #3:         54      #1 AND LA=ENGLISH                  │
│  #4:      38949      HUMAN                              │
│  #5:         41      #3 and (HUMAN in MESH)             │
│  #6:       7530      CASE                               │
│  #7:       7542      REPORT                             │
│  #8:         10      #5 and (CASE REPORT in MESH)       │
│ Find:                                                  │
└──────────────────────────────────────────────────────┘
```

```
┌──────────────────────────────────────────────────────┐
│ SilverPlatter 1.6      MEDLINE (R) (1/91 - 2/91)    Esc=Commands F1=Help │
│                                                        │
│  No.    Records      Request                           │
│  #1:         75      TOXOPLASM*                         │
│  #2:      41902      LA=ENGLISH                         │
│  #3:         54      #1 AND LA=ENGLISH                  │
│  #4:      38949      HUMAN                              │
│  #5:         41      #3 and (HUMAN in MESH)             │
│  #6:       7530      CASE                               │
│  #7:       7542      REPORT                             │
│  #8:         10      #5 AND (CASE REPORT in MESH)       │
│ Find:  and ai=ab                                       │
└──────────────────────────────────────────────────────┘
```

```
┌──────────────────────────────────────────────────────┐
│ SilverPlatter 1.6      MEDLINE (R) (1/91 - 2/91)    Esc=Commands F1=Help │
│                                                        │
│  No.    Records      Request                           │
│  #1:         75      TOXOPLASM*                         │
│  #2:      41902      LA=ENGLISH                         │
│  #3:         54      #1 AND LA=ENGLISH                  │
│  #4:      38949      HUMAN                              │
│  #5:         41      #3 and (HUMAN in MESH)             │
│  #6:       7530      CASE                               │
│  #7:       7542      REPORT                             │
│  #8:         10      #5 and (CASE REPORT in MESH)       │
│  #9:      37505      AI=AB                              │
│  #10:         9      #8 and AI=AB                       │
│ Find:                                                  │
└──────────────────────────────────────────────────────┘
```

Fig. 2.6. SPIRS search in MEDLINE.

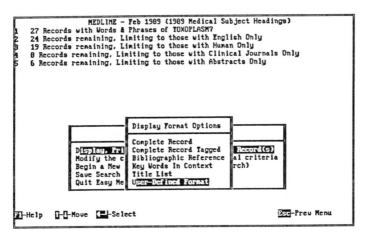
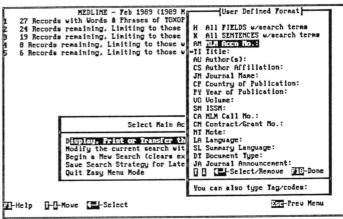
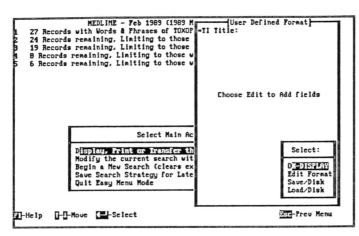
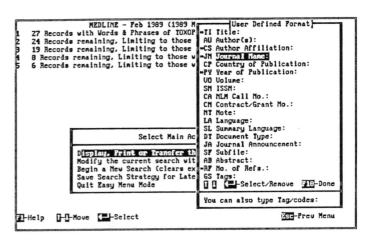

Fig. 2.7. Choosing format option in OnDisc.

Styles of Interface

Apart from the functionality and extent of the menu system, there are differences also in the structure and format of the menus and in the implementation of identical functions. This is the look-and-feel aspect of the menu system, or the style of the interface.

The two major menu styles are the bar menu and the window menu. The bar menu may be in the bottom part of the screen (as shown earlier in figure 2.6), at the top of the screen (as in the Bluefish software shown in figure 2.9), or on the side of the screen (as in EBSCO-CD, shown in figure 2.10).

You can select an option either by typing the first or highlighted character of that option (Q for query, E for exit, and so on) or by positioning the cursor over the option and pressing the Enter key. A second menu bar or a window may then appear with another list of options or with explanations and messages.

SilverPlatter 1.6 MEDLINE (R) (1/91 - 2/91) Esc=Commands F1=Help

No.	Records	Request
#1:	75	TOXOPLASM*
#2:	41902	LA=ENGLISH
#3:	54	#1 and LA=ENGLISH
#4:	38949	HUMAN
#5:	41	#3 and (HUMAN in MESH)
#6:	7530	CASE
#7:	7542	REPORT
#8:	10	#5 and (CASE REPORT in MESH)
#9:	37505	AI=AB
#10:	9	#8 and AI=AB

Commands: HELP FIND INDEX THESAURUS SHOW CLEAR PRINT GUIDE
XCHANGE RESTART OPTIONS DOWNLOAD QUIT G
Press a function key; or type the highlighted letter of a command.

SilverPlatter 1.6 MEDLINE (R) (1/91 - 2/91) Esc=Commands F1=Help

No.	Records	Request
#1:	75	TOXOPLASM*
#2:	41902	LA=ENGLISH
#3:	54	#1 and LA=ENGLISH
#4:	38949	HUMAN
#5:	41	#3 and (HUMAN in MESH)
#6:	7530	CASE
#7:	7542	REPORT
#8:	10	#5 and (CASE REPORT in MESH)
#9:	37505	AI=AB
#10:	9	#8 and AI=AB

SHOW Fields: ALL Records: ALL
TAB between settings to change; RETURN to start with first record; F1 for HELP

SilverPlatter 1.6 MEDLINE (R) (1/91 - 2/91) Esc=Commands F1=Help

FIELDS
Each record in the MEDLINE database is a complete reference to a journal article. Records are divided into the following fields:

TI	Title	CP	Country of Publication
TO	Original Title	AB	Abstract
CM	Comments	MESH	Medical Subject Headings
AU	Author(s)	MJME	Major MeSH Headings
AD	Address of Author	GS	Gene Symbol
SO	Source (Bibliographic Citation)	PT	Publication Type
ISSN	International Standard Serial Number	PS	Personal Name as Subject
		CN	Contract or Grant Numbers
PY	Publication Year	RN	CAS Registry or EC Number
LA	Language of Article	NM	Name of Substance

Press PgDn to continue.

Guide Choices: RESUME INTRODUCTION FIELDS TERMINOLOGY STOPWORDS
EXAMPLES MeSH THEASURUS HELP R
Press PgDn for more; the highlighted letter of choice; or R to resume your work.

SilverPlatter 1.6 MEDLINE (R) (1/91 - 2/91) Esc=Commands F1=Help

No.	Records	Request
#1:	75	TOXOPLASM*
#2:	41902	LA=ENGLISH
#3:	54	#1 and LA=ENGLISH
#4:	38949	HUMAN
#5:	41	#3 and (HUMAN in MESH)
#6:	7530	CASE
#7:	7542	REPORT
#8:	10	#5 and (CASE REPORT in MESH)
#9:	37505	AI=AB
#10:	9	#8 and AI=AB

SHOW Fields: ti,so,ab Records: ALL
TAB between settings to change; RETURN to start with first record; F1 for HELP

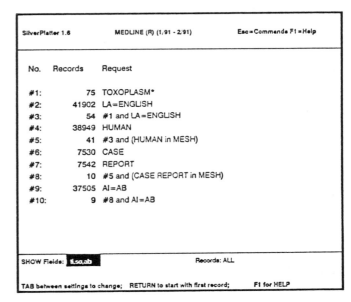

Fig. 2.8. Choosing format option in SPIRS.

Titles Computer Select, February 1991 F1:Help
Browse Log Words Fields Section Copy Print Utility Exit
Display the document represented by the title (ALT-B)
Documents found: 4

1. Adtech, Inc. [Honolulu, HI]

2. Computer Vectors, Inc. [Kailua-Kona, HI]

3. Soft Warehouse, Inc. [Honolulu, HI]

4. UniFORMx, Inc. [Aiea, HI]

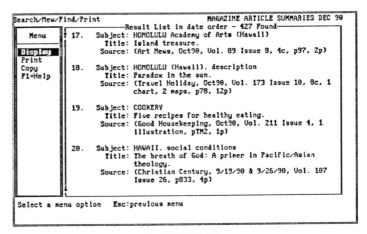

Fig. 2.9. Top bar menu in Bluefish.

```
Search/View/Find/Print                         MAGAZINE ARTICLE SUMMARIES DEC 90
                        Result List in date order - 427 Found
 Menu      17.  Subject: HONOLULU Academy of Arts (Hawaii)
                  Title: Island treasure.
Display          Source: (Art News, Oct90, Vol. 89 Issue 8, 4c, p97, 2p)
Print
Copy       18.  Subject: HONOLULU (Hawaii). description
F1=Help           Title: Paradox in the sun.
                 Source: (Travel Holiday, Oct90, Vol. 173 Issue 10, 8c, 1
                         chart, 2 maps, p78, 12p)

           19.  Subject: COOKERY
                  Title: Five recipes for healthy eating.
                 Source: (Good Housekeeping, Oct90, Vol. 211 Issue 4, 1
                         illustration, pTM2, 1p)

           20.  Subject: HAWAII. social conditions
                  Title: The breath of God: A primer in Pacific/Asian
                         theology.
                 Source: (Christian Century, 9/19/90 & 9/26/90, Vol. 107
                         Issue 26, p833, 4p)

Select a menu option   Esc:previous menu
```

Fig. 2.10. Side bar menu in EBSCO-CD.

An interface may start with a bar menu, continue with a window menu, and then return to the bar style. The window menu may be dropdown (also known as pulldown) or popup. If a window is opened from a top bar menu as in OCSI (figure 2.11), it is called a dropdown menu; if it is opened from a bottom bar as in UMI (figure 2.12) or from a window then it is a popup menu.

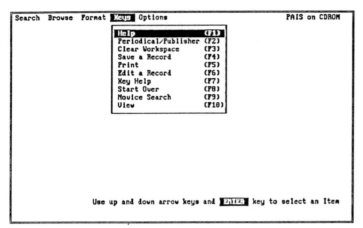

Fig. 2.11. Dropdown menu in OCSI-PAIS.

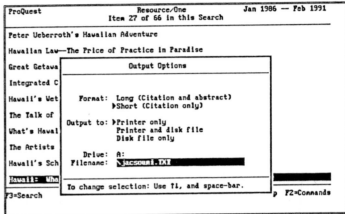

Fig. 2.12. Popup menu in ProQuest.

If the window completely replaces the previous window or bar menu then it is an overlap window, as in Wilsondisc. If two or more windows are kept on the screen, it may be a tiling window, as in the CD450 software of OCLC (figure 2.13), or a cascading window, as in OnDisc. CD-ROM products usually combine these menu styles, as the optimum style always depends on the context and the types of databases.

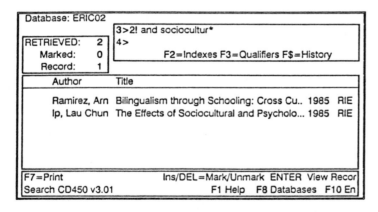

Fig. 2.13. Tiling window in CD450.

Help and Tutorial Facilities

The overall use of a CD-ROM product can be facilitated by a good help system. Structured presentation and context sensitivity make a good help system. The help system is context sensitive if it senses where the user is in the program and gives directions accordingly. We encounter context sensitivity in everyday life, too.

In Paris metro stations, riders press the button of the destination and one or more routes are highlighted on the electronic map from the automatically recognized location to the destination. In the London underground the help information is not context sensitive, but other ergonomic factors such as the color-coding of the lines aid the user (not to mention the friendly Londoners). In a New York City subway station your help is the graffitti-ridden and otherwise vandalized general map. Do not even dream of asking a passenger for context-sensitive guidance.

When you want to know which fields are searchable, or the meaning of a field, or the alternatives for print formats, you typically need information only about that feature. Just as you do not want to read the "Complete Street Guide to Manhattan" to find the direction to SoHo, you may not want to wade through dozens of help screens of SilverPlatter to learn that the predefined bibliographic citation format is to be specified as "citn." You would rather look it up on a short list of options.

The best help systems are not only context sensitive but also give an outline of the appropriate part of the help information, so that you can easily zero in on the relevant issue. Structured help text can compensate for lack of context sensitivity, as in the Bluefish software and ProQuest of UMI, both of which first present a table of contents to help you select the relevant part of the help file. Wilsondisc is not context sensitive, but at least the table of contents of the help file is well structured and easy to read, though it may be slow to get to the point if you have to guess which section would discuss the command important for you. SilverPlatter bombards you with dozens of help screens, though at least you can see that you are on page 2 of a 38-page (!) help screen. Actually the help screens are copies of the printed documentation in SPIRS and show the same limitation as all printed publications: lack of dynamic access to the relevant items. It should have been obvious to the designer of the interface that users need different depth and breadth of instructions in print and online. The often postponed introduction of Version 2 of SPIRS promises a much better structured help file. (Its debut was slated by late 1990, but it still had not been sent to users in the first quarter of 1991.)

EBSCO's help system is the most sophisticated. It is not only context sensitive, but also uses hypertext facilities. This hypertext approach makes it possible to provide concise, well-structured help screens. In EBSCO's hierarchical help system, terms that are highlighted on the screen have a more detailed explanation and/or examples that may be accessed by pressing the Enter key after positioning the cursor over the highlighted term (figure 2.14). This is the equivalent of boldfacing or italicizing words in articles of an encyclopedia, which suggests that the reader look up the article under the typographically distinguished heading. Of course, with the EBSCO-CD help-referencing scheme you do not have to juggle several volumes of the encyclopedia to look up details and samples or background information. Pressing a key lets you jump from one reference

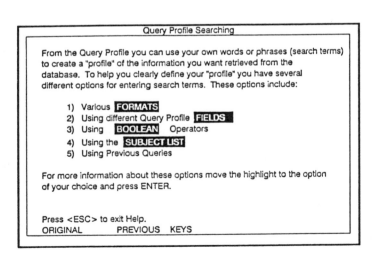
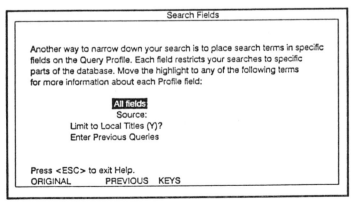

Fig. 2.14. The hypertext help file in EBSCO-CD.

to the other and then back. It is so easy to wander around and return that users feel at ease jumping back and forth in the help file.

A tutorial system built in the CD-ROM product as an option can save a lot of time for librarians by showing users the basics to get started. Furthermore, the tutorial program repeats these steps as many time as the user wants. Even the most cooperative librarian may get bored or tired by repeating explanations a hundred times a day, but the tutorial program does so without difficulty. In SilverPlatter and EBSCO the tutorial is one choice on the main menu options screen. SilverPlatter's approach is better because the tutorial can be invoked at any time; in EBSCO you learn about the availability of the tutorial only at logon time, and you have to trace back to the logon screen to access it.

UMI, Wilsondisc, and Dialog have stand-alone tutorials. Their disadvantage is that you have to exit from the CD-ROM environment and run this tutorial separately. Wilson used to have a tutorial on a separate CD, which could accommodate a lot of records and illustrate all the different databases of Wilson. Its disadvantages were that it cost extra, it was not kept up-to-date, and you had to replace CDs. It was an interesting idea a few years ago, but the tutorial should have been incorporated into each of the real databases long ago.

When the help information misinforms users, shows incorrect examples, or provides wrong explanations, it is particularly annoying. This happens when, in Wilsondisc, the help file claims that the CD-ROM Wilsonline mode is identical to the online command mode. On the contrary, there are no proximity or positional operators and the sort command and many of the print alternatives of the online Wilsonline software do not work in the Wilsonline mode of Wilsondisc.

It also is confusing when the explanation in the help file contradicts the example a few lines later, as illustrated by figure 2.15. The help text in Wilsondisc warns about the importance of the position of the field tag and then uses an example that does not heed the advice. Worse, it is the example that is correct, not the text.

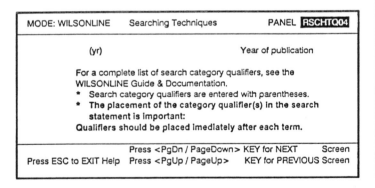

Fig. 2.15. Contradicting help text and example in Wilsondisc.

The help text of LISA gives the nonsense advice to search the "DA" field for publication year (figure 2.16). In LISA the difference between the publication year (PY) and the year when the record gets in the database (DA) is discouraging itself (see chart in figure 3.89). If you use the D = 1991 option to limit your retrieval to articles published in 1991, most if not all of your records will cite articles published in 1990, 1989, and earlier. Use this field to limit retrieved records by the year the records were added to the database.

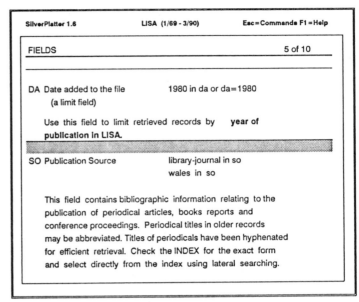

Fig. 2.16. Help information from LISA.

Ergonomics

The ergonomic issues of a user interface cover such areas as the use of menu styles, the choice of colors, the number and mode of display options, the arrangements of explanatory messages, the use of highlighting and reverse video, and so forth. A good menu system may make a software package look and feel better, whereas an ill-designed menu may cripple the otherwise powerful features of the CD-ROM software.

Clothing does not make the (wo)man, but can help to emphasize strengths and soften weaknesses. Analyzing the ergonomics and aesthetics of a user interface is similar to describing at length the clothing in a fashion show. You look at a piece and you like it or not, but you may not be able to explain why one pleases you while another does not. There are no universal rules by which you may judge if an interface is ergonomically and aesthetically appropriate, but there are many published guidelines that lay down some basic concepts of interface designs. To illustrate this subjectivity, I present a list of my impressions of the ergonomic features of one of the best and one of the worst CD-ROM interfaces in my judgment: Dialog OnDisc and SilverPlatter's SPIRS (version 1.6). For illustrations, refer back to the sample search in figures 2.5 and 2.6.

Dialog OnDisc's combination of bar menus and window menus is optimal, as one complements the other. The framing of the options in the menu bar separates them appropriately. The cascading nature of windows balances well between providing as much new information as is digestible and retaining some of the previous menu as a clue for backtracking. The naming of options is clear except for the "Word/Phrase Index," which is confusing because the difference between this and the "Words & Phrases" option is not evident.

The number of options in a window or in a bar is usually not more than eight, a reasonable number. The options are presented vertically in a list format, which is much easier to glance through than a horizontal, enumerative list. Apart from results of human factors research, this is proven by the fact that most people write a to-do list vertically rather than horizontally. If more options are to be presented, they are grouped under a heading with some clues as in "Limit options (English, Human, ...)." The color combination (white letters on a blue background and error messages in red) is visually pleasing. The function keys have informative labels, with the possible exceptions of "Done" to indicate in index browsing that you want no more term selection

("Start search" could be better) and "Transfer" to initiate downloading to diskette, where "Download" could be more informative. The function keys are listed horizontally, but they are well spaced and easily distinguishable.

In SPIRS, the bar menu is overcrowded by too many options. The horizontal arrangement of options aggravates this problem. The green background with yellow foreground text makes the menu bar difficult to read. The system abandons the user too early during searching. Looking up field identifiers or format names from the help file forces the user to leave the search (find) mode. The lack of context-sensitive help and the unstructured, lengthy help file are frustrating. Not all the function keys applicable in a given situation are listed in the menu; for example, the Show (F4) option often is not listed when it would be available.

In spite of these deficiencies many database reviews praise the user interface and ease of use of SPIRS. The different judgments may have to do with different perspectives and relative merits. Compared to command-driven online systems or the cryptic syntax of Unix-based information networks, the user interface of SPIRS is undoubtedly superior. For those, however, who have used OnDisc or some of the Bowker databases, the SPIRS user interface may leave much to be desired.

Ergonomic issues define how easily the user can navigate in the system, which is the key question in judging ease of use. This should be contrasted with ease of learning, which addresses the issue of how easily a new system or a new function in a system can be learned, and depends on both the help system and the navigation facilities.

Navigation Ease

In most major U.S. cities it is very easy to find your way (at least in the downtown area). The gridlike pattern of streets and avenues, the consistent numbering conventions, directional codes in the street numbers, and well-placed and frequent street signs make navigation easy. Similarly, in well-designed interfaces the consistently used function keys, unambiguous prompts, informative labelling of options, directional clues, and context indicators that remind you where you are, where you came from, and where you may go are essential for easy navigation.

Unfortunately, CD-ROM systems have notoriously incompatible interfaces. Your familiarity with one may not help you navigate in another one, and occasionally may even confuse you. Only the F1 key seems to be universally used (to invoke help). Even such a simple task as the indication that you have finished your input ("over" in walkie-talkie lingo) varies wildly from system to system, and sometimes even within one system from function to function. The latter is of particular concern, as it gives an inconsistent feel to the product and may puzzle the user. Dialog and Bowker software packages use F10 or the Enter key to indicate "over," EBSCO uses F2 or Enter, and Wilsondisc requires you to press the End key followed by the Enter key. Many users may miss this double action and keep waiting for the results after pressing the Enter key. In EBSCO-CD at times you have to press the Escape key to proceed. This is confusing since the Escape key is used universally in software packages, including EBSCO-CD to back out or back track.

Ease of navigation requires that you see all of your choices, but only those that are available in that database or in that context. Menus should be not only context sensitive, but also database sensitive. Displaying the thesaurus option in all the SPIRS databases is misleading since SilverPlatter implemented the thesaurus facility only with a few databases. Another case is the display of the "Search by author" option in the CMC ReSearch software used with the Shakespeare database, as the only author in this database is the swan of Avon. Such options tease the user, and in the best case the user gets the message "This option is not available, use the Index option," which is like saying, "Just kidding!"

To navigate effectively in a system you may need to look ahead and see where a given option will lead. This is like looking down a street to see if a landmark building is on the horizon. In this regard the bar menus of SPIRS and Bluefish are more appropriate than most of the window menus, as a one-line message summarizes the effect of the option being highlighted before you activate that option. Very few CD-ROM products give a route map of options in their printed documentation, let alone in their online help file. EBSCO has a very good route map in its manual, which is reproduced in figure 2.17.

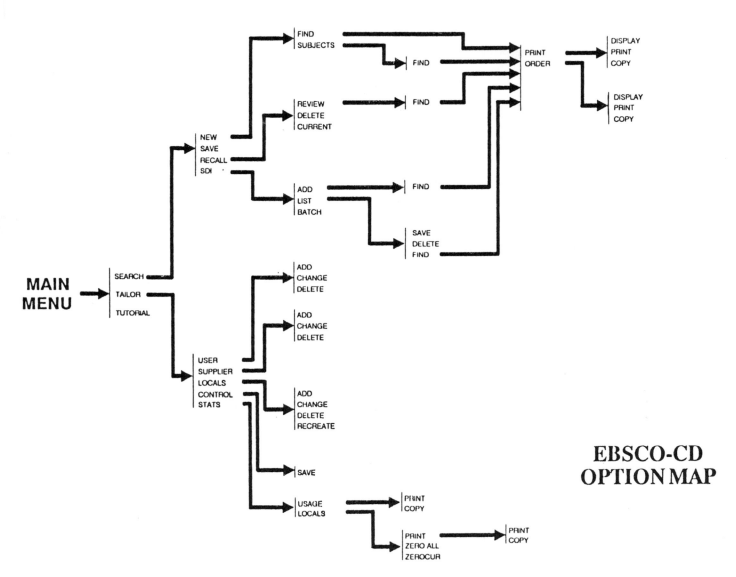

Fig. 2.17. Navigation chart for EBSCO-CD. Reprinted by permission from EBSCO Electronic Information.

Navigating within a record and among records is discussed in more detail under output facilities. Suffice it to say here that in one system you have to press the Page Down key to see the remainder of a long record that could not be accommodated on one screen (SPIRS). In another one (OnDisc) the Page Down key displays the next record, and the down-arrow key displays the remainder of the current record. Some systems (Bowker-CD, ProQuest) use the + and − keys to display the next or the previous record and the arrow keys to go up or down within the record. Again, this is very subjective, but navigation ease and ease of use depend much on intuitivity. A system is intuitive when the action to be taken can be contemplated without looking at a help file or the documentation. Pressing the Enter key to see the next record may seem intuitive (as it is always used to get the system moving). Still, the use of + and − keys to display the next and the previous record, or the up and down arrow keys to move upward and downward within the record, may be better. These pairs imply forward and backward movement, whereas the Enter key has no counterpart key or even a standard name. On many keyboards the Enter key is identified either with the label Return or only by the ◄┘ symbol.

Most systems prevent the users from accidentally navigating themselves out of a search and losing their search results. Usually, confirmation is required in order to quit. In Wilsondisc, however, this applies only to quitting the system but not the Wilsonline mode. Press the Escape key and you are kicked out of the Wilsonline mode losing your search results.

SEARCH FEATURES

In addition to the user interface, search features are the most characteristic capabilities of CD-ROM software. These two are considered flagships of CD-ROM software by both producers and users. This is understandable because though there are other components of CD-ROM software, such as those for sorting, printing, or downloading records, a casual user may never encounter them. No one can avoid the user interface and everyone will certainly use one or more of the search features.

Due to this prominent role, complete CD-ROM software is often called the search software, the access program, or the retrieval engine. The documentation of the Computer Library goes as far as to call the Bluefish software "searchware." Evaluations of search capabilities are the focus of most reviews, analyses, and promotional materials.

The search engine lets you search for those items (records) in the database that meet the criteria specified in a search formula, also known as a query. How effectively you can identify and retrieve relevant items from a database depends on the way you can specify your query and on the way the components of the database are set up and identified.

To evaluate the search capabilities of a CD-ROM software package you must understand the structure of the CD-ROM database. This chapter focuses only on those aspects of the structure of textual databases that are important for evaluation of the retrieval capabilities. Other structural characteristics of databases are discussed in the chapter on dataware evaluation (chapter 3).

Linear and Inverted Files

Most textual databases have two major components: the linear file and the inverted file. In the linear file the records are stored sequentially, one after the other, usually in the order they are added to the database. For this reason the linear file is also called the serial or sequential file. It also is referred to as the master file because it is the one from which the index terms are extracted. This extraction is the inversion process, and its result is the inverted file (also called the index file or dictionary file).

The records of the master file are known by the format that it is most often displayed in (with or without field tag). This format is shown in the top part of figure 2.18. The bottom part of figure 2.18 shows how the master record looks in its native format before it is displayed.

Note that the native format is a string of characters interspersed with field tags (TI, AU), and subfield delimiters and codes (#l, #f). The more tags in the master records indicates the more sophisticated and flexible the search and output features offered by the CD-ROM search software. Our sample record is very lightly tagged for the sake of simplicity. In a real database it is quite possible that the title field be further subdivided into title proper and subtitle components or the citation field be subdivided into subfields of volume and issue number, year and month of publication preceded by subfield codes and delimiters as well.

```
NO:   999
UD:   910615
TI:   Of Buffers and Cards [gambling tips for CD-ROM installation and blackjack]
AU:   Jacsó, Péter
AF:   Graduate School of Library and Information Studies, Univesity of Hawaii
LA:   English
TC:   Practical
JN:   CD-ROM EndUser
VI:   1 (October, 1989): 36-38
DE:   CD-ROM
DE:   software installation
DE:   system configuration
CO:   Microsoft
AB:   Installing CD-ROM applications is often a gamble, but you have some chance for
      controlling the outcome just as in blackjack. You may split, double down, hit or stand in the
      card game. You may increase or decrease the memory usage by changing the values of the
      BUFFERS, LASTDRIVE and FILES commands in the installation game, or you may leave the
      system parameters as they are. The optimal strategy is not to keep drawing as close to 21 or as
      close to the rim of your RAM as possible, but to avoid busting . This requires counting and
      assessing the prevailing conditions, such as the cards dealt and the RAM used by the DOS
      kernel, the device drivers and the adjustable parameters of DOS. In the installation game there
      are no pitch bosses and cocktail waitresses to distract you from keeping a tab.
```

```
■AN999■UD910615■TIOf Buffers and Cards [gambling tips for CD-ROM and blackjack]
■AU#fPéter#1Jacsó■AFGraduate School of Library and Information Studies, Universi
ty of Hawaii■LAe■TCp■JNCD-ROM Enduser■VI1 (October, 1989): 36-38■PD#y89#m10■CD-
ROM%software installation%system configuration■COMicrosoft■ABInstalling.........
................................................................................
.....................keeping a tab.
```

80 character lines   ■AA = field identifier and tag   #a = subfield identifier and code

Fig. 2.18. Master record display and native formats.

You do not usually see this depth of record tagging, but it has an important impact both on the search and output capabilities discussed in this chapter. The extensive tagging of records increases the time, storage requirement, and cost of adding a record to the database, but it pays off in the long run for search power. The more granular the record structure is, the more flexibility it allows in creating the index file. This makes the search facilities of the Resource/One database, for example, far superior to those available in Magazine Article Summaries. Tagging fields and subfields is a prerequisite for a good inverted file.

Think of the inverted file as the most traditional back-of-the-book index or the index in an abstracting journal. These tell you where to find certain terms in the publication. This information may be page number alone, a chapter and page number in a book, or an item number in an abstracting journal, where the main body of the publication is arranged by major subject codes and the items are sequentially numbered.

The index entry is most commonly a subject word, but may also be the name of a person, a corporation, a product, a geographic entity, and so forth. These index entries may be interfiled in one overall index or they may be separated, forming a subject index, a name index, a geographic index, and so forth. Even if index entries are interfiled, some typographical enhancement such as printing personal names in bold or geographic names in italics can help identify the type of entries.

The softwasre that creates the index entries supplies the record identifier for each term extracted from the records in the linear file, and may supply the identifier of the field sequence number of the sentence from which the index term was extracted and even the position of the term within the field, such as first, second, or third term. A very few software packages also tell in which occurrence of a repeatable field the term appeared. The author field is typically a multi-valued, repeatable field, and the index may include the information that the name is from the first, second, or third occurrence of the field.

There are many ways to specify how to create index entries in an index generation program. One possibility is to use an index generation table shown in figure 2.19.

Field tag	Technique	Algorithm	Example
AN	-	-	-
UD			910615
TI	word	-	BUFFERS
AU	subfield	AU=#l, #f	AU=JACSO, PETER
AF	-	-	-
LA	code lookup	LA=[code]	LA=ENGLISH
TC	code lookup	TC=[code]	TC=PRACTICAL
JN	phrase	JN=field	JN=CD-ROM ENDUSER
	word		CD
PD	subfield	YR=19#y	YR=1989
VI	-	-	-
DE	phrase	DE=field	DE=SOFTWARE INSTALLATION
	word		SOFTWARE
CO	phrase	CO=field	CO=MICROSOFT
AB	word		INSTALLING

Stopwords: a, an, and, are, as, at, but, by, for, from, in, is, may, of, no, not, or, such, the, there, to

Word separators: numbers, space, special characters, hyphens, parentheses, comma, semicolon

Fig. 2.19. Index generation table.

This table instructs the software not only which fields and which technique to use in generating the index entries but also the algorithm for generating an entry from the data element in the (sub)field. The examples of index entries in this table are included only for illustration. A real table does not include such information and is much more compact. It is so extensively coded that it is unreadable to the human eye but perfectly adequate for a search program. The interim and final index entries are also more compact and heavily coded. The samples shown in figures 2.18, page 23, 2.19, page 24, 2.20, page 26, and 2.21, page 27 are illustrations not meant to be one-to-one representations of the real storage format. They will be referred to often in this chapter.

The index generation program first creates an interim set of index entries in the sequence as it parses the record. The result of this first step is illustrated in figure 2.20, page 26.

You can check this result by mentally applying the indexing technique and algorithm shown in figure 2.19 to the record shown in figure 2.18. Next the entries are sorted by the terms generated (including the prefix, if any). At the same time the total occurrence of each term generated from the record is calculated (figure 2.21, page 27).

The third step is updating the set of index entries generated from previously added records. The result of this process is not shown here, but the essence is that the new entries update the values in the old ones to create a new inverted file. If there is a new entry, it is inserted in the existing file. Even the slightest difference between two entries will result in a new entry. An extra space or a comma in a name makes it a different entry for the index generation program. Instead of updating an existing entry, a new entry will be created. This results in a polluted and scattered index file in many databases.

For indexes of traditional printed publications the index terms are selected, verified, and consolidated in a rather tedious process by an indexing specialist. In the inverted files (indexes) of databases the selection and mode of indexing are done automatically by the computer using an algorithm (the indexing algorithm), and verification and consolidation are done only on certain fields in the master records, if at all. Because the indexing process is automatic, if a term in the master record is misspelled, it will be entered in the index misspelled, too.

Fields in the master record that are verified are called controlled fields, because they are to use a controlled vocabulary. Typically the descriptor field and sometimes the name fields and some coded fields (such as those for language, document type, or geographic and classification codes) are controlled. The vocabulary may be controlled by a simple authority file that lists the terms to be used by the indexer. A more sophisticated version of the authority file may include cross-references from one form to the other while a thesaurus indicates the hierarchy between terms. These tools help to ensure that various name formats and spellings of terms in the source documents are consistently entered by the indexers into some of the designated fields mentioned above.

The users of a CD-ROM product have no control over indexing, but the search capabilities offered are directly influenced by the indexing algorithm, the indexing technique, and the data elements selected for indexing, as well as by the level of control over the quality of the data elements of the master records. The more information the index file carries, the more time and storage space are required for its creation, but also the more powerful the search facilities may become.

Indexing time is not (or should not be) a consideration with CD-ROM databases. As CD-ROM databases are typically (re)indexed once a week, month, or quarter by the CD-ROM producer, it is irrelevant whether the process takes 20 hours or 50 hours. For the end user it is absolutely irrelevant. The other aspect, the storage requirement, may be relevant in some cases for both the producers and the end users.

Term	Record number	Field tag	Sentence	Field occurrence	Nth word		
999	999	AN	1	1	1		
BUFFERS	999	TI	1	1	2	of	1
CARDS	999	TI	1	1	4	and	3
GAMBLING	999	TI	1	1	5	for	7
TIPS	999	TI	1	1	6	and	11
CD	999	TI	1	1	8		
ROM	999	TI	1	1	9		
INSTALLATION	999	TI	1	1	10		
BLACKJACK	999	TI	1	1	12		
AU=JACSO, PETER	999	AU	1	1	1		
GRADUATE	999	AF	1	1	1		
SCHOOL	999	AF	1	1	2	of	3
LIBRARY	999	AF	1	1	4		
INFORMATION	999	AF	1	1	6	and	5
STUDIES	999	AF	1	1	7		
UNIVERSITY	999	AF	1	1	8	of	9
HAWAII	999	AF	1	1	10		
LA=ENGLISH	999	LA	1	1	1		
TC=PRACTICAL	999	TC	1	1	1		
JN=CD-ROM ENDUSER	999	JN	1	1	1		
CD	999	JN	1	1	1		
ROM	999	JN	1	1	2		
ENDUSER	999	JN	1	1	3		
DE=CD-ROM	999	DE	1	1	1		
CD	999	DE	1	1	1		
ROM	999	DE	1	1	2		
DE=SOFTWARE INSTALLATION	999	DE	1	2	1		
SOFTWARE	999	DE	1	2	1		
INSTALLATION	999	DE	1	2	2		
SYSTEM CONFIGURATION	999	DE	1	3	1		
SYSTEM	999	DE	1	3	1		
CONFIGURATION	999	DE	1	3	2		
CO=MICROSOFT	999	CO	1	1	1		
INSTALLING	999	AB	1	1	1		
CD	999	AB	1	1	2		
ROM	999	AB	1	1	3		
APPLICATION	999	AB	1	1	4	is	5
OFTEN	999	AB	1	1	6	a	7
GAMBLE	999	AB	1	1	8	but	9
YOU	999	AB	1	1	10		
HAVE	999	AB	1	1	11		
SOME	999	AB	1	1	12		
CHANCE	999	AB	1	1	13		
CONTROLLING	999	AB	1	1	15	for	14
OUTCOME	999	AB	1	1	17	the	16
JUST	999	AB	1	1	18	as	19
BLACKJACK	999	AB	1	1	21	in	20
YOU	999	AB	2	1	22	may	23
SPLIT	999	AB	2	1	24		
DOUBLE	999	AB	2	1	25		
DOWN	999	AB	2	1	26		
HIT	999	AB	2	1	27	or	28
STAND	999	AB	2	1	29	in	30
CARD	999	AB	2	1	32	the	31
GAME	999	AB	2	1	33		
YOU	999	AB	3	1	34	may	35
INCREASE	999	AB	3	1	36	or	37
DECREASE	999	AB	3	1	38	the	39

Term	Record number	Field tag	Sentence	Field occurrence	Nth word		
MEMORY	999	AB	3	1	40		
USAGE	999	AB	3	1	41	by	42
CHANGING	999	AB	3	1	43	the	44
VALUE	999	AB	3	1	45	of	46
BUFFERS	999	AB	3	1	48	the	47
LASTDRIVE	999	AB	3	1	49	and	50
FILES	999	AB	3	1	51		
COMMANDS	999	AB	3	1	52	in	53
INSTALLATION	999	AB	3	1	55	the	54
GAME	999	AB	3	1	56	or	57
YOU	999	AB	3	1	58	may	59
LEAVE	999	AB	3	1	60	the	61
SYSTEM	999	AB	3	1	62	as	64
PARAMETERS	999	AB	3	1	63	are	67
THEY	999	AB	3	1	65	the	67
OPTIMAL	999	AB	4	1	68	is	70
STRATEGY	999	AB	4	1	69	not	71
KEEP	999	AB	4	1	73	to	72
DRAWING	999	AB	4	1	74	as	75
CLOSE	999	AB	4	1	76	to	77
21	999	AB	4	1	78	or	79
CLOSE	999	AB	4	1	81	as	80
RIM	999	AB	4	1	84	to	82
YOUR	999	AB	4	1	86	the	83
RAM	999	AB	4	1	87	of	85
POSSIBLE	999	AB	4	1	89	as	88
AVOID	999	AB	4	1	92	but	90
BUSTING	999	AB	4	1	93	to	91
THIS	999	AB	5	1	94		
REQUIRES	999	AB	5	1	95		
COUNTING	999	AB	5	1	96	and	97
ASSESSING	999	AB	5	1	98	the	99
PREVAILING	999	AB	5	1	100	such	102
CONDITIONS	999	AB	5	1	101	as	103
CARDS	999	AB	5	1	105	the	104
DEALT	999	AB	5	1	106	and	107
RAM	999	AB	5	1	109	the	108
USED	999	AB	5	1	110	by	111
DOS	999	AB	5	1	113	the	112
KERNEL	999	AB	5	1	114	the	115
DEVICE	999	AB	5	1	116		
DRIVERS	999	AB	5	1	117	and	118
ADJUSTABLE	999	AB	5	1	120	the	119
PARAMETERS	999	AB	5	1	121	of	122
DOS	999	AB	5	1	123		
INSTALLATION	999	AB	6	1	126	in	124
GAME	999	AB	6	1	127	the	125
PITCH	999	AB	6	1	131	there	128
BOSSES	999	AB	6	1	132	are	129
COCKTAIL	999	AB	6	1	134	no	130
WAITRESSES	999	AB	6	1	135	and	133
DISTRACT	999	AB	6	1	137	to	136
YOU	999	AB	6	1	138		
KEEPING	999	AB	6	1	140	from	139
TAB	999	AB	6	1	142	a	141
910615	999	UD	1	1	1		
YR=1989	999	YR	1	1	1		

Fig. 2.20. Interim unsorted index entries.

Term number	Occurrence	Term	Record number	Field tag	Sentence	Field occurrence	Nth word
1	1	21	999	AB	4	1	78
2	1	910615	999	UD	1	1	1
3	1	999	999	AN	1	1	1
4	1	ADJUSTABLE	999	AB	5	1	120
5	1	APPLICATION	999	AB	1	1	4
6	1	ASSESSING	999	AB	5	1	98
7	1	AU=JACSO, PETER	999	AU	1	1	1
8	1	AVOID	999	AB	4	1	92
9	2	BLACKJACK	999	AB	1	1	21
			999	TI	1	1	12
10	1	BOSSES	999	AB	6	1	132
11	2	BUFFERS	999	AB	3	1	48
			999	TI	1	1	2
12	1	BUSTING	999	AB	4	1	93
13	1	CARD	999	AB	2	1	32
14	2	CARDS	999	AB	5	1	105
			999	TI	1	1	4
15	4	CD	999	AB	1	1	2
			999	DE	1	1	1
			999	JN	1	1	1
			999	TI	1	1	8
16	1	CHANCE	999	AB	1	1	13
17	1	CHANGING	999	AB	3	1	43
18	2	CLOSE	999	AB	4	1	76
			999	AB	4	1	81
19	1	CO=MICROSOFT	999	CO	1	1	1
20	1	COCKTAIL	999	AB	6	1	134
21	1	COMMANDS	999	AB	3	1	52
22	1	CONDITIONS	999	AB	5	1	101
23	1	CONFIGURATION	999	DE	1	3	2
24	1	CONTROLLING	999	AB	1	1	15
25	1	COUNTING	999	AB	5	1	96
26	1	DE=CD-ROM	999	DE	1	1	1
27	1	DE=SOFTWARE INSTALLATION	999	DE	1	2	1
28	1	DEALT	999	AB	5	1	106
29	1	DECREASE	999	AB	3	1	38
30	1	DEVICE	999	AB	5	1	116
31	1	DISTRACT	999	AB	6	1	137
32	2	DOS	999	AB	5	1	113
			999	AB	5	1	123
33	1	DOUBLE	999	AB	2	1	25
34	1	DOWN	999	AB	2	1	26
35	1	DRAWING	999	AB	4	1	74
36	1	DRIVERS	999	AB	5	1	117
37	1	ENDUSER	999	JN	1	1	3
38	1	FILES	999	AB	3	1	51
39	1	GAMBLE	999	AB	1	1	8
40	1	GAMBLING	999	TI	1	1	5
41	3	GAME	999	AB	2	1	33
			999	AB	3	1	56
			999	AB	6	1	127
42	1	GRADUATE	999	AF	1	1	1
43	1	HAVE	999	AB	1	1	11
44	1	HAWAII	999	AF	1	1	10
45	1	HIT	999	AB	2	1	27
46	1	INCREASE	999	AB	3	1	36
47	1	INFORMATION	999	AF	1	1	6
48	4	INSTALLATION	999	AB	3	1	55
			999	AB	6	1	126
			999	DE	1	2	2
			999	TI	1	1	10
49	1	INSTALLING	999	AB	1	1	1
50	1	JN=CD-ROM ENDUSER	999	JN	1	1	1
51	1	JUST	999	AB	1	1	18
52	1	KEEP	999	AB	4	1	73
53	1	KEEPING	999	AB	6	1	140
54	1	KERNEL	999	AB	5	1	114
55	1	LA=ENGLISH	999	LA	1	1	1
56	1	LASTDRIVE	999	AB	3	1	49
57	1	LEAVE	999	AB	3	1	60
58	1	LIBRARY	999	AF	1	1	4
59	1	MEMORY	999	AB	3	1	40
60	1	OFTEN	999	AB	1	1	6
61	1	OPTIMAL	999	AB	4	1	68
62	1	OUTCOME	999	AB	1	1	17
63	2	PARAMETERS	999	AB	3	1	63
			999	AB	5	1	121
64	1	PITCH	999	AB	6	1	131
65	1	POSSIBLE	999	AB	4	1	89
66	1	PREVAILING	999	AB	5	1	100
67	2	RAM	999	AB	4	1	87
			999	AB	5	1	109
68	1	REQUIRES	999	AB	5	1	95
69	1	RIM	999	AB	4	1	84
70	4	ROM	999	AB	1	1	3
			999	DE	1	1	2
			999	JN	1	1	2
			999	TI	1	1	9
71	1	SCHOOL	999	AF	1	1	2
72	1	SOFTWARE	999	DE	1	2	1
73	1	SOME	999	AB	1	1	12
74	1	SPLIT	999	AB	2	1	24
75	1	STAND	999	AB	2	1	29
76	1	STRATEGY	999	AB	4	1	69
77	1	STUDIES	999	AF	1	1	7
78	2	SYSTEM	999	AB	3	1	62
			999	DE	1	3	1
79	1	SYSTEM CONFIGURATION	999	DE	1	3	1
80	1	TAB	999	AB	6	1	142
81	1	TC=PRACTICAL	999	TC	1	1	1
82	1	THEY	999	AB	3	1	65
83	1	THIS	999	AB	5	1	94
84	1	TIPS	999	TI	1	1	6
85	1	UNIVERSITY	999	AF	1	1	8
96	1	USAGE	999	AB	3	1	41
87	1	USED	999	AB	5	1	110
88	1	VALUE	999	AB	3	1	45
89	1	WAITRESSES	999	AB	6	1	135
90	5	YOU	999	AB	1	1	10
			999	AB	2	1	22
			999	AB	3	1	34
			999	AB	3	1	58
			999	AB	6	1	138
91	1	YOUR	999	AB	4	1	86
92	1	YR=1989	999	YR	1	1	1

Fig. 2.21. Interim sorted index entries.

In computer-generated indexes the size of the publication limits the data elements to be indexed, the index terms to be selected, and the mode of indexing. Space has been an important consideration even in computer databases, particularly with personal computers, whose storage capacity was severely limited until quite recently. CD-ROM technology brought relief in this very regard. The 540-megabyte net capacity of a single CD-ROM medium makes it possible to store the full text of the 22-volume Grolier encyclopedia with an index to every word in all the articles, using one-fifth of the capacity of the compact disk.

Yet even this whopping capacity may sometimes prove to be a constraint, as in the case of giant databases with extensive indexing, such as MEDLINE, ERIC, or Library of Congress MARC files, which require three to seven CD-ROM disks to store the complete database. With most databases, however, space is not a consideration and is not an adequate excuse for parsimonious indexing.

The automatic generation and ease of indexing has its dark side, too. Many database indexes are so polluted (with typos and inconsistent or incomplete entries) that the database producers would feel ashamed if they were ever printed. The increase of access points seems to have given a letter of immunity for extremely lax control over quality. Though typos certainly occur in printed publications as well, in the online and CD-ROM environment where the words in the abstract are often used as access points, pollution is a more serious problem. This is discussed in much more detail in chapter 3.

The power of the retrieval engine, and your ability to search a database, depends on how the indexing is done. This boils down to three aspects: (1) which fields are designated for index generation, (2) how the index entries are generated, and (3) what kind of quality control is applied on the fields used for indexing.

In our example in figure 2.18 the accession number (AN), the author affiliation (AF), and the chronological/numerical designation (VI) fields are not indexed. Note, however, that the publication date (PD) field is indexed but not displayed. The year subfield (#y) is used to generate the publication year (YR) index. The month of publication subfield in the normalized form (#m) is not indexed, but it may be used in sorting the output, for example.

Obviously, the more fields used to generate the index file, the more access paths the users will have and the more refined the query may be, but also the more chances there will be for false drops (retrieving irrelevant records). This last aspect can be effectively controlled by the combination of sophisticated indexing techniques and retrieval facilities, which are discussed in the following sections.

Indexing Techniques

The four major indexing methods are word indexing, phrase indexing, code lookup indexing, and marked indexing. The first three are widely used in CD-ROM databases, the fourth one, mostly with in-house databases. Stopwords, used in almost all indexing programs, are also discussed in this section, following word indexing.

Word Indexing

In word indexing every word in the fields designated for indexing is extracted. How a word is defined may vary from database to database or from software to software. Though this is an internal matter, it has a direct impact on the retrieval capabilities. A word may be a purely alphabetic character string delimited by a space or a numeric or special character. In other systems the word may include not only alphabetic characters but also numbers. This is very important in scientific-technical databases, where H_2O should not be separated into three "words" or B1 (as in the vitamin) should not be split into B and 1. In our example in figure 2.18 there are many characters considered to be word separators but the slash, for example, is not one of them. There also are systems in which special characters are not considered word delimiters by the indexing program; therefore, terms such as S&L, I-O, Apple-II +, on-line, AC/DC, and I.B.M. (spelled this way only by the *New York Times* and Bowker) are not split, which makes searching for them much easier. Though as a user you have no control over this, you have to know how such words are indexed to ensure correct formulation of your query. A few systems (Bluefish, EBSCO-CD) automatically take care of this problem by searching for *online* and *on line* when you enter *on-line* in your query, but they are the commendable exceptions. You can avoid much frustration if you understand the rules that govern word extraction in your database. This usually is not documented, but looking at the index file may be telling. There may be limitations also with regard to the maximum length of a word. This, however, is more of a problem with phrase indexing.

Stopwords

Almost all indexing programs use a list to eliminate the generation of index entries for words that are grammatically necessary in a text but do not carry any information on their own. These include prepositions, articles, and conjunctions. These words are called stopwords, though skip-word might be more descriptive. The index program does not stop on encountering them, it just skips them, though it may take note of their presence, which will have important and often subtle implications for the searcher (as in EBSCO-CD).

The justification for use of stopwords is space and the attempt to reduce ambiguity in queries that may use the Boolean operators (AND, OR, and NOT). If a database can be comfortably accommodated on a single CD-ROM disk, there is no motivation to use stopwords. This is the main reason that you sometimes find words in the index of certain databases that are generally considered stopwords in many others. UMI, for example, uses a very short stopword list, and you will find such words as *at*, *on*, and *from* in the index. The other reason for using few stopwords is that what may be a stopword in one database, or in one language, may be an important word in another database or language. An overzealous attempt to cut back on the size of the index file may backfire in searching. If the preposition *at* is considered a stopword you may not be able to search for records about PC AT computers, but only to specify PC, which is far too broad a search. If the special character / is not a word delimiter then you may be better off, because the spelling of this most written about personal computer is often PC/AT. If the word *rather* is put on the stopword list, you will be unable to search for documents about Dan Rather as is the case in the ABI/INFORM database. If the word *one* is on a stopword list you will have a hard time finding records about the remodeling of Air Force One, unless you are willing to wade through all the records about air force issues in general. On the other hand, certain databases may justify putting on the stopword list a word that is not usually a stopword. Because of the hundreds of thousands of love songs, OCLC put the word *you* on the stopword list of the Music Library database.

In our example in figure 2.18 the pronouns are not stopwords as they should be. This can be amended in the next index generation process, however. Good database publishers review and modify their stopword list. UMI, for example, had the word *used* on a stopword list. The users searching for the subject of *used cars* in the RES-1 database retrieved an excessive number of irrelevant records. The word was not removed from the updated documentation, an obvious oversight.

If a database includes many records referencing foreign language materials, such as databases for cataloging and acquisitions support or the PAIS and LISA databases, which have extensive coverage of non-English-language materials, the issue of stopwords is even more critical. If the terms *un*, *los*, *dos*, *di*, and *die* are put on a stopword list because they are articles or possessive pronouns in French, Spanish, Portuguese, Italian, and German, you will not be able to search easily for records about the United Nations (UN), articles about Los Angeles, the DOS operating system, Lady Di, or the film *Die Hard*, at least not easily and unambiguously. As we shall see below, phrase indexing can help in these problems.

Phrase Indexing

This technique takes the content of a field or subfield as it is in generating the index term, also known as (sub)field indexing. The resulting entry is a compound term as a unit entry. This technique is very appropriate for such fields as corporate bodies, descriptors, geographic names, and journal names, where words have a meaning as a group. Phrase indexing retains the intellectual decision that words in a phrase go together. If a software package does not offer phrase indexing, the vocabulary control in searching will be poor or will require too many advanced search operators. Where authority files are used to ensure the consistent form of names and precoordinated terms (such as "boardsailing/study and teaching"), phrase indexing is essential.

Phrase indexing enables you to search for articles about University of Hawaii, freedom of speech, New Mexico, or those published in *Life* magazine unambiguously without the need to use positional and proximity operators (discussed below). You will not retrieve records about Hawaii Pacific University, the president's speech about Nicaraguan freedom fighters, new elections in Mexico, or from the magazines *Outdoor Life*, *Soviet Life*, or *Boy's Life*.

The field used in phrase indexing may be a subfield, such as the place of publication subfield of the imprint field in a cataloging record, or it may be all of the repeated occurrences of a field (such as the descriptor field), which may look to be a single field when displayed. It is important to distinguish this method from the one where the index term is manually marked before indexing. The disadvantage of phrase indexing is that you have to know the exact wording in a compound descriptor or corporate body name. As always, the best solution is if the users have the option to choose, i.e., the fields are both word indexed and phrase indexed. This is called double posting because a compound term is entered in the index as such and also by its component words. In our example double posting is used for the journal name and the descriptor fields shown in figure 2.19.

Code Lookup Indexing

This technique is an excellent tool for improving the quality of the database. Only codes and abbreviations are entered in the master record. There is an auxiliary file which includes these codes and abbreviations along with their full format. When a record is indexed, the equivalent of the code is used to create an index entry. Similarly, when a record is displayed, the equivalent text of the code is located in the auxiliary file and replaces the code while displaying the record. Codes of languages, publication types, abbreviations of publication names, and publishers are primary candidates for code lookup indexing. In our example the language codes and the treatment code fields are indexed this way. This technique ensures consistency and cuts back on data entry time and storage requirements of the master records.

Marked Indexing

This technique is used mostly with databases that have long records, typically full-text databases, or records with lengthy abstracts. An indexing specialist reads the text and marks the words and compound terms in the text that should become index entries. Marking is usually done by enclosing the terms between a special character pair not used otherwise in the text, such as < > or { }.

The advantages of this technique are that it takes less space (there are no separate and redundant index fields) and it is flexible in selecting terms anywhere in the record on an ad hoc basis. The disadvantage is that a human being has to make the marking consistently, a process that is error-prone and slow compared to automatic parsing. Furthermore, there is no controlled vocabulary as in phrase indexing.

These alternatives are not mutually exclusive. They may be used within the same database for different fields, or even for the same field. Dual indexing (or double posting) of some fields is best for users, so they can choose the approach they prefer. These methods can be further subdivided by whether they do or do not use prefixes in generating the index terms. The prefixed indexing method adds a two- to three-character prefix (tag) before the term. The tag identifies the field that the term came from, e.g., AF = Harvard University (if the term was extracted from the author affiliation) versus DE = Harvard University (if taken from the descriptor field). Prefixed indexing is very convenient for the user as it pulls together various name formats and spellings of the same term within the same field. It makes it very easy to scan the neighborhood of the index term and find relevant alternate formats, even if they are recorded incorrectly. This is illustrated in figure 2.22, which is an excerpt from the subject index of the OCLC version of Education Library database.

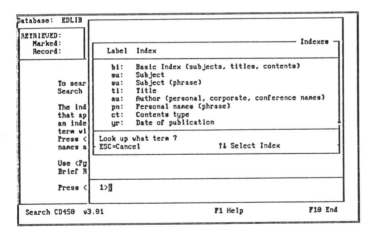 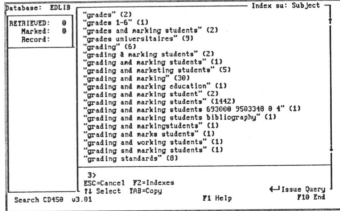

Fig. 2.22. Field-specific index in EDLIB.

Prefixed indexing is simply for the sake of users. From the point of view of the search program, it is irrelevant if the field is identified by a prefix or within the index entry itself (as illustrated earlier in the hypothetical inverted file in figures 2.20 and 2.21). It can identify the source field of the term either way if needed, when you specify in the query that the term must occur in a specific field. Browsing in the prefixed, or field-specific, indexes that are supposed to use some controlled vocabulary tells a lot about the quality of the database. It is surprising that datafile producers or database publishers do not review the prefixed indexes to correct at least the most blatant errors in their databases.

Index Browsing

Browsing in indexes is essential to become familiar with the terminology of a database and to use the right terms in formulating a search. Index browsing is available in most databases, and it is essential for looking up possible terms to be used in the query. Searching without the ability to browse one or more indexes is like driving in an unknown neighborhood without a map. Given the powerful search capability of the Bluefish software, it is strange that this much needed feature is not available. (An indirect way to look into the index is to use truncation. Bluefish displays all the terms with the stem you specify. Of course, this is a far cry from real index browsing.)

In some CD-ROM databases you may browse any of the available indexes, as is the case with the OnDisc databases. Others limit browsing to a few selected fields. Books in Print offers browsing in the publisher index, but not in the Dewey Decimal Code or in the National Library of Medicine subject code indexes. In Magazine Articles Summaries you may only browse in the subject descriptor index, not in the basic index created from words in the title, journal name, publication date, and abstract fields. Sometimes you are not explicitly advised in which index you are browsing, as in the UMI databases, where you have no choice when you browse since there is only one index.

Sometimes the interface level defines the browsing capabilities. In the Wilbrowse mode of Wilsondisc you may browse the subject index (actually you must, as it is the only way to retrieve records), and in the Wilsonline mode you may browse all the indexes, but in the Wilsearch mode you cannot browse at all.

In some systems you can only guess from where the index terms you are looking at have been extracted. The SPIRS software, for example, shows the index with terms culled and lumped together from most of the fields. You learn only from the documentation or the help file that hyphenated terms were extracted from the descriptor, author name, or journal name field, but you do not know from which one. Is the term Religious-Education a descriptor or a journal name? Actually, both—under the same entry.

In other systems you see a list of single words when browsing the index, as in all the UMI databases. This is the consequence of exclusive word indexing. Phrase indexing produces compound terms in the index. Long compound terms may appear truncated in the index list, as the length of the entry is limited to 20 to 30 characters. Browsing in a single-word-only index is disadvantageous when you want to see the complete form of a name or the presence of a descriptor phrase such as "working mother," instead of an entry under "working" and another one under "mother." Single-word listing is even more constraining when you need to know not only the presence of a compound term, but also its posting.

Postings

Most databases show not only the index terms but also the number of records in which they occur. In some systems the total occurrence of the terms is also displayed along with all the entries. The former is called record posting; the latter is term posting. Term posting is always higher than or equal to record posting, as the same term may occur several times within the same record. If prefixed indexing is used and the index is browsable you may see how many times a term occurs in a given field by browsing in the field-specific indexes. This is called field posting.

Posting information in the indexes is a very useful search aid. Postings in single-word indexes are less informative, because a few thousand postings under "New" and under "Mexico" does not imply that there will be any under "New Mexico." Phrase indexing combined with posting information, however, will give a clue whether you need to narrow or broaden a query before executing it. This may spare a lot of time, as the search for the combined occurrences of two or three terms (proximity search) may be painfully slow.

Cross-references and Thesaurus Handling

The more sophisticated CD-ROM products tell you if the term you selected does not exist but there are one or more alternative terms that could be used. This is the traditional "see" referencing. If the original term you entered exists but there are other related terms you are advised about, it is called "see-also" referencing. "See also" is available only with fields using controlled vocabulary or with authority files that specify the exact form of a descriptor, a name, a title, and so on.

In consulting the indexes, the ultimate help is browsing the terms in a thesaurus, a set of hierarchically arranged terms with extensive cross-references from and to narrower and broader terms, synonyms, and non-preferred terms as illustrated by figure 2.23. It shows how the term *Academic Libraries* is accessed and what a printed portion of the thesaurus looks like.

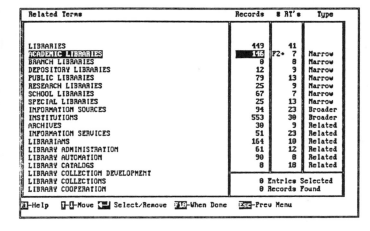

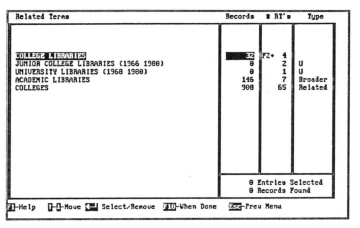

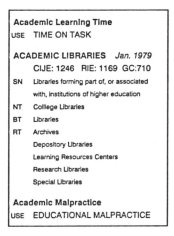

Fig. 2.23. Excerpts from the ERIC thesaurus.

The availability of "see" and "see also" references and thesaurus references in a database depends both on the datafile and on the software. If a datafile has no authority file or a thesaurus, the software cannot help. If the datafile has one of these, the software still may not be able to handle it. Even within a family of products this may vary. Both the ERIC and the MEDLINE files come with a thesaurus file, but SPIRS handles only that of MEDLINE and PSYCLIT as of 1991 (though the ERIC thesaurus has been promised since 1989). Dialog's OnDisc software has been capable of handling the thesaurus of both ERIC and MEDLINE since the beginning. The OCLC CD450 software does not offer thesaurus handling at all.

The extent of thesaurus handling varies from software to software, and this is one of the major differences among the seven implementations of the MEDLINE database. The handling of thesaurus terms may vary even within the same database, depending on which level of interface is used. The Wilsondisc software offers "see," "see also," and thesaurus references. The former two are available only in the browse mode, and the last, only in the Wilsonline mode.

In Wilson browse mode there are three possible results when you enter a term as illustrated in figure 2.24. If the term is a subject heading you see it in the index displayed along with a posting number. If another term is used as a subject heading, you see an asterisk next to the term and a clear instruction for looking up the preferred subject heading. If there is no such term or preferred term for the one you entered, a message appears on the top of the screen. If there are more than 100 records under the subject heading you selected, you are advised to use a more specific subject heading. In the Wilsonline mode you may display the basic index or a field-specific index. If a term is a descriptor (indicated by the DS tag), you may look up its thesaurus relationship as illustrated by figure 2.25.

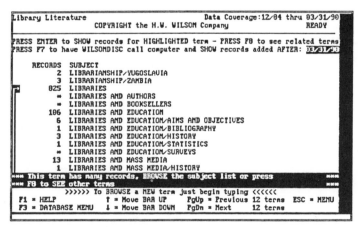

Fig. 2.24. Excerpt from the index in Wilson browse mode.

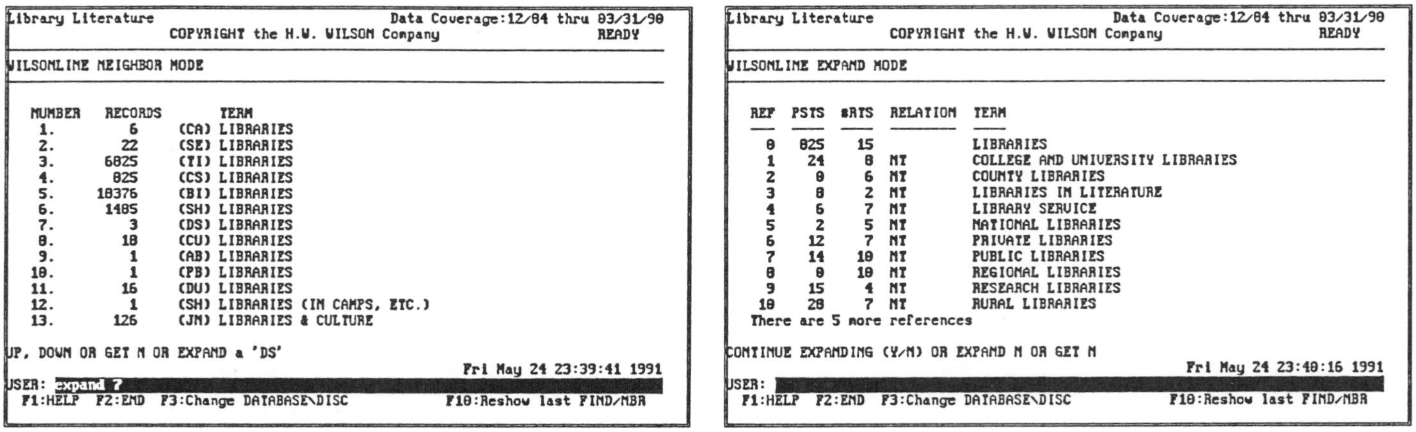

Fig. 2.25. Thesaurus references in Wilsonline mode.

The capability of the software to handle these kind of references is only one side of the coin. To be able to evaluate the thesaurus of the database you have to know the other side, which is the quality of the thesaurus or the non-hierarchical authority file. This is discussed in chapter 3.

In less sophisticated cross referencing systems the postings are not shown as in MAS (figure 2.26).

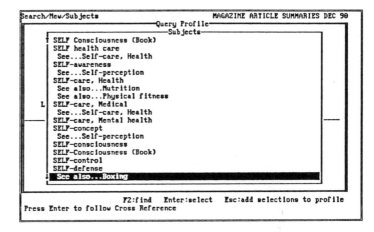

Fig. 2.26. "See" and "see also" references in MAS.

With some CD-ROM products, "see" and "see also" references are offered in the search mode but not in index browsing. The OCSI software has a very valuable feature for handling "see" and "see also" references, though only in the search mode and only in the Ulrich's Plus database. In the Bowker databases you may dynamically modify the search option to enable or disable the automatic inclusion or exclusion of either or both types of references by selecting the appropriate option from a menu, as shown in figure 2.27.

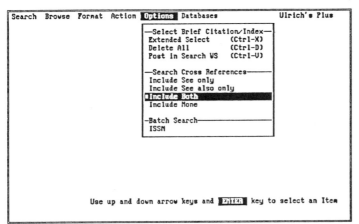
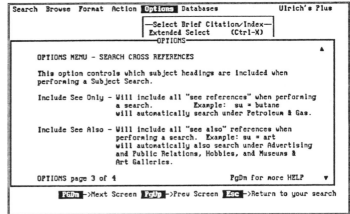

Fig. 2.27. Options for "see" and "see also" reference in Ulrich's Plus.

In the OCSI-PAIS database, if you enter a term that is not a subject heading or is not the only one, then the preferred, or alternate, term(s) is displayed automatically in a window and you may then select one or more of the recommended terms (figure 2.28, page 36).

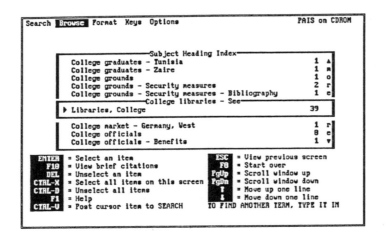

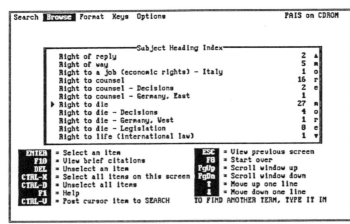

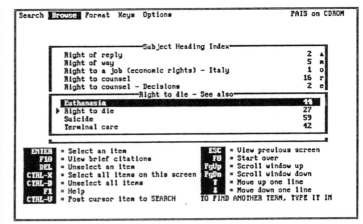

Fig. 2.28. "See" and "see also" reference in OCSI-PAIS.

Having the cross-referencing feature for terms in one field does not imply that it is available for other fields as well. In The Serials Directory of EBSCO, both forms of references are available in the A/I journal title index and the descriptor index, but not in the publisher name and the title proper indexes. To the credit of EBSCO, if you enter the former title of a serial it will automatically retrieve the record with the current title, which includes the former title in a clearly identified field. However, as the field containing the former title is usually the last data element in the record, it may not be apparent why a record was retrieved, particularly if the former title appears only on the second screen of the record. Interestingly, and somewhat confusingly, there are entries in the title index for the variant titles. This underlines the need for a clear explanation in the documentation as to which fields and subfields are used to create the various indexes.

Term Selection and Entry

The purpose of browsing is to find the appropriate terms for a search. Looking at these terms in the index file is useful in itself, but if you have to memorize the spelling and variants of several terms, you may make a mistake when entering them. If you jot them down, or print them out, you slow down the process considerably. However, there are various ways to facilitate term selection and entry. These include term selection from the index, term selection from the record, and hyperlink searching.

Term Selection from the Index

Most CD-ROM software packages allow marking of the terms to be used in searching. A few limit the selection to only one term, which is immediately searched. This is the case in the browse mode of Wilsondisc and ProQuest. The user has no chance to select more than one term, let alone to combine more terms. The software emulates the one-dimensional use of the printed index in the browse mode. Somewhat better is the solution used by ProQuest and EBSCO. You may still select only one term at once, which is then searched, but you may return to index browsing and select another term and combine it with the previous one. This flip-flopping between the index browsing and search modes, however, is inconvenient.

Much better is the solution used by SPIRS, OnDisc, CD450, and the Bowker database family, which all allow you to select multiple terms from the index and then indicate by a special key that you have finished selection and want the search to be executed. The terms selected this way are automatically combined in an OR relationship, i.e., as alternative terms. If the index term was field-specific, so will be the retrieval: if you selected "Lancet" from the journal name index then the records that have this term in their journal name fields are retrieved. If you select the term from the basic index, all records with the term in the fields used to create the basic index are retrieved.

Term Selection from the Record

An interesting and not widely available facility is the selection of terms from the records being displayed. This option, offered by SPIRS, ProQuest, and CD450, is called lateral searching, sideways searching, and pull-mode searching, respectively. On displaying a record you may move the cursor to a term, highlight the term, and search for it in the database. This is a very useful solution, because you are likely to find terms in the records that you have not specified in your original query, and may easily expand your search to records with these terms. What makes this option so attractive is that you can do it without having to jot down the terms, exit the current search, and type in the new terms for a new query.

Hyperlink Searching

A related facility is the hyperlink searching available mostly in encyclopedias and dictionaries. Terms that are (typically) boldfaced, italicized, or preceded by a special character such as -> in printed versions, to indicate the availability of a stand-alone article for the term, can be immediately displayed in a window from within the article you are currently consulting in the CD-ROM database. If this second article also contains terms that you want to look up, you may do so. Backtracking to the original article is very simple: you just keep closing windows of the looked-up terms until you are back at the original. Usually you can see the titles of the previous articles and get a feel for where you are. Figure 2.29, page 38, illustrates a hyperlink chain in Grolier Encyclopedia.

The search starts with an article about Budapest; then we jump to an article about Hungary (now shown); finally in the "Culture" section of the article we position the cursor over the capitalized name "LISZT" indicating an article exists. Press the ALT-L keys to bring up the list of titles; highlight the appropriate line and pressing the Enter key to display the article about Franz Liszt.

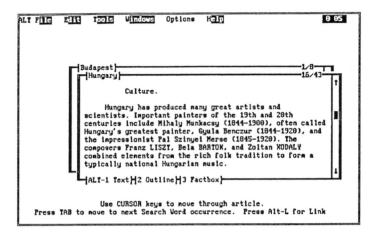

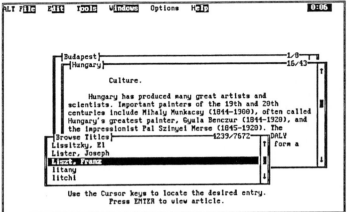

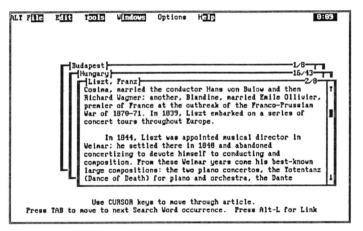

Fig. 2.29. Hyperlink chain in Grolier.

The technique may not be perfect yet. In Grolier the hyperlinked terms are indicated by capitalization, but not all the capitalized terms have a hyperlink, such as acronyms of corporate bodies, which are always capitalized. On the other hand, not all the terms that are article titles themselves are capitalized. In the record about Franz Liszt the name *Richard Wagner* is not capitalized, even though there is an article about him. In spite of these glitches, you will certainly appreciate the ease and speed of hyperlink searching if you have ever kept each of four fingers in different parts of a volume or tried to spread four or five volumes of the encyclopedia on your desk to jockey back and forth between articles.

The difference between hyperlink references and "see," "see also," and thesaurus references is illustrated by figure 2.30 and described below. When using thesaurus or authority list references, you select the related terms before initiating the search, whereas in hyperlink the selection of the related term is done inside the search process. The similarity between the two methods is that both require the pre-establishment of the references and the links by the database producer, and the user has to live with those predefined relations.

The difference between hyperlink searching and lateral searching is that the latter allows the user to pick any term from a record, but does not guarantee that the term will produce additional records, whereas a term being designated as a hyperlink warrants that there is a record (an encyclopedic article) for that term. The exceptions referred to above in Grolier are not significant. Furthermore, from the hyperlink search you can easily trace back to the result of the original query, whereas with lateral searching you initiate a new search and abandon the displaying of records from the original query; typically you have to re-execute the original query to get back to your original records. The similarity is that in both hyperlink and lateral searching you jump to another record from within the record being displayed. A database also may offer more than one type of term selection. In the SPIRS version of MEDLINE you may use the thesaurus to select terms and initiate a search; then you may use the lateral searching from within a displayed record.

	Cross references	Lateral search	Hyperlink search
Pre-established link	Y	N	Y
Any term	N	Y	N
Guaranteed hit	Y	N	Y
Abandon original query	N/A	Y	N
From record	N	Y	Y

Fig. 2.30. Differences among term selection alternatives.

Truncation

Truncation is the facility that allows users to enter only the root of a term followed by a special character, the truncation symbol. The root may be a few characters of a single term, such as "librar?," or a part of a compound term, such as the last name of an author and the first character of his/her first name ("Koenig, M?") or the first two words from a corporate body name ("Chase Manhattan?"). The above described truncation is the most common and is called right-hand truncation. Left-hand truncation is much less common, though it would be useful in many databases to retrieve terms with different prefixes, like entering "$phobia" to retrieve xenophobia, francophobia, and necrophobia or "$pirin" for Kalmopirin, Algopirin, aspirin, and so on. At this writing only Grolier, World Bank's Infofinder, the Bluefish, and Compact Cambridge software packages allow left-hand truncation.

Left-hand truncation is a more difficult function than right-hand truncation because index entries are alphabetically sorted from left to right. To select items with various endings is easy and fast from such a list, because they are adjacent in the inverted file. For left-hand truncation, all the index entries have to be serially scanned. This is a slow process. Left-hand truncation could be made as fast as right-hand truncation if a palindrome index were also created. Because the index file is usually very large, however, this would be feasible only with databases where the palindrome dictionary also could be accommodated on the same disk as the straight one.

Distinction should be made between fixed-length versus variable-length character truncation. In the former, only the specified number of character(s) is truncated; in the latter any character after the root is ignored in finding a match. Premature truncation may result in false drops, particularly if the term is used alone. For example, "manag$" retrieves not only management, manager, managers, and managing, but also Managua. In some CD-ROM products only one type of truncation is allowed, usually variable length, as in the SilverPlatter, Bluefish, and EBSCO-CD products. The majority allow both kinds of truncation. A further, atypical limitation is found in the Bluefish software: you may not combine terms in one statement if you use truncation. This limitation may be overcome by using the set combination command, but it is definitely an inconvenience.

For those who use databases from different publishers it is discouraging to see how many variants are used in different software packages for the same function (figure 2.31, page 40). The question is whether the software would recognize and warn you about an error or would simply return the message "no records found" if you choose the invalid symbol.

SOFTWARE	TRUNCATION				MASKING	
	Specified	Variable	Left	Right	Specified	Variable
Bluefish	?	*	✓	✓	?	*
Bowker-Plus	?	$		✓	?	
CD450	?	*		✓		?
Cambridge		*	✓	✓		
EBSCO-CD		*		✓	?	$
Grolier	?	*	✓	✓		
Infofinder	?	*	✓	✓	?	*
OnDisc Command	? ?	?		✓	?	
OnDisc Menu	? ?	?		✓	?	
ProQuest		? a		✓	?	
SPIRS		*		✓		
Wilbrowse				✓		
Wilsearch	# b	:		✓	#	
Wilsonline	#	:		✓	#	

(a) unsolicited pluralization and singularization

(b) unsolicited singularization in subject field

Fig. 2.31. Truncation symbol alternatives.

Some software packages like Wilsondisc and ProQuest do automatic truncation when a term ends in "s," "es," or "ies." This may be advantageous when a searcher forgets to use both the plural and the singular forms of a term and therefore may miss many relevant records. It is a bonus in ProQuest that the terms retrieved by the automatic truncation are displayed while searching, so the user can see the effect. However, there are situations when this unsolicited truncation backfires. You cannot search for "AIDS" without retrieving everything about "aid," for example. In the Library Literature database using Wilsearch you cannot search for the information retrieval program "CAIRS" without getting every record, which includes terms beginning with CAIR such as Cairo. The software should allow the disabling of automatic truncation either completely or for the actual query. Without this option it is like culinary hospitality turning into forced feeding (as experienced by diet conscious Americans visiting friends in Hungary). The effect of unsolicited truncation is well illustrated by an example: when looking for items about the right to die, the article entitled "Holmes, the Advocate of Civil Rights, Dies at Age 84" was retrieved from Periodicals Abstracts.

A further problem is if the unsolicited truncation is not consistent. In Wilsearch, for words ending in "ss," the last "s" is replaced by a single truncation symbol (e.g., MASS is truncated to MAS# and LOSS to LOS#), except the word *less*, which is searched as "le##," a string that could result in too many irrelevant records. To further confuse the user, the Wilsearch help file claims that the word *less* cannot be searched. Fortunately, the word is searchable; otherwise you would have difficulty searching for articles about less-developed countries.

Far the best solution is when the terms resulting from a solicited or unsolicited truncation are displayed and the user can select the ones needed by highlighting them. This is illustrated by figure 2.32. After entering the truncated term "Surf*", the World Book's Infofinder software displays the terms to be retrieved, and the user highlights the appropriate ones.

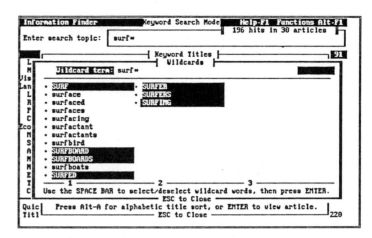

Fig. 2.32. Popup screen of truncated term matches.

Wildcarding (Masking)

A closely related facility is wildcarding, when one or more character(s) within a word may be masked in finding a match. Distinction must be made between single- and multiple-character masking. Depending on the software, "col?r" may retrieve only "color" and not "colour," or it may retrieve both and also the irrelevant terms "collar," "collator," or "columnar." Some systems allow only one type of masking (Bluefish), others use different symbols for the two functions (OnDisc, OCSI), and many do not allow masking at all (SPIRS, ProQuest). Masking is particularly useful to compensate for British and U.S. spelling differences and irregular plurals, such as labor versus labour, (wo)man and (wo)men, foot and feet, thesis and theses, and analysis and analyses. Many user guides and reviews call this feature internal or embedded truncation, which seems to be a misnomer; you can truncate something from one of the two ends. The term *masking* would be more informative, but it does not seem to be used in the literature.

ProQuest also does automatic pluralization, which is uncommon in CD-ROM software. Plural forms are not searched automatically if the singular ends in the vowels a, i, o, or u or if the plural is irregular. Again, automatic pluralization is a good idea, but it may become annoying if users are not given a disable option. If automatic pluralization is combined with unsolicited truncation, articles about any new program are retrieved in a search about news programs, or—unless you use positional operators—ProQuest retrieves everything about commercial banks even if you are interested only in bank commercials.

Boolean Operations

Boolean operations allow the user to define a logic by which the set of records to be retrieved is defined. Three operators are widely used: OR, AND, and NOT. The OR operator between two or more search terms creates a set in which the records include at least one of the terms specified. The AND operator creates a set in which the records include all the terms combined. The NOT operator creates a set whose records do not include the term(s) specified after the NOT operator.

To be more precise, in all of the above cases it is not enough if the search terms appear in the records themselves. They also must be indexed, i.e., they must occur in the inverted file, to meet the criteria. If the month of publication is not indexed, though it is displayed in the record, you may not be able to use it in a Boolean operation to limit your search to the month of publication.

There may be limitations on how many terms you may use in a single query. In Compact Cambridge Menu you may use only two terms in a Boolean operation, which makes it necessary to do stepwise queries if you want to use, for example, three or more synonyms. In the Bluefish software the limit is four. This is reasonable enough, but another constraint of the Boolean operation poses a limit: you may not use truncation in a Boolean expression.

In some other software the length of the query is explicitly limited, e.g., in CD450 the limit is 54 characters. In other cases the number of terms combined in a single query may be implicitly limited by the physical length of the query line (ProQuest) or the width of the template window (EBSCO-CD, Wilsearch). This is not an absolute limitation because the space is enough for four to five terms, and you may break a longer query into smaller units.

You may combine not only several terms but also several operators within a query. If you combine several operators you have to know the order (precedence) of their evaluations, and you may need to explicitly specify the order if the implicit precedence rule is not appropriate for your search. Usually the implied precedence between Boolean operators is NOT, AND, and OR. This is the same principle that you learned in grade-school mathematics:

$$3 * 8 - 2 = 22 \text{ not equal } 3 * (8 - 2) = 18$$

Similarly, the query "Asia OR Africa AND libraries" retrieves different records from the query "(Asia OR Africa) AND libraries". The former retrieves anything about Asia and anything about libraries in Africa, whereas the latter retrieves only those records in which either Asia or Africa appears together with the term *libraries*.

These search facilities allow you to specify quite complex queries, but these are only the basic search facilities that must be available in every CD-ROM software package. However, these capabilities may not be sufficient. A fairly complex query such as

(microcomput? OR (personal and computers) or PC? ?) AND librar? AND (circulation or acquisition?)

retrieves records about the use of microcomputers in libraries for circulation or acquisition purposes. You would need other search facilities if you want to increase the precision of the search, because this query also retrieves records about acquisitions of microcomputers for libraries, which may not be relevant for your interest. These additional facilities, discussed below, include field qualification, proximity operations, and positional operations. The availability of arithmetic operations in the software may increase the precision of your search not in terms of subject, but in other aspects of relevance.

A term used in your query may occur in several fields of the master records. The term *Little* may occur in (1) the name of an author (John *Little*), (2) an institute (*Little* League), (3) a corporate body (the publisher *Little*, Brown), (4) a geographic location (*Little* Rock, Arkansas), (5) the title or the abstract as an adjective (Adam is a *little* child), or (6) as part of a descriptor (*Little* Red Riding Hood).

Elements of a compound term such as *quality of life* or *time management* may occur in different fields or within the same field but not next to each other in this sequence. Their presence within the same records or the same field in itself does not guarantee that those records deal with the issues of quality of life or time management. The word *life* may be in the journal name field and the title reads, "the quality of Japanese cars," or the abstract may include the sentence, "The management of savings in time of economic depression has become a popular rip-off." These records would be obvious false drops. Advanced search facilities can help increase the precision of a search.

Field Qualification

To reduce the chances for false drops (irrelevant records) you must be able to specify in which field(s) the term should occur to qualify for retrieval. In many CD-ROM systems a basic index is used unless you specify otherwise. Sometimes it is also called a keyword index (Bowker-CD) or any-field index (EBSCO-CD).

There are significant differences among CD-ROM products in how this index is created, which fields are used, and how the index terms are generated. In the Wilson databases the basic index is created from single terms in the title field and compound terms in the descriptor fields, but terms in the abstracts are not included.

In databases using the OnDisc and CD450 software the basic index typically also includes single words from the abstract, and the descriptor field is double posted as a phrase index and as a word index. In the ProQuest databases of UMI, only single words are entered in the basic index, though from all the fields of a record.

In the Bowker databases the basic (keyword) index includes terms from every textual field, but not from the coded and numeric fields, such as country codes, language codes, classification codes, and subscription prices. EBSCO-CD lumps together terms from every field without exception in its basic index, whose name (any-field) alludes to this fact.

The content of the basic index depends both on the software and the dataware, so you should not assume that two databases will have the same fields as the source of terms in the basic index just because you are using the same software with two or more databases. If you enter a single term without any qualification it is searched in the basic index. If you enter two or more terms it may be interpreted as an OR operation, an AND operation, a proximity operation, or a positional operation or it may automatically limit the retrieval to exact matches in one or more fields that are phrase indexed. These are discussed under the section on implicit operations.

Usually, however, you may take control and qualify the search to limit the retrieval to records that include the term(s) in field(s) specified by you. This is called field qualification. There are two types of field qualification: suffix qualification and prefix qualification. Suffix qualification is the less common, and it is only available in command-driven systems, such as OnDisc Command and Wilsondisc Wilsonline. After entering the term you specify the tag of the field in which the term should occur to qualify for retrieval. You may define one or more suffixes, as illustrated by figure 2.33.

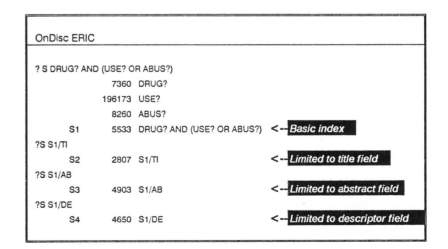

Fig. 2.33. Suffix searching examples.

The software may limit you to using only one suffix, as in Wilsonline and SPIRS. The suffixes (tags) are database specific. It is a unique and convenient feature of ProQuest that you may use not only the full name or the tag of the fields, but (with a few of them) also an alternate tag with which you may be familiar from other systems. For example, SUBJECT, SU, and DE are all acceptable prefixes in the UMI database family. On the other hand, it is a rather unfriendly characteristic of SPIRS that the same fields have different tags in the various databases: JN is used for journal name in PsycLIT, but SO is the tag in LISA for the same field.

In most command-driven systems you also may use prefix indexing (ProQuest, CD450, OnDisc Command). The more sophisticated software packages allow multiple prefixes before the term, which means you do not have to repeat the query with different field tags and then combine the results but may specify all the field tags of interest in one query. Some prefix search examples are shown in figure 2.34.

Software	Query	To retrieve record if term occurs in
OnDisc	cs,jn=drug	corporate source or journal name
CD450	co,jn,su:drug	company, journal, subject
ProQuest	jn (drug) co (drug) su (drug)	journal company subject
Wilsonline	ti (drug) jn(drug) ab (drug)	title journal abstract

Fig. 2.34. Prefix searching examples.

Non-subject fields are also qualifiable, which allows you to specify that a term must occur in the author field. This is particularly important when a personal name is also a commonly used noun or adjective, such as Bush or Black. Though it is possible that a software package provides both prefix and suffix searching, usually a field is either prefix or suffix indexed. It is rather exceptional that a field is searchable in both modes, as is the corporate name in the OnDisc version of MEDLINE.

In the template- and menu-driven system the prefixes either are presented on the workform you use to specify the query (EBSCO-CD, Wilsearch) or have to be entered by you in front of the term (Bowker-CD, OCSI-PAIS). These typically limit the search to one field, unless you use the basic index field cell on the template or the prefix explicitly. Occasionally a field prefix may refer to several fields in the record. The title index in Ulrich's Plus, for example, includes terms from many fields with title information, such as parallel, variant, former, and succeeding title fields, and the documentation makes this clear. The same is true of the MARCIVE version of the GPO (Government Printing Office) database. Its documentation specifies the tags of the MARC fields and also the subfield codes of the (sub)fields used to create the indexes.

The availability of prefixed or suffixed searching is not yet a guarantee for successful searching. The field qualification must be appropriate for the database and for the indexing technique used. A blatant oversight of this hinders even reasonable searching by classification codes in EBSCO's Serials Directory. This type of search is essential in such a database, and the database carries several types of classification codes. Still, records are practically inaccessible by those codes because there is no field qualification for these fields.

Searching in the basic (any-field) index, which lumps together all terms from all fields, would yield unacceptable results. If you want to search for sociological journals and use the Dewey Classification Code 301 for it, you get all the serials of all the publishers located in Miami, whose area code is 301, and those of any publisher whose street address, zip code, or phone number (not only the area code) includes the character string 301. For the same reason, searching by circulation figures or subscription price is hopeless in this database. Sensible searching by LC code is impossible, too. If you want to find home economics serials, whose LC classification code is TX, you get all the serials published in Texas. These are not sporadic false drops, but voluminous ones, and there is no way to eliminate them.

False drops may also result from the fact that only word indexing is used. The journal name field both in the Magazine Article Summaries (MAS) of EBSCO and in all the UMI databases is word indexed, and word indexed only. You may qualify your search by limiting the result to one or more journals. Still, a search for articles published in *Life* magazine retrieves all the records citing *Outdoor Life*, *Soviet Life*, and *Family Life*. Phrase indexing of this field would solve this problem. You may exclude unwanted journal titles by explicitly listing them using the NOT operator, but this is a cumbersome procedure. The database publisher can help to avoid such ambiguities by including value-added information in the records (such as ISSN or unique journal code in this example) and improve the quality of the database. The various methods of doing this are discussed in chapter 4. The lack of appropriate record structuring and the inadequate identification of data elements may prevent the effective use of field-qualified searching even if this facility is available. The characteristics of adequate record structuring are discussed in chapter 3.

Proximity Operations

Proximity operation is a valuable feature for increasing search precision. It allows you to define the exact or maximum distance between two or more terms. There are five levels of proximity: field level, paragraph level, sentence level, word level, and descriptor level. (EBSCO-CD is the only package using character proximity and it seems impractical.)

Field-level proximity specifies that the terms must occur within the same field to qualify for retrieval. If you are unable to specify that the terms *sport* and *science* should both be in the title, or in the descriptor or abstract fields, you would retrieve many articles from *Popular Science* about sports cars. This may happen in MAS, where you can qualify the terms to co-occur in the title or the descriptor field, but not in the abstract field. If you limit the search to these two fields, however, you may miss some relevant items.

In most other software packages more fields can be used for field-level proximity. The difference is in the way you may define the fields. Can you specify one field at a time only, or more than one? In CD450 and OnDisc Command you may specify more fields; in Wilsonline, SPIRS, ProQuest, and most of the template- and menu-driven software you may not.

Even in those databases where more sophisticated field-level qualification is available, you may not be able to filter out all false drops. In the OnDisc version of ERIC the following query specifies that all the terms must occur in the same field.

microcomputers (f) developing (f) countries

This query retrieves the record whose abstract reports that "An investigation has been launched in the Scandinavian **countries** to measure health hazards of those working with **microcomputers**. The study will address allegations that extensive exposure to VDU screens of PCs may lead to **developing** cancer."

Paragraph proximity is similar to field proximity, but it is used in full-text databases where the full-text portion of the records is structured in paragraphs to allow more precise searches. The query above would look like the following in Computer Library and would retrieve the same record as shown above.

microcomputers ANDP developing ANDP countries

In full-text databases, or in databases with long abstracts, the sentence proximity feature is essential. It allows you to specify that terms occur within the same sentence. This may reduce false drops considerably, but not completely. The above query would look like this for sentence-proximity specification:

microcomputers ANDS developing ANDS countries

However, this query would still retrieve articles about "**developing** powerful **microcomputers** by Western European **countries**," though you need items about microcomputers in developing countries.

Word proximity helps filter out such false drops, limiting the retrieval to only those records where these terms occur next to each other or within a few words. The modified query with word proximity would look like this:

microcomputers WITHIN5W developing WITHIN1W countries

meaning that the word *microcomputers* must be within a maximum of five words from the phrase *developing countries*. The operator WITHIN1W makes these two words a phrase, specifying that they must be adjacent. In other software a similar statement could be formulated as shown below:

OnDisc   microcomputer? (5N) developing (W) countr?/ab

CD450   ab:microcomputer* ADJ5 developing ADJ1 countr*

ProQuest   ab (microcomputer? w/5 developing w/1 countr?)

In menu-driven systems you may specify proximity either within a query or by popping up an options window. In the OnDisc Menu software you use the operators *, —, and . to specify field, sentence, and word proximity. In Grolier you pop up the search options window (figure 2.35) to define whether the terms you entered are to be within the same article, paragraph, or sentence or within a distance of *n* words. The implicit proximity is 10 words, but you may change this either for the duration of your search or for good.

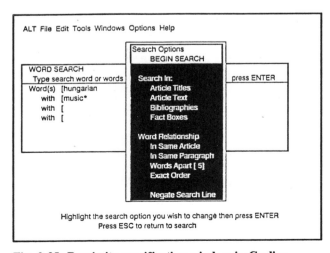

Fig. 2.35. Proximity specification window in Grolier.

Word proximity, as you would expect, is measured by words, except in EBSCO-CD, which does not have any other explicit proximity operator. The default proximity is 50 characters, which is approximately five words according to EBSCO. You may change this proximity value by popping up a window in which the distance may be specified. Proximity is specified by enclosing the terms between square brackets. The query [developing countr*] yields different results depending on the proximity value. This is not only an uncommon way to specify proximity, but also a very subtle one at that, unlikely to be used by users except the most devout.

Word proximity, however, may be a double-edged sword. If you specify too close a proximity you may miss too many useful items, particularly if the result is not zero, which would call your attention to the possible problem. If you enter the query

drug w/3 abuse

you would find a few dozen records where the title or abstract includes "drug abuse" or "drug and alcohol abuse." But you may miss records where "drug, substance and alcohol abuse" is used. Figure 2.36 illustrates the various proximity operators in some software.

SOFTWARE	Field or Paragraph level	Sentence level	Word level	Posi-tional
Bluefish	withinNp	withinNs	withinNw	
Bowker-Plus	field tag			
CD450	with		adjN	
Cambridge	field tag		W/N	
EBSCO-CD	template		[ ]	
Grolier	menu	menu	menu	menu
Infofinder	andNp	andNs	andNw	
OnDisc Command	(f)	(s) (Ns)	(Nn)	(Nw)
OnDisc Menu	*	-	--	
ProQuest	W/seg		w/N	pre/N
SPIRS	with	near	near n	
Wilbrowse				
Wilsearch	template			
Wilsonline	field tag			

Fig. 2.36. Proximity operators.

None of the above queries would prevent false drops of such titles as "Western European countries agree developing joint computer standards." Positional operation may offer some further refinements and increase in precision.

Positional Operations

Positional operators let you specify the order of the terms and, with the most powerful ones, also the proximity of the terms with the specified order. Positional operators can reduce false drops in searches for compound terms, expressions in which adjacency is not sufficient, because the order of the terms makes the difference, such as *nursing home* versus *home nursing*, *jury selection* versus *selection jury*, and *last will* versus *will last forever*.

Positional operators are particulary important with full-text databases or ones with lengthy abstracts. If you are looking for the concept *information retrieval* you may prefer to specify the two words truncated, at maximum three words apart, and in any order that would match such records where "information retrieval," "information storage and retrieval," "retrieval of information," "retrieving information" occurs. You may still have false drops, such as the record whose abstract includes the following: "the black box was never retrieved. Information was leaked by airline employees."

The use of proximity and positional operators may increase the precision of your search, but it also certainly decreases the number of records retrieved. Figure 2.37 illustrates the difference in the number of hits with different proximity and positional operators.

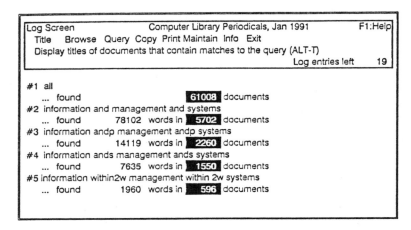

Fig. 2.37. The effects of proximity and positional operators.

The subject of the search, the tolerance for false drops, and the need for completeness should define which operators are used. Adequate facilities in handling the output may influence the query specifications. If it is easy to review relevant parts of the records or to mark records to be selected for inclusion in a printed bibliography, the search strategy may not require sophisticated query operators. Casual patrons are unlikely to be willing to master advanced operations to optimize their searches. It is never a problem if a search feature is available but not used. The problem shows up when a search feature is needed and it is not available.

In OnDisc you may use a KWIC format to display only that part of the record that matches the query. The part may be a full grammatical sentence or a field that includes the term(s) used in the query. In EBSCO-CD you may easily mark records to be excluded from a retrieved set, which is a rare but very useful option as opposed to the general practice where you have to mark records to be included in a printout.

The best way to increase precision is to use in the query precoordinated descriptors presumably assigned to the record by the indexer. It is, however, questionable whether casual users would take the time to study the controlled vocabulary of a database, even if it is available on disk, and whether the descriptors are consistently assigned to all the relevant items. The latter is a tangible measure and one of the criteria in evaluating dataware quality. It is discussed under the heading "Consistency" in chapter 3 on page 138.

Arithmetic Operations

Arithmetic operations are mostly needed in number-oriented databases, such as statistical databases like Consu-stat and directories with lots of numeric data like the Standard & Poor's and Disclosure databases. Here you may want to retrieve records of companies whose sales, profit rate, workforce, assets, or liabilities are equal to, larger than, or less than a specified value.

Just as there often are different ways of writing an author's name, there are various ways to store numbers. The most sophisticated search software packages, such as OnDisc, offer great flexibility in number searching. Figure 2.38, page 50, illustrates the different notations that can be used for the same value. The last screen shows that the same number of records were retrieved by different notations.

Even text-oriented directories may include numeric data by which you may wish to search. In Ulrich's Plus you may want to search for serials having a subscription price or circulation figure less than, greater than, or equal to a given value. Strangely, you may not use the equal to operation but only the other two in the Bowker-CD software.

You also have much less flexibility in specifying numbers. The way Bowker rounds figures up or down when creating the indexes of numeric values may be confusing for the user who does not read the manual. For example, a search for serials with a circulation figure larger than 100,000 copies retrieves also records that have in this field a value between 99,600 and 99,999. These records may be perfectly relevant for the search (as the difference is negligible), but the uninitiated user may be puzzled about why these records were retrieved.

In the CD450 software, used with the ICP Software Database among others, numbers have to be padded to nine digits for searches by price information. This is cumbersome and error-prone. When searching for software costing $100, you have to specify it as "PR: 000000100".

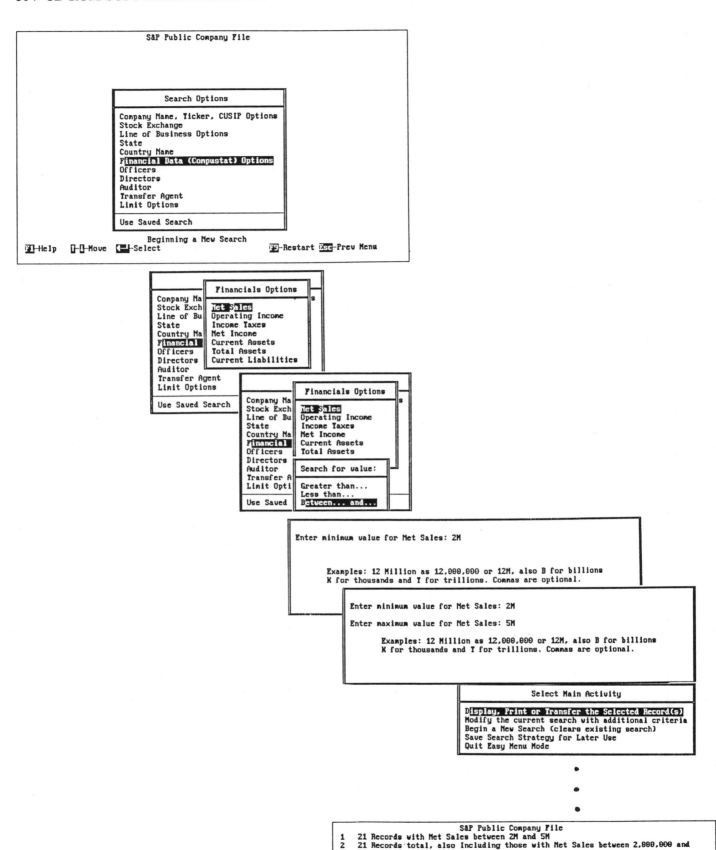

Fig. 2.38. Number searching in OnDisc.

Range searching, available in some systems, allows you to specify in one statement the minimum and maximum values of a field to qualify the retrieval. The syntax of this statement is illustrated in figure 2.39.

Bowker-CD	pr > 50 and pr <101
Dialog OnDisc	pr=50:100
OCLC CD450	pr=000000050/000000100
SPIRS	pr=50-100

Fig. 2.39. Range searching samples.

Range searching is mostly used with numeric fields, but in CD450 you may use it also with textual fields, e.g., "catalog/catalogues." Range searching can be substituted to some extent by truncation, particularly when the length of truncation may be specified.

Even software used with purely textual databases should offer arithmetic operations. The lack of arithmetic operators makes it difficult to limit your search by publication year in EBSCO-CD and ProQuest, though truncation may help in certain situations. For example, in the ProQuest databases of UMI you may limit the search to articles published in the 1990s by simply truncating after the first three digits of the year: DA(199?). But to limit to articles published between 1985 and 1989 you cannot use the shortcut, but have to list the years: DA(1985 OR 1986 OR 1987 OR 1988 OR 1989). In EBSCO-CD any kind of number searching is a sure way to retrieve irrelevant records, because of the way the indexes are generated (as discussed earlier) and the way the data elements are entered and stored in Magazine Article Summaries (discussed in chapter 3).

In systems where you may pick terms from the index easily, range searching may be convenient, as you only have to mark the appropriate numbers on the index list and they are automatically OR-ed together when transferred to a query. If the software leads to a field-specific index or shows the prefix of the field (as do OnDisc Menu and OnDisc Command) the query is unambiguous. Otherwise a number selected from an index (as in SilverPlatter or ProQuest) may or may not be a publication year. If you can easily edit the term(s) transferred from browsing the index and you may use field qualification, this problem is alleviated.

Implicit Operations

Implicit operators are widely used for all kinds of search operations. They take effect automatically, or implicitly. These are very important features of a CD-ROM database used by casual users who do not want to learn various operators, but want only to enter a question and retrieve some records. Human communication is full of implicit operators. If you fix a date on Tuesday for Friday, it will be the next Friday unless you specify explicitly by saying "Friday of next week". If you dial a number on the phone, the implicit area code is the one from which you are calling. These implicit operators are also called default operators, which are taken automatically. The advantage of implicit operators is that you do not have to enter extra operators to specify:

- relationship between terms
- proximity and order between terms
- plural and singular form
- unlimited truncation
- field to be searched

However, there are also disadvantages of implicit operators. They may broaden the search too much (as in the case of unsolicited truncation or pluralization) or narrow it more than you wish (as in limiting a compound term—entered without positional or proximity operator—to the descriptor field).

Implicit operations are not inherently good or bad. The requirements of casual users and search specialists are quite different. What is important is that users be advised about the use of such an operator and have the chance to override this implicit operator. The handling of special characters (slash, hyphen, comma, dot, ampersand); the space character; stopwords (*at*, *from*, *on*, *to*); and words reserved for logical, positional, proximity, and field qualification operators (*and*, *or*, *near*, *in*) is a source of many frustrations, as discussed in the following sections.

Special Characters and the Space Character

The handling of special characters and the space in search statements differs widely. Space deserves special discussion because it is so often used in queries. EBSCO-CD and Bluefish offer the most flexible solutions. When you enter terms like *AC/DC*, *post-mortem*, or *AT&T*, the program searches for the term in three ways: (1) as it is entered, (2) next to each other, and (3) unseparated. This seems to be the most convenient alternative from the user point of view, especially in full-text databases and abstracting/indexing databases, where spelling of the original source is not standardized.

A comma is interpreted by some search software, such as EBSCO-CD and Grolier, as a separator for synonyms, i.e., as an OR relationship. Other software packages give a warning that the syntax is invalid if a comma is used, or look for an exact match of the comma-separated term, or ignore the comma and search for the terms next to each other in either order. If you enter "Paris, Texas" in a ProQuest database it will find all records where the two terms occur within the same field. Wilson, on the other hand, interprets this as an inverted personal name with Paris as the family name and Texas as the first name.

The dot character has particular importance in databases that extensively use the Dewey Decimal Classification system and in numeric databases where the decimal point may make a difference of two orders of magnitude if not used correctly. Most software packages ignore the dots, unfortunately, including those used with library catalogs and directories (EBSCO-CD, OCSI). The CD450 software applies different punctuation rules depending on the database. It is a nice feature of CD450 that by pressing a key combination, the punctuation rules are displayed on the screen.

Understanding how the software handles the space character in compound terms is critical to the realistic evaluation of search results. ProQuest makes its method clear by creating an implicit adjacency operator after two terms are entered next to each other separated by a space ("drug abuse"). OnDisc, however, not only doesn't inform you that it considers this to be the strictest positional operator, but it also limits the search to the descriptor and identifier fields. CD450 accepts such terms and assumes adjacency of the terms, but in any order. EBSCO-CD interprets two terms next to each other as an OR operation.

Automatic Pluralization and Singularization

This facility is often a blessing, as users do not have to enter standard plural and singular forms of a term. However, if the software does not advise you of this feature, let alone allow you to disable it, many unwanted records may be retrieved, as discussed earlier. The ideal solution would be to do truncation and pluralization automatically and provide a message that tells the user how to switch off this feature temporarily.

Handling of Stopwords and Special Words

ProQuest intelligently replaces intervening stopword(s) with the appropriate positional operator (and tells you about it). This is the optimal solution, as illustrated by figure 2.40.

ProQuest	Resource/One	Jan 1986 - Feb 1991
Search Terms		Item Count
(01): dances -> DANCE		942
(02): with -> WITH		Noise Word
(03): wolves -> WOLVE		68
(04): (01) pre/2 (03)		17
Search results in 17 item(s).		
To Display Title List: Press ENTER ESC=Go Back F1=Help F2=Commands		

ProQuest	Resource/One	Jan 1986 - Feb 1991
Search Terms		Item Count
(01): back -> BACK		3206
(02): to -> TO		Noise Word
(03): the -> THE		Noise Word
(04): future -> FUTURE		4314
(05): (01) pre/3 (04)		65
Search results in 65 item(s).		
To Display Title List: Press ENTER ESC=Go Back F1=Help F2=Commands		

Fig. 2.40. Replacement of stopwords by proximity operators in ProQuest.

EBSCO-CD chooses an interesting alternative. It masks as many characters as are in the stopword. For example, if you enter "advertisement to children" the software also retrieves "advertisement of children" and "advertisement by children," but not "advertisement for children," because "for" is three characters. CD450 gives you a message without any clue ("No records found - Try another query"), whereas OnDisc gives a zero result without any clue if you use a phrase such as *quality of life* and it is not a descriptor or identifier in the database.

Many stopwords are database specific, as they may be relevant terms in one database and irrelevant in most others. The term *who* is such a word. As mentioned earlier, it is a noise word in technical databases, but not in many others where it stands as an acronym for World Health Organization. Databases with foreign language coverage present further problems. The Bowker databases have a rather extensive stopword list. This is useful for *Books in Print* and *Variety*, which include mostly English-language text, but may be inconvenient for Ulrich's Plus, which has several thousand French, German, Spanish, Italian, and Portuguese records. When the list of stopwords can be displayed online (as in SPIRS, OnDisc, and CD450), users have more chances to learn what the stopwords are. Grolier does not seem to have been careful enough when it put every single-character "word" on the stopword list. This makes it impossible to search for such terms as *X-ray* or *Malcolm X* because it produces articles about Sugar Ray Robinson and every person whose first name is Malcolm because the single character *X* is ignored. The same problem occurs when the indefinite article *a* is put on a stopword list in many of the SPIRS databases. A search for "vitamin A" retrieves every record that includes the word *vitamin*. OnDisc offers the ideal solution: only the lower-case *a* is put on the stopword list.

A related question is how to handle phrases that include words used to specify logical operation (AND, OR), proximity or positional operation (WITH, NEAR), or field qualification operation (IN). Usually, you have to enclose such phrases in quotes, e.g., "live in companion", "near letter quality", "trick or treat", or "savings and loan". In Wilsondisc mark such a character as "savings a#d loan."

Search Status Display

Some search operations may take a long time to carry out. In such cases, users should be kept informed about the progress of a search continuously. A casual user may not know whether the computer froze or is working hard while nothing changes on the screen. The minimum requirement is to have some sign to indicate that the search is on. Often a flashing message notifies the user, as in the KAWare2 software, and this may irritate some users. It is a better solution when a counter is shown with the number of records retrieved so far. The digits keep increasing as the search progresses. This solution is used in EBSCO-CD, Wilsearch, and Wilsonline. OCSI combines this method with the flashing message.

By far the best method advises the user not only about the absolute progress of the search, but also about the relative progress, or what percent of the search has been completed in a complex search. If you see that the progress is very slow you may interrupt the search or may start doing something else while your CD-ROM software is sweating out the result. SPIRS, CD450, and Bluefish use this method. The former two, particularly the software from OCLC, often seem unable to cope with the speed of the search, and the displayed progress rate is much behind the actual.

A related question is what happens when you interrupt a lengthy search. Most software packages lose the set retrieved for the query in progress. Wilsondisc and EBSCO-CD are the exceptions. Both allow viewing of the records retrieved until the interruption, a very useful feature.

SET AND QUERY MANAGEMENT

Information retrieval systems typically work on sets. Sets represent groups of records that meet the criterion or criteria specified in a query. Creating, modifying, reexecuting, and saving queries are important features of CD-ROM software, as they are pivotal for the heuristic type of searching characteristic of both online and CD-ROM retrieval. These features are even more encouraged in the latter by the lack of pressure of connect time-based charges. Though actual usage is not a factor for license fee payments, the administrator of the CD-ROM database services may wish to have some statistical information about the use of the CD-ROM databases and other related resources for making decisions regarding the renewal of a subscription, the scheduling of the service, and so on. This chapter considers the related capabilities of the software.

Set Building

For complex subject searches, the preferred way of specifying a query is to create subsets of related concepts in a stepwise fashion and then combine these sets and narrow them by limiting to specific fields or restrict the search by additional, non-subject criteria like language, publication period, document type, and so on. This approach allows you to gradually build your query, see the partial results, and modify your query accordingly.

To make this stepwise search convenient, effective, and flexible you must be able to refer to the partial results and use the resulting set of one query in a new query. If you have to repeat the previous query and add other query elements to it, the process is very slow and error-prone. Almost all the software packages automatically identify the result of a query by a set number. A former version of the IAC software did not provide any means to build sets because it used pre-coordinated descriptors, which was believed to compensate for the lack of Boolean operators, field qualification, and set limiting. After several years of defending this concept, IAC modified its software to allow these features, which in turn necessitated set building.

Set building may depend on the mode of user interface being used. No set building is available in the Wilbrowse mode of Wilsondisc, but sophisticated set building is offered in the Wilsonline mode, and a rather uncommon form of set building is available in Wilsearch. It is uncommon because you have to explicitly request after each step to identify the set retrieved by a query and assign a name to the set for later use. Only the most recent query is kept automatically, under the name "Last." It would be much better if queries were automatically kept also in the Wilsearch mode. EBSCO-CD, which uses a fill-in-the-form approach to query formulation that is similar to the template mode of Wilsondisc, offers adequate set building and manipulation, so the Wilsearch approach is not inherent to template-driven software.

The various software packages manage sets in different ways, and some packages have considerable limitations in set handling. The syntactical differences in referring to a set are not surprising. Figure 2.41 illustrates how to combine a set (identified as set number 7) with a term.

Bluefish	#7 and smoking
CD450	7! and smoking
OnDisc	ss s7 and smoking
ProQuest	[7] and smoking
SPIRS	#7 and smoking
Wilsonline	7 and smoking

Fig. 2.41. Syntactical differences in set referencing.

If you do not observe the syntactical rules you do not get error messages, but you do get irrelevant records. If you omit the set symbol most software packages search for the number in the index file and retrieve all the records that include the specified number. Some software packages, such as OCSI, do not allow the combination of set numbers and terms, though you may combine terms with terms and sets with sets. This is a definite inconvenience.

The most typical limitations on the number of sets that may be created during a search session are usually not a problem. The 99-set limit of SPIRS and OnDisc is generous enough; Wilsondisc's 50-set maximum is also a reasonable limit. In a few packages, however, the set limit is too low. Both OCSI and ProQuest allow only 12 active sets. In the former this limit is particularly straining, because every element in a query is assigned a set number. You can easily run out of set numbers even with a fairly simple search, such as the publications of the U.S. Senate Judiciary Commission about conflict of interest issues published between 1985 and 1989. In ProQuest, the result of the query is assigned a set number; its elements are identified only by temporary numbers. Bluefish offers a limit of 24 sets and it numbers only the complete queries, not their partial results. OnDisc Command offers the best solution: it allows 99 sets, and the user may define whether to assign a set number to each element of a query or only to the result of the query itself. SPIRS, CD450, and Wilsonline provide no options for set numbering as every element of a query has a set number.

In those software packages that have low limits for sets, it is important how the set-exceeding situation is handled. OCSI handles the situation better when set numbers have been used up. It warns you and offers you the chance to define which set(s) should be deleted to proceed. ProQuest simply deletes, without any warning, the $n - 12$th set, and you learn about it only when you try to combine a deleted set with a current one.

The size of the set your queries generate is usually limited only by the available memory or hard disk space on the computer, depending on where the temporary sets are stored. A notable exception is the KAware software, where the size of the set may not exceed 32,000 records. In itself this is not necessarily too bad, but it is hardly acceptable in the Directory of Library and Information Professionals, which uses this software. Two criteria (gender and the United States as country of residence) often would be useful in searching this database, but they would generate a set larger than the limit of the software and therefore cannot be used at all. Less constraining but still inconvenient is the limit in Grolier Encyclopedia, where only the first 50 records matching a query can be retrieved. Often you may modify the search and make the result more precise. Many times, however, there are no alternatives, and you just wonder what records have been missed. If you search for "firsts" by women, the software tells you there are over 100 articles in which the terms "first woman," "first women," or "first female" occur but shows you only the first 50 articles. This search cannot be refined or reformulated in any other way.

If the memory or hard disk space is not enough for the search being executed the systems behave differently. Some just freeze, whereas others give a cryptic message. Few clearly indicate the source of the problem. Interestingly, ProQuest gives a clear message when it runs out of hard disk space, but only a code number when the memory is insufficient.

CD450 and KAware have what may seem to be a size limitation, but it is not. The limitation is related to the number of terms generated by a truncated term or a range query. This limit is 300 and 200 terms, respectively, and may be a constraint when you search by a truncated decimal classification number, by a date range, or by a too-short stem that has many individual values and endings. Doing these kinds of search in two phases should solve the problem, however.

Domain Searching

A special version of set combination is domain searching. If you select a set and combine it with a series of other sets or terms one-by-one in a stepwise fashion, then you are actually working in a domain of the database that you repeatedly specify in the queries. If you want to limit your subject searches to a given publication period, language, document type, set of sources, and so on, you may select that subset of your database first, have a set number assigned to it, and combine all the following queries with that set. A faster and more convenient mode is domain searching, in which you define a subset of the database and specify it as a domain. All subsequent searches are then *automatically* limited to that domain, which may be any subset selected by you. KAware and Bluefish offer domain searching. The only disadvantage of domain searching is that if you do not release the domain on a public access CD-ROM workstation, all subsequent users limit their searches unknowingly to the domain you defined, as this option requires explicit release or restarting of the application.

In SilverPlatter the implicit domain for a query is the set created by the previous query. You may start a query with a Boolean operator without first identifying the set number with which you want to combine the newly entered term or set number. This query is automatically applied to the last set. For example, you could specify the following query sequence:

headache

and vascular

and smoking

Predefined Sets

In the simple set combination and in domain searching you define the set or the domain. In many CD-ROM products, however, there are sets available that were defined during database creation. The criterion to select a subset was defined by the database producer, and you may refer to it after you have selected a set. The predefined set may be a subset of English-language records, foreign language records, items with abstract, items added in the most recent update, articles published in clinical journals, and so on. This facility is called "restrictor" in CD450 and "limit option" in SPIRS and OnDisc. The advantage of predefined sets is the speed of searching. Because the records meeting the criterion have been pre-selected, the program does not have to make a search to select those. The following two OnDisc searches produce identical results, but the first query makes the search much faster.

1. ss headache
    limit1/clinical

2. ss headache and dt = clinical

OnDisc allows you to set a limit for all subsequent queries until you explicitly lift the limit, which makes this feature very similar to domain searching. The only difference is that in domain searching you may freely define any subset you like, whereas in OnDisc you have to live with sets predefined by the publisher of the CD-ROM database.

Predefinition is an important distinctive criteria. ProQuest databases have many useful categories by which you may refine your search, including the types of journals (academic, health, business) and the length of articles (long, medium, short), but these are not predefined sets. The software has to select the records with such criteria each time you make a search, and this slows down the process considerably.

Query Log Display

Using previous sets is feasible if you can easily identify the set numbers and the queries belonging to them. Some systems keep the search history in front of you until a limited number of sets is reached (OCSI, ProQuest, OnDisc Menu); these are the active sets. When a set is not on the screen it is not active any more and cannot be used in the query. SPIRS displays the last 20 queries whenever you enter the search mode using the Find command. You also may refer to set numbers not visible any more if you can remember the set number correctly. SPIRS has no facility to display the full search history. In Bluefish and Wilsonline you see the last 10 to 12 queries and may easily scroll up and down in the log screen by using the arrow keys.

In EBSCO-CD, OnDisc Command, and CD450 the complete search history (query log) can be displayed upon request. To do this you have to use a command, such as DS (Display Set) in OnDisc Command; a function key, such as F3 in CD450; or a special character, like the ? in EBSCO-CD. If the list cannot be accommodated on one screen, you may scroll down and up. Grolier doesn't have a query log; World Book's Infofinder does.

Query Modification

Using a previous query may be a significant time saver. If you want to field qualify a complex query or to add another term to it, it is convenient if you can modify the former query rather than retype it. To modify a query other than the last one you may have to make the desired query the current one. In some systems (OnDisc Command, SPIRS) you refer to the set number to make a former query the active one and combine it with additional terms. In CD450 and Bluefish you may use the above method or point to the query to be modified on the history log, which brings it to the query edit line. In ProQuest you may scroll queries through the query editing line (but only the last 11), and when the one you need is displayed you just start editing it. In Wilsearch you have to save the query and assign a name to it to use it later. This is a rather inefficient way of query modification, and if you forgot the name you assigned to the query, there is no way to find it.

Query Re-execution

Query re-execution is the process of evaluating a query formulated earlier in the session, either in another volume of the same database or in another database that uses the same software. The first alternative is often needed when you are using a multi-volume database (such as ERIC, MEDLINE, or ABI/INFORM) and you wish to run the same query against backfiles. The second alternative is needed when more databases of the same product family may contain items relevant for your search, possibly from a different aspect or from different sources. After searching ABI/INFORM you may wish to execute the very same search in Dissertation Abstracts, or you may want to repeat a search in Wilson's Arts Index that you did in Humanities Index.

The software should provide the means not only to change the disk, but also to keep your queries after changing databases and refer to them by their set numbers. Almost all the software packages that are used in several databases have this capability, making it surprising that OCSI, which is used with the Bowker family of databases, offers only disk changing and not query re-execution. Compact Cambridge also was not capable of multi-platter searching without the need to re-enter the query until quite recently. Other differences are mostly in the specifics of query re-execution. In OnDisc Command and CD450 you simply replace the disk and then enter "BX" or press F8 followed by the name of the database. In SPIRS you may re-execute queries in a different volume of the same database but not in another database, which means you cannot re-execute in Psychological Abstracts a query made in Sociological Abstracts. You do not even need database specification in ProQuest, but you may not change disks midstream; instead, you must go back to the main menu to replace the disk. Wilsondisc offers the most adequate solution for query re-execution. You indicate during the search, by pressing F3, that you want to re-execute the query in another disk and you are coached through the process by appropriate messages.

If the CD-ROM database is available for the public then changing disks may not be a desirable feature. In Wilsondisc you may customize the system to request a password for this function. In SPIRS you have to make the decision whether to allow disk changing at installation time, which is much less flexible.

Query Saving

Queries are usually kept by the software automatically, but only temporarily. They are or may be lost if you initiate a new search (OnDisc Menu) or exceed a specific number (ProQuest), change to another database (OCSI), or exit the system (all software). Some software packages allow you to save a query permanently (until you explicitly delete it) for re-execution in another database or in another session. EBSCO-CD is the most careful: it warns you every time you leave the software that there are queries that you may wish to save before exiting. Most other software packages do not provide this feature but do provide means to save queries. In addition to EBSCO-CD, you may save a query in OnDisc Command, KAware, and Wilsondisc (except in the browse mode).

Query Listing and Review

Query listing is the facility to display the names of the queries you have permanently saved, and query review lets you look at the content of the query specified. In EBSCO-CD these are two different options on the menu, whereas in OnDisc Command you use the same command for both (Recall). If you don't provide a filename, Recall lists all the saved queries; if you do provide a filename, it lists the content of the query saved under that name. In Wilsearch you may save a query, but you cannot list or review saved queries.

SDI Services

EBSCO-CD offers the facility of selective dissemination of information (SDI), which is an extension of query saving. SDI allows you to save a query to run it whenever an update disk is received. On executing this special query you are prompted to enter a start date and an end date of publication, to retrieve from the disk only articles published in the specified date range. This facility is meant to update bibliographies prepared from earlier editions of a database. The idea is good but the implementation may not be perfect.

Assume that the June edition of Magazine Article Summaries included citations up to the May issues of most of the journals scanned, except a few. You update earlier bibliographies using the June issue of MAS by specifying the range as 910501-910531, specifying the range to cover the previous month. The July issue of MAS makes up for the missing May citations of those few titles that did not make it into the previous issue of MAS. These, however, will not be included in your SDI listings because now you will specify the range as 910601-910630. If every citation gets in the database without any delay this is not a problem, but this is unlikely to be the case. Another inconvenience of this kind of SDI facility is that there is no way to look at the results before they are printed; you cannot specify the destination of the SDI outputs (let alone look at them while retrieved), as they go directly to the printer.

Much better is the solution used by OnDisc for the same purpose. An SDI query is just like an ordinary query, which you may save. The only trick is that you specify in the query that the search be limited to the records entered since the last update of the disk. All records that were added during the preparation of the last disk include the special value 9999 in the update field (which will be changed by the producer when the next issue of the database is prepared). To limit a search to the most recently added items about arthritis you use the following command: ARTHRITIS? AND UD = 9999. In OnDisc Menu you select the limit option named "Latest items only" to restrict your search to the most recent additions. Obviously, this facility is available only with databases that are updated (bibliographic databases) rather than reloaded (directory databases).

Statistical Information Gathering

Statistical information gathering is a valuable unique facility in EBSCO-CD. Though there are other CD-ROM software packages that gather statistical information, they are used with special databases. The software used with the Business Periodicals OnDisc full image database collects information about the pages printed from each source journal for royalty payment accounting; the software used with the Supercat cataloging support database collects statistics about the number of items cataloged, the card sets printed, and so on.

Wilsondisc has a limited facility to record the session time, the average response time, the total number of I/O operations, and a few other technical details. This logging is limited because data is kept only for the last session, and the information is not particularly useful for the database administrator. Wilson has announced that it will release a new version of Wilsondisc that will collect more relevant information.

The statistics collection facility in EBSCO-CD is unique with abstracting/indexing databases and directories. These can give insight into the usage pattern of the database and assist in collection development decisions. The usage statistics collect data for a flexibly specified period about the number of searches (sessions), queries, hits, saved searches, bibliographies prepared, average hits per query, and average citations per bibliography. Comparing the last two, for example, may give you an idea what percentage of the retrieved records proved to be relevant enough to be included in the bibliographies. As most computers now come with a real-time clock built in, the average search (session) time and query execution time along with usage chronology could be easily collected.

The feature named "local title statistics" provides three types of statistical information about titles identified as held locally by the library when the database is installed. The only difference is in the time period reported. This feature informs you how many times records from a particular journal title were printed or copied to disk since the installation of the database, since the period defined by the library, or in the current search session. You also have great flexibility in deciding whether to include all titles held in your library, only those to which you subscribe, or only the ones you get as a nonsubscription item. You may decide the content of the statistics by including any or all of these elements: title, ISSN, notes, subscription, date range, the three statistical counts, and the share of the title out of the total prints or disk copies. You may even sort the output by title, ISSN, or descending order of the statistical counts. All of this is in a menu-driven mode with the possibility to send the output to disk or to the printer. It is perplexing that these features are not available for sorting and defining the content of records resulting from bibliographic searches.

OUTPUT FEATURES

Search features of CD-ROM software seem to get much more attention than output facilities both from software developers and from product reviewers.[3] This is somewhat understandable as the users have their first encounter with CD-ROM software through the user interface and then the search engine, and these are what influence their opinions and preferences the most. Quite often all a user needs is some simple form of printed output to take to the shelves to find an item in the collection or to take to the librarian to request an interlibrary loan. These kinds of output do not require any sophisticated capability.

However, search results often are to be kept by the searcher or forwarded to the end user or a fellow worker. In such cases the ultimate purpose of making a search is to produce a clean, well-structured output with as much information as is optimal for the end user. Moreover, many output capabilities (primarily the display features) have a direct effect on optimizing or simplifying a search. If a user can quickly review the results in a short format or easily find the sentence in which the search term(s) occur, it is easier to judge the adequacy of the search and modify the query if necessary.

What features make the set of output facilities outstanding? Again, it must be emphasized that there is no universally valid answer to this question. It depends on the type of database and the type of user. Abstracting/indexing databases and full-text databases need different capabilities, as do textual databases versus ones with mostly numeric data. Casual first-time users and online veterans have widely differing expectations and needs. The set of features discussed below represents the most often needed capabilities in managing the output of a search.

The output features of a product encompass the capabilities to display, print, and transfer (download) the results of a search. On one extreme are software packages that provide extensive features in all three areas; on the other are packages with very limited display options, barely acceptable print facilities, and no means at all to transfer (download) records in different formats. The most important output capabilities include:

- definition of the output set and operation
- automatic short-entry hit list
- built-in format alternatives
- user-definable format alternatives
- record layout specification

- navigation within and between records
- marking of items to be output
- sorting of records
- downloading capabilities

The quality of these functions is evaluated in light of ease of use, power, efficiency, and level of user control.

Defining the Output Set and Operation

In most CD-ROM products the output operations apply to the set retrieved by the most current search query. This is based on the assumption that you keep refining your search formula until you arrive at the appropriate number of records. Some programs (e.g., EBSCO-CD and the Wilbrowse mode of Wilsondisc) automatically start to display the records retrieved with the last query.

The majority of software packages require you to initiate the displaying of records. OnDisc, SPIRS, Compact Cambridge, Bluefish, ProQuest, and the Wilsearch and Wilsonline modes of Wilsondisc belong to this category. The difference is how intuitive the step is. Some packages give clear instructions, whereas others rely on your intuitivity. KAware, for example, expects that you would find out that you have to select the Screen option on the main menu to display the set of records retrieved by your last query. By default all the software packages display the result of the last query. Often, however, you may prefer to display or print one of the previous sets. Four alternatives are available.

1. The least preferred one is when you have to re-enter the complete query to reproduce an earlier set. In the worst case within this category, you cannot even see the search history when repeating the query that produced the set you want to display, and if it was a complex query the process is error-prone. No search history is displayed, for example, in the Grolier Encyclopedia or in Utlas-CD, so you have to re-enter and re-execute the desired query. If you can display the search history it makes the query re-creation easier, but it still may take a long response time to re-evaluate the query if it was a complex one. Slightly better is the solution when you may refer to a previous set by its set number (i.e., you do not have to retype the query), but the query still has to be executed again to reproduce the set. This is the case with OCSI.

2. In most CD software you may make a previous set the active one and then apply the output operation, without executing the query again. You have to enter the set number of the query itself (SPIRS, EBSCO-CD) or use an option meant specifically for this purpose (KAware). This group of alternatives seems to be the best compromise in terms of ease and performance.

3. Somewhere in between these solutions is the one used by Wilsearch, where you may make an earlier set active. It has, however, two disadvantages. First, you have to remember the name of the stored query, and the software does not offer any help for this. The other disadvantage is that the query has to be re-executed. In Dialog OnDisc Menu, you may activate a previous set, but you have to indicate that you want to back up to a previous query line by having the system delete everything up to that query.

4. In some CD-ROM software you may directly specify the set number in the output operation itself. This is used in the command mode of Dialog OnDisc and by Wilsonline. This possibility obviously is available only to those who have mastered the command language of the software.

Automatic Short-entry Hit List

If your search query retrieved more than a few records, it is highly desirable to be able to look at the results in a short format to quickly judge the adequacy of the query. There is, of course, no guarantee that all the short-entry record formats will help you in judging the adequacy of your search, but typically they are likely to give you a good idea. The ProQuest, OCSI, OCLC CD450, and Bluefish software packages provide this feature. A few of them are illustrated by figures 2.42 and 2.43.

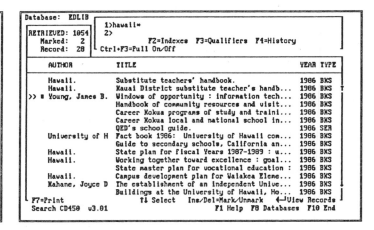

Fig. 2.42. Short-entry hit list in ProQuest.　　　　Fig. 2.43. Short-entry hit list in CD450.

If the search resulted in only one hit then the complete record should be displayed without imposing the unnecessary stop of looking at the short format. This is typical for known item searches characteristic of cataloging support databases, and all of them are capable of doing this. Software packages used with other types of databases are not so uniform in this regard.

Most systems automatically display a list of one-line (occasionally two-line) entries of the records retrieved in case of multiple hits. The content of the short entries usually is not under user control and is not document sensitive. As shown in figure 2.44, in Bibliofile the title, author initials, page number, country code of publication, and publication year are included for the records. For serials, an ISSN and a form indicator (print or microfiche) would be more useful than author and pagination information, which typically do not apply to serials.

78	LIBRARIAN'S GUIDE TO MICROCOMP	WO	1983		US:NY	209	m	4
79	LIBRARIAN'S HELPER OF DAILY ACTI	CO	1974		UK:EN	142	m	1
80	LIBRARIAN'S IN FOREIGN LANDS	SE	1977		UK:EN	60	m	1
81	LIBRARIANSHIP AND LITERATURE		1970		UK:EN	4	m	1
82	LIBRARIANSHIP AND THE PURSUIT	AL	1974		US:NJ	16	m	1
83	LIBRARIANSHIP AND THE THIRD WO	HU	1977		US:NY	374	m	1
84	LIBRARIANSHIP AND THERAPY	LI	1968		UK:EN	61	m	2
85	LIBRARIANSHIP AS A PROFESSION	RE	1969		Philipp	140	m	1
86	LIBRARIANSHIP AS CAREER	SO	1970	2d Ed.	SAfric		m	1
87	LIBRARIANSHIP AT A FOUR YEAR UN	CO	1981		US:NB	295	m	3
88	LIBRARIANSHIP FOR TOMORROW		1969		Austra	114	m	1
89	LIBRARIANSHIP IN CANADA 1946		1968		CN:BC	205	m	1
90	LIBRARIANSHIP IN PAKISTAN	KH	1974		Pakista	214	m	3
91	LIBRARIANSHIP IN THE DEVELOPING	AS	1966		US:IL	95	m	1
92	LIBRARIANSHIP IN ZAMBIA	ZA	1969				m	1
93	LIBRARIANSHIP INFORMATION WORK	LI	1970		UK:EN		m	1
94	LIBRARIANSHIP OF THE GERMAN DE	KE	1981		Germa	20	m	4
95	LIBRARIANSHIP OVERSEAS	LI	1964		UK:EN	86	m	4

Disc 4: 0

F1 SEARCH MARC   HITCOUNT = 95

78. . . . . Au Year-Year   Place Pages Subject   Type

Press the ENTER key to continue.

Fig. 2.44. One-line entries in Bibliofile.

The adequacy of the information in these short records depends on the database. The grading of this capability should reflect how useful the information is to deciding whether the query was appropriate. Severely truncated titles and author initials are perfectly acceptable in cataloging support databases because the items (or their surrogates) for which catalog records are sought are in hand for matching. In some abstracting/indexing databases, however, a longer title field at the expense of author information may be preferable.

Encyclopedic databases list the titles of the articles that match the query. This often may not be informative enough and is likely to puzzle the user, but there is no viable alternative. In figure 2.45 the article titles were displayed in response to a search on "Honolulu" in Grolier Encyclopedia. The reason for retrieval of many of the articles is obvious, but you may wonder why Bette Midler shows up until you display the full record, which says that she was born in Honolulu.

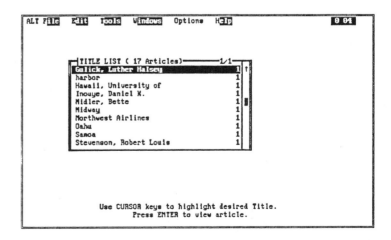

Fig. 2.45. Article title displays in Grolier Encyclopedia.

It is an extra bonus if the short record provides some additional information. Books in Print uses a code in the short entry to indicate if an item may be ordered from Ingram. The Computer Library of Ziff-Davis puts an asterisk next to the short entry of records to indicate if the full text is available (figure 2.46). Strangely, even software packages that have automatic short-entry display format may not offer such a built-in alternative format for printed output.

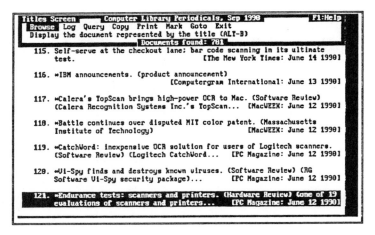

Fig. 2.46. Full text indication in short-entry displays in Computer Select.

The purpose of the short-entry list is to have as many items on one screen as possible, typically between 15 and 20. Some systems, although they automatically provide the short-entry versions of the records retrieved, present only one record per screen. The KAware software of the Directory of Library and Information Professionals database has this shortcoming. This seems to fly in the face of the idea to see at a glance as many records as possible, without the need to intervene to get these short records displayed one-by-one.

Other systems provide the full record as the only record format available. Wilsondisc is such a system, except in the Wilsonline mode, where the user may specify short-entry display. This single format may be appropriate for most of the Wilson databases, which feature short index records, but it is not for Readers' Guide Abstracts and Business Periodicals Abstracts, the alternate version of Business Periodicals Index.

Of course, no single format would satisfy all users all of the time. Most software packages offer two methods for alternative formats, via built-in and/or user-definable formats.

Built-in Alternative Formats

With a few exceptions (like Wilsondisc), all the packages offer at least two predefined, built-in formats: a short/medium one and a complete one. SilverPlatter has an ALL format (which includes every data element in the record) and a CITN (citation) format predefined. The records of the UMI databases may be displayed in two predefined formats (short and long). Records from the PAIS database may be displayed in five predefined formats. The CD450 software used with the abstracting/indexing databases of OCLC offers three to five predefined formats depending on the database. OnDisc also provides this, featuring even more predefined formats.

These formats differ in the amount of information presented, but not in the layout of the record. This approach is mostly used by abstracting/indexing databases. A laudable exception of these run-of-the-mill alternatives is the software used by EBSCO, with which records may be presented in the shape of an interlibrary loan or photocopy request form. PAIS deserves special mention in the abstracting/indexing category for offering a unique feature. In whatever format you choose to display a bibliographic record, you may add to that format detailed information about the publisher by the press of a key. (This feature is available with the Books in Print database but not with its sister publication Ulrich's Plus, even though the latter uses the same OCSI software.)

It would be nice if abstracting/indexing databases would offer one or two citation formats according to the conventions of the *Chicago Manual of Style*, Turabian, the American Psychological Association, or the Modern Language Association, to mention those most widely used. Unfortunately, as of this writing none of the databases offer this convenience. Instead, you have to transfer the records to some information management software to format the records with an appropriate template. The best known of those products that can accept CD-ROM records and re-format them into one of the standard citation formats are Bibliolink, with ProCite, and Library Manager.

The New Grolier Encyclopedia and World Book have an outline format for longer records that includes the chapter headings and subheadings of the article. In Grolier the user must initiate the activation of the outline format by pressing a function key. In World Book the outline format is automatically displayed next to the main body of the text (figures 2.47 and 2.48).

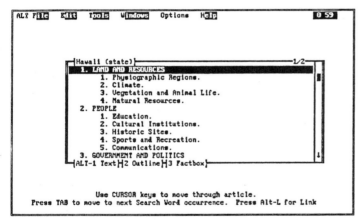

Fig. 2.47. Grolier's outline format.

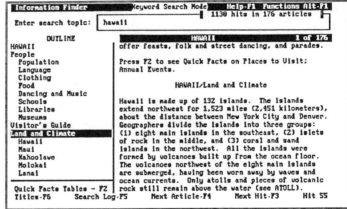

Fig. 2.48. World Book's outline format.

Given the special nature of full-text databases, they have to offer some nonconventional method in specifying the data elements to be included. The software used with the Grolier Encyclopedia lets you specify if you want the complete article, the paragraph where the cursor is located, or the current screen to be output (figure 2.49, page 66). The limitation is that you have to specify your preference item by item, as the format does not apply to all the records in the set.

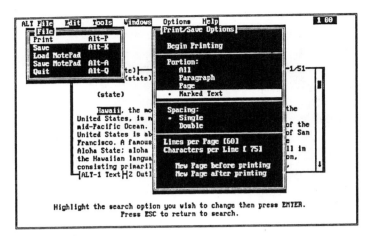

Fig. 2.49. Output alternatives in Grolier.

The Bluefish software used by the Computer Library is more flexible. It lets you define globally for a set to output (1) the complete text, (2) only those paragraphs that contain (one of) the search term(s) you used, or (3) only the portion of the text marked by you (figure 2.50).

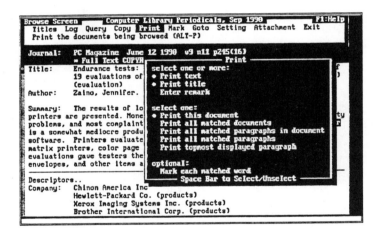

Fig. 2.50. Format options in Computer Library.

These options apply only to printing or downloading the output, not to its display. However, the first and second alternatives apply to all the records in the current set. Obviously, marking portions of records cannot be global, but has to be done in every record of the set. Marking parts of records, however, is an important feature, as some records take dozens of pages when printed completely.

It is regrettable when a database does not offer a format that seems obvious from the purpose of the database. The Directory of Library and Information Professionals is meant to be used among others to produce mailing lists, but it does not offer a mailing label format. Equally inconvenient is the built-in display format of the DiscPassage software, used by—among many others—the Shakespeare database, which includes the full text of Shakespeare's works. The only format available displays/prints a full passage of the text (hence the name?) even if most often you would need only the paragraph or sentence that includes the quotation you are looking for. This inconvenience is aggravated by the fact that no alternative format is available.

User-defined Format Alternatives

No matter how many formats are supplied by the software, there will always be users who want to specify their own formats. There are two approaches to meet this requirement. In the less convenient approach the librarian who installs the product may specify a single user format during installation. The OCSI software follows this method. This is a half-hearted solution because it only allows the addition of one more predefined format, and only when installing or re-installing the database. The only advantage is that it is the librarian who may define the format instead of the software producer or database publisher.

In some systems you do not have to re-install the system, but you must use a special customization program to specify a format, which means the format is not specified during searching. The CD450 is such a program. Its format specification facility is so powerful and complex that it could be hardly used by casual users, however. The librarian may define not only the data elements to be included in a format, but also the punctuation (figure 2.51). Moreover, the librarian may specify several formats from which the user may choose during the search.

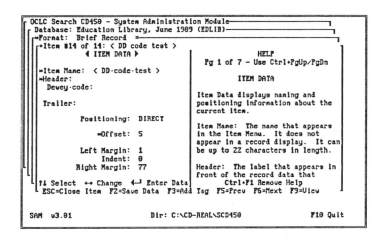

Fig. 2.51. Format customization in CD450.

In an environment where the database is always used by the same person(s), as, for example, in technical services, this is an acceptable solution. It is unlikely, however, that in public services the format specified by the librarian would satisfy all users, who still may not improvise a format. For them the user-specified format is just one more built-in format. Though many casual users would not want to specify a format, it makes a system flexible if formats can be user-defined.

In the more sophisticated approach the end users themselves may specify their preferences for the data elements to be included in the records. However, they typically have no control over the layout of the records. There are also differences in the implementation of this definable format specification.

The software used by SilverPlatter allows you to improvise a format, but you have to remember the tags of the fields or display them first by using a function key. To do so, however, you first have to leave the screen where you specify the field tags and then return to it after looking up and memorizing the tags you need. This is the same problem you face when a footnote essential to understand the text you are reading is relegated to the back of the chapter or the book, and you have to jump back and forth between the footnoted text and the footnote.

Much better are those software packages that display the data elements and their tags on the same screen where you have to specify the format. This is analogous to having the footnoted text and the footnote on the same page. For example, OnDisc and Compact Cambridge open a window that lists all the fields used in the database, and the user simply has to mark the ones to be included (figure 2.52).

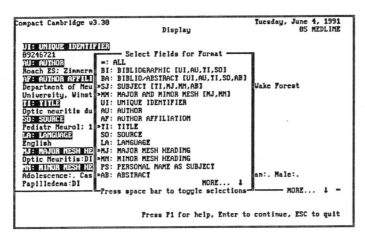

Fig. 2.52. Picking data elements for user-defined format in Compact Cambridge.

Specification of Record Layout

Though the displayed/printed content of the record may be changed by the user in many software packages, the specification of record layout is almost always out of user control, at least with bibliographic databases. Typically, the user may not even specify the sequence of the fields, let alone their arrangement, juxtaposition, indentation, etc. SilverPlatter lets users define the indentation of continuation lines, but that is all. The CD450 software allows the specification of the sequence of the data elements also, though not during the search and display process.

Directory databases offer slightly more flexibility in record layout. OCSI can display records in the PAIS print publication format and in the detailed bibliography form layout, as shown in figure 2.53.

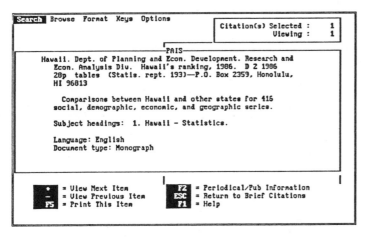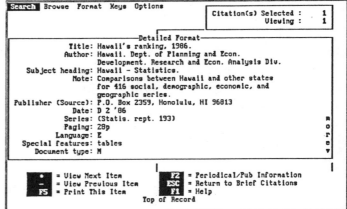

Fig. 2.53. Record layouts offered by OCSI-PAIS.

OnDisc offers limited user control over record layout but only in the directory databases using the Report format. The user may define the sequence of the fields and their length. The corollary is that the length of the records may not exceed 255 characters and must be in one line, and the maximum length of a field is 50 characters. The user may truncate certain fields, like the name of the company or its banking or law firm, to squeeze more data elements into one line.

Cataloging support databases shine in the area of user control over specifying record layout. Displaying and printing records in proofreading sheet, catalog card, and spine label layout is very common. The question is what additional layout control is available for the users. Bibliofile, for example, offers the utmost in layout specification. You may define such refined parameters as where to break and truncate the Dewey classification number or the cutter number, where to display and print the Library of Congress card number, the ISBN, how much vertical and horizontal margin should be left, etc. The user may specify 99 different formats. Similar features are offered in Gaylord's Supercat and OCLC's CATCD450 software. At the other extreme within this category is the CATSS software of Utlas, which does not even allow changing the single-spacing of record printout. Those who have to enter or modify fields in the proof-copy printout of catalog records would certainly consider this a gross negligence.

Navigating within and between Records

One disadvantage of computer-based searching is that you often feel you are dealing with a black box. This has implications not only for the search process itself, but also for the displaying of the result of your search. With the printed encyclopedia, abstracting/indexing journal, or bibliography you get some spatial impressions as soon as you look at the source or take it in your hand. You can easily gauge the length of an article and can visually scan the text even if it is several pages long. Typography and indentation of text also give a lot of clues. In computer-based searching, on the other hand, you look at piecemeal information of 20 to 25 lines and 60 to 80 characters per line, sort of peeping into the full record. The software can somewhat alleviate this "window vision" by facilitating navigation within and between records.

Navigation within Records

When you look at the records displayed you may wonder why a seemingly irrelevant record was retrieved. It is of great help if the term you used in the query is highlighted using either a different color, reverse video mode, or underlining. SPIRS, OnDisc, ProQuest, and Bluefish apply this technique, but it is not available in Wilsondisc. This is useful even in relatively short records because the screen may be crowded, and your term may be buried in the abstract or among the descriptors. Unfortunately, only SPIRS offers highlighting in the printed output, though it could be a useful feature.

In full-text databases this kind of highlighting is imperative but not completely sufficient. If a record spans over several screens you may not want to go sequentially from screen to screen, but rather to look only at screens that display those portions of the records that include your search term. The most sophsiticated systems offer the option of jumping from the first occurrence of (one of the) search term(s) to the next by the press of a key on the keyboard. In the Bluefish software, for example, you have to press the right or left arrow key to jump to the next or the previous occurrence of the term, respectively. The same purpose is served by two special formats in Dialog's OnDisc to display the sentence or the paragraph in which (one of) the search term(s) occurred.

This section on built-in formats has shown that encyclopedic databases offer an outline view of the articles and that you may zoom into selected portions of the article very easily. Full-text databases also need this outlining feature, but it requires that the source text be appropriately structured. This is not reasonable, however, to expect from databases that include the full text of one or more magazines or newspapers that are not necessarily structured. However, when the full-text materials of the CD-ROM database emanate from the same body, such outline formats should be available. Longer materials usually have tables of contents, which are appropriate for outlining if they may be displayed in the same way as the outline format in the encyclopedias and which serve as a stepping-stone to get to the appropriate section of text.

Navigation between Records

Most of the software packages display the records in some sequential order, i.e., in a linear fashion. If you wish to see more records on the same screen, you may choose a shorter format, thus creating more chance that two or more records may be displayed simultaneously. However, you may not define the sequence of the records that are displayed simultaneously. These will be the adjacent records in the set retrieved.

Occasionally you may want to look at two records that may not be adjacent in the result set, such as when you wish to compare in an encyclopedia the fact boxes of two countries or the bibliographic citations of two articles. Even if sorting were possible, it would not be satisfactory because a sort algorithm may not be able to file next to each other the duo, trio, or quartet of the records you would like to see simultaneously.

Grolier offers a rather unique solution. You may open two windows and look at two different articles of your choice on the same screen. Of course, you will see less than half of the information shown on a full screen, and the window vision problem is accentuated. The advantages, however, offset this. You may scroll up and down in both windows independent of each other until you find the portion of the records to be compared. You may display in both windows the capsule format of two encyclopedic entries, as shown in figure 2.54, which compares the fact boxes of Hungary and Portugal.

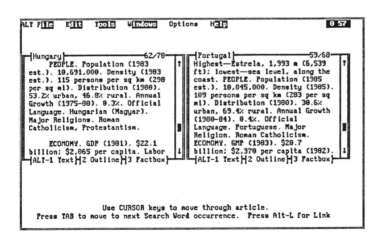

Fig. 2.54. Windowed display of two records in Grolier.

Another facility in Grolier Encyclopedia makes it very easy to switch between and/or enlarge windows. With the press of a key you may move another article (which you have looked at previously) into one of the active windows or zoom out a window into full screen. Selecting another article is very easy because, though the windows are stacked behind each other, their title tabs are visible, as shown in figure 2.55.

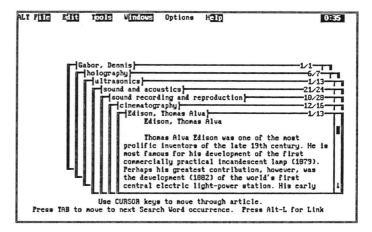

Fig. 2.55. Stacked windows of records in Grolier.

A similar solution is available in the software used by the Supercat cataloging support database of Gaylord. You may display two records simultaneously to easily find, for example, what is the difference between two records retrieved by the same ISBN. This is a superb solution for a common problem in finding the adequate MARC record for a book. You use a search key you hope will result in a single hit, but still you get several records. Comparing MARC records just by displaying them on the screen consecutively is very inefficient. The split window display helps a lot, and the software was made intelligent enough to highlight the differences between the two records automatically (figure 2.56).

```
Entry on CD: 2                  |  Page Number:   3
                    | SuperCAT |  |  Hit Count: 240+
Search Queue: 0 entries         |
TITLE                    AUTHOR         YEAR       TYPE
Hawaii                   Sunset         1969       BK
Hawaii                   Sunset         1975       BK
Hawaii                   Sunset         1984       BK
Hawaii                   Tabrah, Ruth M. 1984      BK
Hawaii                   Tabrah, Ruth M. 1980      BK
HAWAII                   THOENE, ALMA E 1968       BK
HAWAII                   THOENE, ALMA E 1968       BK
Hawaii                   Thompson, Kathle 1987     BK
Hawaii                   [United States  1958      MP
Hawaii                   United States   1983      MP
Hawaii                   Wallace, Robert 1973       BK
Hawaii #1                                1983       MP
Hawaii, 1985             Bostwick, Jeri  1985      BK
Hawaii 1969 boating guide Rand McNally and 1968    MP
Hawaii 2000; continuing experiment i Governor's Confe 1973  BK
Hawaii 200 Congress II   Hawaii 200 Congr 1973     BK
```

```
Control No: 67-004414        pre: ac    Leader: dam1.
Entered 740123 Dates s 1968 .... Ctry nyu Ill abc. Aud . Rep . Cont b...
Gov . Conf 0 Fest 0 Indx 0 Main 1 Fic 0 Bio . Lng eng M/S ..

043  |`an-us-hi
050 0 |`aDU623.2`b.T5
082  |`a919.69
100 10|`aThoene, Alma E.
245 10|`aHawaii,`cby Alma E. Thoene. Illustrated with photos.
260 0 |`aNew York,`bF. Watts`c[c1968]
300  |`a58 p.`billus., maps, ports.`c23 cm.
504  |`aBibliography: p. 56-57.
520  |`aAn introduction to America's Island State: its geography, people,
      |agriculture, and industries.
651 0|`aHawaii`xDescription and travel.
```

```
Control No: 68-010188 /AC/r8 pre:    Leader: nam1.
Entered 850821 Dates s 1968 .... Ctry nyu Ill abc. Aud j Rep . Cont b...
Gov . Conf 0 Fest 0 Indx 0 Main 1 Fic 0 Bio . Lng eng M/S ..

043  |`an-us-hi
050 0 |`aDU623.2`b.T5
082  |`a919.69
100 10|`aThoene, Alma E.
245 10|`aHawaii,`cby Alma E. Thoene. Illustrated with photos.
260 0 |`aNew York,`bF. Watts`c[c1968]
300  |`a58 p.`billus., maps, ports.`c23 cm.
504  |`aBibliography: p. 56-57.
520  |`aAn introduction to America's Island State: its geography, people,
      |agriculture, and industries.
651 0|`aHawaii`xJuvenile literature.
651 1|`aHawaii`xDescription and travel.
```

```
            Current Record    68010188
LDR     nam1
001     68010188 /AC/r8
008     850821s1968   nyuabc j b   00010 eng
651 0  `aHawaii`xJuvenile literature.
651 1  `aHawaii`xDescription and travel.
            Active Record # 2 ac 67004414
LDR     dam1
001     ac 67004414
008     740123s1968   nyuabc   b   00010 eng
651 0  `aHawaii`xDescription and travel.
651    is missing.
  Record compare complete... F1: Restart Compare, F9: Previous Screen
```

Fig. 2.56. Automatic highlighting of differences in Supercat.

You may rotate in one window a maximum of eight records while in the other window one record is kept "anchored." This is user-friendliness at its best.

Stepwise moving between records is fairly universal among CD user interfaces even to the extent of function key implementations. The user may go (1) one line up and down within a record by using the up and down arrow keys, (2) one screen up and down by using the PgDn and PgUp keys, and (3) to the next or previous record with the + and − keys, respectively. All these are rather intuitive steps. The CD450 software is one of the few exceptions. The F5 key displays the previous record and the F6 key the next one.

It is inconvenient that with the Wilsondisc software you may not go backward so simply to display the previous record. As the navigation key is the Enter key, it has no counterpart. You have to press a function key and then specify the record number within the set to which you want to go. On the other hand, Wilsondisc allows you to jump back and forth by specifying the number of the next record to be displayed, so you do not have to proceed sequentially one by one. (This feature is common in the command-driven systems.)

This jumping back and forth not only is available, but also is impressively fast with the EBSCO-CD software because it seems to use the so-called caching technique. It keeps fetching records from the CD into the memory while you are looking at a record. This is the reason that you hear your CD working even while you are reading the record being displayed. This period would be an inactive time for the computer and the CD reader otherwise (except in a networked environment). EBSCO-CD makes the most intelligent use of this time. If the user does not want to look at any more records then it was a superfluous transfer, but it caused no harm. If the user wants to look at the next record it is there instantly. Compared with the painfully slow record navigation with the ProQuest or the OCSI software, the solution of EBSCO-CD makes jumping back and forth in a database lightning fast.

All of the software used with encyclopedias and the citation indexes of the Institute of Scientific Information offer the hyperlink facility. This is considered to be primarily a search facility and is discussed above under "Search Features." However, because some implementations of hyperlink also are closely related to record display, it is briefly mentioned here, too.

From a record being displayed you may jump to another record even if that record is not in the retrieved set. You may not use just any word in a record as a stepping-stone, but only those that are specially marked (highlighted, underlined, or capitalized) or that occur in a specially designated part of the record (figure 2.57). You may position the cursor on any such terms, and the associated article will be displayed when you press the Enter key.

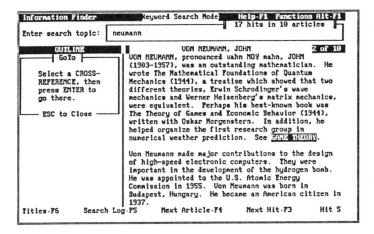
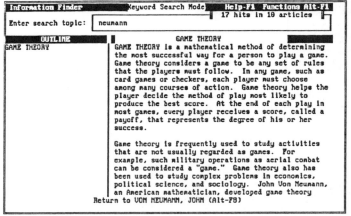

Fig. 2.57. Hyperlink feature of World Book.

A more limited but still very useful version of this hyperlink feature is available in OCSI. While you are looking at an article citation from PAIS you may display the record describing the publisher of the journal by the press of a function key, as illustrated by figure 2.58. This "kangaroo" record structuring makes the publisher names awesomely consistent in the PAIS database. The publisher record is created once; thereafter, only its short identifier is entered with the article records. Whenever an article citation is displayed and the user wants to see the data pertaining to the publisher, the data is loaded from the publisher record. This solution would help the inconsistency of journal names, publisher names, and geographic names in many abstracting/ indexing and directory databases.

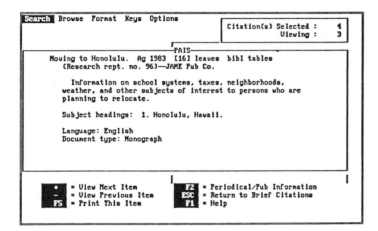
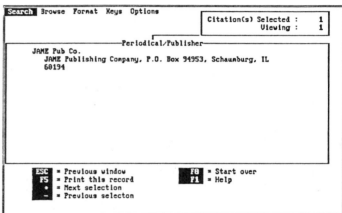

Fig. 2.58. Kangaroo record display in OCSI-PAIS.

Interestingly, other databases that use the OCSI software do not use this feature across the board. It is available in Books in Print, but not in Ulrich's. In spite of the potential of this record-linking capability for consolidation, publisher names are discouragingly inconsistent in both Bowker databases.

A new and popular feature pioneered by EBSCO and then adapted by IAC, UMI, and Wilson offers a hyperlink from records on the CD-ROM to pieces of information defined and stored by the user on the hard disk. It is called the collection hot-link. If you wish to do so, you may indicate for each title abstracted/indexed in the database whether your library has a subscription for that title. In the UMI implementation of this collection hot-link feature the system administrator may go one step further by indicating additional information such as holding statements or the retention/circulation policy.

The KAware software lets you add a few lines of information to *any* records you retrieve from the CD-ROM. This appendage is stored on the hard disk but is linked with the record on the CD-ROM. Whenever such a CD-ROM record is displayed the comment lines you added are appended to the displayed version of the record. This technique, if adopted by the other software producers, may make the personalization of database records as suggested by Koenig a reality.[4] This kind of customized merging of linked CD-ROM and hard disk records would be extremely important in catalog records. The original MARC record could come from the CD-ROM, and the overriding and location-specific data elements (local call number, mode of acquisition, circulation status, and so on) could come from the hard disk in a manner absolutely transparent to the user.

Format Switching and Retention

It is an asset if the software offers many alternate built-in and user-defined formats, but also to be considered is how easy it is to switch between formats or to retain the preferred format across searches.

In SPIRS the output format can be changed dynamically by specifying the tag of the fields, but the problem is that each time you perform a display or print operation you have to specify the format again, because it changes back to the default.

The ProQuest software used by the UMI family of databases offers a better alternative. The database administrator may define the preferred output format at any time. The user may change to the alternate format, which remains in effect until explicitly changed or until the application is restarted.

OCSI employs a simple method to switch between formats. The user initiates the format switch by pressing the ALT + F key combination. A dropdown menu is displayed (figure 2.59). The user moves the highlight to the format to be chosen and presses the Enter key. The format remains in effect within the search session until it is explicitly changed.

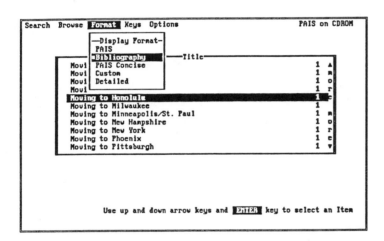

Fig. 2.59. Format switching in OCSI-PAIS.

The same applies to the menu mode of Dialog's OnDisc software. In OnDisc not only are the selection and switching among the formats very easy, but also you may save the user-defined Report format beyond the session, which is very handy. This feature also should be made available with bibliographic databases of DIALOG.

OCSI also allows specification of a default format. The constraint is that this specification may be done only at installation. In most other software packages you do not have a choice to select a default format across search sessions. Whenever you exit from a CD-ROM database, your format preference is lost.

In the command mode of Dialog's OnDisc software you have to specify the format by using a number identifying it. You may also use tags to identify the fields, and you may combine predefined formats with additional field tags. If you do not specify the format, the default is Format 2, which is the full record without the abstract. There is no way to designate another format as the default.

Marking Items for Output

After viewing the short-item list, you may want to display the records in a longer format (if alternate display is available), but you may not necessarily want all the records. Specifying the format was discussed above. This section focuses on how you can mark records to be displayed in another format or to be included in the printout or download file.

There are two major options for the display version. You move the cursor to the record you want to display and press an appropriate key. The record marked is displayed. Pressing another key takes you back to the short-entry list. You move up or down to the next item to be displayed and proceed as above, jumping back and forth between the short and full formats.

In the other approach, you first mark all the records you want to display in the long format and then you indicate that you are through with the selection. The marked records are displayed in the long format in a row. This is obviously a more convenient way because you may still mark only a single record if you wish. It is possible in both cases that between the marking and displaying of records you have to specify the alternate format. It seems preferable to define the format first and then to mark and display the records.

Systems that use command mode may offer you the option of specifying in the display command the records to be displayed by their sequence number within the retrieved set. Usually you may specify a consecutive range, a series of non-consecutive numbers, or a combination of both.

The command "TYPE 12/TI,JN/1,4-6,9" in OnDisc displays the title and journal name of the first, fourth, fifth, sixth, and ninth records from set 12. A similar feature is available in the menu mode of OnDisc, but this is far less convenient than marking the records as you proceed.

SilverPlatter has the same feature of specifying record numbers, but the limited space to enter record numbers makes it even less convenient. If you have a dozen non-consecutive records to be displayed, printed, or downloaded you have to repeat the operation a few times. The beauty of the marking system is that you do not have to jot down the numbers of the records and then re-enter them in the command or in reply to a prompt.

When you want to print out the results of a search it is even more important to be able to easily select records to be retained or discarded. Even the best searches will produce a set that may include some items you do not find appropriate for inclusion in the final output. You may refine your search to eliminate those items, but that is rather inefficient. Some systems do not allow selecting items from the output. KAware2 and Wilsondisc (except in the Wilsonline mode) belong to this category.

Probably the best solution is offered by EBSCO-CD. In addition to the above described positive marking, you may do negative marking. This means that you mark those records you want excluded from the printed output. This is a very reasonable approach, as it is often likely that most of the items in the output set are correct hits, making it easier to mark only the exceptions. The default meaning of marking in EBSCO-CD is the traditional one: you mark the records to be included in the printout. You have to switch to the exclusion mode if you want to mark the records to be excluded. This useful feature, however, is not obvious for the casual user.

Sorting

An essential feature of automated library systems is the powerful sorting capability. One of the most disappointing deficiencies of almost all CD-ROM software today is the lack of the ability to sort the output by one or more criteria. The implied sort criteria is most often the accession number. Quite often this is equivalent to the reverse chronological order of publication, but you had better not bet your home on it. There is no guarantee that the datafile producer processed the source documents in chronological order, which would ensure that the more recent sources have a higher record number. This is particularly difficult when foreign sources, or notoriously late-appearing conference proceedings, are processed. A better solution is when some other data element is used for the automatic sorting of the results. OCSI-PAIS, for example, sorts the output by publication year, which results in a reliable and predictable sequence. This is, however, a built-in sort algorithm, not one in which the user can choose the sort criterion.

Of the most widely used software only Dialog's OnDisc offers sort facilities. In its menu mode you may sort the output by one criterion; in the command mode, by two criteria. The criteria are database-specific and they satisfy any reasonable user requirements. The how-to aspect of sorting is as user-friendly as most of the other facilities of the menu mode of OnDisc. The user simply presses a function key to indicate sorting and then selects the sort criterion from the options presented. This includes not only the selection of the sort key, but also the choice between ascending or descending sort, as illustrated by figure 2.60.

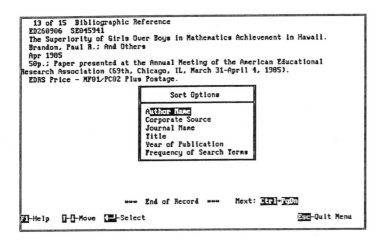

Fig. 2.60. Sorting in Dialog's OnDisc.

The software packages used with directory databases fare somewhat better in general than the bibliographic databases. The output from Books in Print is sorted by the title proper of the books. Ulrich's Plus sorts the output by country code and, within country code, alphabetically by title proper. Computer scientists who like to give a name to the dozens of sort algorithms would probably label it the "patriotic sort algorithm," as all the U.S. titles come first. The Serial Directory of EBSCO arranges the records by key title.

The KAware software also offers convenient sort facilities. Output from the Directory of Library and Information Professionals database, for example, can be sorted by the employer's name, zip code, city, and state in addition to a default sort key, which is the name of the biographee.

Sometimes the software packages are able to sort the output but the database publisher chooses not to offer this possibility. This is the case with the CD-Answer software used by the Baker and Taylor directory of books and also by the Arctic and Antarctic Regions bibliographic database. The former database does not offer sort options, whereas the latter does.

In the group of encyclopedic databases, World Book offers the sorting of records alphabetically by title or by the frequency of those search term(s) in the article that have been used in the query. The latter is the default, and only, sort possibility in Grolier. The Bluefish software used with the Computer Library (among others) has an interesting sort option. You may sort the terms retrieved by a truncated term either alphabetically or by frequency of occurrence, but you may not sort the output of a search.

At least a single-level sort key specification by the user should be available in every CD-ROM software package. Many users would like to sort results from an abstracting/indexing database by journal title, author, or document type; the output from a product directory by sales volume, zip code, or price; a listing of books or serials by classification code or number of copies printed; and so on. Sorting is a time-consuming process but is an essential requirement in a computerized environment.

Downloading Features

Many limitations of CD-ROM software can be overcome if the output can be downloaded to disk in a format appropriate for uploading into a word processing, spreadsheet, or information storage and retrieval program. Though this is a two-step process it certainly can offer significant post-processing possibilities. Reformatting of record and page layout, adding of comments, weeding out unwanted records or fields, or sorting the output can be easily done with mainstream programs.

However, it requires two to tango. The CD-ROM software must be able to export records in a format that can be imported by the host software for post-processing. Unfortunately, too many software packages lack appropriate downloading features. "With one or two exceptions, the laserdisk database publishers have not released fully developed downloading features. Also, downloading could be made much simpler, if database producers provided better instructions."[5]

More than a half-dozen transfer (data exchange) formats are widely used by potential host software. These are the (1) fixed-field, (2) comma-and-quote delimited, (3) tagged, (4) MARC image and communications, (5) WK1, and (6) DBF formats for textual and numeric information. Figures 2.61 through 2.66 illustrate some of these data exchange formats, which are briefly described below. Graphics files have their own A-B-C soup of common exchange formats, such as the PCX, TIFF, and EPS formats. Though it is true that even unstructured output, also often referred to as plain ASCII format (figure 2.61), can be imported by most of the potential host software for post-processing, it is inefficient to have to manually format each record of a sizable output every time.

```
1 CBI
Rank, Hugh
The pep talk; how to analyze political language
Counter-Propaganda Press 1984  215P  $11.95
ISBN: 0-943468-01-09  LC: 83-15318
DEWEY DECIMAL NO.  808\.042  LC CLASS NO.  PE1431


SUBJECTS COVERED:
English language/Rhetoric
Persuasion (Rhetoric)
```

Fig. 2.61. Plain ASCII format.

The fixed-field output is far from ideal. A fixed amount of space is allocated for each data element (figure 2.62, page 78). There will always be many records in which space is wasted or data elements are truncated because of the basically variable-length nature of data in most CD-ROM databases. This unsophisticated format is inefficient for bibliographic records whose data elements are inherently of variable length. It could be appropriate, however, for some directory types of databases where the length of the majority of fields may be predicted fairly accurately.

```
The Peptides: Analysis, S Udenfriend, S  $117.00 11/1985 0123042070
Pepys                      Bryant, Arthu   $8.95 08/1985
Pep Talk: How to Analyze   Rank, Hugh     $11.95 03/1984 0943468019
Pepe Botellas              Gardeazabal,    $11.00    1984 0317467603
Peppers: The Domesticated Andrews, Jean   $40.00 11/1984 0292764863
Peptide Hormones, Biomemb Bolis, Liana    $59.50    1984 0306418169
Peptides, Hormones & Beha Nemeroff, C.   $150.00    1984 0883311747
The Peptides               Udenfriend, S  $112.00 11/1984 0123042062
Pepys at Table             Driver, Chris   $18.95 08/1984 0520053869
Pepper & Salt              Havner, Vance    $4.95 12/1983 0801042763
PepperTide                 Weyland, Jack   $10.95 02/1983 0877479674
```

Fig. 2.62. Fixed-field format.

The other formats are more sophisticated and they have one thing in common: all allow the programmed parsing and recognition of records and data elements within a file. In all the structured formats the data elements are unambiguously identified by marking or delimiting characters.

In the comma-and-quote delimited output the data elements are separated by a comma and are enclosed between quotes. If a data element is absent a comma and a pair of quotes is still present as a placeholder (figure 2.63). Comma-and-quote delimited records are accepted by spreadsheet, database management, information storage and retrieval, and graphics programs. This format is appropriate also for word processors if you want to do mail-merge functions, using mailing list information downloaded from a directory database.

Company	Year Started	Number of Employees	Sales
-------	-------	---------	-------------
AIR CANADA	1937	22,100	$1.94 Bil
AIR CARGO, INC.	1941	186	$52 Mil
AIR WISCONSIN, INC.	1965	NA	NA
AIRCAL INC.	1967	1,900	$375.40 Mil
ALASKA AIRLINES, INC.	1937	3,165	$468.26 Mil
ALOHA AIRLINES, INC.	1946	900	$77.17 Mil
AMERICAN AIRLINES, INC.	1926	43,800	$5.86 Bil

```
"","","Number","",""
"","Year","of","",""
"Company","Started","Employees","Sales"
"AIR CANADA","1937","22,100","$1.94 Bil"
"AIR CARGO, INC.","1941","186","$52 Mil"
"AIR WISCONSIN, INC.","1965","NA","NA"
"AIRCAL INC.","1967","1,900","$375.40 Mil"
"ALASKA AIRLINES, INC.","1937","3,165","$468.26 Mil"
"ALOHA AIRLINES, INC.","1946","900","$77.17 Mil"
"AMERICAN AIRLINES, INC.","1926","43,800","$5.86 Bil"
```

Fig. 2.63. Comma-and-quote delimited format.

In the tagged format (figure 2.64) the data elements are preceded by a field identifier (tag), which may be an alphabetic or a numeric code, such as AU for author or 245 for title proper. These tags identify the field unambiguously. The tagged file format is accepted by many textual information management systems.

Fig. 2.64. Tagged format.

The MARC format deserves special mention as it has been the backbone of library automation for 30 years. Distinction must be made between the MARC image and the MARC communications formats. The MARC image format (figure 2.65) is the one that may look familiar to many librarians. It is the image you see on your display when using online bibliographic utilities and CD-ROM databases for cataloging support. However, this is for the human processing of records. Computer programs that process MARC records expect records in MARC communications format (figure 2.66). This format is much more compact and has two additional components: a leader field, which includes among others the length of the record, and a directory with information about the tag, start position, and length of each field in the record.

Fig. 2.65. MARC image format.

Fig. 2.66. MARC communications format.

This distinction is important because the library automation programs that are capable of accepting MARC records typically require MARC communications format. They cannot accept, for example, the MARC image format of BIP Plus and Ulrich's Plus databases. On the other hand, a few library automation programs (such as the Midwest Library System) are capable of accepting records in the MARC image format but cannot import records in the MARC communications format.

The WK1 format and the DBF format are the absolute standards with spreadsheet and database management programs. They were introduced by the Lotus 1-2-3 spreadsheet program and the dBASE-II database management program. Every competitor wanted to make sure that their program could accept Lotus and dBASE files, and this helped these two native formats become the de facto standards.

Typically, statistical databases and directories with predominantly numeric data offer the downloading of records in these formats. For a database like Disclosure, downloading sets of records in WK1 format is second nature. The Bluefish software of the Computer Library also allows downloading of records in this format. It is a full-text database, and such databases usually omit tables of the original article, but Computer Library makes many of the tables available from a separate file in both formats. This is a good interim solution until CD-ROM software is capable of handling tables wider than 80 positions, the width of the typical display monitor.

The formats used to exchange textual and numeric data between programs represent "law and order" compared to the chaotic scene in the graphics world. There are several implementations of the major graphics exchange formats. PCX, TIFF, and EPS format files are accepted by many word processors and presentation graphics programs. Fortunately, most of the predominantly graphical CD-ROM products, such as the National Portrait Gallery database or the NEC Clip Art 3-D database, are capable of transferring images, drawings, clip art, and line art in one of these formats. Whereas the downloading of records from numeric and textual CD-ROM databases to other packages is a secondary function, it is essential with all of the graphical CD-ROM products.

You use CD-ROM software to find and look at the appropriate graphics, but then you must download them to transfer into a word processing, desktop publishing, painting, or business presentation graphics program. The purpose of the transfer may range from simple insertion into a report as a logo to sophisticated post-processing such as rotating, shrinking, enlarging, clipping, and so forth.[6]

Regretfully, not all the CD-ROM software packages offer an adequate choice of transfer formats. Some do not allow downloading to disk at all. Ironically, the software packages with the most powerful output capabilities have the most transfer formats, and the ones that have the most modest search and output capabilities offer no downloading at all or only in an unstructured format.

The software packages used with the InfoTrac databases and the Newsbank database ignore downloading. The Compton's Encyclopedia allows downloading, but it is limited to the textual part of articles and to a frugal 120 lines. The same restriction applies to direct printing. This volume limitation also applies to a complete session. If a user prints two segments of an article totalling 100 lines, the next person has only 20 lines left. To reset the limit, the system must be reloaded, which is an unacceptable practice on a public access CD-ROM workstation and is very inconvenient in any context.

This is not the best way to prevent plagiarism or copyright infringement. Users should be warned to refrain from both, and copyright notices should be included in the text (as is done by Grolier and the Computer Library), but the software should not police the user by imposing unrealistic limitations. Ironically, the recommended hardware bundle for the Compton database includes a color matrix printer (at least in Hawaii). Given the fact that no images can be printed or downloaded, it is difficult to understand the logic behind this.

CD-ROM software packages still have a long way to go in output capabilities. Until they can boast decent post-processing capabilities they should provide the raw data in the most common exchange formats. This, of course, assumes that the user has access to and is willing to learn the use of an appropriate host program. The real solution would be to enhance the CD-ROM software by post-processing facilities as illustrated by the KAware software, which allows users to do sophisticated cross-tabulation functions on records retrieved from the DLIP database.

This makes it a snap to create a two-dimensional table (figure 2.67) to show in which state reside alumni with Master of Library Science (MLS) degrees granted at the University of Hawaii between 1982 and 1987. (The values in the ROW variable of the table are short enough to also display the 1980 and 1981 graduates. You may move both horizontally and vertically with ease.) It is unfortunate that this excellent software feature is marred by the incompleteness of data in this database.

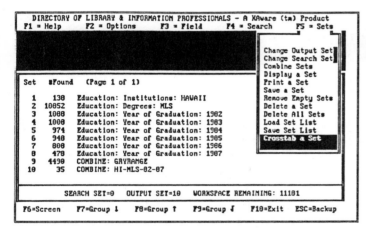

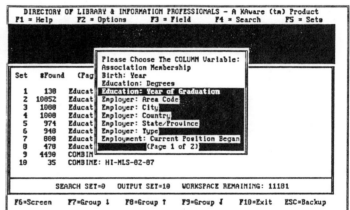

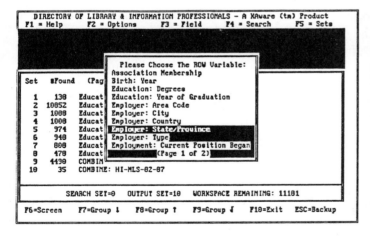

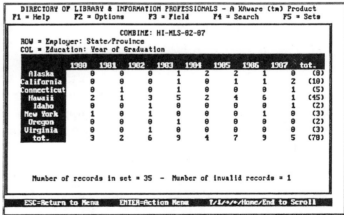

Fig. 2.67. Cross-tabulation with KAware.

FUTURE CD-ROM SOFTWARE DEVELOPMENTS

The clear trend of software development is to add new features, both implementing what others have successfully developed and coming up with new ideas. It may be obvious from the previous sections that some software packages could be hardly improved, whereas others need to implement features that now are considered basic. These developments are certainly welcome, but there is one that may be the most important. This is the implementation of the common command language (CCL). It is the one feature that could do the most for increasing the use and popularity of CD-ROM applications, making them as common a fixture in the library and the office as a photocopy machine.

Just as many people would never need the sophisticated features of photocopiers, telephones, and VCRs, most users may not need advanced search capabilities but just a quick and simple query to retrieve relevant data. The most often heard complaint about using CD-ROM databases is the need to learn a new user interface or command language to use another database that features a different software. Patrons may refrain from searching a database if it has a different command structure for navigating and searching than they are familiar with. Libraries, in turn, may give preference to a database that is less adequate to the clientele in terms of content and quality than its competitors just because it sports the same software as the existing databases in the library. Datafile producers may choose a software not on its superiority for handling their datafiles but simply on the assumption that most potential users may be familiar with the software used in similar databases.

It would be naive to believe that software producers would abandon their own products and work jointly to develop a superlanguage. It is not impossible, however, that a CCL interface could be developed in addition to the proprietary part of the existing CD-ROM software. This would not be without precedence. The online industry faces the same problem, and CCL has achieved modest results both in Europe and in the United States.[7] Even if the CD-ROM software producers do not offer CCL capabilities, there is a chance that an independent entrepreneur will develop a program that will translate CCL commands into SPIRS, OnDisc, Compact Cambridge, Wilsonline, and other commands.

Richard Kollin, who has been the pioneer of many innovative services, has developed and successfully operated such a system in the online arena. His Easynet service allows users to use any of the databases of over a dozen online services without knowing anything about their command language and protocol. The first version of Easynet "interviewed" the users about their information need, selected the most appropriate database for it, translated the question into a query, submitted it to the online service, and presented the result to the user. Later, Easynet implemented a CCL that supports many features of the draft standards of the National Information Standards Organization (Common Command Language for Online, Interactive Information Retrieval) and of the International Standards Organization (Commands for Interactive Searching).

The CD-ROM environment is even more appropriate for this kind of operation as the time needed to interview the user, formulate a query, and translate it or a query specified in CCL into the command language of the host system is not as critical as in the online environment, where the meter is ticking. (In the original Easynet the user was charged a flat rate regardless of the communication time, but in many of its current implementations you are paying by the time.)

There is, however, another problem. Your PC has to accommodate both the original CD-ROM software and the translator program and must perform a carefully orchestrated pas de deux in a limited space. With the ever-increasing appetite of CD-ROM applications this may be a tall order, but there is hope. More and more PCs are bought or upgraded to 1 or 2 megabytes of memory capacity, which is a prerequisite for this type of dynamic program switching. Second, the latest version of DOS 5.x releases more conventional memory for application programs by moving systems software components into the memory area beyond the 640K barrier. Third, application programs are being rewritten for the Windows environment, whose major feature, apart from the graphical interface, is switching between tasks.

The Windows software of Microsoft (and its alternatives that were introduced with much less hype, such as Hewlett-Packard's New Wave and Geo's Geoworks) also deserve attention in discussing the possible future developments of CD-ROM software from another point of view. More and more word processing, spreadsheet, database management, business graphics, and telecommunication programs will be released for the Windows environment. CD-ROM software will not be an exception. Even without the above described task switching the Windows environment will provide much more uniformity than presently available in the interface part of the CD-ROM software, as well as note taking and other advanced output features.

Currently there are very few Windows-compliant CD-ROM software packages. The software used with the Facts on File database and the Windows Personal Librarian program of I-Mode Retrieval Systems have been running in the earlier versions of Windows and are being upgraded to the Windows 3.x environment. KnowledgeSet Corporation introduced in 1991 the Windows 3.x version of its Graphics Knowledge Retrieval System (GKRS). Microsoft released the long-overdue, updated version of Bookshelf as a new product in the Windows environment rather than in the DOS environment. Other CD-ROM software no doubt, will follow suit.

REFERENCES

1. Martin Brown. *Human-Computer Interface Design Guidelines*. Norwood, NJ: Ablex Publishing Corporation, 1988.

2. Greg Kearsley. *Online Help Systems: Design and Implementation*. Norwood, NJ: Ablex Publishing Corporation, 1988.

3. Péter Jacsó. "Data Transfer Capabilities of CD-ROM Software. Part I." *CD-ROM Professional* 4 (January 1991): 63-66.

4. Michael Koenig. "Linking Library Users: A Culture Change in Librarianship." *American Libraries* 21 (October 1990): 844-47.

5. Kathy Jackson. "Downloading Provisions of CD-ROM Software—Are They as Good as They Should Be?" *Laserdisk Professional* 1 (September 1988): 76-79.

6. Péter Jacsó. "Data Transfer Capabilities of CD-ROM Software. Part II." *CD-ROM Professional* 4 (March 1991): 61-66.

7. Carol Tenopir. "A Common Command Language." *Library Journal* 114 (May 1, 1989): 56-57.

3

CD-ROM DATAWARE
EVALUATION

INTRODUCTION

The previous chapters of this book addressed the software component of CD-ROM products. In this section the characteristics of the dataware component are discussed. This delineation of the two components is very typical in the evaluation and selection process for practical reasons. When you are looking for a database, the primary question is the scope, coverage, content, and quality of the database — all of which are dataware characteristics.

In shopping for a CD-ROM database you should always look first for the appropriate dataware component and only thereafter at the software component. Your primary approach is to find a database that covers the preferred sources in a given subject area and provides sufficient information. If the dataware component is identical, or almost identical, across several databases then the emphasis shifts to the software component. This is the case with such multi-publisher databases as ERIC or NTIS, where the dataware is practically identical. The same applies to the various Bible databases on CD-ROM.

This is not as much the case with databases that use datafiles from the Library of Congress or the National Library of Medicine. One reason for this is the sheer size of the datafile, which prevents the publisher from making a database out of it on a single CD-ROM disk. Although the source datafiles sent from these government agencies to the commercial publishers are identical, the dataware reflects the preferences of the database publisher. The database publisher determines what to include from the source datafile and how to split the records across disks, such as whether to group them by language, document type, or publication period.

On the other extreme, there might be absolutely unique databases, such as the Birds of America database, the Science Citation Index, or the full text of Shakespeare's works, that come with a software you may like or dislike. If you want access to that data badly, you must also accept the software.

The most typical situation is when a discipline, a subject field, or a market segment is served by several databases that offer different features and specialties in both the software and the dataware components of the CD-ROM product. If you want bibliographic information about business publications, you may choose the ABI/INFORM database of UMI or the Business Periodicals Index of Wilson. If you want factual data about business enterprises you may choose Moody's 5000 Plus, Standard & Poor's Corporate Database, Disclosure's Corporate Database, or One Source/Corporate from Lotus. The subject is identical, but both the software and the dataware are different.

Certain subject areas have an abundance of databases (such as the field of life sciences) featuring different software and dataware as well as databases that offer the same software with various dataware. Agriculture, medical science, and biology are such fields. There are numerous abstracting/indexing databases, directories, full-text, and image databases for agriculture, and there is also an impressive assortment of life sciences databases published by SilverPlatter that use the same software. Some of the major CD-ROM databases with agricultural coverage are listed in figure 3.1, and figure 3.2 shows the assortment of the life sciences databases offered by SilverPlatter.

Dataware	Software
Agriculture Data Dissemination Service	Supermap
AGRISTATS	QUACC
AGRIBUSINESS USA	OnDisc
AGRICOLA	ROMware
	CD450
	SPIRS
AGRICULTURAL STATISTICS	SEARCHER
AGRICULTURE LIBRARY	CD450
BIOLOGICAL & AGRICULTURAL INDEX	Wilsondisc
BIOSIS	SPIRS
CABCD	SPIRS
CRIS	CD450
	SPIRS
PESTICIDE DISC	PERGAMON-CD
AGRIS	SPIRS
FOOD,AGRICULTURE, AND SCIENCE	KAware-2
FOOD SCIENCE AND TECHNOLOGY ABSTRACTS	Compact Cambridge
	SPIRS
FOOD/ANALYST	QUACC
AQUATIC SCIENCES AND FISHERIES ABSTRACTS	Compact Cambridge

Fig. 3.1. Agricultural CD-ROM databases.

```
AGRICOLA on SilverPlatter
AGRIS
Biological Abstracts on Comapct Disc
CAB Abstracts
CANCER-CD
CHEM-BANK on SilverPlatter
CRIS
Excerpta Medica CD: Cardiology
Excerpta Medica CD: Drugs & Pharmacology
Excerpta Medica CD: Gastroenterology
Excerpta Medica CD: Immunology & AIDS
Excerpta Medica CD: Neurosciences
Excerpta Medica CD: Psychiatry
Excerpta Medica Library Service
FSTA
HealthPLAN-CD on SilverPlatter
MEDLINE on SilverPlatter
NURSING & ALLIED HEALTH (CINAHL)-CD
OSH-ROM on SilverPlatter
PEST-BANK
TOXLINE on SilverPlatter
TROPAG & RURAL
```

Fig. 3.2. SilverPlatter's life sciences databases.

Using some criteria to evaluate and compare the different dataware is essential when you have several options. When the software is the same, the only decisive factor is the dataware. As with the evaluation and comparison criteria for software, the prevailing conditions at the user site (the collection, the clientele, the budget, and the availability of other printed, online, and CD-ROM sources) are to be considered when evaluating the dataware, as these factors determine how appropriate the database is in the given environment.

The following sections introduce various dataware evaluation criteria and use examples to illustrate the points. The criteria are grouped into three categories.

Scope	size, source, period, language, and geographic coverage
Content	descriptive and value-added information, informativeness, and record structure
Quality	authenticity, accuracy, completeness, and currency

Many of these criteria are the same discussed in some of the essential textbooks on reference used with printed indexes, abstracting journals, and directories.[1,2] After all, the majority of CD-ROM databases grew out of printed publications. The delivery medium does not bring any change, for example, in the quality of the abstract or in the accuracy of data, but it does offer some unique methods for evaluation and also some unique perspectives.

For example, the completeness of records in terms of mandatory data elements, such as the area codes in a directory or the publication dates in a bibliographic database, are very easy to check in most CD-ROM databases, but not in their printed equivalents. The same applies to the consistent format of use of such data elements.

A criterion that may be essential in the print medium may lose its relevance in the CD-ROM medium, such as the quality of the paper in an encyclopedia. With others the emphasis may shift. The index terms and codes assigned by the indexer may be the exclusive subject access point in a printed abstracting journal, and therefore their consistency and adequate use is absolutely essential. In a CD-ROM database these are also significant criteria, but the accessibility of data by words in the title and in the abstract may somewhat lessen their importance. When the search specification can be easily and quickly changed to limit or expand the search to certain fields and to specify proximity and positional requirements, there is a different perspective to evaluating the quality of indexing.

Many criteria and methods are applicable to and available in the online version of the publications, but the CD-ROM version provides a much more cost-effective way to evaluate the criteria using the methodology because of the usage-independent subscription or purchase cost of a CD-ROM database. The emphasis here is on the criteria and methods as applicable to the CD-ROM version of publications. Whenever possible generally applicable methods for dataware evaluation are discussed. Examples are mostly taken from widely used databases whose printed or microfiche equivalents have been in use in many types of libraries and whose content is obvious to anyone without any specialization or that, due to their subject orientation, are particularly relevant for librarians, the target audience of this book. The most frequently used databases in the examples are listed in figure 3.3 and are referred to by their acronyms.

MAS	Magazine Article Summaries
RES-1	Resource/One
RGA	Readers' Guide Abstracts
LIBLIT	Library Literature
LISA	Library and Information Science Abstracts
PAIS	Public Affairs Information Service
COMPLIB	Computer Library (Ziff-Davis)
DLIP	Directory of Library and Information Professionals

Fig. 3.3. Sample databases.

The first six databases are bibliographic, the seventh is a combination of the bibliographic and full-text type, and the eighth is a directory type. Examples are used extensively both to demonstrate the methods and to comment on the findings. Some criteria are relevant only for bibliographic databases and not for directories or full-text databases and vice versa. Whenever this is not obvious it is noted.

The samples chosen also demonstrate the real-life situations of choosing between two or more alternatives or evaluating the only one to decide whether it is worth the price. It is emphasized that these criteria, methods, and analyses are also important when you do not want to choose from alternatives but to learn about the characteristics of a single candidate database.

Database evaluation methods also depend much on the software. The sample databases feature software packages that are used with numerous dataware; therefore, many of the methods may well be adopted to evaluate other dataware. Once you learn how to check the completeness of records in Reader's Guide Abstract, you may apply the process to the other 17 dataware packages available with the Wilsondisc software. Once you read about the technique to evaluate the currency of LISA, you may use it with most of the other databases published by SilverPlatter.

Occasionally other databases are also used to illustrate a specific method or feature. Some of the texts recommended here may take a long time, but mostly computer time and not your time, and they are to be done only once or twice. Most important, they do not incur extra charges as in the online environment. A very important byproduct of accessing data on CD-ROM is that it opens unlimited possibilities for exploring databases.

The best way to learn about a database, however, is to explore it systematically, via searches specifically meant to verify and evaluate the dataware component of the database. You may get very good impressions about a database just by casual use, but a well-based decision necessitates that you get hard facts, tangible data about the databases that its producer may not volunteer. Doctors may get important impressions about patients by looking at them, talking with them, and taking their pulse and temperature, but they also need blood analysis and X-rays to form a sound diagnosis. The usage-independent price of CD-ROM databases encourages the types of searches recommended here, which are impossible with printed/microfiche publications and unaffordable with online databases.

If you are spending several hundred or several thousand dollars on a CD-ROM product you may want to take a few hours to get data for diagnosing the potential candidates or to learn about the one you expect to buy or license. You do not have to use all the criteria discussed below, as some may not apply to all databases or may not interest you. You do not have to present your findings in charts, tables, and graphs, which are amply used in this book to facilitate the explanation of criteria or pinpoint the diagnosis.

You may not necessarily have available all the potential candidates for direct evaluation, or you simply may not have the time to do it. Many CD-ROM publishers will send a database for evaluation (see chapter 7). The evaluation period may range from a few weeks to three months. These criteria may provide a systematic approach for the evaluation. Even if you are not going to do the analysis, these criteria may give you some ideas as to what should be asked from database publishers, file producers, or fellow users.

If you wish to formalize the evaluation and make its results easy to compare and present to others involved in the evaluation and selection process, it is recommended that you use the chart in appendix 2, which is to be completed similarly to the software evaluation chart discussed in chapter 2 of this book. Fill out one chart for each database evaluated. You may add your own criteria and omit ones irrelevant for you or for the type of database.

SCOPE OF THE DATABASE

The scope of the database includes such aspects as its subject field, size, composition, the type of sources covered (publications, corporations, persons, products), the language, and geographic and time coverage: the width and depth of coverage. The scope of the database should primarily match the scope of interest of the user community, the target audience to be served. A database with wider and deeper coverage is not necessarily better per se, because it may overwhelm the users. Adequacy depends entirely on the needs of the would-be users. No one doubts that the MEDLINE database has a much wider and deeper coverage in the field of medicine than the Health Index database of IAC, which in turn has a wider and deeper scope for users interested in health science issues than that offered by the databases of primarily general interest periodicals like RGA, RES-1, or MAS. A critical issue in judging the adequacy of the scope of a database is the primary users. The special library of a research-oriented clinic, the university with a medical faculty, the college with a nursing school, or the public library would have different opinions about the adequacy of the scope of the above databases.

Another critical aspect in evaluating the scope of the database is your collection, interlibrary services, and possibly the collections of neighboring libraries where patrons may easily go for a document not available in your library. High school students usually need some materials immediately about the subject of their term paper that is due the next day. For them the scope of the database is adequate if locally available titles are covered. Researchers may prefer a much broader coverage, however, including foreign language sources, and may accept some delay in getting the source documents if they seem to be relevant from the citation and document acquisition is part of the project budget. Users in a public library may be disappointed if most of the citations they found in the database are from sources not available in the library and an inter-library loan request would take a week or two and cost a couple of dollars for each article.

This aspect of the scope of dataware does not apply to full-text databases, to directories, or to those special bibliographic CD-ROM databases that come bundled with the microfiche or microfilm versions of *all* the source documents covered. Such databases include the TOM database from Information Access Company or Newsbank Electronic Index from Newsbank, Inc.

The criteria in judging the scope of the dataware includes the evaluation of the following characteristics:

- subject field
- size
- source coverage
- period coverage

- depth of coverage
- language coverage
- geographic coverage

Subject Field

The subject field of a database may be universal, as in Grolier Encyclopedia or the Bibliofile database; discipline-specific, as in the International Encyclopedia of Education, Sociofile, or Legal Literature; or field-specific, such as Water Resources Abstracts; or it may focus on a highly specific area, such as the Renal Tumor in Children database. The subject field is the first filter in your search for the most appropriate CD-ROM database.

The majority of abstracting/indexing databases are discipline-oriented, though there is an increasing number of databases of general interest periodicals, such as the ones that are used below as examples. Discipline-specific databases may have a broad subject field with relatively thin coverage or a narrow subject field with fairly deep coverage. The Applied Science and Technology Index covers — among many other disciplines — mathematics, physics, computer science, technology, and applications across many areas, whereas the Computer Library focuses on computer technology issues, with an emphasis on microcomputers.

Directories may be discipline-independent, such as the Serials Directory; discipline-specific, such as DLIP; or field-specific, such as the Physician Data Query, which contains references to physicians and health-care organizations providing oncological disease care or treatment.

Full-text databases are usually highly specific in their subject field, if for no other reason than the capacity of the CD-ROM medium to store the full text of the original source documents. The specificity varies from the Oxford Textbook of Medicine, which covers the entire range of internal medicine, to Pediatrics, which is the CD-ROM equivalent of the monthly journal of the same name. In between is the Yearbooks On Disc database, which contains the full text of 10 medical yearbooks. A full-text database also may be universal in subject, as are the Facts on File database and the World Book encyclopedia.

Quite often you may be familiar with the subject fields covered by the printed or microfiche equivalents of the CD-ROM database. In such a situation it is very likely that the CD-ROM version has the same subject field. Usually, the prefaces of the printed indexes give a much better description of the subject field of the publication than do the manuals, promotional brochures, and ondisk help files of the CD-ROM products. This is illustrated by the preface, product catalog information, and ondisk guide information of LISA (figures 3.4-3.6).

Scope and Coverage

LISA's scope is world-wide with the coverage of primary material in over twenty languages.... LISA includes abstracts for periodicals, papers in conference proceedings and multi-author works, books and reports....

The subject fields covered include library science, information science and subject disciplines which are likely to be of interest to librarians and information workers, e.g., bookselling, publishing and reprography.

Fig. 3.4. Excerpt from the LISA printed preface.

LISA

Core data for the information sciences
Abstracts of the world's literature in librarianship, information science, and related disciplines as compiled by Library Association Publishing, Ltd. Coverage includes references on library management and materials, as well as new technologies in such areas as teleconferencing, videotext, databases, online systems, telecommunications and electronic publishing. Covers the complete database from 1969 with over 81,000 citations from 550 periodicals. These periodicals are from 100 countries and are published in over 30 languages. Updated semiannually.

	Single user	Multiuser
Annual subscription (1 disc)	$995	No additional charge
Special price for subscribers of other SilverPlatter databases	$750	,,

Fig. 3.5. The SilverPlatter catalog entry for LISA. Reprinted by permission from SilverPlatter Information.

SilverPlatter 1.6	LISA (1/69 - 3/90)	Esc=Commands F1=Help

FIELDS   1 of 1

The LISA Database

The LISA Database on this disc contains summaries of the world's literature in librarianship, information science and related disciplines. LISA is compiled by Library Association Publishing.

    For HELP: press F1
    To FIND (search):   press F2

    For search examples: press e
    For record and field descriptio press f
    For an explanation of LISA ter   press t

Guide Choices: RESUME INTRODUCTION FIELDS TERMINOLOGY STOPWORDS
                EXAMPLES   HELP

Type the highlighted letter of a choice; or R to resume your work.

Fig. 3.6. The LISA ondisk preface.

Database Size

One of the characteristics most prominently advertised by database publishers is the size of their database. Though this data is important to know and is one of the few quantitative data that is readily available for dataware, you need to approach it with a grain of salt. The number in itself does not necessarily tell the whole story. Much depends on the composition of the database and the method of counting.

It is easy to "pump up" an abstracting/indexing database by including records that may be irrelevant for most users in the long run. Inclusion of announcements of forthcoming events, new products, conference calendars, or brief news items may be relevant for users of daily updated newspaper databases but not for users of quarterly updated sci-tech databases. Including all letters to the editor may increase the size without adding substance. This concept is discussed and illustrated in the section on depth of coverage.

Many cataloging support databases inflate the size of the database by failing to distinguish between the number of unique titles versus the number of records and also count the outdated, corrected, or otherwise duplicate, triplicate, or quadruplicate records, as in the CD-CATSS Serials database from Utlas. There are 400,000 records in this database, but a very significant portion of them represent incomplete and outdated records.[3]

Directories have their own way of creating and counting records. The number of records in software directories, for example, may warrant a closer look to determine if different versions, releases, and editions are described in separate records and whether outdated versions and releases are still kept in the database.

In the case of a directory of CD-ROM databases much depends on what constitutes a record (entry). All are versions of MEDLINE lumped together in one entry? Is every disk of a multiple-disk dataware a separate record? How are databases such as Book Reviews Plus handled? (The last is not available independently but only as a combination with Books in Print Plus, which is also available alone.) What about such CD-ROM products as the Arctic and Antarctic Regions, which combines six databases, none of which is available separately?[4] What about the OncoDisc database, which is a superset of several databases, some of which are available from different publishers separately?

Depending on how the directory is set up the size of these directories may be quite different, and the number of records in competing databases may be easily misinterpreted. You face the same problem with the printed editions, but in the CD-ROM versions of these directories the claims are easier to verify.

The size of the database should always be considered along with the period coverage, the geographic and language coverage, and the qualitative features, such as the accessibility of the individual items and the flexibility with which these may be displayed and/or printed. There are various methods to learn about the size of a database, and these are illustrated when the completeness of the records is discussed below in the section on dataware quality.

The size of the database should always be put in perspective, literally. There are three dimensions of a database: (1) its width tells you how many sources it covers, (2) its length informs you about how long it goes back in time, and (3) its depth tells you to what extent it covers the sources. Databases of the same size may have quite different dimensions as illustrated in figure 3.7.

There are databases which cover many sources but provide only relatively shallow coverage of the titles. There are others that are very selective about their sources but provide cover-to-cover indexing. A third group has both wide and deep coverage but go back for only a limited period of time. A discussion of these three dimensions follows. The results are often graphically represented in order to emphasize the differences among the sample databases. Your emphasis may be different, and the evaluation should be always made in relation to your library's collection and patrons.

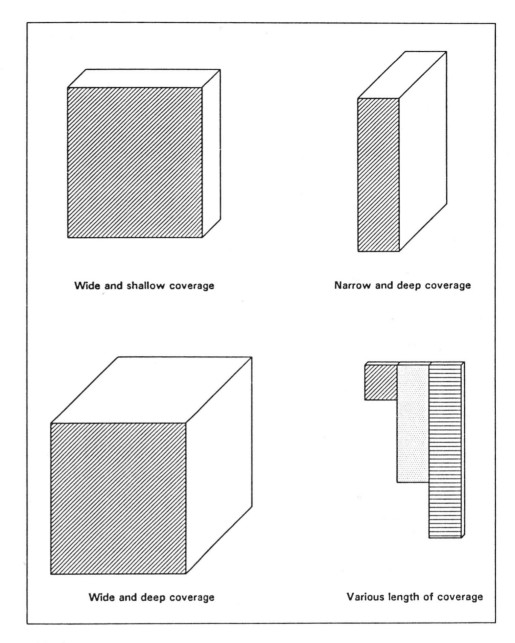

Wide and shallow coverage

Narrow and deep coverage

Wide and deep coverage

Various length of coverage

Fig. 3.7. Database dimensions.

Source Coverage

Almost all database publishers and/or file producers will provide some information about the number of sources covered. In abstracting/indexing databases this means the number of journal titles, conference proceedings, monographs, and the like covered by the database. LIBLIT covers approximately 200 journal titles and about 100 monograph titles a year. LISA covers 550 journals and several conference proceedings, but does not include books. The numbers of titles covered by LIBLIT, LISA, RES-1, MAS, RGA, and other comparable databases are illustrated by figure 3.8, page 92. The sheer number of titles indicates uniqueness, but only a detailed title list would inform you how important the sources are for you.

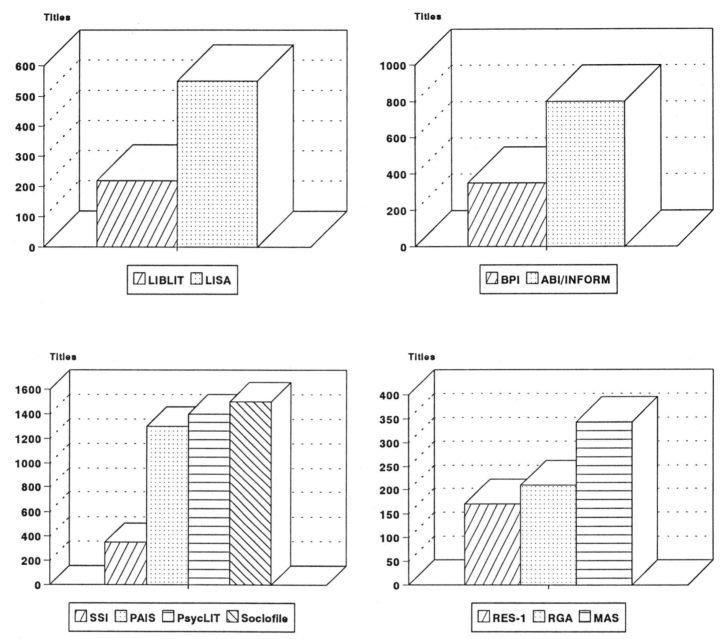

Fig. 3.8. Comparison of numbers of titles covered in various databases.

Most database publishers will provide a list of the titles they scan for abstracting and indexing, or you may find the list in the front or back of the printed publication. If this is a fairly short list of 100 to 200 titles you may easily assess its relevance to you by comparing it with other lists and with your collection. If time permits, it is useful to make a complete list of all the titles. Figure 3.9 illustrates an excerpt from such a list that compares titles covered by three databases that abstract/index general interest periodicals. Recently, EBSCO has doubled its source coverage. This seemingly impressive growth rate should be taken with a grain of salt, however, as the following discussion indicates.

R	M	W	Title
	M		321 Contact
R	M		50 Plus
R	M		80 Micro
R			ABA Journal
	M	W	Ad Astra
	M	W	Aging
	M		Air Progress
	M		Alaska
R	M	W	America
R	M	W	American Artist
	M	W	American Craft
R	M	W	American Film
		W	American Health
R	M	W	American Heritage
R	M	W	American History Illustrated
	M		American Libraries
	M		American Rifleman
	M	W	American Scholar
	M		American Scientist
		W	American Spectator
		W	American Visions
	M	W	Americana
	M	W	Americas
		W	Antiques
	M	W	Antiques & Collect. Hobbies
	M		Archaeology
	M	W	Architectural Digest
	M	W	Architectural Record
	M		Arithmetic Teacher
	M		Arizona Highways
	M	W	Art News
	M	W	Art in America
	M		Arts & Activities
R	M	W	Astronomy
R	M	W	Atlantic
R	M	W	Audubon
	M	W	Aviation W. & S. Techn.
	M		BMX Plus
	M		Backpacker
	M		Barron's
R	M	W	Better Homes & Gardens
	M	W	Bicycling
R	M	W	Bioscience
R	M	W	Black Enterprise
	M		Bon Appetit
	M		Book Report
	M		Boston Magazine
	M		Boy's Life
	M		Bride's
R	M	W	Bull. of Atomic Scientists
	M		Business Month
R	M	W	Business Week
R	M	W	Byte
	M		California Business
	M	W	Car & Driver
	M		Career World
	M	W	Center Magazine
		W	Change
R	M	W	Changing Times
	M	W	Channels
	M		Chicago
R	M	W	Children Today
R	M	W	Christian Century
	M	W	Christianity Today
	M		Cobblestone
	M		Colonial Homes
R	M		Columbia Journalism Rev.
R	M	W	Commentary
		W	Common Cause Mag.
R	M	W	Commonweal
R	M	W	Computel
	M	W	Congressional Digest
	M		Connoisseur
R	M	W	Conservationist
R	M	W	Consumer Reports
	M		Consumers Digest
R	M	W	Consumers' Res. Mag.
		W	Contemporary Digest
	M		Cosmopolitan
	M	W	Country Journal
	M		Country Living
R		W	Courier
	M		Crafts & Things
	M		Creative Computing
	M		Creative Ideas for Living
	M		Cricket
	M		Cruising World
	M	W	Current (Washington, D.C.)
	M		Current Events
	M		Current Health 1
R	M	W	Current Health 2
R	M	W	Current History
	M		Current Science
	M	W	Cycle
	M		D & B Reports
	M		Dance Magazine
	M		Datamation
R	M	W	Department of State Bull.
R	M		Design for Arts in Education
	M		Dirt Bike
	M		Discover
	M		Dissent
	M	W	Down Beat
	M		Dr. Dobb's Journal
	M		Earth Science
R	M	W	Ebony
R			Economist
R	M	W	Education Digest
R	M		Electronic Learning
R	M		English Journal
	M	W	Environment
R	M	W	Esquire
R	M	W	Essence
R	M	W	FDA Consumer
	M		Family Computing
	M	W	Family Handyman
R	M	W	Family & Home Office Comp.
	M		Farm Journal
	M	W	Field & Stream
R	M	W	Film Comment
R			Financial World
	M	W	Flower & Garden
	M	W	Flying
	M	W	Focus (New York, N.Y.)
R	M	W	Forbes
R	M	W	Foreign Affairs
R	M	W	Foreign Policy
	M		Forthcoming Books
	M	W	Fortune
	M		Futurist
	M	W	GQ
	M		Games Magazine
		W	Gentlemen's Quarterly
		W	Glamour
R			Golf Digest
	M	W	Good Housekeeping
	M	W	Gourmet
	M	W	HG
R	M	W	Harper's Bazaar
R	M	W	Harper's Magazine
R	M		Harvard Business Review
R	M	W	Health
R	M	W	High Fidelity
		W	High Technology Business
	M		Highlights for Children
	M	W	History Today
		W	Holiday
R	M	W	Home Mechanix
R	M	W	Home Office Computing
	M		Horizon
	M		Horse & Rider
	M		Horticulture
	M		Hot Rod
R	M	W	House & Garden
	M		House Beautiful
R	M	W	Humanist
	M		Ideals
	M		Inc.
	M		Instructor
	M		Instrumentalist
R	M	W	International Wildlife
R	M	W	Jet
R			Journal of American History
R	M		J. of the Am. Medical Assoc.
R	M	W	Ladies' Home Journal
	M		Lancet
	M		Learning
	M		Library Journal
R	M	W	Life
	M		Los Angeles Magazine
R	M	W	Maclean's
	M		Mademoiselle
	M		Magazine Antiques
	M	W	McCall's Magazine
	M		McCall's Needlework & Crafts
	M		Metropolitan Home
	M	W	Modern Maturity
R	M		Modern Photography
R	M	W	Money
R	M	W	Monthly Labor Review
R	M	W	Mother Earth News
	M		Mother Jones
	M	W	Motor Boating & Sailing
R	M		Motor Trend
R	M	W	Ms.
	M		Musician
	M		NATO Review
R	M	W	Nation
R	M	W	Nation's Business
R	M	W	National Geographic
	M		National Geographic Traveler
	M	W	National Geographic World
	M	W	National Parks
R	M	W	National Review
R	M	W	National Wildlife
R	M	W	Natural History
	M		Nature
R	M	W	New Choices for the Best Years
	M	W	New England Business
	M	W	New England Journal of Medicine
	M		New England Monthly
	M	W	New Leader
	M	W	New Perspectives Quarterly
R	M	W	New Republic
R	M	W	New York
	M		New York Review of Books
	M		New York Times (Daily & Sun.)
		W	New York Times Book Review
	M	W	New York Times Magazine
	M		New Yorker
	M		News for You
R	M	W	Newsweek
	M		Nibble
		W	Occupational Outlook Quarterly
	M	W	Oceans
	M	W	Odyssey
R	M	W	Omni
	M	W	Opera News
	M		Opus
	M	W	Organic Gardening
R	M	W	Outdoor Life
	M		Outside
	M		Ovation
	M		Owl
	M		PC World
	M		Parade
R	M	W	Parents
	M		Penny Power
	M		People
R-		W	People Weekly
R	M	W	Personal Computing
	M		Petersen's Photographic
R	M	W	Phi Delta Kappan
	M		Philadelphia Magazine
R	M	W	Phychology Today
	M		Physics Today
	M		Popular Computing
R	M	W	Popular Mechanics
R	M	W	Popular Photography
R	M		Popular Science
	M	W	Prevention (Emmaus, Pa.)
	M	W	Progressive
	M	W	Publishers Weekly
	M	W	Radio-Electronics
	M		Ranger Rick
R	M	W	Reader's Digest
	M		Reading Teacher
	M		Reading Today
	M	W	Redbook
R	M	W	Road & Track
		W	Rodael's Org. Gardening
R	M	W	Rolling Stones
R	M	W	Runner's World
	M		Sail
R	M	W	Saturday Evening Post
R	M	W	Scholastic Update
	M		School Arts
	M		School Library Journal
	M		Science
R	M	W	Science
	M		Science Digest
R	M	W	Science News
R	M	W	Scientific American
R	M		Sea Frontiers
		W	Sea Secrets
		W	Senior Scholastic
	M	W	Seventeen
R	M	W	Sierra
	M		Single Parent
	M		Ski
R	M	W	Skiing
	M	W	Sky & Telescope
R	M	W	Smithsonian
		W	Society
	M		Sojourners
	M	W	Southern Living
R			Soviet Life
	M		Space World
R	M	W	Sport
R	M	W	Sport Illustrated
R	M	W	Stereo Review
	M		Succesful Farming
	M	W	Sunset
	M	W	TV Guide
	M		Teaching
R	M	W	Technology Review
R	M	W	Teen Magazine
	M		Tennis
	M		Texas Monthly
R	M	W	Theatre Crafts
R	M	W	Time
	M		Town & Country
	M		Trailer Life
R	M	W	Travel Holiday
	M	W	UN Chronicle
	M	W	UNESCO Courier
	M	W	US Catholic
R	M	W	US News & World Rep.
R	M	W	USA Today
		W	Update
		W	Utne reader
	M	W	Vanity Fair
	M		Venture
		W	Video
R	M	W	Video Review
	M	W	Vital Speeches
R	M	W	Vogue
	M	W	Washington Monthly
	M		Washingtonian
	M	W	Weatherwise
	M	W	Weight Watchers Mag.
	M		Western Horseman
	M	W	Wilderness
	M	W	Woman's Day
R	M	W	Women's Sport & Fitness
	M	W	Workbench
R	M	W	Working Woman
R	M	W	World Health
R	M	W	World Press Review
R		W	World Tennis
R	M	W	Writer
	M		YM
	M		Yachting
	M		Yankee
	M		Zoobooks

R	RES-1	136
M	MAS	295
W	RGA	203

Fig. 3.9. Title-specific source comparison in MAS, RES-1, and RGA.

This title-by-title comparison is particularly feasible and important when the number of sources is only a few hundred and you are comparing similar databases. Note that this list simply indicates if a title is covered, but does not indicate the time period, let alone the depth of coverage of those titles. This is discussed in the sections "Period Coverage" and "Depth of Coverage," below.

The number of titles covered by the databases is not necessarily an ace argument for one of them. How many of the titles in your collection are covered may be just as important to you. There is a vast difference between the titles covered by MAS (295 titles), RGA (203 titles), and RES-1 (136 titles), but when they are compared with your collection this difference may shrink significantly. Figure 3.10 shows how many of the 150 titles held in a neighborhood library are covered by the three databases of primary relevance for this collection. You are unlikely to find a 100 percent coverage of your collection in any database, because you certainly have sources of exclusively or primarily local interest.

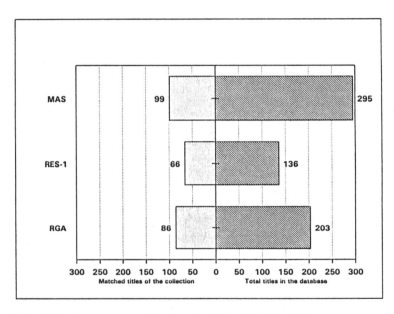

Fig. 3.10. Coverage vs. collection in MAS, RES-1, RGA.

There are databases where the list of sources abstracted/indexed is so extensive that it makes up a volume, such as BIOSIS or MEDLINE. When the sources covered are in the thousands, your only feasible option is to use the list of titles in your collection or a subset of it (e.g., the list of most frequently consulted or the most expensive titles) to see what percent of those are covered by the databases evaluated. The title selection does not need to be statistically representative but should reflect your and your patrons' interests.

Sometimes a database is offered in two versions on the basis of source coverage. This is typical of the mega-databases. EBSCO has a Core MEDLINE and a Comprehensive MEDLINE database, where the distinction is in the number of titles covered. Dialog offers a Clinical Collection subset of MEDLINE.

The source coverage may be analyzed in terms of the types of sources covered. Though the databases of general interest periodicals cover magazine-type sources almost exclusively, it may be a particularly valuable asset of MAS and RES-1 that they also cover the *New York Times* newspaper. LISA has a much stronger coverage of conference proceedings than LIBLIT, which offers records about only those individual conference papers also published in a journal and covers proceedings as monographs. Also, LISA has some coverage of research reports while

LIBLIT has none. LIBLIT covers book reviews extensively; LISA doesn't cover them at all. LIBLIT claims to cover unpublished theses accepted by library schools, which may be an asset, but only 45 theses turn up, and all of them are from the University of North Carolina at Chapel Hill. The question is which source types are important to you and are present in sufficient number in the database.

This aspect of source coverage may be easily checked in many of the abstracting/indexing databases. Many software packages allow you to browse in the document (publication) type index, which is the fastest way to get this information. Figure 3.11 illustrates excerpts from this index of some databases that feature the OnDisc and Wilsondisc software. Note that the Compendex database is only a small sample, but it illustrates the technique well.

OnDisc	Compendex	Sample database
Ref	Items	Index-term
E3	613	*DT=COFERENCE PAPER
E4	45	DT=CONFERENCE PROCEEDINGS
E5	45	DT=CP
E6	4	DT=DISSERTATION
E7	4	DT=DS
E8	16,367	DT=JA
E9	16,367	DT=JOURNAL
E10	78	DT=MC
E11	78	DT=MONOGRAPH CHAPTER
E12	16	DT=MONOGRAPH REVIEW
E13	16	DT=MR
E14	613	DT=PA
E15	24	DT=RC
E16	24	DT=REPORT CHAPTER
E17	286	DT=REPORT REVIEW
E18	286	DT=RR

*** End of Index ***

Library Literature   Data Coverage: 12/84 thru 03/31/90
COPYRIGHT the H.W. WILSON Company   READY
WILSONLINE NEIGHBOR MODE

NUMBER	RECORDS	TERM
1.	19	(CT) AUTOB
2.	2191	(CT) BIBLI
3.	464	(CT) BIOGR
4.	99	(CT) BKEXP
5.	170	(CT) EXHIB
6.	39089	(CT) FEATU
7.	347	(CT) INTRV
8.	468	(CT) OBITU
9.	543	(CT) PRODR
10.	1	(CT) PROFL
11.	2305	(CT) SPECH
12.	90	(CT) SYMPO

UP, DOWN OR GET N OR EXPAND a 'DS'

USER n a: (ct)
F1:HELP   F2:END   F3:Change DATABASE\DISC   F10:Reshow last FIND

Fig. 3.11. Browsing document-type indexes in OnDisc and Wilsondisc.

Other software packages let you search by document type, but this not only usually takes longer than index browsing, it also requires you to know the terminology used to identify the types of documents included. This applies to all the databases featuring the SPIRS software. In the databases with the Wilsondisc software the index browsing takes longer than the searching, and in either case of searching you have to know the rather mysterious codes. You do not have to know codes to browse in Wilsondisc. These include *ana* (analytic), *art* (article), *blk* (blanket reference), *brv* (book review), and *frv* (form review) instead of the widely used categories shown above.

As more and more CD-ROM databases outgrow the capacity of a single CD-ROM disk, it is likely that in addition to the current practice of splitting records by publication date among two or more disks, the type of publication will be an alternative dividing line. It is very likely that in the near future someone will offer a journal-only version of the ERIC database with an optional second (or third) disk covering the report type of ERIC documents.

In directory databases the source coverage is more difficult to evaluate. In the case of abstracting/indexing databases there might be a consensus on the scope of core journals of general interest or library and information science, or biomedicine, and you may compare the list of titles covered in the database against this core list or against your own collection. But what represents a good source coverage in a who's-who publication or a product directory?

In directory databases there is no way to group records by sources similar to the grouping of individual articles under journal names in abstracting/indexing databases. In directory databases each record is a separate source.

If there are competing products then you may look at the number of sources covered. There are, for example, three software directories on CD, each covering computer programs for mainframe, mini, and micro computers. All of them ignore game programs, shareware programs, and utilities in the public domain. Some allowance is to be made for one of them focusing on business software. The sources covered by these three databases are as follows: ICP Software Database, 15,000 titles; Business Software Database, 11,500 titles; and Datapro Software Finder, 18,000 titles.

The difference is even more striking in the sources covered by four directories of publicly held companies. Moody's 5000 Plus includes data about slightly more than 5,000 publicly owned corporations; Standard & Poor's, 9,000; Lotus One Source/Corporate, 12,000; and Disclosure, 12,000. The relative merit of source coverage is apparent in these figures. Of course, there are significant differences in record content, quality, and price among these databases.

Sometimes the printed equivalent or the manual may provide a hint about the source coverage of the CD-ROM database, if there is no benchmark to compare it with. DLIP includes data about 44,000 to 45,000 library and information professionals. But is it good coverage? Considering the statement in the introduction of the printed publication that 80,000 individuals were sent requests to answer a questionnaire a 55 percent source coverage is hardly satisfactory.

If there is no relative figure to compare the source coverage, you may wish to do actual searches in the database to get an impression about it. In a serials directory check for the presence of non-obvious titles referred to in a bibliography or randomly selected from a catalog. In a company directory search for companies discussed in some business publications. You may not have the time or inclination to select a statistically significant sample for testing; down-to-earth methods may work fine. Some searches were done to double-check the source coverage of DLIP; the results clearly confirmed the above 55 percent source coverage estimate, as illustrated by figure 3.12.

Search by	N=	Found	Rate
Authors in 1988 issues of			
Online Magazine	107	60	56%
Library Journal	76	43	56%
Laserdisk Professional	54	22	41%
U. S. library and information			
Specialists in author's Rolodex	96	51	53%
Columbia University Library School Faculty	12	10	83%
Rosary College Library School Faculty	8	4	50%
University of Hawaii Library School Faculty	9	4	44%
IFLA Personal Affiliates	186	78	42%
Total	548	272	49%

Fig. 3.12. Source coverage in DLIP.

In full-text databases the source coverage is unambiguous, as usually only a few sources are included.

Period Coverage

Databases differ significantly in retrospective coverage. Even the same datafile may come in different versions of date coverage. The versions of MEDLINE by various publishers come with different time-span coverage as illustrated by figure 3.13. As some publishers specify the time span relative to the current data (last two years, for example), the comparison shows the retrospective coverage as of January 1991.

Publisher	Database	From
Aries	KnowledgeFinder MEDLINE	10 years back
BRS	Colleague MEDLINE	1976
CD Plus	CD Plus Medline	1966
CSA	Cambridge MEDLINE	1976
DIALOG	OnDisc MEDLINE	1984
	MEDLINE Clinical Collection	1984
Digital Diagnostics	Bibliomed	1985
EBSCO	Core MEDLINE	3 years back
	Comprehensive MEDLINE	1966
SilverPlatter	SPIRS MEDLINE	1966
	MacSPIRS MEDLINE	1966

Fig. 3.13. Period coverage of MEDLINE versions.

Many publishers, however, have their database on a single disk and you get the equivalents of all the back issues of the abstracting/indexing journal when you subscribe. This in itself is a valuable feature. If you subscribe to the print version you do not automatically get back issues.

Period coverage may have a significant impact on the cost of subscription, as is discussed below in relation to pricing. Many publishers split databases on the basis of time periods and offer these separately or as a combination. There may be a current disk and one or more backfile disks. It is advantageous to decide how much retrospectivity you want, considering the obsolescence of the literature in the specific field, your collection and preservation policies, and, of course, your budget. You should find out the period coverage of the complete set and of the individual disks.

Splitting the database by time period is usually done out of necessity, as even the capacity of a compact disk may not be enough to store all the records and index files of a mega-database. Different time coverage also is offered, however, for marketing purposes, when the file could be accommodated on a single disk.

The start date of coverage by the database usually indicates the earliest year of publication of *some titles* in the database, and by no means suggests that all the sources are covered from that date onward. This is obvious if a title started publication later than the start period of the database. The earliest possible issue of the magazine *PC Sources* may be 1990 regardless of whether the database claims coverage from 1986 onward. However, titles that have been published for a long time are not necessarily covered from the start year of the database. *Library Journal* has been covered in MAS only since 1989, even though the database start year is 1984.

The best database publishers provide a title list that clearly indicates from which year they cover a particular journal and in which year they stopped abstracting/indexing a title. The source list of RES-1 indicates the start date only. MAS indicates clearly both the beginning and ending date of coverage for each title, though there are some errors in the list. It fails to indicate the end of coverage for *50 Plus, American Photographer*, and a few other titles, but includes their continuation titles.

Database publishers may do additional retrospective coverage of a title even after the database is released, and you must consult with the producer to find out about such plans. UMI started the Resource One database from 1988 onward when it debuted, but gradually increased retrospective coverage for most titles from 1986.

Of course, there are no guarantees that all the titles will continue to be abstracted in the future, but the track record of the publisher may give you some impressions about your chances. One database may be fast in picking up new titles and dropping others, while the competing database may not jump so quickly on new titles, but once the datafile producer has picked a title, it will stick to it.

Database publishers should include the start year and end year of coverage for each publication in a file on the CD-ROM disk, so that anyone could easily check it. Ask the database publisher for such a title list in print. If that is not available, then make a search by some titles. The resulting set is usually in descending chronological order. Looking at the first dozen titles in the list and then jumping in at the end of the result list to display the records can provide important hints. Alternately, you may combine journal names and publication year for such a search. Figure 3.14 shows the results of such searches. It shows the superiority of RGA and MAS (but there's a catch to MAS).

If the number of titles is within reasonable limits, modify the chart in figure 3.8 to look like the one in figure 3.14 by including the start and end years for each title or for the most important titles in your library. If no dates are indicated, the journal is covered as implied by the overall database coverage, e.g., 1983 in RGA, 1984 in MAS, and 1986 in RES-1.

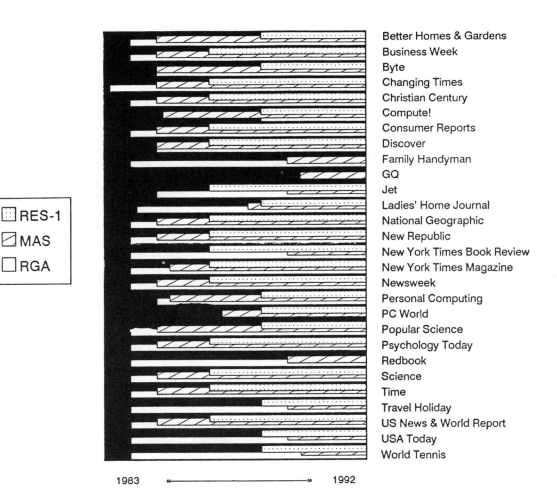

Fig. 3.14. Title and date coverage in MAS, RES-1, and RGA.

Do not always take date coverage as stated by the publisher at face value. MAS claims coverage from 1984 with most titles even though it only sprinkles the database with a few records from the 1984 (and often the 1985, 1986, and 1987) issues of these titles. Technically the statement is true, but practically it may be misleading. Figure 3.15 illustrates this with data for a few titles. To get this figure, make a search by some journal titles and combine it with different publication years.

The coverage of six of the seven sample titles is minimum to say the least. This is clear even by MAS' own standard in its coverage of the same titles in 1989 and 1990 and becomes very marked compared with RGA's substantial coverage. (See figure 3.16.) MAS indicates in its promotional brochure if coverage of a title does not start from 1984, but none of these titles are marked. This shallow coverage of core journals in a three- to four-year period makes one skeptical about the announcements from MAS regarding the rate of increase in its source coverage.

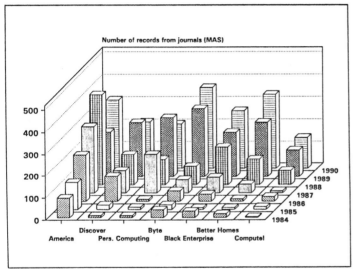

Fig. 3.15. Sporadic coverage of titles in MAS.

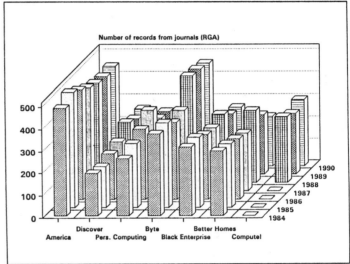

Fig. 3.16. Even coverage of titles in RGA.

Extended retrospectivity may be particularly valuable if your journal retention period coincides with the date coverage in the database. This can be evaluated only on a title-by-title basis by selecting a few of the most frequently used titles in your collection and comparing their retention period (in print or microform) with the retrospective date coverage in the database. In the example, illustrated in figures 3.15 and 3.16 extended retrospective coverage of *National Geographic* magazine, *Time*, *Newsweek*, and some other titles is important because the retention period for these titles is between five and ten years in my neighborhood library (figure 3.17).

The importance of retrospective coverage also depends on the needs of the subject field. It may not sound good that the Computer Library database goes back only to the 12 months preceding the beginning of your subscription, but actually it is not bad at all. In the field of computer technology anything older than a year or two is likely to be history. In light of this extremely rapid obsolescence of computer literature, the five to six years of retrospective coverage in the Computer Database of IAC does not

Retention period in years	Title	RES-1 Start	MAS Start	RGA Start
		8601	8401	8301
2	Better Homes & Gardens	8801	8401	8301
3	Business Week	8601	8401	8301
2	Byte	8801	8401	8401
3	Changing Times	8601	8401	8203
3	Christian Century	8601	8401	8301
1	Compute!	8801	8403	8801
5	Consumer Reports	8601	8401	8212
3	Discover	8601	8402	8401
2	Family Handyman		8901	8212
1	GQ		8907	
3	Jet	860113	8901	8401
2	Ladies' Home Journal	8801	8705	8303
Forever	National Geographic	8601	8401	8301
3	New Republic	8601	840109	8301
1	New York Times Book Rev.	8601	890101	8301
3	New York Times Magazine	860105	8405	8301
10	Newsweek	8601	840102	8301
1	Personal Computing	8801	8406	8401
2	PC World	8801	8606	
3	Popular Science	8801	8401	8301
3	Psychology Today	8601	8401	8301
2	Redbook		8901	
3	Science	8601	8401	8301
10	Time	8601	8401	8301
1	Travel Holiday	8801	8902	
3	U.S. News & World Report	8601	8401	8301
3	USA Today	8801	8901	8301
3	World Tennis	8801	8907	8301

Fig. 3.17. Retrospective coverage versus retention.

seem that much of an advantage in itself, unless the clientele in your library is interested in the less recent computing literature.

In the field of library and information science the obsolescence of the literature is much longer, depending on the subjects. Still, the 20 years of period coverage of LISA is not necessarily three times as good as the seven-year retrospectivity of LIBLIT. The Wilson product compensates for the much shorter retrospectivity by indexing twice as many items for the past four years (figure 3.18). This may be due either to covering more sources (wider coverage), as discussed above, or to selecting more items from the same sources (deeper coverage), which is discussed after this section. These two factors determine the extent of coverage.

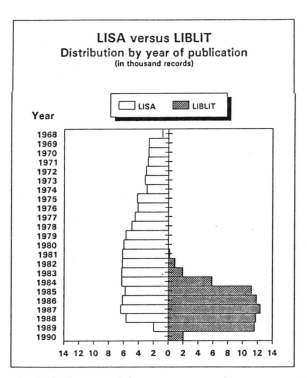

Fig. 3.18. Retrospectivity versus extent of coverage.

Published figures about the obsolescence and half-life of literature in various disciplines clearly indicate that the aging of literature is quite different, for example, in physics[5] and in musicology.[6] Your personal experience with users and knowledge of collection use patterns may be the most relevant in evaluating the date coverage of CD-ROM databases. The end of period coverage indicates the timeliness of the database, which is discussed in the section about "Currency" on page 155, as it has more to do with qualitative than with quantitative features.

In directory databases the retrospective coverage is not necessarily relevant because most directories are intended to provide current data rather than historical. The importance of retrospective coverage depends on the nature of the directory. You need the current price and features of a product, the current address and phone number of a company or a person, and so on. Directories usually are not cumulated but updated. It is another question if the records in the database also keep older data for cross-reference and tracing purposes. This is the case, for example, with the Ulrich's Plus and the Serials Directory databases. If a journal has changed title a new record is created under the new title, and this record includes information about the former title. The journal is retrievable under either title, but only one record is kept.

In certain situations retrospective coverage may be an asset in a directory. For example, in company directories, it may be valuable to know not only the most recent financial indicators of the companies, but also their past performance. Apart from the number of companies, the retrospective coverage of their financial indicators makes a significant difference between the various company directories. Due to the special nature of updating directory entries rather than cumulating them, retrospective coverage may be considered as a criterion of record content.

In full-text databases the situation is often similar to abstracting/indexing databases, though much fewer sources are included and it is likely that the retrospective coverage for all the full-text documents within the database is even. This is the case with the Computer Library, which includes the full text of 11 journals for the past 12 months. It is very likely that retrospective coverage in full-text databases is an explicit price factor, i.e., you pay by the time period covered.

This is the case with the Consumer Reports database, which comes in two versions in terms of time period covered, one with coverage from 1982 and the other, from 1985. (Interestingly, and uniquely, the version with the longer time span also offers two modes of interfaces versus the single user interface of the version with shorter time period coverage.)

Depth of Coverage

The source and period coverage indicate the width of coverage. The depth of coverage indicates to what extent titles are abstracted/indexed. It is one thing to abstract and index the same core titles, and it is quite different how selectively those same titles are processed. This may vary not only from title to title but also for the same title across the years. There may be general rules of exclusion and inclusion published in the CD-ROM manuals, as is the case with RGA and LIBLIT, but they may not be specific and tangible enough. The selection policy published in the documentation of RES-1 is exemplary, but it is the exception rather than the rule. It succinctly explains and justifies the criteria for selecting the sources and then lists the types of documents included (figure 3.19).

Periodical selection

Resource/One contains abstracting and indexing to 130 popular journals, as well as to the *New York Times Current Events Edition*. Resource/One editors have selected journals from a wide range of subject areas, including science and technology, education, the arts, consumer issues, health, business and current affairs. Together, these resources meet a broad range of information needs.

The database is an excellent starting point for many types of projects. Students find the database helpful in writing research papers in the social and natural sciences, as well as in the humanities. The inclusion of the *New York Times Current Events Edition*, an indexed collection of important articles from one of the nation's most respected news sources, makes the database even more useful in researching contemporary issues.

Resource/One is also a source for less traditional kinds of information. Teachers and librarians find reviews of books, audio and video recordings, movies and computer equipment. Students involved in extra-curricular activities find instructional articles on tennis skills, football strategy and photographic techniques.

Source publications are selected for inclusion after a careful review of the following resources:

- *Magazines for Libraries* and *Magazines for School Libraries* by Bill Katz and Linda Sternberg Katz. Because librarians often consult the Katz publications in building their core collections, periodicals listed there as basic reference sources are given priority for inclusion in Resource/One.

- **Circulation data.** Journals with large circulations were given preference because of their widespread availability and readership.

- **UMI serials requests.** Statistics on microform and reprint requests compiled by UMI/Data Courier's parent company, University Microfilms International, are assessed to determine the usefulness of various publications to researchers.

The New York Times Current Events Edition

Indexing and abstracting of the *New York Times Current Events Edition* is included in Resource/One to make the database even more useful for researchers seeking information on current affairs. The *Current Events Edition* includes national and international news, editorials, analyses, features and profiles from the United States' "newspaper of record." About 10% of the full *New York Times* is included, which gives users access to the information they need most.

The *Current Events Edition* is available in microform from UMI. *New York Times* records contain a FULLTEXT field, which gives the fiche and frame number of the article in the microfiche *Current Events Edition*.

Fig. 3.19. Selection policy for RES-1. Reprinted by permission from University Microfilms International.

(Figure 3.19 continues on page 102.)

Article selection

Feature articles and stories from every publication are selected for inclusion in Resource/One. The outstanding criterion for article selection is whether an item has research value that will endure over time.

Features, commentaries, editorials and the most significant new articles from the *New York Times* are selected for inclusion in the *Current Events Edition*.

The selection policy for other publications is broader. From these periodicals we index:

- Columns
- Editorial cartoons
- Editorials
- Features
- Fiction, essays and poems
- Instructional material
- Letters from prominent individuals
- News items that include some background or story development
- Obituaries of well known people
- Recipes.

Short articles that have a general title and common authorship occasionally are included and indexed as a single record.

Reviews

Reviews of books, movies, television and radio programs, live performances, art exhibits, restaurants and recordings are included in the database. Each review is classified as FAVORABLE, MIXED, UNFAVORABLE, NO OPINION or COMPARATIVE.

Letters

In selecting letters, the status of the writer is of primary consideration. Letters from leaders in all three branches of government are included, as are those from candidates for public office. Letters from authors, corporate executives, actors, the heads of professional associations and members of the clergy also are considered for inclusion.

Editors also consider the length and content of the letter. Pieces in the "Correspondence" sections of academic journals, for instance, are often short articles in themselves. These are indexed, as are letters from relatively unknown people that make substantive contributions to controversial subjects. Letters that simply announce a stand on an issue usually are not selected.

Topical material

Material that is extremely topical or of relatively low research value usually is not included in the database. Excluded on this basis are:

- Advertisements or articles in advertising supplements
- Box scores
- Calendar (coming events) items
- Columns that skip from subject to subject without a unifying theme
- Crossword puzzles and other games
- Horoscopes
- Letters from people who are not generally known by the public
- Obituaries of less-prominent individuals
- Product announcements
- Question-and-answer columns without a unifying theme
- Reader response surveys
- Stock price tables

Material of limited topical interest is excluded because it would be obsolete by the time it reaches the researcher. Stock quotations, horoscope predictions and announcements of upcoming events all lose value soon after publication.

The article selection criteria provide clear and easy access to the most valuable material in popular journals published today, and will maintain the usefulness of Resource/One for researchers in the future.

Fig. 3.19—*Continued*

Some database publishers do not provide any information about the selection policy, and the only way to find out is to explore the database by test searching. No selection guidelines are published for MAS, for example. The best and most reliable way to learn about the comprehensiveness of a database is to do searches by journal titles, document types, authors, and a few simple subjects.

Searching by journal title tells you how many records are in the databases from the same journal. Due to the different time periods covered, the search should be limited to a period covered by all the databases. Figure 3.20 illustrates the findings by journal title searches limited to 1988 as the publication year.

The most popular titles in the local library were selected and grouped into four categories. The results clearly show that with the exception of a single title, RES-1 provides the most in-depth coverage among the three databases, followed closely by RGA. MAS is doing well in the Current Affairs category but is only an also-ran in the other three categories. The depth of coverage may vary significantly from year to year, so it is advisable to conduct searches over two or three distinct time periods.

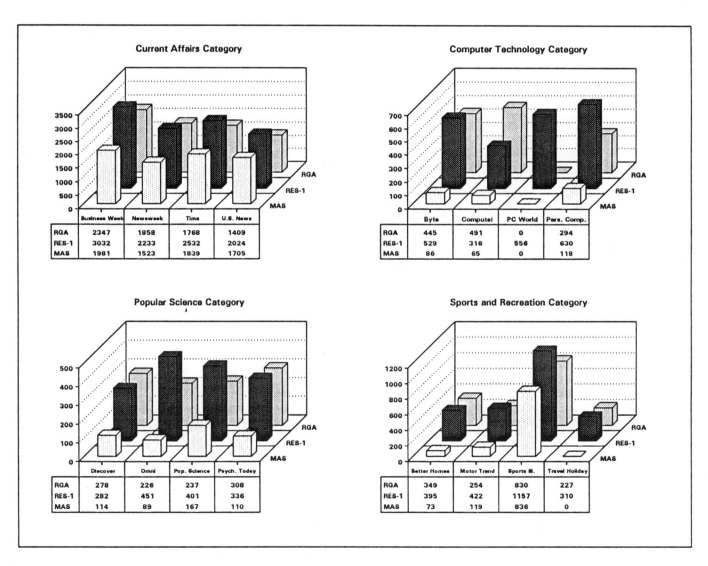

Fig. 3.20. Sample title coverage for one year in MAS, RES-1, RGA.

Be careful with title selections. Avoid journals that have changed titles or that have titles consisting of one or more words that may be part of another title (such as *Tennis* versus *World Tennis* or *New York Times* versus *New York Times Magazine* versus *New York Times Book Review*). *History* as a search term may pick up records from *Journal of American History*, *Journal of Contemporary History*, or *Natural History* in MAS and RES-1. The best way is to search such titles by ISSN, but many databases are inconsistent in using this standard number, and the result may be misleading.

Depth of coverage can be checked by doing author searches. Choose productive authors, senior writers, persons who have regular columns, and names that are rather unique. Be sure to spell names according to the database conventions, including spelling variations. If the author search cannot be made field-specific (as in Magazine Article Summaries), avoid names that may be common words and therefore may be retrieved from the basic index, such as Brown, Will, and White.

Differences in results of author searches may be the consequence of the databases not covering the same period or the same sources. If you have already analyzed these criteria, then limit your search to a period and sources covered by all the databases. Our sample author search was limited to the 1983 to 1989 period covered by both LIBLIT and LISA. It reconfirmed earlier finding that the coverage of LIBLIT is deeper than that of LISA. It also revealed some other characteristics after looking at the records summarized in figure 3.21.

LISA absolutely ignores book reviews and editorials but has better coverage of the feature articles and conference papers of Tenopir and Desmarais. It is surprising that Raitt's articles published in a British journal got less coverage in LISA than in LIBLIT. Tenopir's and Beiser's columns in *Library Journal* and *Wilson Library Bulletin* were spottily covered in LISA. A detailed analysis of Tenopir's columns shows that once LIBLIT started to index her column, it continued to do so unfailingly (with the sole exception of the September 1985 column). LISA, however, did not have a consistent policy. Knowing Tenopir's editorials I fail to find a justification for this pattern in LISA. (See figure 3.22.)

1983-89

	Raitt		Tenopir		Desmarais		Beiser		Nicholls	
	LIBLIT	LISA	LIBLIT	LISA	LIBLIT	LISA	LIBLIT	LISA	LIBLIT	LISA
Conference paper	3	3		3						
Editorial/column	12		45	30			6	3		
Database review	6	2			11	12	1	1		
Book review	62		3		2					4
Book, book chapter	2	1	2	1	1					
Feature article	11	8	9	12	17	19	8	6	13	10
Report										
Total	96	14	59	46	31	31	15	11	18	12
Items in both	8		30		18		3		8	

Fig. 3.21. Results of author searches.

TENOPIR'S EDITORIALS (1983 - 1989)

	1	2	3	4	5	6	7	8	9	10	11	12
1989		■●	■	■●	■●	■●		■	■	■		
1988		■	■●	■●	■	■	■		■	■●	■●	
1987		■●	■●	■	■	■			■■		■	
1986		■	■	■●	■	■●	■●		■●	■	■●	■●
1985	■	■●	■●	■●	■●	■●		■		■●	■	
1984			●		●		●	●	●		●	●	■●
1983			●			●			●		●	

Legend					
22	■	Only LIBLIT	20	▨	No column was published
11	●	Only LISA	9	▢	Neither in LIBLIT or LISA
23	■●	Both LIBLIT and LISA			
		Two editorials in September, 1987			

Fig. 3.22. Pattern of coverage of Tenopir's columns.

Subject searching can also provide an overall feel for the depth of coverage. Again, you may wish to limit the search to a time period to make the comparison easier. Choose topics that represent a key interest of your patrons. Use queries of single-word concepts that are nevertheless unique enough to make sure that results would be relevant without the need to look at the records themselves. Do not use single words that may be part of a journal title (travel), a geographic location of a publisher (Hawaii), or whose spelling is dubious or different in British and U.S.

English, as these may distort the results. Figure 3.23 illustrates the results of some broad subject searches over three periods using single terms.

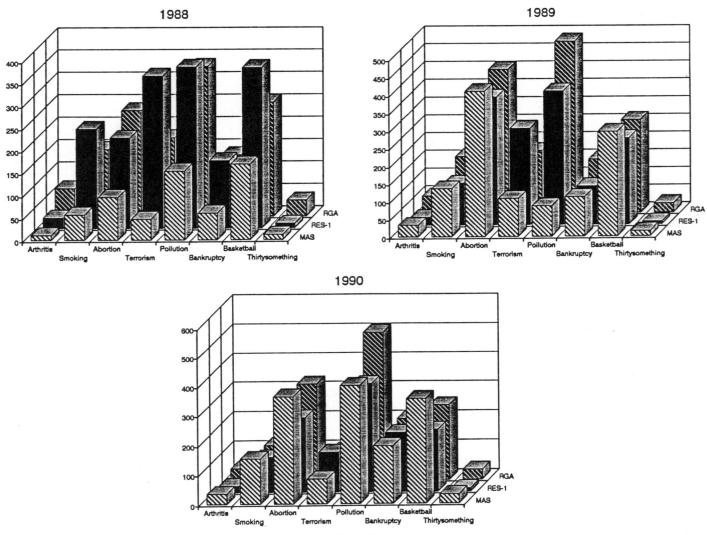

Fig. 3.23. Broad subject searches for three periods in MAS, RES-1, RGA.

Significant differences may result if one database has abstracts and the other does not. This is the case with LISA versus LIBLIT. The same terms pick up many more records from LISA than from LIBLIT, because the former has long abstracts (see figure 3.24, page 106).

This is, of course, a fair advantage, and it is very useful to see how much greater the results of a search can be when a database offers abstracts, but it may distort the result of the analysis from the viewpoint of comprehensiveness. Figure 3.25, page 106, shows the result when the search terms (appropriately truncated when necessary) were limited to the title field and the same period was used. It reconfirms the previous findings that LIBLIT provides deeper coverage. This method eliminates most of the differences due to indexing for the evaluation by depth of coverage. Obviously, you cannot do this search when limiting to title field is not possible, as in MAS.

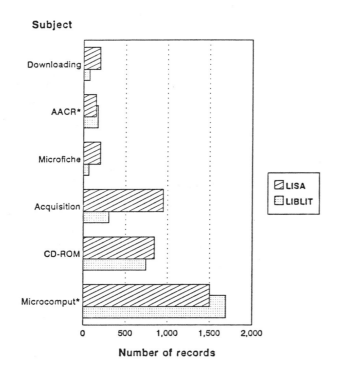

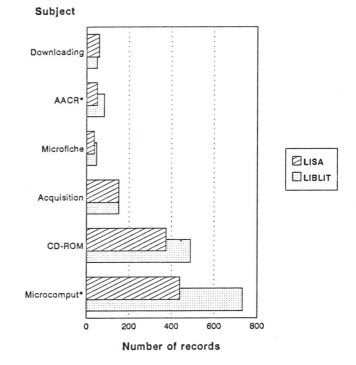

* Term entered with appropriate truncation symbol

Fig. 3.24. Broad subject searches in LISA and LIBLIT.

Fig. 3.25. Subject searches limited to title field and by period in LISA and LIBLIT.

The depth of coverage can be quickly checked by making searches for one or two specific issues of a given journal title, if that level of searching is readily available and is unambiguous. Figures 3.26 and 3.27 illustrate the results of searching by specific issues of some popular journals.

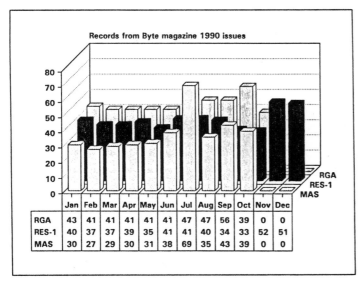

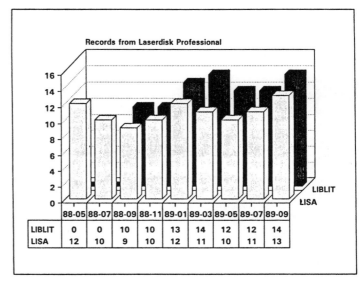

Fig. 3.26. Issue-level search results in MAS, RES-1, RGA.

Fig. 3.27. Issue-level search results in LISA and LIBLIT.

A comparison of the figures may be telling in itself, but if you want to use a benchmark and not just the performance figures relative to each other, compare the hits from the issue on item-level basis with the issue itself in hand to see which articles, columns, types of contributions, etc., were left out in each database. If you do this with a couple of issues you are likely to see a pattern, which may be more informative than the published statement about the selection policy. Figure 3.28 illustrates the item-level analysis of the October 3, 1988, issue of *U.S. News and World Report*. This is one of the few analyses that take much of your time, but it may be worth it. It may also reveal gaps of comprehensiveness in all the potential databases and may prompt you to create a small in-house reference database of the valuable but forgotten items, such as the information-rich and current "Vital Statistics" items in *U.S. News and World Report*.

COLUMN	TOTAL	RGA	RES-1	MAS
Letters to the Editor	14	0	1	0
Currents	6	6	6	5
- People Making News	3	0	0	3
Washington Whispers	1	0	0	8
U.S. News	5	4	4	5
On Politics	1	1	1	1
Cover stories	6	2	6	6
Tomorrow	4	0	4	4
World Report	4	3	3	4
Worldgram	3	0	3	3
Business	5	3	4	5
- Briefings	1	1	1	1
- People to Watch	3	0	0	2
Economic Outlook	6	0	2	4
Horizons	6	3	3	3
On Language	1	1	1	1
News You Can Use	7	3	7	7
- Eye on Wall Street	2	1	1	1
- Vital Statisctics	5	0	0	0
Editorial	1	1	1	1
TOTAL	84	29	48	64

Fig. 3.28. Item-level analysis of an issue of *U.S. News and World Report*.

It is quite revealing to see that only MAS includes items from certain departments of the magazine or that only RGA ignores all the items from the "Tomorrow" and "Worldgram" sections. This item-level analysis would also explain the much higher global number of items in MAS in the last year than in the other two databases.

If this analysis is too time-consuming, limit it to certain categories of article types. Usually there is no significant difference in selectivity regarding feature articles, but there is in terms of covering reviews, commentaries, obituaries, letters to the editor, recipes, inset stories, news items, etc. Choose some issues and find out the coverage of some of these items that are relevant to you.

If the database is easily and unambiguously searchable by article types, you may do this type of analysis on a much larger scale, as illustrated by figure 3.29, page 108. Note that MAS is excluded from this comparison because it has no separate field for article type and is not unambiguously searchable by words in the summaries describing article types. Selectivity by article type may vary even within a database family. Wilson claims to include significant letters to the editor in LIBLIT but generally excludes this type of document in Business Periodicals Index. The latter also excludes articles of less than one column, whereas the LIBLIT literature does not mention this restriction, though it seems to be applied.

```
┌──────────────────────────────────────────────┐   ┌──────────────────────────────────────────────┐
│ProQuest          Resource/One   Jan 1986 — Dec 1990│ │ProQuest          Resource/One   Jan 1986 — Dec 1990│
│                                                │   │                                                │
│    Previous Activities            Item Count   │   │    Previous Activities            Item Count   │
│                                                │   │                                                │
│[ 1]  ty (commentary)                 21952     │   │[13]  ty (recipe)                       895      │
│[ 2]  ty (editorial)                   8191     │   │[14]  ty (review)                     49524      │
│[ 3]  ty (editorial cartoon)            177     │   │[15]  ty (speech)                       839      │
│[ 4]  ty (feature)                    98189     │   │[16]  ty (book)                       30974      │
│[ 5]  ty (fiction)                     1067     │   │[17]  ty (arts)                         530      │
│[ 6]  ty (general information)        15196     │   │[18]  ty (audio)                       4803      │
│[ 7]  ty (instructional)               1555     │   │[19]  ty (movie)                       2531      │
│[ 8]  ty (interview)                   2064     │   │[20]  ty (performance)                 1517      │
│[ 9]  ty (letter)                       293     │   │[21]  ty (product)                     5725      │
│[10]  ty (news)                       40193     │   │[22]  ty (restaurant)                   134      │
│[11]  ty (obituary)                     730     │   │[23]  ty (television)                  1213      │
│[12]  ty (poetry)                       976     │   │[24]  ty (video)                       2097      │
│                                                │   │                                                │
│                                                │   │                                                │
│Search term(s): ty (poetry)                     │   │Search term(s): ty (video)                      │
│                                                │   │                                                │
│To Search:  Enter key word or phrases, press ↵. │   │To Search:  Enter key word or phrases, press ↵. │
│                          F1=Help  F2=Commands  │   │                          F1=Help  F2=Commands │
└──────────────────────────────────────────────┘   └──────────────────────────────────────────────┘
```

Fig. 3.29. Global search results by some article types in RES-1.

Depth of coverage does not apply to directory databases, where one record provides information about one source. How much information is available per source is a criterion for record content and is discussed in "Content and Structure."

For full-text databases the depth of coverage criterion is often the same as for abstracting/indexing databases, and many of the methods described there may be used. In some types of full-text databases, like encyclopedias and dictionaries, the depth of coverage is meaningless for the same reason as for directories.

Language Coverage

Abstracting/indexing databases may include a significant number of citations to foreign language documents. This may be either an asset or absolutely irrelevant, depending on the user community. One of the major differences in the scope of LIBLIT and LISA is the much broader coverage of non-English-language sources in the latter. Figure 3.30 illustrates the language coverage of these two databases by some major languages and/or by languages important to this author.

LANGUAGE	LISA 01/69 - 03/90		LIBLIT 12/84 - 03/90	
TOTAL ITEMS IN DATABASE	99966	100.0%	65441	100.0%
Chinese	230	0.2%	25	0.0%
Danish	1706	1.7%	498	0.8%
Dutch	1705	1.7%	405	0.6%
Finnish	736	0.7%	304	0.5%
French	2847	2.8%	1053	1.6%
German	8144	8.1%	2467	3.8%
Hungarian	1087	1.1%	3	0.0%
Italian	727	0.7%	286	0.4%
Norwegian	960	1.0%	769	1.2%
Portuguese	697	0.7%	204	0.3%
Polish	967	1.0%	256	0.4%
Russian	5000	5.0%	2686	4.1%
Spanish	448	0.4%	50	0.1%
Swedish	1036	1.0%	87	0.1%

Fig. 3.30. Language coverage in LISA and LIBLIT.

The documentation usually does not provide quantitative information about the distribution of items by the language of the original document, but you may easily find this out by browsing the field-specific language index (LIBLIT) or, if the software does not allow such index browsing, by making a few searches by the language names important to you (LISA).

In many databases the software lets you limit your search by two language categories: English versus non-English. Even if you do not want to compare one database with another, it is worthwhile to find out its language coverage, as too many citations of non-English-language documents may disappoint your user community. Furthermore, foreign language title words may weirdly coincide with your English-language query. A keyword search for articles about the right to die in PAIS will retrieve German-language items where *die* is the definite article in almost every title and the subject heading is, for example, "right-wing movement." PAIS has substantial coverage of foreign language publications and the importance of this coverage is underlined by the elegant software solution, which automatically displays the list of languages if you want to limit your search by language(s), as illustrated by figure 3.31.

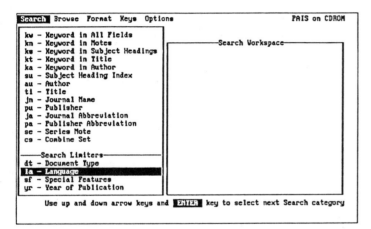 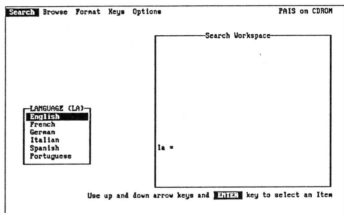

Fig. 3.31. Language searching in PAIS.

Language is the organizing criterion in some cataloging support databases that split the datafile into English- and non-English-language segments. These usually can be licensed separately, as with Bibliofile and Supercat.

The same considerations apply to some directories, but typically language is not a characteristic of the sources included in directory databases. In those directories where language is important, it is usually possible to browse in or search by the language index. It is perplexing that you cannot search, let alone browse, by the language of the serials in Ulrich's; you may search but not browse by language in The Serials Directory.

In full-text databases the language is typically obvious from the title of the database, as in Grolier Encyclopedia, Microsoft's Programmer Library, Facts on File, Federal Taxation Library, Die Bibel, Juridische Bibliotheek Deel I, or Le Monde. This may not always be so, however. The JUSTIS CD-ROM database contains only English-language documents of the Commission of the European Communities. On the other hand, the FABS Reference Bible includes the full text of six English, one German, one Latin, and two Spanish Bibles. Though the Shakespeare database is only in English, it includes both the queen's English and the modern English versions of his works.

Geographic Coverage

Geographic coverage may be a function of language coverage, but there is not necessarily a direct relationship between the two. Both the Computer Database of IAC and the Computer Library of Ziff-Davis cover only English-language documents, but the former includes many more Canadian, British, and European sources. On the other hand, wide language coverage also implies broad geographic coverage, as in the case of MEDLINE, with worldwide coverage, versus the United States-only coverage of Health Index.

In abstracting/indexing databases the geographic coverage usually refers to the countries of publications covered. Databases that abstract or index many sources originating from outside of the United States usually indicate in the records the country of publication. This usually can be checked by browsing in or searching by the country index. Again, browsing in the prefixed indexes, as in the databases using the OnDisc or Wilsondisc software (see figure 3.32), provides a much easier and often faster way to explore geographic coverage than in those databases where this data element is only searchable and that require that you know the exact names and spellings of the countries or their codes (SPIRS).

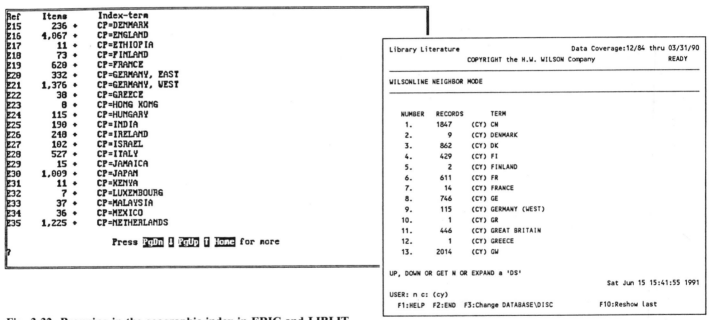

Fig. 3.32. Browsing in the geographic index in ERIC and LIBLIT.

On the other hand, geographic coverage may be the most international in a database that abstracts/indexes only U.S. sources. All the records in the AGRIBUSINESS database cite documents published in the United States; still, these documents cover practically every country in the world from an agricultural production aspect at least.

Some abstracting/indexing databases indicate by their title the scope of their geographic coverage, such as the Arctic & Antarctic Regions. In other cases the producer of the datafile is indicative of the geographic coverage, as with the KIT database of the Royal Tropical Institute, the AGRIS database of the United Nations, or the LILACS database of the Pan-American Health Organization.

As geographic names are often used as descriptors and occur in title and abstract fields, it is feasible to make simple subject searches to explore the geographic coverage of a database. Be as careful with geographic subject searches as with topical searches, using synonyms and positional and proximity operators and also being aware of homonyms to increase recall and to avoid false drops like "New England" instead of "England" or "danish," the pastry, instead of "Danish," related to Denmark, in a general periodical index including many recipes, or "china," the porcelain, instead of "China," the country. It may be appropriate to limit the search to the title or the title and descriptor fields and to a period available in all the databases compared.

Figure 3.33 shows the results of searching for names of some European countries and other regions in PAIS, ABI/ INFORM of UMI, and Business Periodicals Index of H. W. Wilson. Searches were limited to the title and descriptor fields and to citations from the period 1986-1988.

Much of what was said about abstracting/indexing databases applies also to directory databases, but there are also some additional features in terms of geographic coverage. In some directories geographic coverage refers to the country of publication of the original documents. This is the case with Ulrich's Plus and The Serials Directory (TSD). The promotional materials of the former suggest coverage of serials from 188 countries, and the latter boasts coverage of more than 200 countries.

It would be very easy to verify these claims and take a glance at the geographic distribution of records if you could browse in the index. Unfortunately, this is not possible in either database. You may do a search by the country codes listed in the user manuals. Be careful, however, because in the Serials Directory more than 20,000 records do not carry a country code. This may distort not only your findings, but also the normal search results if someone is using this access point, either alone or in combination with other search criteria.

	BPI	ABI	PAIS
	86-88	86-88	86-88
Sweden or Swedish	205	143	102
Norway or Norwegian	116	91	164
Denmark or Danish	52	63	28
Finland or Finnish	64	129	71
Iceland or Icelandic	24	14	15
Portugal or Portuguese	48	50	115
Spain or Spanish	280	162	71
Italy or Italian	264	216	84
Hungary or Hungarian	46	27	65
Austria or Austrian	62	58	29
Poland or Polish	74	76	72
Europ*	2095	1526	1399
Asia*	318	396	337
Africa*	542	269	637
Japan*	2937	2058	765
China or Chinese	761	783	512
Canad*	1821	1177	853
Austral*	413	401	291

* The appropriate truncation symbol was used

Fig. 3.33. Geographic subject searches in BPI, ABI, PAIS.

Despite this serious limitation EBSCO fares better in U.S., Canadian, Chinese, Indonesian, and South Korean serials, whereas Ulrich's has the lead for all other countries and regions (figure 3.34, page 112). If it is important for you to know what the real country coverage is you may use additional search techniques. For example, to maximize the recall of a search in the Serials Directory, make a query in the publisher field, using the name of the country and one or more of its major cities, which may be publishers' headquarters. In the case of Malaysia and Thailand this trick increased the recall by 50 percent with negligible false drops.[7]

In other directories geographic coverage may refer to the headquarters of the companies included (Standard & Poor's) or the country of residence of the persons included (Directory of Library and Information Professionals—DLIP). Database descriptions are not too informative in this regard, either. Some may gild the lily by boasting about worldwide coverage, and users may get false impressions. In DLIP many countries are represented by a single entry, and less than 10 percent of the records refer to professionals outside of North America. Even Great Britain, whose Library Association has over 20,000 members, is represented by 34 individuals.

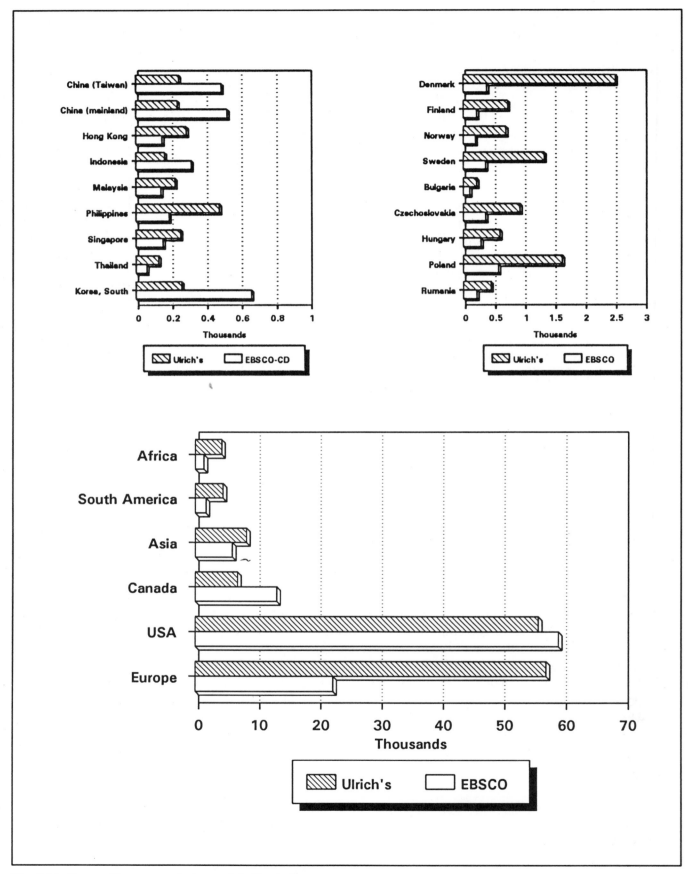

Fig. 3.34. Geographic coverage in two serials directories.

Though you may browse the geographic index in DLIP, it includes no postings (figure 3.35), so you have to make the search one by one. (In spite of the limitation that you don't see postings in the index, it is still easier than having to type in the names of the countries.) The results clearly prove that this is basically a North American directory, and searchers should know this before trying to use it to locate librarians in Europe, Asia, Africa, or Latin America.[8] To the credit of the database publisher, the most recent advertisements clearly state the geographic scope of the database.

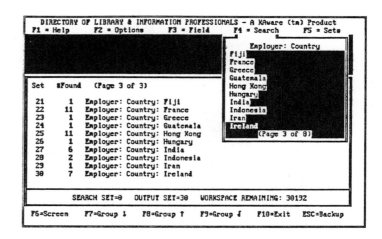

Fig. 3.35. Search by country name in DLIP.

Browsing the field-specific country index or searching by a few countries may be more informative than the documentation of the database (and may reveal discouraging inconsistencies and typos that have a serious impact on retrievability).

Geographic coverage does not necessarily imply U.S. versus non-U.S. coverage. The PhoneDISC USA CD-ROM directory is available in separate East and West editions, with the geographic split-line being the Mississippi River.

More and more CD-ROM directories focus on a particular region or country (other than the United States). Disclosure offers a company directory covering European corporations. The Wer Liefert Was (Who Supplies What) database provides information about German manufacturers and service providers; similar databases cover Austrian and Italian companies. The Swiss, British, and German CD-ROM versions of telephone and zip code directories were published long before the first U.S. phone directory hit the market. (This may have been almost the only positive side-effect of government-controlled telephone services in most European countries.) The French, British, German, and Italian equivalents of Books in Print are available for those who want information about titles published in these countries.

Just as there is a clear trend in subject specialization of CD-ROM databases, there is also a tendency to publish databases with a given regional focus. This is particularly true with directory-type databases and may reflect the fact that users are less willing to pay for bundled data that is not directly relevant to them. An interesting example for specialization by language and geographic area within a subject field is the Psyndex database which covers only German language source documents originating from Austria, Germany, and Switzerland. Quanta Press released the Middle East Diary CD-ROM database the summer of 1991.

Full-text databases may or may not have a geographic slant. General encyclopedias should provide worldwide coverage. *Time* magazine on CD-ROM certainly has a wide international scope, but the emphasis on the United States is obvious. In the case of such world-renowned sources as the *Los Angeles Times* or the *Washington Post*, this mixture of global coverage with emphasis on a region or metropolitan area may be taken for granted. This is even more so the case with such regional sources as the *San Jose Mercury News*. Some full-text databases in a well-defined subject area have international coverage of scattered geographic regions. The JUSTIS database covers legislative materials in the countries of the European Economic Community.

CONTENT AND STRUCTURE

The structure and content of the records define how the information can be indexed by the database creation software, presented by the retrieval software, and interpreted by users. Databases differ significantly in the amount of information carried in a record and also in the structuring of the data elements that make up the records.

Certain content criteria are crucial in printed indexes and abstracts, such as the arrangement of entries in the main part of the publication and their filing, but irrelevant on the CD-ROM media, where only a few items may be seen on the screen at a time and the filing order of the records is indifferent. Other criteria, such as the format or layout of the records, have accented importance in the CD-ROM environment where the user is confined to reading screen by screen.

Some of these criteria depend as much on the software as on the dataware and were already discussed under "Output Features" in chapter 2. A few criteria, such as the ease of reading records, depend also on hardware issues. Although typographic wizardry is possible only on very expensive monitors, the CD-ROM database may compensate by displaying records in a variety of formats, by including informative labels in front of data elements, and by not resorting to crowded presentation in minuscule type sizes, which is characteristic of many printed sources.

Scope of Data Elements

The scope of the data elements that should be included in a record is very much database-dependent. The CD-ROM medium may not seem to necessitate more information than the printed version of the abstracting/indexing or directory publication, but it does. This "extra" information is not primarily for display, but for searching purposes. What is obvious for the human eye when sequentially scanning the text of records must be made explicit for the computer program for retrieval purposes, such as the language of the cited item or the type of document abstracted.

It is possible that not even the most detailed display or print format would include all the data elements available and searchable in a record, albeit they could be useful. The date of the update, for example, is not visible, though it is in the records and is searchable. When you evaluate the content of a record you have to realize that not all the searchable elements are displayable, and more often not all the data elements displayed are searchable, let alone unambiguously. In some CD-ROM products, as in the databases published by SilverPlatter, you may get information about both of these categories of data elements by the press of a key (figure 3.36). Both categories should be considered in evaluating the scope of data elements.

Requirements for record content vary not only among database types, but also among databases within the same category. Obvious content differences exist between referral, abstracting/indexing, and full-text databases, but also between an abstracting/indexing database of business publications and one of life sciences publications. The former requires distinct data elements about the widely used company identifiers and product/service categories (such as DUNS number, Stock Exchange Symbol, or SIC code), whereas the latter requires distinct data elements of taxonomic codes, genus and species names, etc.

```
SilverPlatter 1.6            LISA  (1/69 - 3/90)           Esc=Commands F1=Help


FIELDS                                                              1 of 10

Each item or document in LISA, called a record, is a complete
reference to an article in a journal, a conference proceedings, etc.
Every record is devided into fields, or information categories.
Highlighted fields are limit fields. The LISA fields are:

TI    Title                         AB    Abstract
TO    Original (non-English         FH    Feature Headings
      Title                         DE    Descriptors
AU    Author(s) and other           CC    Classification Code
      names                         DA    Date added to file
ED    Editor                        AN    Abstract Number
SO    Publication Source            XR    Abstract Numbers for Parts of
PY    Publication Year                    Composite Works
LA    Language


The CITN for SHOW and PRINT includes: ti, to, au, ed, so, an.
Press PgDn for a discussion on field searching and limit fields.

Guide Choices:    RESUME   INTRODUCTION   FIELDS   TERMINOLOGY   STOPWORDS
                  EXAMPLES       HELP
Press PgDn for more; the highlighted letter of choice; or R to resume your work
```

Fig. 3.36. List of data elements displayed in Guide of USA SPIRS.

It is hardly possible to give a complete list of data elements in databases. It is much better to make an inventory of the typical data elements of records in the databases to be compared. Figure 3.37, page 116, illustrates the data elements in four abstracting/indexing databases of general periodicals. The Canadian Business and Current Affairs database is included for this part of the evaluation because it illustrates very well some of the points discussed.

The mere presence of a data element does not imply that it is searchable, let alone unambiguous as we shall see later in this chapter. The chart in figure 3.37 simply indicates if a data element is present in the record and in what part of the record. Notice the highly unstructured nature of MAS which lumps together distinct pieces of information in the "Summary" and "Source" fields as opposed to the highly structured nature of RES-1. This has a significant effect on the ease and quality of searches. We focus on the information content of the records first and then examine how appropriate the records are in identifying an item and how informative the records are.

The data elements can be divided into essential and optional data elements. The absolutely essential data elements for retrieval and identification are rather obvious. In an abstracting/ indexing database they include the title; source document name; and volume, issue, and page numbers. This is descriptive information and constitutes a minimal citation. It is appropriate to identify the source item but rarely provides enough to judge the relevance of the item, let alone to retrieve this item predictably. This last would require other kinds of information, such as subject headings, classification codes, etc.

If any of the essential elements are absent from the record, it is very difficult to judge the adequacy of the retrieval. Newsbank is an exceptional database in that the direct result of a search is at most three subject headings of the records retrieved, but quite often only one or two, plus the microfiche locator code (figure 3.38, page 116). Neither title nor source information is displayed; instead, you must look up the item in the microfiche file to find out if the records retrieved are relevant for your search. This product is an index to the Newsbank microfiche file, rather than a stand-alone database.

Newsbank cannot be used on its own, whereas all the other abstracting/indexing databases supply a basic citation that provides at least the title and the source. Undoubtedly Newsbank has a far broader source coverage (more than 450 newspapers) than the other newspaper indexing/ abstracting databases, most of which feature only five to eight sources. Furthermore, Newsbank provides the full text of the articles on microfiche as part of the service, whereas the other abstracting/indexing databases may not deliver the document in any form.

In a company directory the absolutely essential elements include the name, address, phone number, and line of business of the company. In a product directory the name of the product and its producer are the minimal data elements.

In full-text databases, by definition, there is no minimum set of data elements. Full-text databases "contain records of the complete text of an item, e.g., a newspaper article, a specification, a court decision, or a newsletter."[9]

It is seldom the set of essential data elements, but the variety and quality of optional data elements that make the difference between competing databases and enhance the retrieval and identification of the items described. These factors are usually referred to as value-added information. In full-text databases the "extras," or optional data elements, may include images; line drawings; tables; charts; and, occasionally, sound, animation, and full-motion video.

	CBCA	MAS	RES-1	RGA
Accession number	AN	-	NU	AN
Company	CO	Summary	CO	CS
Title	TI	Summary	TI	TI
Title enhancement	TI	Summary	-	TI
Corporate Source	CS	n/a	n/a	CA
Author	AU	Summary	AU	AU
Publication date	PD	Source	DA,PD	YR
Publication year	PY	Source	DA,PD	YR
Journal name	JN	Source	JN	JN
ISSN	-	Source	SN	IS
Language	LA	n/a	n/a	n/a
Publisher	PU	-	-	PB
ISBN	BN	-	-	BN
Special features	SF	Source	SP	PD
illustration	✓	✓	✓	✓
map	-	✓	✓	✓
photograph	✓	✓	✓	✓
table (chart)	-	✓	✓	✓
graph	✓	✓	✓	✓
portrait	-	-	-	✓
Series	SE	-	-	SE
Notes	NT	-	-	SE
Named person	NA	Summary	NA	PS
Trade (product) name	TN	Summary	PR,PN	SH
Descriptors	PE	Descriptor	DE,SU	DE,SH
Length of article	-	-	LE	-
Record type	SF	-	AT	RT
Article type	SF	-	AT	CT
Journal code	-	-	JC	-
Journal group	-	-	JG	-
Volume	JN	Source	VO	JN
Issue	JN	Source	IS	JN
Pages	JN	Source	PA	JN
Abstract	-	Summary	AB	AB
Dewey code	-	-	-	DD (1)
LC class number	-	-	-	LC (1)
LC card number	-	-	-	LN (1)
Full text	-	(2)	-	-

(1) For book reviews only and very sporadically
(2) For Magill's book reviews

Fig. 3.37. Data elements in CBCA, MAS, RES-1, and RGA.

```
Current  AIRLINES                                    3196
Search   bankruptcies and failures        213   NewsBank              x Index
             American Airlines             38        January 1981 - April 1990
 ┌ Headings ─────     No. of Articles ┐
                  ┌─ Sub-headings ──── No. of Articles ┐
                                                ┌─ Sub-headings ──── No. of Articles ┐
 AIRLINES
 AIRLITE ALUMINUM C   bankruptcies and f    American Airlines                38
 AIRPLANE HIJACKING   bankruptcy impact     attitudes and opinions            1
 AIRPLANES            black owned           bankruptcy impact      ■          2
 AIRPORTS             certification         Bar Harbor Airways                1
 AIRSTREAM CO         chairmen              Bass Aviation Inc.                1
 AJELLO CARL          chairman's attitud    bomb threats impact               1
 AKAHANE GEORGE       charter airlines      Braniff International Airways     19
 AKAKA DANIEL         charter lines         California: San Francisco         1
 AKANA BERNARD        charter services      Colorado: Denver                  2
 AKEBONO BRAKE INDU   commuter airlines     Continental Airlines             74
 AKERLAND GUSTAV      concentration and     contract negotiations             5
 AKERS JOHN           cooperation agreem    contract ratification             2
 AKHSHARUMOVA ANNA    deregulation impac    contract rejections               2
 AKIHITO CROWN PRIN   divestitures          contract settlements              2
 AKIHITO EMPEROR 2F   economic impact on    Delta Air Lines                   3
 ALABAMA              employees             Delta Airlines                   17
 ALABAMA A M UNIVER   establishment

  Press SEARCH to search the highlighted Sub-heading or PRINT REF to print.
```

```
Current    AIRLINES                          Last    ALOHA AIRLINES
Search       bankruptcies and failures       Search
                American Airlines

        January 1981 - April 1990
 ───── NewsBank          x Index  ─────── Microfiche Locator Code ──────
        unionization                          1988      TRA 4 :E12
                                              1988      TRA 65:F7
     American Airlines
        captain, woman                        1986      TRA 69:E12
        contract concessions                  1987      TRA 7:D3
        contract negotiations                 1983      TRA 6:A11
                                              1983      TRA 6:C13
                                              1981      TRA 118:D4
                                              1987      TRA 7:D4
                                              1987      TRA 81 D5
        contract ratification                 1983      TRA 6:A12
        contract rejection                    1985      TRA 35:F11
        contract settlement                   1987      TRA 15:B7
                                              1985      TRA 28:A1
        contract settlements                  1983      TRA 11:B5
                                              1983      TRA 65:A4
                                              1983      TRA 65:B14

 ─ Press LINE FORWARD or BACK, HEADINGS for headings list, PRINT REF to print. ──
```

Fig. 3.38. Search results in Newsbank.

Value-added Information

The battery of value-added information may make one database far superior to others. They significantly enhance the searchability and informativeness of the records. The various types of value-added information are not readily available from the source. Some are fairly easy to create, such as language, country, document-type identifiers, and article content codes. Others may require much more intellectual effort, like the selection of the most appropriate descriptors, classification codes, or the creation of summaries. There also might be exceptions to this rule, such as when the author's abstract is taken without modification from the source document.

The differing amount of value-added information is quite obvious in figure 3.39, which illustrates the minimalist record with some value-added information from the Canadian Business and Current Affairs database and the richly enhanced records from RES-1. Somewhere in between are the MAS and RGA records, in terms of quantity of value-added information. The qualitative aspect of value-added information is discussed separately.

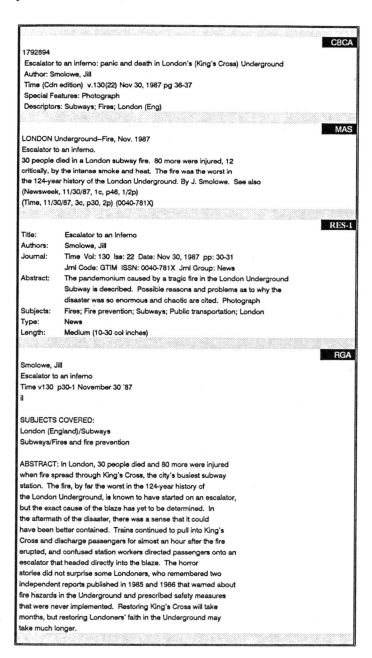

Fig. 3.39. Comparing records from CBCA, MAS, RES-1, and RGA.

Even in such relatively simple types of databases like those for general interest magazines there may be numerous pieces of value-added information. Subject headings and abstracts are the most prominent ones, and the lack of abstracts in CBCA is noteworthy, though only in this context. So is the single subject heading in MAS, which is in sharp contrast with the average of three to four headings in the others. This parsimonious subject heading assignment has a negative impact on searching MAS, because you must search the whole record to ensure that you do not miss too many relevant items by doing subject-heading-only searches. This technique, however, often results in irrelevant hits. There is no interim solution, such as searching in the subject heading and title fields but not in the abstract.

On the other hand, MAS includes side references to other articles related to the topic searched that are not included in the database. This is a very satisfactory solution. Almost identical news items do not inflate the database, and the user is advised where else the event was reported. Another unique feature of MAS in this group is the inclusion of the full text of *Magill Book Reviews* in more than 2,000 records. This is just a prelude to the introduction of a new EBSCO database, "MAS with Full Text," which includes the complete text of over twenty-five popular magazines.

Only RES-1 includes a special journal code used by UMI, which may seem redundant next to the journal name and the ISSN of the magazine but actually is important value-added information for searching. The journal code is invaluable in searching for records from journals whose title (and ISSN) have changed, since the UMI code remains the same during the lifetime of the serial. Furthermore, it can be used for titles consisting of a word that is part of another title, such as *Life* or *History*.

The use of the code can significantly reduce the response time in searches for titles that consist of common words, such as *New York Times* or *Children Today*. These words would produce very large temporary sets for "New," "York," "Times," "children," and "today," whose creation and then combination and restriction to the title field is a slow process. Using the appropriate code makes the search eight to ten times faster, as the codes are unique and single terms.

To add to all this, the code is intuitive, as in most of the cases it is created by the first three characters of the magazine title preceded by the letter G, e.g., the code for *Time* is GTIM, for *Newsweek* it is GNEW, and so on. Even if users do not look up the codes in the user manual, there is a good chance that they will find out the algorithm.

Both MAS and RES-1 include not only the traditional pagination information, but also the length of the article either as number of pages (MAS) or as number of columns and length category (RES-1). The convention of MAS seems less ambiguous, but this information is searchable only in RES-1, a significant advantage. In searching for a widely discussed topic, you may limit your results in RES-1 to long articles. As for record display, there is hardly any difference from this point of view.

RES-1 has another unique data element that indicates in what type of magazine the original article appeared. Each journal covered is assigned to one or more of the following journal groups: academic, arts, business, commentary, health, lifestyles, news, sci-tech, or socioenvironmental. If you want to limit search results to citations from consumer-type journals, you may use the journal group to do so without the need to list the titles individually and then combine the result with the results of the topical search. This is a unique type of value-added information also from another perspective. Usually individual records are analyzed to provide value-added information. In this case the journal title records are assigned value-added information, not the individual article records.

RES-1 and MAS offer another type of value-added data that resembles the one described above in technique. This is the local information that may be provided by the librarian when installing the application. Each journal title may be assigned local information, such as the status of subscription or holding statements, which is automatically appended on displaying the citations. In MAS you can limit your search to such titles, too.

This may be a minor point, but you may find the use of specific illustration types (chart, graph, photo, map) in the RES-1 and MAS databases much better than the generic code "il" used in the Wilson databases to indicate that some illustrations are available in the original article (figure 3.40). Though Wilson has specific illustration types, their application seems to be very sporadic. MAS specifies the number of each type of illustrations and even makes a distinction between black-and-white versus color photographs, but its coding of the illustrations may not be immediately obvious for the user and may not be searched as unambiguously as in RES-1.

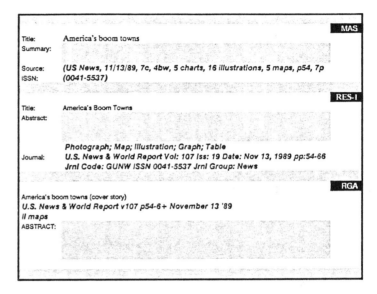

Fig. 3.40. Citation excerpts from records in MAS, RES-1, and RGA.

RGA and MAS (and occasionally CBCA) offer title enhancement when the original title is not informative enough. Though this problem is usually overcome by the use of subject headings, abstracts, and other types of value-added information, title enhancement is particularly useful in RGA because in the most commonly used Wilsearch mode titles are searchable, but abstracts are not. Title enhancement could be especially valuable when displaying short-title-only lists for the quick scanning of the results, but neither RGA nor MAS offers this display format. In the Wilsonline mode RGA has a title-only display format, but it does not include the title enhancement. RES-1 does have title-only display format but does not provide title augmentation. This is an ironic discrepancy between software and dataware.

Some types of value-added information are only applicable in specific record types. ISBN, LC card number, and Dewey Decimal Classification codes are included in the Wilson databases, but only with book reviews and not consistently. In RES-1, another well-implemented feature applies only to records citing review articles. In a subfield of the review type field the conclusion of the review is indicated by one of five possible categories (favorable, unfavorable, mixed, no opinion, or comparative). You may very easily find out if a film or book has gotten more positive than negative reviews, as illustrated by figure 3.41, page 120. You do not even have to read the abstract to get a quick scorecard.

```
ProQuest              Resource/One          Jan 1986 — Feb 1991

    Previous Activities                        Item Count

[ 1]  ty(movie review and favorable)             1069
[ 2]  ty(movie review and unfavorable)            541
[ 3]  ty(movie review and mixed)                  399
[ 4]  ty(movie review and comparative)            705
[ 5]  ty(movie review and no opinion)              27




Search term(s): ty(movie review and no opinion)


To Search:  Enter key word or phrases, press ←┘.   F1=Help  F2=Commands
```

Fig. 3.41. Searching by review conclusions in RES-1.

The differences between the information content of records in LISA and LIBLIT are obvious at first glance (figure 3.42). LISA is far more rich in content, not only providing a lengthy abstract but also assigning many more subject headings on the average. It is another question how redundant, and overwhelming, these subject headings often are.

More data is not always better as illustrated by the LISA records. Not only are the descriptors usually redundant and repetitious, but also they are often too broad. The sample record in figure 3.42, for example, has the descriptor "subject indexing" repeated twice and is part of the term "computerized subject indexing" as well. The article has nothing to do with subject indexing, by the way. This kind of indexing is very characteristic of LISA.

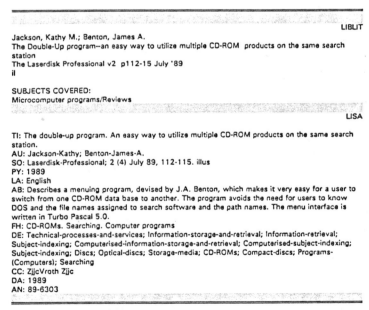

Fig. 3.42. Comparing records in LISA and LIBLIT.

Directory databases also feature many data elements of value-added information. The Serials Directory boasts to have more information about serials than its nearest competitor. This is certainly true for language code (which does not exist in Ulrich's Plus, the obvious nearest competitor) and classification codes. The Serials Directory has UDC and NLM for many (but far from all) records. It also has more records with CODEN and LC classification codes than does Ulrich's Plus. It is, however, questionable how much value these codes add in reading a record. They certainly could significantly improve the retrieval process if they were consistently applied and unambiguously searchable, which is discussed in the next section.

The Lotus One Source company directory provides more value-added information, more financial data, and more analytic reports than are available in the Standard & Poor's Corporations directory at about three times the price. The availability of references in the Lotus product to journal articles about the companies is in itself an asset that may spare the subscription fee for a separate indexing/abstracting CD-ROM database for business periodicals.

The newcomer Bookfind database will certainly pose a challenge to the market hegemony of Whitaker's Bookbank database of British books in print if for no other reason than its inclusion of table of contents and extensive summaries of the books, as illustrated by sample records of the oft-cited work on full-text databases in figure 3.43.

Full-text databases also offer unique and not immediately obvious value-added information. Many might be tempted to believe that there may be no information that could add value to the full text. Many researchers have proved that this is not so, and the availability of full text does not eliminate the need for value-added information.[10,11,12]

BookFind-CD FULL FORMAT LIST

Series: New directions in information management, 21
FULL TEXT DATABASES
By Carol Tenopir (Associate Professor, School of Library Information Studies, University of Hawaii, USA); Jung Soon Ro (Associate Professor, Department of Library Science, Hannam University, Korea).
Greenwood Press, 30 September 1990
Bibliography, index
HARDBACK UK £30.95 NET 0-313-26303-5
UK trade orders to: Eurospan Group of Publishers
Tel: 071-240 0856

   This book incorporates an overview of the current status of full text databases with explanations of past research pertinent to full text and offers information regarding the future of full text. The major online systems that offer full text are described, with five systems highlighted - DIALOG, Mead Data Central's LEXIS and NEXIS, Westlaw, STN International, and BRS. The book features an extensive bibliography that includes articles specifically about full text databases, as well as citations to research studies that use methodology particularly appropriate to full text research.
   The first two chapters of the book describe in detail the major online systems that currently offer full text. Chapter three provides an overview of the search and display features on the major online systems that are particularly suited to full text searching. Chapters four, five, six and seven focus on full text searching. Chapter four introduces and provides an overview of the types of full text research that have been done. The next three chapters describe in detail the methodology and findings of some full text research projects undertaken by the authors. Chapters eight and nine bring together the practical aspects of the research described in the preceding chapters and offer advice for searchers, database producers and online developers. The information is of immediate use for searching today's full text database, but also offers ideas for improvement in the near future. The final chapter focuses on the future of full text research. The book can also be used as a supplemental text.

CONTENTS: Online systems and full text databases; system features for full text searching; research on full text database retrieval; retrieval performance in Harvard Business Review; applicability of ranking algorithms to full text retrieval; research on full text magazines; implications for research for searchers; implications of research for database producers and online vendors; future research needs and directions.

SUBJECT: C200: Specific computer hardware and operating systems

Readership: research, professional
New entry: R

BOOKBANK

```
        ISBN: 0 313 26303 5              Availability:  ip
       Class: General   New Class: Computers, General
    Author 1: Tenopir, Carol
    Author 2: Ro Jung Soon
       Title: Full Text Data Bases.
    Physical: 23cm.295. Cloth
   Publisher: Greenwood Press, London :  Aug 90
       Price: £35.95*
```

Fig. 3.43. Sample records from Bookfind and Bookbank.

Apart from the most common value-added information, such as subject descriptors, document type codes, and abstracts, there may be other, less obvious data elements. It may not be immediately apparent why the ticker symbol field is added to records in the Computer Library that cite articles discussing a company's marketing plan, finances, or new product line. This code is usual in corporate directories, but not in a technology-oriented abstracting/indexing and full-text database. Still, it is valuable when you want to search for company information in articles and the company name is used inconsistently by the sources or is not searchable without an excessive amount of false drops. This is the case with AT&T, which is an extremely difficult acronym to search in a full-text database. Of course, you first have to know or find the ticker symbol ("T" in the case of AT&T), usually from a record retrieved by some other means. Then, in the field-specific query you can use the following statement to get all citations of articles dealing with AT&T: "ticker ANDS T".

This database offers other uncommon value-added information. One common disadvantage of full-text databases is that they still cannot reproduce the original charts, tables, line drawings, and graphics. Reading a *PC Magazine* product comparison article as a full-text record in the Computer Library is a far cry from reading the original with its superb charts and tables, which convey extensive information in a succinct way. It is, however, a good sign that many of the articles from *PC Week* that contain much less graphically demanding tables are now available also in the CD-ROM database as special, so-called attachment records. These can be downloaded either as a spreadsheet or as a database file. A similar type of value-added information is the utility programs published in computer magazines, many of which are available in separate attachment records in source code and executable format for downloading.

More and more full-text databases go beyond the inclusion of plain text. The Facts on File database has maps along with some of the text. World Book includes tables that many consider difficult to handle on display, but its Infofinder software handles them flawlessly. The latest edition of Grolier Encyclopedia incorporates black-and-white and color images in varying quality. The Birds of America database includes not only the images of the birds but also their call sounds. Audio and video types of value-added information characterize Compton's Encyclopedia and the Mammals database of *National Geographic* magazine.

It is likely that with the increase of storage capacity and the progress in data compression and display techniques more and more full-text databases will offer the image equivalent of the text. Though the image of the text is not searchable, it may retain the layout and typography of the original publication. While the coded text in ASCII form will be searched, the facsimile image of the original will be displayed. In evaluating full-text databases this will be an increasingly important criterion.

Informativeness

Many of the database evaluation criteria are objective, using tangible, factual data. The informativeness of database records, however, is a very subjective criterion. It depends on many of the factors already discussed. Clear pagination style may convey useful information about the real length of the original document. Having a value-added field for this information makes it even more simple, as in the UMI databases. The listing of specific types of illustration (chart, graph, cartoon) in Resource One is much more informative than the generic (and coded) notation "il" in the Wilson databases.

Informativeness of the contents of records depends on the number and type of descriptors assigned to the record, on the availability of augmented titles, and on the abstract. Descriptors are essential for effective searching, but they are also useful to indicate the focal points of the article. The single descriptor assignment of Magazine Article Summaries cannot compare with the informativeness provided by the three to five subject headings in Reader's Guide Abstracts and

Resource One. On the other hand, the number and redundancy of subject headings in the LISA database may reduce the informativeness.

Title augmentation is a valuable asset both in MAS and in RGA. It adds explanation to an otherwise uninformative title and may even supply the bottom line of the article (as shown below in the RGA record about the Marfan syndrome). Any marked titles could come in handy for those who want to quickly scan the title lines first and then decide to read the abstract, if there is any. It is even more important in databases where abstracts are not available, as in the Reader's Guide to Periodical Literature. The quality of the abstract is probably the most important issue of informativeness. The abstract may help to decide whether it is worthwhile to read the original article; occasionally, it may even substitute for the original.

One of the classic works on abstracting defines the "ABC" of abstracts as accuracy, brevity, and clarity.[13] The type of the abstract, according to Tenopir and Lundeen, may be indicative, informative, critical, or special purpose: "Indicative, or descriptive, abstracts tell the reader what she or he will find in the original document. Informative abstracts are intended to substitute for the original document and often include a summary of findings and/or parts of tables. Critical, or review, abstracts provide evaluation of the contents of a document, including the abstractor's opinion on its quality and worth. Special purpose abstracts are geared to a specific group of users and relate information of interest to them."[14]

It is very difficult to define what makes an abstract a good, informative one; it is easier to demonstrate it. Figure 3.44 illustrates records from three databases for the same article.

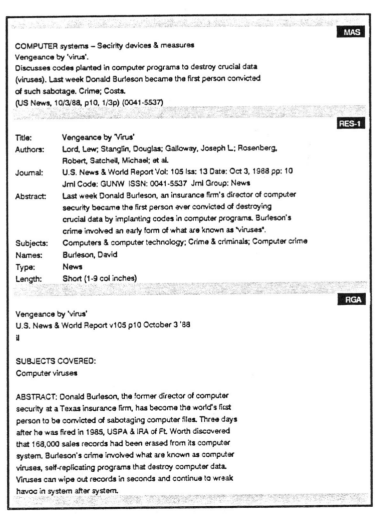

Fig. 3.44. "Virus" article from three databases.

The one from RGA is a perfect example of an informative abstract that answers the four W's: who, what, when, and why. The abstract of MAS does not provide many crucial details and there's a typo in the subject heading, and the one of RES-1 makes no mention of the fact that the culprit was fired a few days before this crime. Only this information makes the meaning of the title clear.

Another example illustrates other differences for an editorial (figure 3.45). The abstract of MAS focuses on one particular event and gives the most details, whereas that of RES-1 does not mention the actual case but summarizes the thoughts of the author well. RGA combines these two approaches and also illustrates that the length of the abstract does not necessarily have an impact on informativeness.

The third sample, shown in figure 3.46, illustrates some exceptionally valuable features of RGA.[15] It is the only abstract that reports the conclusion of the article, i.e., that there is no proof that Lincoln had Marfan syndrome. The other two abstracts leave out this key information. The same informativeness also applies to the explanation of the essence of Marfan syndrome. RGA succinctly explains it, RES-1 merely indicates that it is a genetic disorder, and MAS gives no hint about the implications of the disease. RGA even includes the punchline as title augmentation, so it cannot escape your attention.

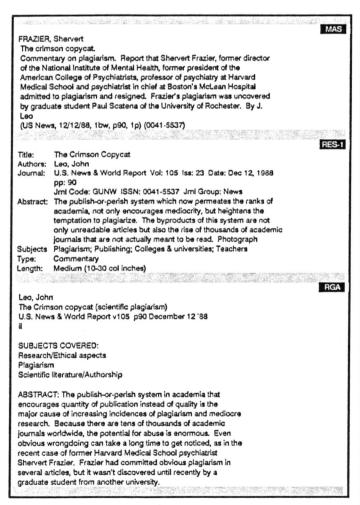

Fig. 3.45. "Copycat" article from three databases.

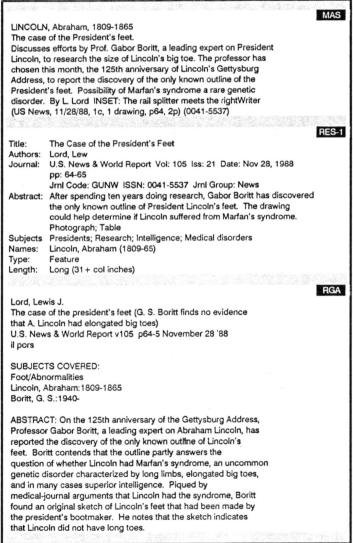

Fig. 3.46. "Marfan syndrome" records from three databases.

To evaluate the informativeness of the abstracts, look at a few dozen records citing articles you can read yourself for comparison. You may also find that in spite of its name, not all the records have abstracts in RGA. This would be acceptable for the year 1983 because the label on the compact disk clearly indicates that abstracting began in 1984, but there are almost 10,000 records from 1984 onward without abstracts. This figure excludes RGA's book review records that have no abstracts. This is understandable because RGA would then have to cannibalize Wilson's Book Review Digests database. It also happens in all three databases that the abstract adds absolutely nothing to the records, which is true, for example, of all book reviews in RES-1 and MAS, most of the poem citations and many recipe records in all three databases, as illustrated by figure 3.47.

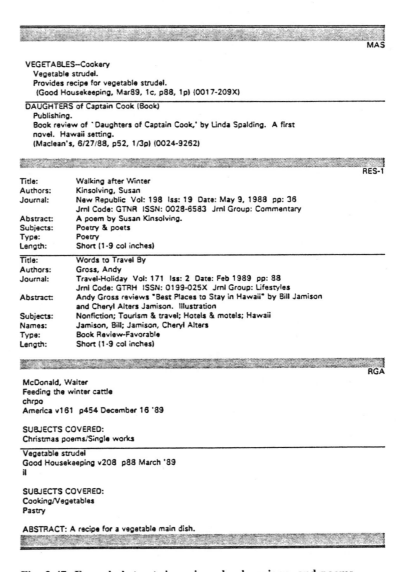

Fig. 3.47. Formal abstracts in recipes, book reviews, and poems.

Directory databases usually have no abstracts but there may be annotations, descriptions, or summaries that provide narrative information about the person, company, product, or whatever else is the subject of the directory.

Style and readability are important criteria in judging the quality of the abstracts. Evaluating these two criteria is very taxing to do manually using the classic methods and algorithms of

Kinkaid and Gunnings. Hardly anyone could afford to analyze more than a dozen records for this purpose. CD-ROM databases, together with word processing and style-analyzer programs, make it a snap. You can retrieve hundreds or thousands of records in a few minutes and pass them on to style checkers like Grammatik or Rightwriter for analysis. Both of these software programs provide the most important readability measures of the analyzed text and explain them in the software documentation. Figure 3.48 illustrates the analysis of the records indexing the items from the same issue of *U.S. News and World Reports* in three databases. The analysis was done by the Grammatik software.

Criteria	MAS	RES-1	RGA
Flesch-Kinkaid grade level	8	7	8
Gunnings' Fog Index equivalent high school reading level	12 senior	10 sophomore	11 junior
Flesch reading ease score description of style	48 Difficult	60 Fairly difficult	48 Difficult
Passive voice	0	9	1
Avg. sentence (# of words)	4.2	6.6	5.1
Avg. word length (# of syllables)	1.83	1.66	1.81
Avg. paragraph (# of sentences)	1.1	0.9	0.9
Number of abstracts analyzed	64	47	30

Fig. 3.48. Results of abstract analysis.

This process is particularly easy if the CD-ROM software allows the downloading of specific data elements from the records, such as the abstracts in our case. Wilsondisc, SPIRS, OnDisc, and Compact Cambridge all allow for this. In the other software where you also get those data elements that you do not need, you have to use a word processor to filter out the title, access number, journal citation, and similar data elements before passing the downloaded file to the style analyzers. Carol Tenopir and I are currently working on a paper that will report on the findings of the automatic analysis of readability of abstracts from various databases. Figure 3.49 shows the result of analyzing 1,000 abstracts of LISA comparing their readability indexes with three other documents as a yard stick.

Abstracts or summaries are also very important in full-text databases. Abstracts provide an efficient tool "to judge relevance quickly and efficiently," as "few searchers want to read ... every word of any document."[16] The summary portion of a full-text record of over ten screens is shown by figure 3.50.

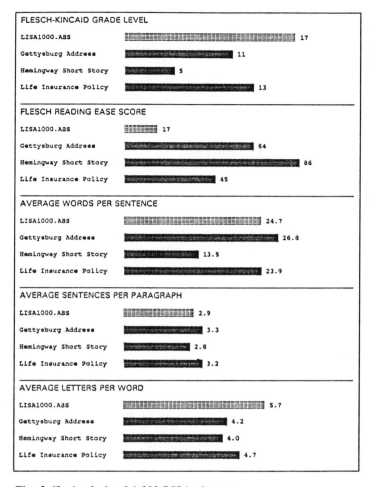

Fig. 3.49. Analysis of 1,000 LISA abstracts.

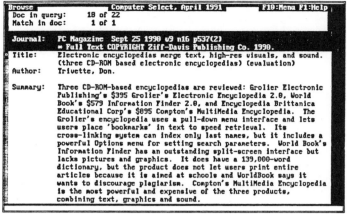

Fig. 3.50. The summary portion of a full-text record in Computer Select.

Record Structure

Record structuring has two facets of interest to users: external structuring and internal structuring. The former has an obvious impact on how fast the user can digest the information presented, in addition to aesthetics. The more information there is in a record, the more important it is to structure the records appropriately so the user can read them effectively. This is a very subjective criterion, but looking at the sample records displayed above, it is hardly arguable that the records of UMI databases are better structured than those of EBSCO or Wilson, due to the more appropriate indentation and clear labelling of data elements. The display format is also important from the viewpoint that only seldom may the user redefine the external structure. Limitations of user control over record layout are discussed in "Output Features" in chapter 2.

In the external structuring of records typography may play an important role. Capitalization of the first or only word in a descriptor as used by EBSCO may be preferred by some because it adds emphasis. The automatic boldfacing of the descriptor when printed also helps in finding an essential data element in the records. Those who are accustomed to seeing the descriptors at the end of the records may prefer the UMI solution in RES-1. Wilson's typography for descriptor strings is considered by many to be unsightly. The use of a slash to separate the descriptor from its subdivisions is unusual for those used to card catalogs and forces strange notation for slashed terms, e.g., OS\2 and PC\DOS instead of OS/2 or PC/DOS as used in the literature.

The same applies to the citation style. None of the abstracting/indexing databases offer one of the several traditional styles of citations (e.g., *Chicago Manual of Style*, American Psychological Association, or ANSI). It would seem obvious for the American Psychological Association to use their widely known citation format for PsycLIT on SilverPlatter. The only movement in this direction is seen in one of the Wilson databases, which otherwise are the most restrictive in display and print formatting. In the Index to Legal Periodicals database the citations conform to the Uniform System of Citation published by the Harvard Law Review Association.

Publishers of printed indexes and abstracts have devised their own bibliographic citation format. Many databases have printed counterparts, and users may be familiar with the citation style of the printed publication. No matter whether it is good or bad, what counts is that the style is known by the user community. While the printed indexes and abstracts cannot allow the subscriber to choose from several formats, the CD-ROM versions should do so. This choice should mean not only shorter or longer records, but also different layout and arrangement of elements.

Regretfully, many database producers have not put any effort into devising different options for output formats, even if the software is capable of handling different formats. Printed indexes typically are very terse in bibliographic citations for space reasons. But what may have been justified with thousands of items per volume should not apply for item lists or short bibliographies, which should spell out cryptic codes. You appreciate this when patrons do not keep coming back to ask you what is the meaning of "por" and "il" at the end of the citations in the Wilson databases. These should be resolved into easily understandable terms during printing and displaying of records, such as *portrait* and *illustration*.

Directory databases and cataloging support databases are much more flexible in external record structuring. Bowker and the Library Corporation are to be commended for offering functionally different record layouts such as printed directory, catalog card, order form, cataloging worksheet, or spine label formats. Standard & Poor's records can be formatted flexibly into tabular format by the user, who may also define the sequence and length of each data element in this format.

The best way to judge the adequacy of the record structure and the citation style is to print out two or three records from each database and show them to potential users for comments. Studying some samples also helps to spot the differences in other conventions, such as the exclusion of all authors from the record if there are more than three authors (Wilson databases) versus the UMI convention to list five authors and use "et al." to indicate contributions by further authors.

As mentioned at the beginning of this section, another aspect of record structuring has significant impact on indexing, and thus on searching and also on record display and printout. This aspect is the internal structuring of the records, which usually is not visible to end users. Deep structuring and tagging of records is the key to efficient searching and output capabilities. Deep structuring means records with granular structure, i.e., records are divided into distinct data elements and these are further subdivided into their component elements. Tagging means the identification of these elements within the records and within the fields.

If the component elements of the bibliographic source, for example, can be clearly identified by the software, then the required components may be selected for indexing (searching) and for displaying. This internal structuring is not identical to the external one. The human eye can easily distinguish between the elements of chronological and numerical designation of a journal issue and the page numbering, but computer programs cannot necessarily make such distinctions.

The coarse internal structuring of records makes it impossible in SPIRS to display only the journal name (without the volume number, issue index, or pagination information) along with the title of the article. Good compartmentalization of records in the databases of UMI makes it simple to search not only by the year but even by the month or day of publication in RES-1, Periodicals Abstracts, or Newspaper Abstracts. Similarly, there is no ambiguity in searching by the name of a person as author versus subject in the UMI databases.

Lack of granular record structure and (sub)field-specific indexing make it difficult to conduct an unambiguous search by such an often needed criterion as publication year in MAS or to distinguish between, for example, Bernstein as author versus Bernstein as subject. The same may make confusing the browsing of the journal name index in RGA, LIBLIT, and in all the Wilson databases. There are entries for each issue of each journal, but they are not in apparent order, as illustrated by figure 3.51. For example, the index gives the false impression that *Discover* magazine has not been indexed between 1985 and 1989. The journal names and the chronological designation of the issues are like Siamese twins, and the sort program apparently handles them as a simple character string. The odd date designation backfires here. Using the number of months and leading zeros for both the volume numbers and months could make the index easier to understand. Seasonal issues, however, would still present some problems.

```
Readers' Guide Abstracts                      Data Coverage: 1/83 thru 12/31/90
                     COPYRIGHT the H.W. WILSON Company                  READY

WILSONLINE NEIGHBOR MODE


    NUMBER   RECORDS        TERM
      1.       26      (JN) DISCOVER/11/JL '90
      2.       18      (JN) DISCOVER/11/MR '90
      3.       25      (JN) DISCOVER/11/MY '90
      4.       29      (JN) DISCOVER/11/N '90
      5.       23      (JN) DISCOVER/11/O '90
      6.       29      (JN) DISCOVER/11/S '90
      7.       18      (JN) DISCOVER/5/AG '84
      8.       18      (JN) DISCOVER/5/AP '84
      9.       16      (JN) DISCOVER/5/D '84
     10.       16      (JN) DISCOVER/5/F '84
     11.       13      (JN) DISCOVER/5/JA '84
     12.       21      (JN) DISCOVER/5/JE '84
     13.       14      (JN) DISCOVER/5/JL '84

UP, DOWN OR GET N OR EXPAND a 'DS'
                                                   Mon Jun 10 12:49:56 1991
USER:
   F1:HELP  F2:END  F3:Change DATABASE\DISC              F10:Reshow last FIND/NBR
```

Fig. 3.51. Haywire index entries in LIBLIT.

Coded data storage may be a blessing if it is transparent to the user and if the software can manage it appropriately. Much information may be stored in a coded form, invisible to the user, that is uncoded during displaying and printing of records automatically or by user solicitation. For example, it is enough to store in the records the ISSN of the journal from which an item is abstracted and to create one single record for the journal. Establishing the link between these records via an element common in both records makes is possible to display and print the full title of the serial when a citation is displayed.

This is not only an efficient method of storing repetitive data only once in full, but it also helps to create a consistent database. It is likely that this coding (shown in figure 3.52, page 130) is what makes the document type, language, journal name, and publisher index so clean in the PAIS database. (It is also very convenient to the user, who can display the record in steps as illustrated earlier by the kangaroo record display in figure 2.58.)

Notice that in the SPIRS version of PAIS the solution is not so convenient. The user has to remember the code exactly, exit the bibliographic database, log into the directory database, and then enter the code to retrieve the publisher record. By this time the user may have forgotten the code.

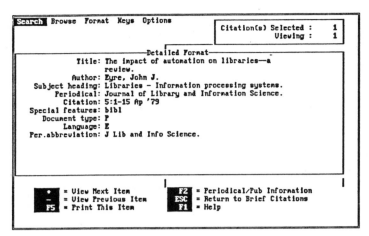

Fig. 3.52. Record linking through coded data in OCSI-PAIS.

Good external structuring and grouping of information are essential when extremely long directory records are to be displayed. The records in Standard & Poor's and Disclosure provide extensive amounts of information that would be overwhelming without the good grouping and structuring.

For internal structuring the same applies as to abstracting/indexing databases, but to an even larger extent. A directory is very likely to be searched by area codes, state codes, zip codes, product category codes, and so on. For the database creation software to make unambiguous entries in the index (inverted) file, the record must be as much granular as possible. Even granular record structure may not help if the index is a single lump-all-field type, i.e., if it includes terms from all or most of the fields.

Full-text databases need clear paragraph numbering not only in the internal record structure but also externally. This allows the user to jump back and forth several paragraphs at once, not only a screen at a time. The outline format in the Grolier Encyclopedia and the World Book is an ideal navigation tool. This is feasible with full-text databases where records are created by strict editorial rules as for the structuring of articles, but would require significant intellectual investment in full-text databases of multiple sources.

DATAWARE QUALITY

Quality of the data has been an important issue since the early days of the online era. Unfortunately, not much has been done by the dataware producers to improve it. Repeated pleas and criticism by industry pundits for increased quality control seem to go unheeded.[17,18,19] The CD-ROM era has not yet changed this situation. It is very likely, however, that concerns of database quality will surface more and more, because with the CD-ROM medium it is easier and cheaper than ever to systematically explore the inconsistencies, incompleteness, and poor quality control in general.

Users are able to do quality checking and comparisons during a test period, i.e., prior to committing themselves to a product. They may decide not to license a CD-ROM database because of quality problems specified in a tangible manner. With the lack of connect time pressure, many may feel able to do some detective work on seeing suspicious results and may find skeletons in the closet. It is hoped that database publishers will improve the quality of their products or put pressure on dataware producers if the related problems are reported to them regularly. As databases are usually licensed for a year, no publisher may take a user base granted for the next year.

Users have to realize that quality control requires time and extra effort, and quality improvements often may be achieved only at the expense of quantity and currency. This may be the reason that one database has less current items than another or costs two times as much even though the size and scope of the databases are very similar.

Erroneous records are easy to find even through casual use. However, to verify the claims in product brochures and other promotional materials and systematically review the quality of a database, the best method is to do "test searches" specifically meant to explore glitches, inconsistencies, and incompleteness, all of which may significantly influence search results. Such test searches can also sharpen your search ability and make you aware of the limitations of the database.

Many of the quality criteria discussed below also apply to the online or printed counterparts of the CD-ROM database. You may wish to consult reviews of the other versions. The accuracy of data or the informativeness of the abstracts requires the same analysis irrespective of the medium. However, certain criteria (such as completeness and consistency) are much easier to evaluate in the CD-ROM medium; therefore, these are discussed and illustrated in much more detail.

Quite often, you may anticipate quality by knowing who the datafile producer is. Cleveland and Cleveland note in writing about the quality of abstracts that "Authoritativeness is closely related to the prestige of abstracting services, and this prestige comes by performance over a period of time."[20] The same applies on a larger scale to the quality of the whole dataware. Nevertheless, even companies with a high reputation may produce less than perfect files, and the CD-ROM medium is the ideal tool to check them out.

Authenticity

Many CD-ROM producers have established their authenticity long before the CD-ROM era, when their printed or microfiche versions were introduced to the market. H. W. Wilson has unparalleled name recognition in the library world due to its printed publications and online services. UMI established itself with its microfiche services before launching Periodical Abstracts, Dissertation Abstracts, and Newspaper Abstracts on CD-ROM. The Library Corporation (Bibliofile) and General Research Corporation (Laserquest) served libraries with microfiche catalogs for a long time before offering CD-ROM products. Gaylord (Supercat) and Follett (Alliance Plus) had recognized names in the library world not only for library accessories but also for cataloging and circulation software. WLN (Lasercat) may have been less well known than OCLC (the CDCAT 450 and CD450 database family); still, it has garnered a superb reputation for the high quality of its database.

Users may feel more comfortable with producers that have a track record in the field, like H. W. Wilson, Bowker, or OCLC. Still, a newcomer on the CD-ROM market may start with the aura of authenticity without any significant historical print, microfiche, or online publications. EBSCO published at almost the same time the printed and CD-ROM versions of the Serials Directory a few years ago, but had immediate authority because of their extensive background in serials jobbing. It can be assumed that some of their data is more accurate than that in a competitive database, which has to rely on the publishers' replies to questionnaires for such data as publisher address, subscription price, or current title. EBSCO, on the other hand, is in daily working contact with thousands of serials publishers and must verify the data constantly. (It is another question that an ill-designed indexing strategy, discussed later, cripples access to the otherwise impressively information-rich, current, and accurate dataware in the Serials Directory.)

Accuracy

Accuracy is difficult to analyze on a systematic basis, particularly in text-oriented databases. Still, the CD-ROM medium offers a good opportunity to learn about certain types of inaccuracies. These are, of course, also present in the printed and online versions. However, the printed versions usually do not offer as access points the most error-prone fields, such as words in the abstract or the full-text portion of the records, or the numeric data elements, such as the price field in a product directory. Online databases can help you learn about inaccuracies, but the connect time fee is a deterrent.

Typographic inaccuracies (typos) are easy to spot if the software offers field-specific index browsing. It is important to make a distinction between the accuracy of fields with controlled vocabularies (descriptors, coded data) and fields with free text (title, abstract, full text). Misspellings in the free-text fields are less critical than typos in fields with controlled vocabulary. A term that is misspelled or spelled inconsistently in the title or abstract is less of a problem if it is correctly available as a descriptor, as illustrated by the excerpt from RGA in figure 3.53. As the term *toxoplasmosis* is correctly spelled as a subject heading, it is not critical (though it is unsightly) that in the abstract the name of the parasite spelled twice as *taxoplasma*.

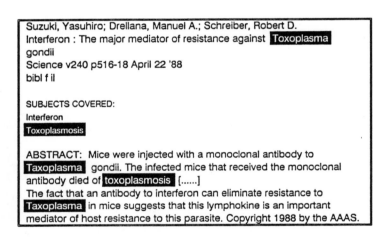

Fig. 3.53. RGA abstract with typo.

Inaccuracies in fields using controlled vocabularies are the most critical, particularly when an alternate field is unlikely to store the same information. Language codes, document type codes, classification codes, and publication years are such fields. Subject headings have a somewhat different status as the descriptor may occur correctly in the title or the abstract. On the other hand, users tend to take for granted the formal accuracy of subject headings. It is shown below that this is not always the case. When value-added information is minimal, the accuracy of the essential fields becomes much more important. A review of Bertolucci's film will not be retrieved in the Canadian Business and Current Affairs (CBCA) database because of the typo "Last Emporer" in the title field, which is the only source for the film's title (figure 3.54).

```
1807806

The Last Emporer // Review

Author: O'Toole, Lawrence, REV
Macleans v.100(50) Dec 14, 1987 pg 66
Special Features: Photograph
Descriptors: Movie reviews
```

Fig. 3.54. Misspelling of a title in CBCA.

Field-specific index browsing clearly shows how polluted the contents type field is in EDLIB versus the impeccable publication type field in ERIC (figures 3.55 and 3.56).

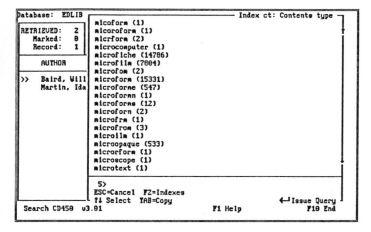

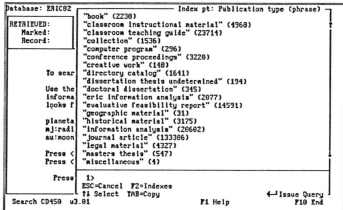

Fig. 3.55. Misspelling of content-type index in EDLIB.

Fig. 3.56. Clean publication-type index in ERIC.

If the software does not allow field-specific index browsing (as in the SilverPlatter databases), you may not be able to decide whether the misspelling is important or not. It is not clear, for example, in figure 3.57 where the term "Goverment" comes from as the index lumps together terms from many fields.

	SilverPlatter 1.6	ERIC (1/83 - 12/89)	Esc=Commands F1=Help	
			Occurences	
			Word	Record
	GOVERMENT		7	7
	GOVERMENT-UNIVERSITY-INDUSTRY-ROUNDTABLE		1	1
	GOVERMENTAL		1	1
	GOVERN		159	155
	GOVERNALI		1	1
	GOVERNALI-JOSEPH-F		1	1
	GOVERNANCE		2578	1634
	GOVERNANCE-		899	899
	GOVERNANTI		1	1
	GOVERNANTI-MICHAEL-P		1	1
	GOVERNED		186	172
	GOVERNEMENT		1	1
	GOVERNEMENTS		1	1
	GOVERNEMNT		3	3
	GOVERNER		1	1

FIND:
Type a search then press Enter (<—).   Use the INDEX (F5) to pick terms.

Fig. 3.57. Typos in SPIRS-ERIC.

In some databases, such as those from UMI, you may check field-specific inaccuracies even if the software does not offer the facility to browse the index terms generated from one or more specific fields. Instead, you can browse the single-word index and see that it includes a lot of typos and inconsistent spellings, though you do not know which fields contain these words (figure 3.58, page 134).

A good tool is to search for a truncated term defining the field tag. ProQuest, for example, lists the various terms retrieved and you may see if there are inconsistencies in the critical fields (such as the descriptor field in figure 3.59). The result shows that the descriptor is always correct and that the different spellings come from the other fields.

ProQuest	Resource/One	Jan 1986 – Feb 1991

Word Index	Count
GOVERMEMT	1
GOVERMENT	20
GOVERMENTAL	1
GOVERNEMNT	6
GOVERNING	171
GOVERNMANT	2
GOVERNMEMT	1
GOVERNMENT	15000
GOVERNMENTAL	3057
GOVERNMET	1
GOVERNMMENT	1
GOVERNMNET	1
GOVERNOR	772
GOVERNORSHIP	24
GOVERRNMENT	1
GOVFATHER	1

Type letters, use arrow keys. Press ENTER
F1 = HELP

To Search: Enter key word or phrases, press ENTER.   F1 = Help F2 = Command

Fig. 3.58. Polluted word index in RES-1.

Search terms	Item Count

(01)   gover? ->   GOVERNING   2
                    GOVERNMENT   9200
                    GOVERNMENTAL   2909
                    GOVERNOR   332
        gover? ->   (5 matches)   12220

Search results in 12220 item(s)

To Display Title List: Press ENTER.   ESC = Go Back   F1 = Help F2 = Commands

Fig. 3.59. Truncated search in the descriptor field of RES-1.

Many times the file producer may not be blamed for inaccuracies. It may receive the data erroneously or the source that is abstracted/indexed may be inaccurate. In figure 3.60 the misspelling of the name is the result of sloppiness in the source document, whereas in figure 3.61 the abstractor or the data entry operator made a typo.

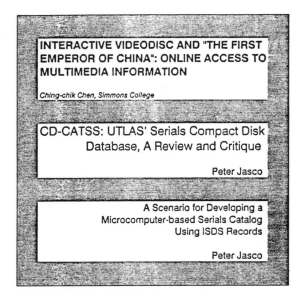

Fig. 3.60. Name misspellings in the source document.

TI: Micro-based optical videodisc applications
AU: Ching-*chi*-Chen; Chen-Ching-*chi*
SO: Microcomputers-for Information-Management; 2 (4) Dec 85, 217-240. illus

TI: MICRO-CDS/ISIS: a bibliographic information management software from Unesco
AU: Ja*csco*, Peter; Szuecs, Andras; Varga, Sandor
SO: Microcomputers for Information Management, 3(3) Sept 86, 173-198. illus

Fig. 3.61. Name misspellings by the A/I service.

There is a dilemma often faced by file producers. If the source is obviously erroneous (e.g., an obvious misspelling of a name or a million figure quoted instead of a billion), should it be corrected and should the correction be indicated? The answer varies from one datafile producer to another. In the example in figure 3.60 LISA spotted the misspelling of this author's name in the source once; Wilson both caught it and corrected it as shown in figure 3.62.

```
TI:   CD-CATSS: UTLAS' Serials  compact disk database; a review and critique.
AU:   Jacso, Peter
SO:   Serials Review, 15 (4) Winter 89, 7-18. illus
```

```
Jacso,  Peter
CD-CATSS: UTLAS' serials compact disk database, a review and critique
Serials Review v15 no4 p7-18 +  '89
charts il

Jacso,  Peter
A scenario for developing a microcomputer-based serials catalog using ISDS
records
Serials Review v13 p25-34 Winter '87
```

Fig. 3.62. Spelling correction by the A/I service.

The source document may publish a correction in the next issue, but if the file producer abstracts and indexes only feature articles and major communications, the user of the database may never be aware of important corrections. A very rare exception is the RES-1 database, which includes letters and notes to and from the editor if these concern an error.

Inaccuracies in directory databases that include a lot of numeric data may have more negative effects and they are more difficult to explore systematically. Unless you know the mandatory structure, or the plausible range of values in a field, it is not much help to browse a field-specific numeric index. However, if you do have this knowledge, then displaying part of an ISSN index in an abstracting/indexing database or the sales figure field in a company directory may provide some feeling about the accuracy of the data. Obvious inaccuracies from the numeric indexes of EDLIB are illustrated in figure 3.63.

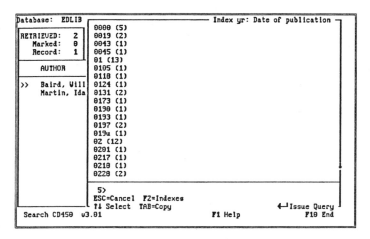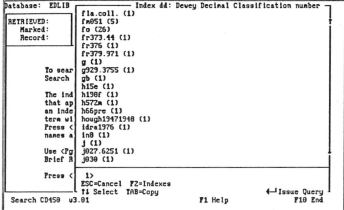

Fig. 3.63. Excerpts from numeric indexes of EDLIB.

Even if you cannot expand all the field-specific numeric indexes (as in the databases using the OCSI software), you may do some plausibility searches and then look at the records to verify the data. In a plausibility search you look for values in a field that are outside the likely valid (plausible) range. In a who's-who database of living personalities you may search for records where the year of birth field is less than 1900 or greater than 1970 since not too many people that old or young may be included in such a database. In those databases using numeric classification codes (PscLIT, Sociofile, Disclosure, etc.) a search for values in the classification field is below or above the valid classification numbers. (All of the above databases fared extremely well with this test.) In a serial, book directory, or catalog look for the Library of Congress classification codes starting with the letters "O" or "X" or "Y" that are not valid in the LC classification system. In a directory with U.S. geographic coverage search for state codes starting with "B," "E," "J," "X," "Y," or "Z." Figure 3.64 illustrates a plausibility search in the OCSI-PAIS database.

Note that there are no records with a publication year larger than 1991, but there are ten records which have a publication year less than 1970, the year this database started. Even if all these years were wrong, this is a negligable amount of incorrect data. The short-entry display records indicate *immediately* the obvious typos (figure 3.65).

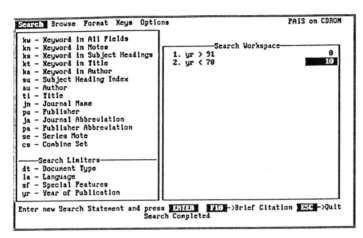

Fig. 3.64. Plausibility search in OCSI-PAIS.

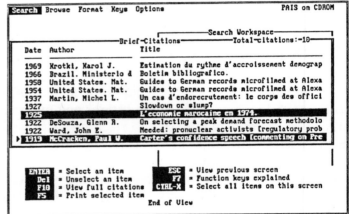

Fig. 3.65. Obvious typos in the publication year fields.

Other times, you may accidentally bump into obviously erroneous data, such as the subscription price of *Biological Abstracts* being stated as $4. A look at the detailed record reveals that a decimal point is misplaced. (See figure 3.66.) This type of error may prompt you to search for a couple of titles whose subscription price you may then compare with your actual subscription figure or with those of the competitor.

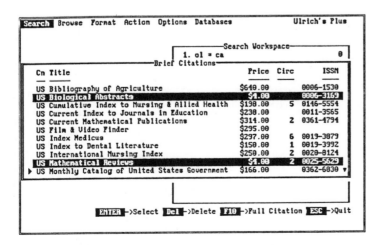

Fig. 3.66. Inaccurate price information in Ulrich's Plus.

The same applies to the field that includes the number of copies distributed of a serial. Searching for the most highly circulated serials can produce some unexpected results, as discussed in a recent article.[21] Many journals now regularly publish their circulation data in the issues themselves. Comparing a few of these with circulation figures in the record may help to get a feeling about the accuracy of this data. If you want to use this database for reference only, it may not be relevant to know how accurate these figures are, but if you want to use it as a collection development tool, then you must know both the accuracy of this data and whether it is available in all the records or only occasionally. The latter aspect relates to the completeness of records, which is discussed later. Though the same types of inaccuracies show up also in the printed directories, numeric data is not an access point in the print versions. Also, only a few minor differences do not necessarily indicate a problem.

Inaccuracy of numeric data can have much more serious implications. Dosage data of medications in a pharmaceutical directory comes to mind immediately. Ruth Pagell and Ann Mintz cite some disheartening examples of inaccuracies in numeric data when they really count and may hurt business.[22,23] The use of wrong exchange rates resulted in nonsense results. A search in the Dun & Bradstreet European Market Identifiers database ranked three Greek companies one, two, three of top food companies. The number one company featured a sales figure four to five times greater than the giants Unilever and Nestle. This was due to an exchange conversion error. The same kind of error occurred a few months earlier, naming three Yugoslavian companies to the first three positions. The error was reported to the file producer, and all that changed after the reload of the database was that the Yugoslavian companies dropped to positions four through six as the top spots were taken over again by the three Greek firms. When results are so obviously wrong the searcher may have a clue, but in many other cases there is no way to learn about the inaccuracies of numeric data.

Directory databases also include the same type of textual inaccuracies as were discussed with abstracting/indexing databases. A good way to get some information about inaccuracies is to look up records about something or someone with which you are very familiar and see how accurate the records are. If the data element by which you want to search the database is itself inaccurate then you need an alternative method.

In DLIP one of the most important data elements (and the only one that is always present) is the name of the person. But if the name is misspelled, you may not know whether it was not retrieved because of the inaccurate name form or because there is no record about the person in the database. In checking the database for the names of professors at the School of Library Service of Columbia University, it was suspicious that two names were missing out of ten.[24] When searching by affiliation, it turned out that these persons are included, but their names are misspelled. Further searches for names of acquaintances revealed similar inaccuracies, as illustrated by figure 3.67. These should have been spelled correctly as Eres, Romanansky, Rorvig, and Petherbridge. This is rather discouraging in a who's-who type of database where the personal name is a very common (and, in this database, often the exclusive) access point.

In the above situation the responsibility for the inaccuracy lies with the file producer because the names were supplied on questionnaires or cards completed by biographees, the most accurate sources. On the other hand, the file producer may not have been in an enviable position in deciphering many handwritten questionnaires.

Full-text databases present the same types of inaccuracies described above, but on a larger scale. If you look at a few records of the Computer Library you find that the number of typos is much higher in the full-text part of the records than in

```
DIRECTORY OF LIBRARY & INFORMATION PROFESSIONALS

Data Copyright (c) 1988  Research Publications

• • • • • • • • • • • • • • • • • • • • • • • • • • • • • • • • • • • •
RECORD #1 OF 4
NAME:             Fres, Beth Krevitt
• • • • • • • • • • • • • • • • • • • • • • • • • • • • • • • • • • • •
RECORD #2 OF 4
NAME:             Romanasky, Marcia Canzoneri
• • • • • • • • • • • • • • • • • • • • • • • • • • • • • • • • • • • •
RECORD #3 OF 4
NAME:             Rorveg, Mark E.
• • • • • • • • • • • • • • • • • • • • • • • • • • • • • • • • • • • •
RECORD #4 OF 4
NAME:             Tetherbridge, Guy
```

Fig. 3.67. Inaccurate names in DLIP.

the summaries or in the titles. Though no index browsing feature is available with this database, you may peep into the index by using a truncated term. It is even better if you use character masking, as illustrated by figure 3.68.

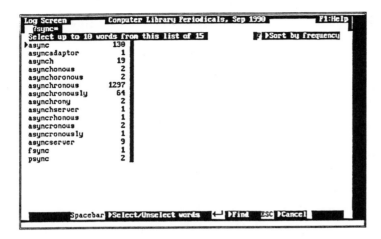

Fig. 3.68. Excerpts from the index of Computer Library.

This is not a specialty of the Computer Library, but it is very characteristic of most full-text databases. Typos, though unsightly, do not hamper the reading of the text. It is the retrieval of records that may be hampered by typos. Blair and Maron found that pertinent records were not retrieved from full-text databases due to typographical errors.[25]

Time-honored methods and tools are available in or with the database to improve consistency in indexing and recall in searching. Publishers of directory databases and encyclopedias do extensive record editing to consolidate spelling variations, among other inconsistencies. Publishers of abstracting/indexing and full-text databases (except encyclopedias) cannot be expected to do this. As these databases process hundreds of thousands of documents from thousands of different sources, it would be a herculean task. The best that may be expected is that the datafile producers apply standards and use a controlled vocabulary, a thesaurus, or an authority file of some format for as many data elements as possible. This is the key for database consistency.

Consistency

Ideally, every element in a database should be entered by applying some standards. This would apply to names of persons, corporate bodies, geographic entities, subject descriptors, journal titles, chronological and numerical designations, and so on. Some of the standardization, such as that for pagination, helps only in reading a record with ease and improves the look and feel of a database. Others can have serious impact on retrieval efficiency.

While you certainly would not search a database by page number range, it is important that the pagination information be consistently presented, including punctuation, indication of non-continuous pages, and so on. Most data elements, however, require more than that level of standardization. Databases that apply some controlled vocabulary or authority file offer the best chances for consistency. These include the unified forms of names, codes, words, and phrases that are used to describe and index a document or whatever the subject of the database is.

Authority files are meant to standardize various name formats, spelling, and terminology and thereby simplify the search process tremendously. Users do not have to be concerned about possible synonyms, acronyms, or spelling variations of terms describing their subject if they can choose the most appropriate terms for their information needs. This is based on the assumptions that the authority file is readily available for the searchers and that the indexers used the same terms consistently. Only indexing consistency is dealt with here; access to the authority file is discussed in "Accessibility" in chapter 4. Indexing consistency itself has two aspects: format and content consistency.

Authority files may range from a simple list of terms to a sophisticated hierarchical thesaurus that includes broader and narrower terms, synonyms, codes, and scope notes that explain the use of the terms. In between the two are the authority files, which provide "see" and "see also" references but are not organized in a hierarchical way. Most databases feature this kind of authority file, though quite a number have a full-blown thesaurus, such as the various Wilson databases, ERIC, or PsycLIT.

The problem is that these authority files too often are limited to subjects and do not always include personal, corporate, or geographic names. Another problem is that the authority file is not accessible readily from within the application or may not be available at all for the users.

The format consistency can be checked easily if you browse field-specific indexes. Browsing the publisher-name index field where possible in any database is revealing. Search for such publishers where inconsistencies may occur, such as "John Wiley and Sons." The sample searches in Book Review Digest, RGA, and PAIS yield impressively good results. In Books in Print Plus and Ulrich's Plus there is definitely room for improvement. Excerpts from some of the publisher indexes are shown in figure 3.69.

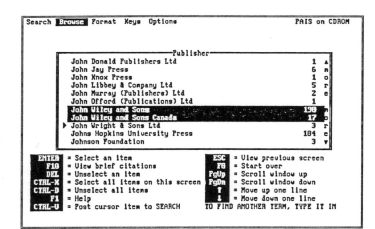

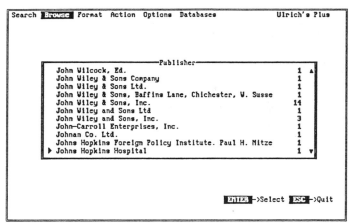

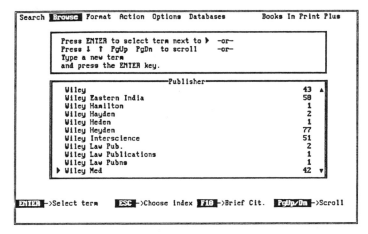

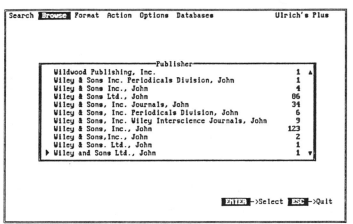

Fig. 3.69. Excerpts from publisher indexes in PAIS, BIP, Ulrich's.

Such a check is more difficult if there is no possibility for field-specific index browsing since variant name formats may be interspersed with terms from other fields. This is the case with the SilverPlatter databases. Still, browsing some of the authors' names in LISA quickly reveals inconsistencies (figure 3.70). It is true that these inconsistencies may also come from the various source documents, but the file producer could use a name-authority file to eliminate such discrepancies as done by LIBLIT (see figure 4.2 for the same author's names).

SilverPlatter 1.6	LISA (1/69 - 3/90)	Esc=Commands F1 =Help
Word	Occurence	Records
KOENIG	45	40
KOENIG-L-MARULLI	2	2
KOENIG-M	1	1
KOENIG-M-E-D	3	3
KOENIG-MICHAEL	4	4
KOENIG-MICHAEL-E-D	26	26
KOENIG-W	1	1
KOENIGSBERG	2	1
KOENING	1	1
KOENING-MICHAEL-E-D	1	1
RAITT	33	30
RAITT-D	4	4
RAITT-D-I	7	7
RAITT-DAVID	7	7
RAITT-DAVID-I	9	9
RAITT-DAVID-IAIN	1	1
RAITT-MILDRED-O	1	1

Fig. 3.70. Excerpts from the author-name index in LISA.

The content aspect of indexing consistency applies to subject terms and codes. The quality of indexing depends on how consistently the terms are used and how appropriately the index terms describe the subject of the documents or the business line of a company or indicate the category or functional characteristics of a product. Content consistency of indexing is a particularly difficult issue with databases covering either a very broad subject area — like general periodical indexes, book and serials directories, and catalogs — or a long period during which the index terms significantly changed.

To test the consistency of usage of index terms, make some sample searches such as a subject search, a search for a person or a company, or a search for a geographic location. Make sure that the term is not a homonym or a name that may be part of some other term. Look at the records to find out some pattern of indexing in relation to terms in the title and in the descriptor field. The easiest way is to select a term that has an exact equivalent in the authority file. Then make another search in which you specify the term to occur in the title but not in the descriptor field.

Look at the records retrieved to see if, in your judgment, the term should have been assigned. A few such searches should give a rather reliable picture of indexing consistency, though it is to be understood that this is only the tip of the iceberg. Results are illustrated by a few examples in figure 3.71. Records searched in LIBLIT and LISA included the terms *CD-ROM*, *CDROM* or *CD ROM* in the title but not in the descriptor field.

LIBLIT

CD-ROM: an overview of US developments
Automation of library processes
Information brokers

CD-ROM usage and prospects: an overview
no descriptor at all

The media and the message (moving from microfiche to CD-ROM)
Information retrieval

A CD-ROM database product for oncology
Information systems/Special subjects/Cancer

Design considerations for CD-ROM retrieval software
Information systems/Design
Microcomputer programs

The CD-ROM medium
no descriptor at all

CDROM--dej`a vu . . . or voil`a
no descriptor at all

CD-ROM: how the users react
Information systems/Special subjects/Audiovisual materials
National Information Center for Educational Media

Strategies for libraries (when using CD-ROM)
Reference services/Automation

An online searcher's perspective
no descriptor at all

CD-ROM: is the future now?
no descriptor at all

CD-ROM in a sci-tech library?
Reference services/Automation
Scientific and technical libraries/Reference services

Oh, say can you CD-ROM?
no desriptor at all

Pertinent comparisons between CD-ROM and online
no descriptor at all

CDROM activities at Microsoft: an interview with Thomas N. Lopez, vice president, CDROM Division
Lopez, Thomas N.
Microsoft Corporation

Fig. 3.71. Lack of obvious descriptors in LIBLIT and LISA.

LISA

TI: Evaluation of CD-ROM teleconference: over 6,000 returns.
DE: Services; Reader-services; Information-work; Information-communication; Teleconferencing; Telecommunications; Data-transmission; Conferences; Computers; On-line-computers; Computer-conferencing; Satellites

TI: Information retrieval on a microcomputer: the evaluation of software for personal information systems and for CD-ROM products.
DE: Data-processing; Computers; Evaluation; Programs-(Computers); Microcomputers

TI: From microfiche to CD-ROM: converting the Human Relations Area Files full-text database.
DE: Technical-processes-and-services; Information-storage-and-retrieval; Information-retrieval; Subject-indexing; On-line-information-retrieval; Computerised-information-retrieval; Searching; Searching; Computerised-information-storage-and-retrieval; Microfiches; Information-services; Data-bases; Conversion; Ethnography; Social-anthropology; On-line-information-retrieval

TI: AMIGOS and CD-ROM technology: how a multi-state network integrates CD-ROM technology into its services.
DE: Technical-processes-and-services; Information-storage-and-retrieval; Information-retrieval; Subject-indexing; On-line-information-retrieval; Computerised-information-retrieval; Searching; Searching; Computerised-information-storage-and-retrieval; Telecommunications; Data-transmission; Cooperation

TI: PAIS International: print, online, CD-ROM.
DE: Technical-processes-and-services; Information-storage-and-retrieval; Information-retrieval; Subject-indexing; On-line-information-retrieval; Computerised-information-retrieval; Searching; Searching; Computerised-information-storage-and-retrieval; Data-bases; Information-services; Computerised-information-services; Magnetic-tape; Social-sciences

TI: The electronic branch library: using CD-ROM and online services to support off-campus instructional programs
DE: Branch-libraries; University-libraries; Technical-processes-and-services; Information-storage-and-retrieval; Information-retrieval; Subject-indexing; On-line-information-retrieval; Computerised-information-retrieval; Searching-; Searching-; Computerised-information-storage-and-retrieval; Telecommunications-; Data-transmission

TI: Information retrieval-databases online or on CD-ROM-a question of today and tomorrow
DE: Future-developments; Technical-processes-and-services; Information-storage-and-retrieval; Information-retrieval; Subject-indexing; On-line-information-retrieval; Computerised-information-retrieval; Searching-; Searching-; Computerised-information-storage-and-retrieval; Data-bases; Information-services; Computerised-information-services; Magnetic-tape

The printout is slightly edited for legibility, but the content of both the title and the descriptor fields are kept as they are in the original records. There are negative symptoms in both databases. It is surprising that many records in LIBLIT have no descriptor assigned at all let alone the most appropriate one. In LISA the omission of the appropriate descriptor is perplexing in light of the large number of inappropriately broad and repeatedly-used descriptor terms. Usually such omissions occur when the subject term was not introduced at the time the records were created. This, however, does not apply to these records which date from the period when the descriptor "CD-ROM" was already an accepted term in both databases.

A similar test was made in the PAIS database looking for items with "Hawaii" or "Hawaiian" in the title but not in the descriptor either as a term in itself or a geographic qualifier for another term. Figure 3.72 shows a surprisingly high ratio (one-third of the records retrieved by the first query). The listing of the titles clearly show that the descriptor "Hawaii" should have been assigned to most of these records.

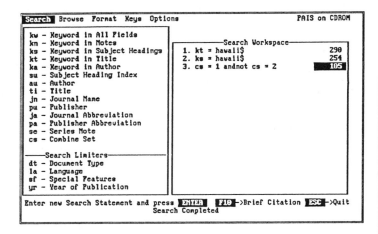

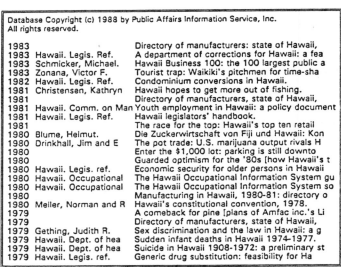

Fig. 3.72. Lack of obvious descriptors in PAIS.

To the credit of PAIS, the short-entry list also shows that all these records originate from the period before 1984 when a different descriptor list and assignment policy were used. These discrepancies are unavoidable in an older database.

The consistency of index assignment can also be done by searching for some items about a clearly defined event and then looking at the descriptors. Such a sample search was made in the demonstration subset of the CBCA database about the tragic fire in the London Underground. All the records retrieved are news items and are dated from the same two-week period after the fire (figure 3.73). This is important because there may not have been any change in the controlled vocabulary or in the indexing conventions in such a short time span.

The indexing is inconsistent and the two records that have been assigned only a single descriptor are practically irretrievable by any reasonable query for this subject. In the other three databases (MAS, RES-1, and RGA) the indexing was consistent and adequate.

Title	Journal	Issue	London (Eng)	Fires	Subways	Fires-Great Britain	Great Britain
UK police doubt arson caused fatal subway fire	Calgary Herald	Nov 21,1987	■	■	■		
Reports say (London) subway fire warnings were ignored	Calgary Herald	Nov 22,1987	■	■	■		
Full inquiry ordered into (London subway) tragedy	Calgary Herald	Nov 20,1987	■	■	■		
Fire safety on subway questioned	Globe and Mail	Nov 20,1987	■	■	■		
Swift spread of flames in station baffles London subway officals	Globe and Mail	Nov 20,1987	■	■	■		
London subway bans smoking, tobacco ads	Globe and Mail	Nov 25,1987	■	■	■		
Raging fire claims 32 in (London) subway	Calgary Herald	Nov 19,1987	■	■	■		
Police don't suspect arson in subway fire	Montreal Gazette	Nov 21,1987	■	■	■		
"Coctail" of gases suspected in subway fire	Globe and Mail	Nov 21,1987	■	■	■		
35 killed, 80 hurt in UK subway fire	Globe and Mail	Nov 19,1987	■		■		
Killer fire (in London subway) sparks ban on smoking	Calgary Herald	Nov 25,1987			■		
Subway inferno kills 32:"catastrophe" strikes London underground	Halifax Chronicle Herald	Nov 19,1987	■				
(London) subway fire inquiry announced	Winnipeg Free Press	Nov 20,1987	■	■	■		
Britain to hold public inquiry into subway fire that killed 30	Montreal Gazette	Nov 20,1987	■	■	■		
32 dead in London subway blaze	Montreal Gazette	Nov 19,1987	■	■	■		
Escalator carried commuters into inferno of flames, smoke	Toronto Star	Nov 19,1987	■	■	■		
UK fire chief says blaze began on subway escalator	Toronto Star	Nov 20,1987	■	■	■		
Escalator problems cited in subway fire	Toronto Star	Nov 21,1987	■	■	■		
Flaming horror in London subway (King's Cross)	Macleans	Nov 30,1987			■	■	■
An inferno in the London Underground	Newsweek	Nov 30,1987			■	■	■
Escalator to an inferno: panic and death in London's Underground	Time	Nov 30,1987			■	■	■
Total occurrence of each descriptor			17	15	20	3	3

Fig. 3.73. Inconsistent indexing for London subway fire in CBCA.

A possible justification for the lack of an obvious descriptor is if a more specific term was introduced in the authority file and used by the indexer. Change in the authority file is inevitable to reflect changes in the area covered by the database. The changes may be minor and sometimes may be easily achieved by adding an appropriate subdivision to a major subject heading, or they may be comprehensive and affect the complete authority file, as happened when the Standard Industry Classification (SIC) code system went through a complete renovation.

The problem is that new terms and codes are introduced in upcoming records but are not changed retrospectively. It is exceptional that in 1991 the American Psychological Association mapped back in every relevant record from 1974 the five new descriptors introduced since 1989. Usually, users have to know during what time period a particular term was applied. Some database producers make this information available in the printed thesaurus. It is up to the software and the database publisher to decide whether such information will be available also with the database on the disk. Scope notes and use periods are indicated in the printed ERIC thesaurus, for example, but they are not available even in an excellent implementation of ERIC, that of Dialog OnDisc, which otherwise offers flexible access and navigation in the term hierarchy. Neither of the two other ERIC versions offers thesaurus access at all, although SilverPlatter has been promising it since 1989.

It usually takes some time until a new term becomes a descriptor. However, once it has been introduced it should be used consistently. Wilson, who has a well-earned reputation for quality control in indexing, also provides some disappointing examples. The terms "Cambodia" and "Kampuchea" were both used as descriptors until 1991. The fact that there was no cross-reference in the controlled vocabulary from one term to the other made this even worse. Figure 3.74 illustrates that there are no records under the heading "Cambodia" as a single-term descriptor.

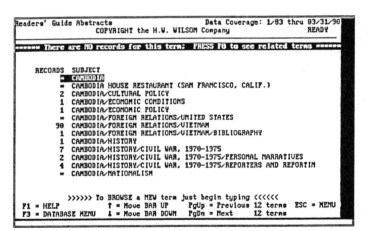

Fig. 3.74. Indexing anomaly in RGA.

When the user looks up the list of related terms, "Kampuchea" is not included either. Still, when searching in the Wilsonline mode for subject headings, both terms appear. After much investigation users may find out that "Kampuchea" is used in book reviews, but they are most likely to miss these relevant items due to indexing inconsistency.

The specificity of the descriptors is usually a function of time and developments in the areas covered by a database. A few years ago it was enough in the LISA or LIBLIT databases to assign the term *computers* to an article dealing with any type of computers. Now it is likely that a more specific term, such as *IBM PC* or *Macintosh*, will be used.

Datafile producers often are "trigger-happy" introducing new terms only to abandon them a short time later. Browsing the descriptor index may indicate this type of inconsistency. When you see that many terms have only two to five associated records that are not typos, this may be the case. In MAS there are a good dozen records with the specific subject heading:

"Kuwait. Iraq invasion, 1990 - Public opinion"

and then there is a single record for this descriptor:

"Kuwait. Iraq invasion, 1990 - Public opinion, **Bahraini**"

It is one thing if the authority file includes appropriate terms and the software leads you to that via references, and it is another question whether the indexer chooses the most appropriate terms. Assigning only too specific terms may result in missing important items in retrieval. Assigning too broad index terms may yield many irrelevant items. In addition, what may be too specific at a given time may be too broad a short time later.

As discussed earlier, much depends on the search features of the software used. In databases where only the indexer-assigned terms can be searched (Magazine Index, Wilsondisc browse mode), the appropriate selection and consistent use of index terms is absolutely critical. In databases where the queries can be easily and quickly changed to limit or expand the search to certain fields or to specify proximity and positional requirements the indexing quality is not as critical.

There is no such thing as a universally good authority file. What may be perfect for a database with a fairly broad subject coverage, such as the Applied Science and Technology Index, may be unacceptably general for a highly subject-specific database, such as the Computer Library. A database using the Library of Congress Subject Heading List may be the dream of a librarian from technical services, but may overwhelm the casual user. Hierarchical, number-based classification systems may overcome many of the problems associated with text-oriented authority files, but they must be combined with free-text searching; otherwise, casual searches without consulting the classification system are not possible.

This type of combining textual and coded terms is excellently implemented in some company directories, such as Disclosure and Standard & Poor's, where a search can be done by the primary or secondary SIC codes or by their textual equivalents. With either approach both the SIC code and its text equivalent are shown. On the other hand, in the Agribusiness database using the same OnDisc software, only the SIC codes are browsable and searchable but not their text equivalents. Both databases have SIC codes, but what a difference there is between the two alternatives (figure 3.75, page 146).

S&P Public Company File

```
      Search Options
Company Name
Stock Exchan    Line of Business Options
Line of Busi
State           General Description of Business
Country Name    All SIC Codes
Financial Da    Primary SIC Description
Officers        Primary SIC Codes
Directors
Auditor
Transfer Agent
Limit Options
```

```
      Search Options
Company Name
Stock Exchan    Line of Business Options
Line of Busi
State           General Description of Business
Country Name    All SIC Codes
Financial D
Officers        Search Method
Directors
Auditor         Select items from a list
Transfer Ag     Enter start and end of range
Limit Optio
```

```
All SIC Codes: 737                                          Records
7349   (Building maintenance services, nec)                    1
7361   (Employment agencies)                                   1
7363   (Help supply services)                                  2
7370   (Computer and data processing services)                21
7373   (Computer integrated systems design)                    1
7380   (Miscellaneous business services)                       2
7383   (News syndicates)                                       2
7384   (Photofinishing laboratories)                           1
7389   (Business services, nec)                                1
75     (Auto repair, services, and parking)                    5
7510   (Automotive rentals, no drivers)                        1
7530   (Automotive repair shops)                               2
7532   (Top & body repair & paint shops)                       1
7538   (General automotive repair shops)                       2
7549   (Automotive services, nec)                              1
76     (Miscellaneous repair services)                         2
7699   (Repair services, nec)                                  2
78     (Motion pictures)                                       9
7812   (Motion picture & video production)
7819   (Services allied to motion pictures)
7822   (Motion picture and tape distribution)

                                        0  Entries Selected
                                        0  Records Found

F1-Help  ↑-↓-Move  ↵-Select/Remove  F10 When Done  F9-Restart  ESC-Prev Menu
```

AGRIBUSINESS U.S.A.sm Database. Mar-May 1988

```
      Additional Search Options
S
         Words & Phrases
         Company Name
         Company City
         Company StatE
         SIC Code Options
Word/Phr
Agribusi   Trade Name
Geograph   Author N    Document TYpe
Author N   Journal     DUNS Number
Journal    Title Wo    Named Person
Title Wo
Date of
Limit Options
Additional Search Options
```

```
      Additional Search Options
S
         Words & Phrases
         Company Name
         Company City
         Company StatE
         SIC Code Options
Word/Phr
Agribusi   Tra    SIC Code Options
Geograph   Doc
Author N   DUN    Select items from a list
Journal    Man    Enter start and end of range
Title Wo
Date of
Limit Options
Additional Search Options
```

```
SIC Code Options: 737                     Records
7313                                          6
7319                                         12
7342                                          9
7371                                         42
7372                                          1
7373                                          4
7375                                          3
7379                                          1
7382
7391                                         77
80                                            1
8062                                          1
81                                            1
8111                                          1
82                                           11
8211                                          1
8221                                          1
8222                                          7
8299                                          2
83
8322

                                  0  Entries Selected
                                  0  Records Found

F1-Help  ↑-↓-Move  ↵-Select/Remove  F10 When Done  F9-Restart  ESC-Prev Menu
```

Fig. 3.75. SIC codes with and without text equivalents in Standard & Poor's and Agribusiness.

The too loose or too narrow nature of terms is a problem not only with subject descriptors but also with other kinds of value-added information. Assigning descriptors or codes to the records by the type of the original documents is a useful feature in both the Reader's Guide Abstracts (RGA) and the Resource One (RES-1) databases, but it is missing from Magazine Article Summaries (MAS). On this level RGA seems to offer too few options, while type classification categories in RES-1 are more numerous, better, and much more easily understandable, as illustrated by figure 3.76.

Article type list

Arts/Exhibits Review-No Opinion
Arts/Exhibits Review-Favorable
Arts/Exhibits Review-Mixed
Arts/Exhibits Review-Unfavorable
Arts/Exhibits Review-Comparative
Audio Review-No Opinion
Audio Review-Favorable
Audio Review-Mixed
Audio Review-Unfavorable
Audio Review-Comparative
Book Review-No Opinion
Book Review-Favorable
Book Review-Mixed
Book Review-Unfavorable
Book Review-Comparative
Commentary
Editorial
Editorial cartoon
Feature
Fiction
General Information
Interview
Instructional
Letter
Movie Review-No Opinion
Movie Review-Favorable
Movie Review-Mixed
Movie Review-Unfavorable
Movie Review-Comparative
News
Obituary
Poetry

Product Review-No Opinion
Product Review-Favorable
Product Review-Mixed
Product Review-Unfavorable
Product Review-Comparative
Performance Review-No Opinion
Performance Review-Favorable
Performance Review-Mixed
Performance Review-Unfavorable
Performance Review-Comparative
Recipe
Restaurant Review-No Opinion
Restaurant Review-Favorable
Restaurant Review-Mixed
Restaurant Review-Unfavorable
Restaurant Review-Comparative
Speech
Television Review-No Opinion
Television Review-Favorable
Television Review-Mixed
Television Review-Unfavorable
Television Review-Comparative
Video Review-No Opinion
Video Review-Favorable
Video Review-Mixed
Video Review-Unfavorable
Video Review-Comparative

Fig. 3.76. Article-type categories in RES-1.

In a further classification within the review categories, RGA becomes excessive (and cryptic) by giving unnecessarily specific options (like oratorio review), whereas RES-1 is unambiguous even though it has less specific categories, as illustrated by figure 3.77. In RGA the codes must be used in entering the query, and they are inconsistent in format and hardly mnemonic. The user is likely to have to consult the print documentation to use these codes.

Article Contents

In the periodical indexes, there are 5-letter codes that describe special types of article contents. To limit a search to specific article contents, use the 5-letter code with the (ct) qualifier. Example: **find batman and mpicr(ct)**

Code	Contents	Code	Contents
autob	autobiography	oprar	opera review
ballr	ballet review	oprtr	operetta review
bibli	bibliography	oratr	oratorio review
biogr	biography	phonr	phonograph record
bkexp	book excerpt		review
cases	legal case	poems	poetry
chrpo	Christmas poem	prodr	product review
chrst	Christmas story	profl	corporate profile
chsto	children's story	radpr	radio program
dancr	dance review		review
datab	database review	recip	recipe
detst	detective story	rokor	rock opera review
dityw	do-it-yourself work	scifi	science fiction
drama	drama	shsto	short story
dramr	drama review	softw	computer software
exhib	exhibition		review
featu	feature article	spech	speech
fictn	fiction	statu	statute
intrv	interview	sympo	symposium
mpicr	motion picture review	telpr	television program
muscr	musical comedy review		review
obitu	obituary	viddr	videodisc review
		video	videotape review

Record Types in Bibliographic Files

Searches may be limited to specific record types. Use the 3-letter mnemonic with the (rt) qualifier. Example: find stock# and blk(rt)

Code	Record Type	Code	Record Type
ana	analytic	lit	literature
art	article	mon	monograph
blk	blanket reference	nbm	non-book material
brv	book review	rep	reproduction
frv	form review		

Fig. 3.77. Article-content and record-type categories in RGA.

A look at the postings of some index terms (figure 3.78) indicates that H. W. Wilson itself may not have meant this depth of classification of review types. It adds further confusion in Wilson databases that book reviews are to be searched as record type while other reviews are to be searched as article content type, i.e., with two different field tags.

Review type code	Review type name	No. of items	Percent in total
ballr	ballet review	531	3%
dancr	dance review	248	1%
dramr	drama review	2230	11%
mpicr	motion picture review	8934	43%
muscr	musical comedy review	851	4%
oprar	opera review	1373	7%
oprtr	operetta review	30	0%
oratr	oratorio review	27	0%
phonr	phonograph record review	2887	14%
radpr	radio program review	70	0%
rokor	rock opera review	6	0%
telpr	television program review	2871	14%
viddr	videodisc review	21	0%
video	videotape review	478	2%

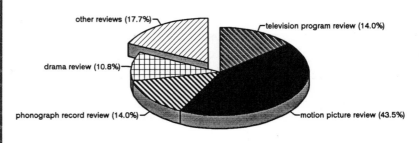

Fig. 3.78. Distribution of records by review types in RGA.

It is exceptional that the data on the CD-ROM medium has some improvements of accuracy or consistency, though this happened with a multi-publisher database. The GPO (Government Printing Office) database has a rather bad reputation for inaccurate, redundant, and inconsistent data.[26] The same datafile is received by all the CD-ROM publishers. One of its derivative dataware versions, the one published by MARCIVE, boasts a greatly improved file compared to the as-is versions by SilverPlatter, OCLC, and Wilson. The GPO database was recently dropped from Wilson's repertoire for database quality problems among others.

Your expectations for content consistency of indexing may be higher in directory databases simply because the records of directories typically go through updating as their subjects keep changing. The descriptive and subject characteristics of an article or a conference paper do not change after publishing, but the characteristics of people, organizations, and products (the typical subjects of directories) keep changing names, titles, addresses, prices, and so on. An abstracting service would not change the country-of-publication data in existing records when there is a change in the name of a country, whereas the publisher of a directory should make that change in every record.

Publishers of directories proudly announce how many records have been updated in addition to adding new ones. If there is a change in the classification and coding system or in the terminology of the authority file, these changes may be implemented in all the records along with the other changes at the regular intervals. While it is understandable that index and abstract records are not updated retrospectively when the authority file is modified, all directory records should reflect such changes.

In full-text databases the same applies to both the format and content consistency of indexing as in the abstracting/indexing databases. The only difference is that you have more chances for retrieval even if the codes or descriptors are not assigned consistently, as your terms may occur in the full text. Obviously, extending your search to the non-controlled vocabulary part of the records may also increase the number of false hits.

Record Completeness

One of the most apparent advantages of CD-ROM databases is their accessibility by a great number of individual and combined access points. Printed A/I publications and directories present the items arranged by one major criterion, such as subject category, classification code, subject heading, or author name, and provide indexes at the end of the publication by some other criterion, such as title, affiliation, product name, or company location. Printed publications are inherently limited in providing access points, if for no other reason than the sheer bulkiness of extensive indexing. CD-ROM products, on the other hand, typically offer a plethora of access points that may be combined by the users to their hearts' content.

However, it is exactly this power of access that may prevent users from finding relevant items, if the data elements so proudly advertised as access points are not consistently present in all the records. Format wise inconsistencies of these data elements may also hinder access, but they often may be explored by browsing the indexes, using truncation, and so on. Absence of mandatory data elements is a much more serious problem because there is no cure for the consequences of missing data elements.

Completeness of records is the sole responsibility of the producers of A/I datafiles. All data elements are typically available from the source or are to be assigned by the producer of the file, who should make efforts to provide all the value-added information to the records.

Compilers of directory files are in a more difficult situation. They have to rely on questionnaires completed by individuals (for a who's-who database) or by corporations (for a product or company directory). They are at the mercy of the suppliers of the source information for record completeness (and accuracy as well). Nevertheless, tracing missing data and verifying suspicious data are part of the business of compiling directories, and for the end users of the product, excuses for record incompleteness (and inaccuracies) are irrelevant.

The absence of publication year data in a large proportion of the records in a database is a significant limitation. By limiting a subject search to a given period, you may miss many records that otherwise would qualify but were ignored because in absence of a publication year they did not meet the query specification.

When the gender of the biographee is absent in every other record in the DLIP database, the result will be misleading if you limit a search by gender, e.g., in searching for female faculty members at library schools. When the LC classification code is absent from 80 percent of the Ulrich's Plus records, it is hardly an access point to rely on. (To the credit of the publisher, the latest promotional material of Ulrich's Plus makes this lack clear.)

A few publishers other than Bowker also include warnings in their printed product documentation about incompleteness of records, but most do not. At the same time, the product brochures list every data element by which the database may be searched—more or less. Even if the printed documentation warns about incompleteness, it may not help the casual user who uses only the typically scanty ondisc documentation, which can be displayed on the screen, and the help files.

It is a much more appropriate solution when these fields carry a notation like "NA" (for not available) if the data is absent. When browsing an index the user then is automatically alerted to the incompleteness, as illustrated by an index browsing example from Disclosure (figure 3.79).

Bowker uses another solution in Books in Print Plus for a similar situation. If the year of publication (which is a mandatory field) is not available the value "9999" is assigned to that field. This way those records can be retrieved if desired, with the understanding that they may not have been published in the period to which the search is limited. It is not a perfect solution because the publication year field is not browsable, and therefore the user may not know about this practice. Still, it could offer a way to alleviate the problems resulting from record incompleteness, though the concept is not implemented consistently.

Even with this provision, 10 percent (about 70,000) of the records in the January/February 1991 edition did not have publication year data (figure 3.80). The total number of records was determined by doing a fully truncated search in the title and keyword fields, which are supposed to be present in every record. It was a long search because the range of values in both fields is very large.

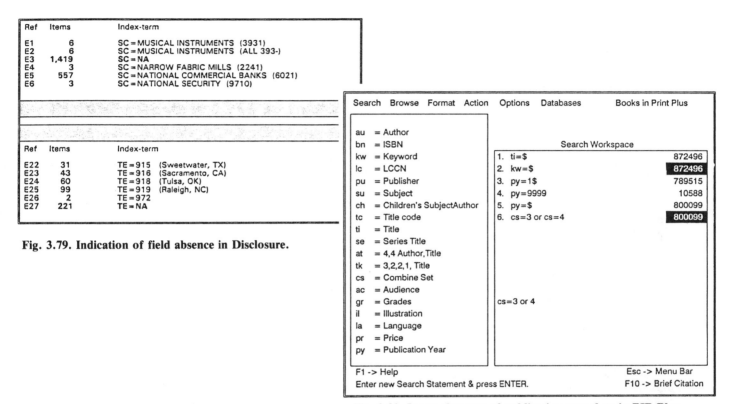

Fig. 3.79. Indication of field absence in Disclosure.

Fig. 3.80. Incompleteness of publication year data in BIP Plus.

In evaluating record completeness, a clear distinction must be made between data elements that must be present in all records versus those that are to be provided only when applicable. There are fields whose absence in many records is normal. Not all books or articles have named authors, not all serials have ISSNs, and only a fraction of them have CODEN codes, but all items must have a title, publication year, journal or conference proceeding name, and at least one descriptor in an abstracting/indexing database or a product name and producer name in a product directory. The scope of mandatory data elements is database-dependent, and you must be familiar with it to make reasonable completeness verification searches.

It would be highly desirable for database publishers to advertise not only the access points to their products, but also the percentage of records that have these access points. This would be similar to the mandatory Food and Drug Administration (FDA) labelling of foods and medications to protect consumers against misunderstanding the claims of producers. Until this FDA type of labelling is widely used, the best advice is "buyer beware" and verify record completeness by some sample searches. You may not be able to verify the presence of all the mandatory fields in a database, but checking a few fields should be indicative enough.

The possibility and ease of such verification searches depend both on the software and on the dataware. The best chance to make verification searches is when the dataware is highly structured and has prefixed indexes and the software offers field-specific browsing and searching as well as truncation facilities with no minimum stem required (full truncation).

Expanding on or searching by fields that are supposed to be present in every record tells a lot about record completeness. The best candidates for this verification are those fields that may have only a few values, such as the document type, publication year, or language fields, which you may easily specify in the query. Often you also may be able to browse the indexes of those fields with limited unique values (i.e., the language, document type, publication year, gender, status fields) and find out the number of postings for each value assigned to the field. If the totals in these fields match or almost match, the records are complete in terms of these data elements.

Figure 3.81 illustrates the results of browsing in the publication year and record type fields of the LIBLIT database from Wilson. The result shows that 1,807 records are without the publication year data element. Similar checks can be done in all of the Wilson databases, and other fields with a limited range of values, such as language and content types, are also possible candidates for completeness checking.

```
Library Literature                          Data Coverage: 12/84 thru 03/31/90
              COPYRIGHT the H.W. WILSON Company              READY
   WILSONLINE NEIGHBOR MODE

   NUMBER   RECORDS        TERM
     1.         2      (YR) 1959
     2.         1      (YR) 1979
     3.         7      (YR) 1980
     4.       147      (YR) 1981
     5.       882      (YR) 1982
     6.      1922      (YR) 1983
     7.      5048      (YR) 1984
     8.     11178      (YR) 1985
     9.     11838      (YR) 1986
    10.     12133      (YR) 1987
    11.     11459      (YR) 1988
    12.      9624      (YR) 1989
    13.       393      (YR) 1990
                                               total: 64634

   UP, DOWN OR GET N OR EXPAND a 'DS'

   USER: n 19:(yr)
     F1:HELP  F2:END  F3:Change DATABASE\DISC      F10:Reshow last FIND/NBR
```

```
Library Literature                          Data Coverage: 12/84 thru 03/31/90
              COPYRIGHT the H.W. WILSON Company              READY
   WILSONLINE NEIGHBOR MODE

   NUMBER   RECORDS        TERM

             BEGINNING of NEIGHBOR terms (or stopped by user)

     1.      5639     (RT) ANA
     2.     45455     (RT) ART
     3.       467     (RT) BLK
     4.     10673     (RT) BRV
     5.      3207     (RT) MON
                                               total: 65441
             END of NEIGHBOR terms (or stopped by user)

   UP, DOWN OR GET N OR EXPAND a 'DS'

   USER: n * (rt)
     F1:HELP  F2:END  F3:Change DATABASE\DISC      F10:Reshow last FIND/NBR
```

Fig. 3.81. Browsing in the field-specific indexes of LIBLIT.

You may browse in the prefixed indexes of those databases that feature the CD450 software of OCLC. A caveat is that many of the prefix indexed fields are not phrase indexed but word indexed, so you may not automatically add up the postings. Do not add postings twice or more even if they appear twice or more: in figure 3.82 both the terms *sound* and *recording* appear 4,390 times in the document type index due to word indexing of the term *sound recording*. The same applies to "archival manuscript material" and "machine-readable data file."

If the software offers full truncation with prefixed fields you may also do completeness checking even on those fields that have nearly a million unique values, such as the title field in the Books in Print database. Though such a search will take several hours, you do not have to sit through it. Such searches may be initiated before you go out for lunch or leave the library in the evening.

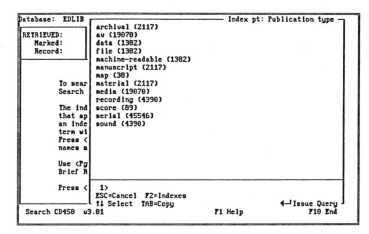

Fig. 3.82. Browsing in the publication-type index of EDLIB.

Figure 3.83 shows how impressively complete the OCSI-PAIS database is in terms of key data elements. A completeness verification search is easy in the OCSI-PAIS version because full truncation of prefixed fields is possible in this software. We are searching for records that have title, document type, language code, and publication date field. Then, we select those with document type "p" (periodical article) and the ones that have some data in the journal name field. It is apparent from the result that:

1. only nine records have no language code
2. only one record has no title field
3. only two journal article records have no journal name field
4. only twenty-six records have no publication year field
5. only thirteen records have no subject field

An identical search is not possible in SPIRS-PAIS because in field-specific searches truncation is not permitted. However, knowing the document type and language codes, part of the completeness checking test can be done as shown in figure 3.84.

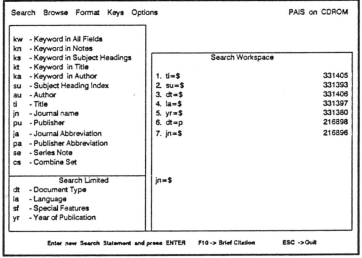

Fig. 3.83. Completeness verification searches in OCSI-PAIS.

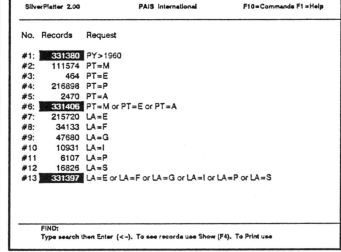

Fig. 3.84. Completeness verification searches in SPIRS-PAIS.

These verification searches always must be database-specific for two reasons. First, it is quite possible that the most common value of a field is intentionally omitted in the records. In the NTIS database the country of publication and the language fields are absent if their value would be "USA" and "English", respectively. These are called default (automatically assumed) values. In MEDLINE, this convention applies only to the language field. In ERIC there is no such convention, i.e., both the language and the country of publication field should be present in all the records.

You must be careful, because the default value convention may vary even among databases of the same database family. The Private Companies file of Standard & Poor's always indicates the country of the company headquarters, whereas the Public Companies file does so only if the country is other than the United States.

The other aspect of database dependency in these searches is that you may find appropriate fields for verification of completeness, even if neither prefixed index browsing or full truncation are available. There may be only one or two such fields, but even these may give important clues.

You may do very revealing searches in all the UMI databases using the publication year and the article length fields. The former may be truncated, and the latter accepts only three values (long, medium, or short). Figure 3.85 shows that only a very few records have no publication year in the RES-1 database.

In databases using the SPIRS software you may need some extra finesse because you can do field-specific searching in only a few fields, and if you do so you may not combine it with any truncation. Still, there are ways of doing completeness verification searches, as illustrated in figure 3.86.

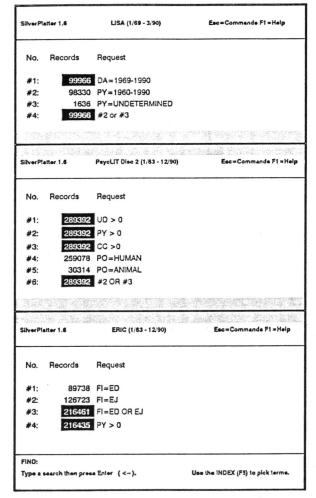

	UMI Resource/One Ondisc - - Jan 1986 to Dec 1990	
	Previous activities	Item Count
[1]	length (short)	42383
[2]	length (medium)	92967
[3]	length (long)	106314
[4]	[1] or [2] or [3]	241664
[5]	da(1986)	25297
[6]	da(1987)	25675
[7]	da(1988)	77203
[8]	da(1989)	59294
[9]	da(1990)	54091
[10]	[5] or [6] or [7] or [8] or [9]	241560

	Search terms	Item Count
(01)	19? -> 19	5433
	1900	39
	1982	6
	1986	25297
	1987	25675
	1988	77203
	1989	59294
	19891989	1
	1990	54091
	19901989	1
	19? -> (9 matches)	241607

Fig. 3.85. Completeness verification searches in RES-1.

Fig. 3.86. Completeness verification searches in SPIRS.

In LISA you may use the publication year and the date-of-entry fields for verification. As the date-of-entry field in most databases is generated automatically, you may count on its presence. Since these are numeric fields you may use the greater-than operator and the value zero to allow for possible typos (which, of course, may also pose problems) when verifying the completeness of these fields. In ERIC all records must belong either to the CIJE or the RIE subset of the database. In Psychological Abstracts either the term *human* or the term *animal* must be assigned to all documents.

Currency

The currency of abstracting/indexing databases indicates how fast a record becomes available on CD-ROM after the source document was published. The simplest way to check the currency of an A/I database is to make a few searches by journal title and to look at the results, which are usually (though not always) presented in backward chronological order, with the most recent citation displayed first. Use weekly and biweekly publications to pinpoint differences more sharply. The results of figure 3.87 are based on searches made in the December 1990 issue of MAS, RES-1, and RGA and clearly illustrate that RES-1 is somewhat ahead of RGA in all the titles examined, and MAS has the longest time lag.

Many databases may be subscribed to at different update frequencies. Make sure that in such situations you compare the currency of identically updated databases: don't compare the quarterly updated version of MAS with the monthly updated version of RES-1. In some cases one database is offered only on a quarterly basis (The Serials Directory) whereas the competition is available on a bimonthly basis (Ulrich's). This in itself becomes a currency evaluation consideration.

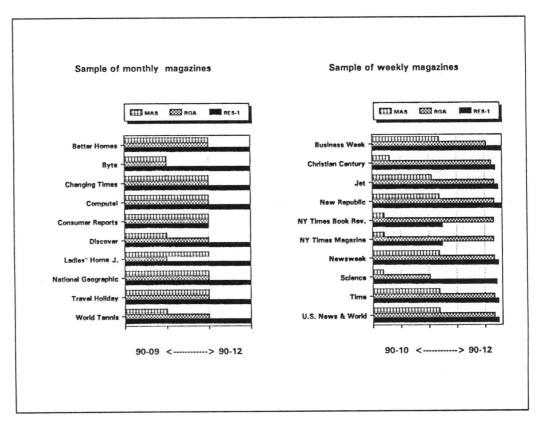

Fig. 3.87. Results of currency searches in MAS, RES-1, RGA.

The determination of currency has always been an important criteria in evaluating abstracting/indexing services, but there have also been limitations on the number of samples one can analyze in order to draw a conclusion and on the precision of the results. Often it is not possible to tell if there has been a significant difference between the cover date and the actual issue date of a journal or in which month of a three-month period (identified by the season) a quarterly magazine was issued.

Though these limitations remain with the CD-ROM versions of abstracting/indexing databases, there are unparalleled possibilities for checking database currency in many of the CD-ROM versions. Records usually include an update date that indicates when the record was entered in the database. This may be simply the year, the year and the month, or the full calendar date. If this data element and the publication year are searchable, you may do searches that reveal a lot about the currency of databases. Furthermore, you may do such searches for a group of items selected by a query. It may be a group of journals, the set of non-English language items, a group of items from a given publication year period, the combinations of these, or whatever set you can create by searching the database. The time invested in such an analysis will vary only slightly regardless of the size and composition of the sample records. You may even do this analysis for the absolute sample, the complete database. Figure 3.88 illustrates such a search in LIBLIT and LISA.

Fig. 3.88. Currency searches in LIBLIT and LISA.

The syntax of the query is obviously different, but the technique is the same. We are searching by year of entry and combine those sets with descending years of publications in order to find out how many items have made it into the database in the same year as their original year of publication. Though the result is not the traditional currency measure (i.e., the number of months between the publication of the primary item versus the availability of the record in the database) it is very telling (figure. 3.89).

One might argue that this technique does not make a difference between an item published in December 1990 and made available in the database in January 1991 versus the one published in January 1990 and made available in the December 1991 issue of the CD-ROM database. This is

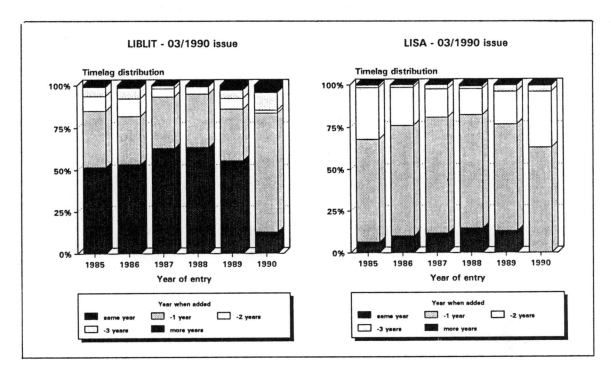

Fig. 3.89. Currency chart of LIBLIT and LISA.

true, but these extreme cases will level off with a very large sample. Also, you have to realize that the date of entry is not necessarily the date of availability of the CD-ROM itself. Wilson updates its database twice a week but distributes it only quarterly. LISA has a monthly update of its file, but the CD-ROM database is distributed only every six months. This makes the currency results even less rosy. With all these reservations the timelag between the two databases is very emphatic, LIBLIT faring far better than LISA.

There may be several reasons for this marked difference. LISA, for example, adds a good quality abstract to almost every record and that takes a significant amount of time. Abstracting conference proceedings may also be a significant delay factor, as many conference proceedings are notoriously late.

The other reason for the delay may be that for the British A/I journal all the U.S. titles are foreign titles, and these were predominant in the sample. Ironically, LIBLIT has more recent articles from the British bimonthly periodical "The Electronic Library" than does LISA. Covering foreign sources is often a delaying factor in any database. If sources include materials from developing and far-away countries as LISA does, the delay is likely to be even longer. These sources also are most vulnerable to publication delay, though you do not have to look abroad for journals with cover dates much earlier than their actual publication dates.

These factors have a negative impact on the overall currency of the database and are beyond the control of datafile producers. This should be borne in mind when doing title-blind searches, such as when you search by the combination of publication date versus data entry date without regard to the titles.

Apart from the significantly longer timelag in LISA, in general, it is also very discouraging that the March 1990 issue of the LISA CD-ROM database did not have a single item from the same year. Given the semi-yearly update of LISA this means that the user has to wait a minimum of nine months to get a record in the database. This seems excessive, even if abstracts are added to each record.

Figure 3.90 shows the timelag distribution in PsycLIT and Wilson's Social Science Index (SSI). Here again, the delay factor is due to the fact that PsycLIT adds substantial abstracts and other, more value-added information than SSI. It is also interesting to see that after a period of decreasing currency, PsycLIT has been on the improvement track since 1988.

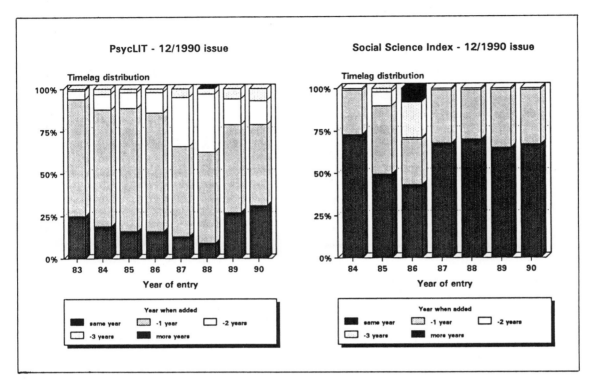

Fig. 3.90. Currency chart of PsycLIT and Social Science Index.

Such searching is not only software dependent but also database dependent. It would have been interesting to make a currency search in Sociofile, but the date of entry is not available in that database. It is possible that one version of a database includes this information, and the others do not. The Dialog ERIC dataware carries this information; the SilverPlatter and OCLC ERIC dataware do not. Using the Dialog OnDisc software it was possible to make this timelag analysis for the journal articles and the reports separately. The results shown in figure 3.91 confirm the general notion that reports get into the ERIC database much later than journal articles.

In directory databases currency indicates how quickly changes that take place in the object are reflected in the record, e.g., price reduction of a product included in a product directory, change of the headquarters of a corporation in a company directory, a new version or release of a program in a software directory, change of affiliation or address in a who's-who database, cessation or launching of a title in a serials directory, and so on.

In directory databases the best way to check the currency is to make some known-item searches. In a company directory, search for companies that had some changes in management not long before the CD-ROM database was published; in a software directory, search for relatively new programs or ones that had a recent version or release update, to see if these changes show up in the records; in a serials directory, check for some new titles, recent title changes, and so on.

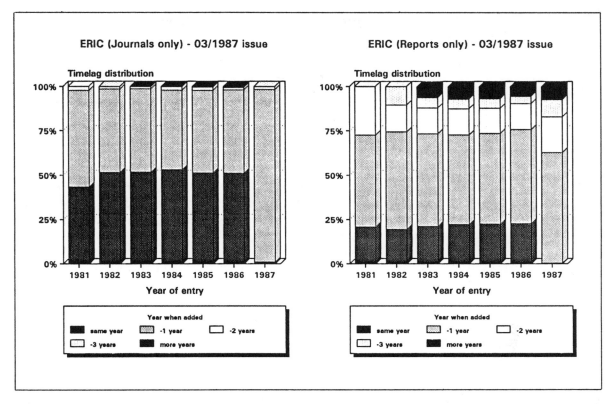

Fig. 3.91. Currency chart for ERIC journals and report records.

You should select the items to be checked with regard to the update of the CD-ROM database, which itself may have a direct impact on the currency of the information. If an item missed the March issue of LISA, the next chance is the September issue, whereas LIBLIT is published quarterly. If an item misses the December 1991 issue of RGA, the next chance is March 1992 and January 1992 with RES-1. With MAS it depends on the update frequency you subscribe to.

Other perks bundled with the subscription to a CD-ROM database may also have significant impact on currency. H. W. Wilson offers free access to the online version of the database that you receive on CD-ROM; you pay only for the telecommunication costs. This makes the quarterly published CD-ROM version of RGA competitive in terms of currency with the monthly issues of both RES-1 and MAS, as RGA is updated twice a week online and the other two are not available online at all. The biweekly online update of LIBLIT delivers the *coup de grâce* in terms of currency to the twice-a-year updated LISA.

Currency of the database is never to be evaluated, let alone idolized, in itself, but rather in light of other features, such as coverage, information quantity and quality, and cost. It is easy to be current with a few dozen titles, no abstracts, minimal value-added fields, and mediocre indexing. Also, you may not expect currency from an inexpensive database as much as from an expensive one. Some databases are available on different update plans, and you may pay twice as much for the monthly update option as for the bimonthly, and it may not be worth it.

FUTURE CD-ROM DATAWARE DEVELOPMENTS

The most visible development in CD-ROM dataware is likely to be the provision of graphical information (charts, graphs, and still and moving images) with textual data. With many databases this will be the most important novelty. The availability of the trademarked images in the Trademarkscan database featuring the OnDisc software will make it an extremely valuable product of the Dialog family.

Generally speaking, CD-ROM databases with images will open an even more fierce competition to their online versions because online transmission of images takes an excessively long time. The ever-improving compression technology will make it possible to store significant amounts of graphical information without the current disk space penalties. Information Access Company already manages to have 1.2 gigabytes of data on a standard CD-ROM in the Magazine Rack database.

Text information also will be stored as graphical images, which will make the reading of full-text records much easier. For example, charts or graphs displayed on the screen can be enlarged for better legibility and readability. The Business Periodicals Ondisc, General Periodicals Ondisc, Agent Orange, and Acid Rain CD-ROM databases have been pioneering this text image approach, and there will be many more such databases. CD-ROM databases will increasingly incorporate multimedia information, mixing in sound and moving images as prototyped by the Compton's Encyclopedia or the Birds of America database.

From another perspective, it is likely that the race will continue for the title of the largest database in the life sciences, the humanities, or the business field. Also, database publishers will not only strive to add more and more records to their databases but also to make them more comprehensive in terms of the document and information types included. EBSCO now includes not only more general interest periodicals and more articles, but also the full text of Magill's Reviews. Bowker has been doing that for years by optionally combining Books in Print with Book Reviews, but for an extra price.

The Computer Select database from Ziff-Davis since the beginning of 1991 has included software, hardware, and company directory information in addition to abstracts and the full text of journal articles and a computer technology glossary. It is a wonderful one-stop shop including the most important titles and types of sources for those involved or interested in the microcomputer industry. The next step will probably be the inclusion of the charts, tables, and other pictorial materials from the prestigious sources covered. At its price below $1,000, Computer Select is likely to lead the field of producers who include only one type of information, such as the Datapro's Software Finder, the Computer Database, or the Computer-Specs database.

Bowker has been a pioneer in combining different types of material and information into one database. Its Children Reference Plus database includes directory and full-text information about books, journals, videotapes, computer programs, and other types of material meant for children along with complete bibliographies and with the full text of reviews of juvenile materials. The mixing of information types may be even more stretched in the future. The European Business Database includes journal articles, hotel directories, and airline and train schedules for major European countries, and the software can even optimize the scheduling of a business trip.

An interesting example of pulling and blending records from sources of different datafile producers into one database is attempted by Cambridge Scientific. Its PolTox database incorporates records of pollution and toxicology subject content from its own five databases, from TOXLINE, and from the Food Science and Technology Abstracts databases.

On the other hand, subject or geographical subsets of mega-databases will develop. SilverPlatter started to publish series of the Excerpta Medica mega-database, such as Excerpta Medica CD: Gerontology and Excerpta Medica CD: Psychiatry. As it becomes clear that the one-size-fits-all concept may not work with a large segment of the potential market, more and more special databases will appear. Users who are reluctant to pay megabucks for mega-databases may be willing to buy the less expensive subsets.

Many CD-ROM databases already piggy-back on the nearly 5-million-record datafile of the Library of Congress. This, however, may be overkill for many. Follett launched the Alliance Plus database, which is a 300,000-record subset that includes items of primary interest for school libraries, but the price ($900) may still not be attractive enough. Enter Brodart's Precision One database, in 1991 with a 1-million-record subset for school and public libraries with a price tag of $300. This trend may continue.

Continuing decreases in the cost of producing a CD-ROM database may lead to such special CD-ROM products as the disc/in/DISC database from Helgerson Associates, which is the CD-ROM supplement to the periodical of the same name. A subscription includes both formats at a cost of $3/issue.[27] As this book went to press, Helgerson Associates went out of business. It is hoped that many of its excellent publications will continue to be made available, although Linda Helgerson will be sorely missed as author and editor.

In addition to traditional CD-ROM publishers various government units, societies, associations, and small businesses will publish thousands of CD-ROM titles very soon on their own. This makes even more important the implementation of more user-friendly software and a common command language as discussed at the end of chapter 2.

REFERENCES

1. Donald B. Cleveland and Ana D. Cleveland. *Introduction to Indexing and Abstracting*. 2nd edition. Englewood, CO: Libraries Unlimited, 1990.

2. William A. Katz. *Introduction to Reference Work, Volume I: Basic Information Sources*. New York: McGraw-Hill Publishing Company, 1987.

3. Péter Jacsó. "CD-CATSS: Utlas' Serials Compact Disc Database, a Review and Critique." *Serials Review* 15 (Winter 1989): 7-18, 58.

4. Peter Brueggeman. "Arctic & Antarctic Information." *CD-ROM Librarian* 5 (December 1990): 39-43.

5. Usha Gupta. "Obsolescence of Physics Literature: Exponential Decrease of the Density of Citations to Physical Review Articles with Age." *Journal of the American Society for Information Science* 41 (June 1990): 282-87.

6. R. Longyear. "Article Citations and Obsolescence in Musicological Journals." *Notes* 33 (March 1977): 563-71.

7. Péter Jacsó. "Coverage and Accessibility in Ulrich's and EBSCO." *Serials Librarian* 20 (January 1991): 1-35.

8. Péter Jacsó. "Directory of Library and Information Professionals." *Laserdisk Professional* 2 (July 1989): 63-73.

9. Carol Tenopir and Jung Soon Ro. *Full Text Databases*. Westport, CT: Greenwood Press, 1990.

10. Karen Markey, Pauline Atherton, and Claudia Newton. "An Analysis of Controlled Vocabulary and Free Text Search Statements in Online Searches." *Online Review* 4 (September 1980): 225-36.

11. Carol Tenopir. "Search Strategies for Full Text Databases." In *Proceedings of the Annual Meeting of the American Society for Information Science, Atlanta, October 1988*. Medford, NJ: Learned Information, 1988: 80-86.

12. D. C. Blaire and M. E. Maron. "An Evaluation of Retrieval Effectiveness for a Full-Text Document-Retrieval System." *Communications of the ACM* 28 (March 1985): 289-99.

13. Harold Borko and Charles L. Bernier. *Abstracting Concepts and Methods*. New York: Academic Press, 1975.

14. Carol Tenopir and Gerald Lundeen. *Managing Your Information: How to Design and Create a Textual Database on Your Microcomputer*. New York: Neal-Schuman, 1988: 85.

15. Marilyn Reppun, personal communication, summer 1990.

16. Carol Tenopir and Jung Soon Ro. *Full Text Databases*. Westport, CT: Greenwood Press, 1990.

17. Reva Basch. "The Secret World of SF = ." *Database* 14 (February 1991): 13-18.

18. Carol Tenopir. "Database Quality Revisited." *Library Journal* 115 (October 1, 1990): 64-67.

19. Martha Williams. "The Quality of Information." Keynote speech at the National Online Meeting, May 1, 1990, New York.

20. Donald B. Cleveland and Ana D. Cleveland. *Introduction to Indexing and Abstracting*. 2nd edition. Englewood, CO: Libraries Unlimited, 1990.

21. Péter Jacsó. "Coverage and Accessibility of Ulrich's and EBSCO-CD." *Serials Librarian* 20 (January 1991): 1-35.

22. Ruth Pagell. "Sorry, Wrong Number: Exchange Rates and Sales Figures." *Online* 14 (November 1990): 20-21.

23. Anne P. Mintz. "Quality Control and the Zen of Database Production." *Online* 14 (November 1990): 14-23.

24. Péter Jacsó. "The Directory of Library and Information Professionals." *Laserdisk Professional* 2 (November 1989): 63-73.

25. D. C. Blair and M. E. Maron. "An Evaluation of Retrieval Effectiveness for a Full-Text Document-Retrieval System." *Communications of the ACM* 28 (March 1985): 289-99.

26. Judy Myers. "The Government Printing Office Cataloging Records: Opportunities and Problems." *Government Information Quarterly* 2 (January 1985): 27-56.

27. Linda Helgerson. "It's About Time." *DISC Magazine* premier issue (Fall 1990): 12-13.

CHAPTER

4

CD-ROM DATABASE EVALUATION

It was discussed earlier that a CD-ROM database is a combination of the software and the dataware. The ideal integration of the two makes a good database. The evaluation of the database was split into two parts to provide a structured approach and to emphasize the software and the dataware ingredients of a database. Some criteria, however, cannot be easily classified as software or dataware evaluation criteria because they depend so much on the interplay between dataware and software or because they apply to the product as a whole. There is no separate cost for the software and the dataware or for the support of the dataware and the software. Furthermore, the integration of the software and the dataware is the key to the accessibility of the database. The following group of database evaluation criteria are discussed in this chapter:

- accessibility
- documentation and user support
- installation and customization
- costs and terms of use

ACCESSIBILITY

Delivering hundreds of thousands of records on a 4.75-inch disk is the highlight of CD-ROM products. Simply delivering data on CD-ROM, however, does not automatically offer appropriate and flexible access to the gargantuan amount of information. In fact, it may simply offer a saving of the time and inconvenience inherent in browsing through dozens of volumes of the printed equivalents or in consulting microfiche and microfilm forms of abstracting/indexing and other information sources. Apart from the cumulation of large amounts of data, accessibility is the key both in online and CD-ROM databases, but it should not be considered as a given in either.

For example, the major weakness of the InfoTrac database family from IAC has been the lack of versatile access to the data. The only access points to the records until 1991 were the precoordinated subject headings, as in the microfiche version and in most printed indexes. For the first six years of the products a user cannot search by a combination of words in the title, in the abstract, or in the descriptors. Nor can a search be limited by date or document type. IAC defended this type of very limited access for six years, claiming that most users would not need Boolean logic, field-specific access, and other sophisticated search features. But by 1991, IAC decided to offer a version that incorporates many of the above features.

Flexibility of access should be a primary consideration when choosing any CD-ROM database. The flexibility and the overall quality of access depend on both the software and the dataware. The criteria by which accessibility can be reviewed include the choice, precision, and reliability of access points and the ease of access.

Choice of Access Points

The choice of access points is the most strongly advertised feature of CD-ROM databases. Generating access points to records on a CD-ROM database is a question of free disk space and time needed to create the inverted file. With the whopping capacity of CD-ROMs, space may not be at a premium except in the case of megafiles that require more than one disk. A large number of CD-ROM databases do not fill even one-third of the approximate 540-megabyte net capacity of a disk even if every word in every field of the records is indexed (inverted) by the database creation software. The time needed by the software to create the index file is not critical either. It makes no difference for the publisher whether it takes 12 hours or 16 hours to generate the inverted file (the index entries or access points) when it is done only once a month or twice a year, depending on the update frequency of the database. The time needed for generating the access points is a minor issue among the hassles inherent in the process of producing a CD-ROM database from the source datafile.

Because it is so easy to generate access points, it is often overdone. There is hardly any likelihood that someone would search for programs in a software directory by the street address or the name of the marketing representative of the software developer, but these still are offered as access points. If someone would like to know who are the software producers in a geographic area to compile a mailing list, access by telephone area code and zip code would be more than enough.

This generosity poses no harm for the end user, unless the number of access points makes it difficult to see the forest for the trees or results in ambiguous access points, as in the EBSCO databases discussed below. The choice of access points is determined by (1) the availability of the data element used as an access point in the record, (2) the mode of indexing, and (3) the level of user interface.

The adequacy of choice of access points is always datafile- and dataware-dependent. It is obvious that no software can help if the file producer does not include a data element in the records. Also, the sheer amount of access points does not compensate for the lack of an important one. The choice of access points is impressive in the Ulrich's Plus database but the lack of access by the language of the serials is a blatant omission when a significant part of the records refer to non-English-language journals. Access by various classification codes is not possible in Books in Print Plus.

In LISA accessibility by document type is woefully missing, as is accessibility by country of publication. In a database that has such a wide geographic coverage of sources, the latter is a much needed search criterion. For a time searches in LISA could not even be limited by publication year, which is now available.

In some databases one or more access points apply only to specific types of records. It is obvious that conference location may be an access point only for conference-paper-type records; it is less obvious that only book reviews can be searched by classification number in the Wilson databases.

The way one database publisher indexes the datafile to create the dataware may have significant impact on accessibility. For example, Compact Cambridge made the gender and age groups in MEDLINE records a prompted access point; in SilverPlatter's MEDLINE these are not access points let alone prompted ones.

It is disadvantageous that in RGA the month of publication is not a distinct access point. The data is available within the bibliographic source field, and when the record is displayed the user can see this information. However, it is not a separately indexed data element. Consequently, you may not be able to limit a subject search to documents published in a given period within a year. If you wish to search for articles about Kuwait and Iraq published in the three months before the invasion, you cannot do so.

The irony is that Wilson carefully normalizes every date into its own standard (though somewhat odd-looking) numerical and chronological designation format, so the field could easily be made searchable. However, this normalized date format is tacked onto the journal name. The source citation **Newsweek v113 p6-7 October 23 '89** is transformed into the following index entry: **NEWSWEEK/113/O 23 '89**. The consequence is that the month is not a distinct access point.

RES-1 creates the three-letter standard code of the month (APR, MAY, JUN) of publication irrespective of the original format and offers it as a distinct access point. MAS enters into its inverted file the month as it appears on the original document. The consequence of this is that searching by month is possible in MAS, but not in a standardized format.

Sometimes the level of the user interface determines the access points. In the beginner mode of MAS you may not search by journal title. In the Wilbrowse mode of Wilsondisc, the only access points are the subject headings, while in Wilsearch mode you may also search by title words, author names, journal names, and Dewey classification codes. Only the Wilsonline mode offers the words from the abstract and the publication year as access points. (It is another matter that the help menu incorrectly states that you may search by publication year in the Wilsearch mode.)

Precision of Access Points

The precision of access points is a criterion to evaluate how unambiguously you can search the database, which means retrieval of only those records that are pertinent to the query. In addition to the obvious prerequisite, i.e., the availability of controlled vocabulary, the precision of access also depends on (1) the structuring of the records and their data elements, (2) the mode of indexing, and (3) the search facilities. The first two are dataware characteristics and the third is a software feature.

To make an unambiguous search you often must qualify the term. However, it is not sufficient that the software offers this possibility; the data also must be structured appropriately. You must be able to distinguish between John Updike as the subject versus the author of an article. You can do this in RGA and RES-1 by qualifying the term to occur in the named person versus the author field.

In MAS, however, the type of record, the author, and the abstract of the article are lumped together in the summary field. The index-generation program creates an access point for every word in the summary field (as shown in figure 3.37), and they become indistinguishable when searching. In this case the precision of access points depends on the dataware, because the software would be capable of doing field-specific searches, as proven by the EBSCO version of MEDLINE and by the fact that even in MAS the terms from the journal citation data are searchable separately.

The lack of precise access points prevents you from making an accurate search in MAS about the subject of conducting business in New York. Because you must search in a global index that takes its entries from any field in the records, you will retrieve all articles from *Business Week* or the *Nation's Business* that mention New York in the abstract and every article from the *New York Times*, *New York Times Magazine* and the *New York Times Book Review* that mentions business in the abstract.

Database conventions used in the spelling of author names may have serious impact on the precision of searching, which may be hopeless if there is no separate author index. Searching for articles by Ching-Chih Chen in LISA is a frustrating experience because her name is spelled in many different ways, as illustrated by figure 4.1, page 166.

In addition, the LISA record includes two or three variations of her name, adding to the confusion and the uncomfortably crowded record structure and creating a very user-hostile solution. There seems to be no logic when and how often a name is repeated in variant formats. The correct, or authoritative, format of the name may be present in the record, but the dataware is not structured in a way to let the software distinguish between authority and variant formats.

TI: ASIS '87: Proceedings of the 50th ASIS Annual Meeting.
AU: Dick-R.; Girill-T.-R.; Stirling-K.-H.; Chen-Ching-chih; Chen-(ed)-Ching-chih; American-Society-for-Information-Science.-Annual-meeting-(1987)

TI: Quantitative measurement and dynamic library service
AU: Ching-chih-Chen(ed); chih-Chen,-Ching; Chen,-Ching-chih

TI: Hypermedia information delivery: the experience of the PROJECT EMPEROR-1.
AU: Chen-Ching-chih; Project-Emperor

TI: Potential of videodisc technology for international information transfer
AU: Chen,-Ching-chih; EMPEROR-project

TI: The potential of the interactive videodisc for international cooperation as documented by Project Emperor-1
AU: Ching-chih-Chen; Chen,-Ching-chih; Emperor-project

TI: Sample interactive courseware development on the use of PROJECT EMPEROR-I videodiscs
AU: Chen,-Ching-chih; EMPEROR-I-Project

TI: Interactive videodisc and 'The First Emperor of China'-online access to multi-media information
AU: Chen,-Ching-chik; EMPEROR-project

TI: Online information and interactive videodisc technology: case presentation about PROJECT EMPEROR-1
AU: Chen,-C-C

TI: Factors in decision making for automated systems
AU: Tebbetts,-D-R; Chen,-Ching-chih; Ching-chih-Chen; Chen,-Ching-chih

TI: CD-ROM survey in American academic and college libraries
AU: Chen,-Ching-chih; Ching-chih-Chen

TI: Libraries and CD-ROM
AU: Ching-chih-Chen; Chen-Ching-chih; Library-Corporation-(USA); Biblis-File

TI: Micro-based optical videodisc applications
AU: Ching-chi-Chen; Chen-Ching-chi

TI: Libraries in the information age: where are the microcomputer and laser optical disc technologies taking us?
AU: Ching-chi-Chen; Chen,-Ching-chi

TI: Microcomputers: independence and information access for the physically handicapped
AU: Regern,-Shari-S; Ching-chih-Chen; Chen,-Ching-chih; Chih-Chen,-Ching

TI: Products of graduate library and information science schools: untapped resources?
AU: Ching-chih,-Chen; Raskin,-Susan; Tebbetts,-Diane-R; Chih-Chen,-Ching; Chen,-Ching-chih; Raskin,-S; Tebetts,-D-R

TI: Microcomputer use in libraries in the US: current and future trends
AU: Ching-Chih-Chen; Chen,-Ching-Chih; Chih,-Chen-Ching

TI: A regional investigation of citizens' information needs in New England
AU: Ching-Chih-Chen; Chen,-Ching-Chih; Chih-Chen,-Ching

TI: Hardware and peripherals
AU: Chen,-C-C; Goldstein,-C-M; Grosch,-A-N; Noerr,-P-L; Bivins-Noerr,-K-T; Noerr,-K-T-Bivins

TI: A citation analysis of the Bulletin of the Medical Library Association
AU: Chen,-Ching-Chih; Chen,-Ching-Chih

TI: An investigation of the continuing education needs of New England health sciences librarians
AU: Chen-Ching-chih; Ching-chih,-Chen

TI: Using circulation desk data to obtain unbiased estimates of book use
AU: Morse,-Philip-M; Chen,-Ching-chih

Fig. 4.1. Haphazard name formats in LISA records.

If the producer of the datafile is not capable of creating a name authority file with cross-references, then at least the variant formats should be put into a separate field. This way the author field would not be further contaminated. It is enough of a difficulty that names of corporate bodies and projects share this field with personal author names. The variant author name format is valuable, but should be in a separate field, which could then be used as a search qualifier and displayed if so specified by the user. The optimal solution is when the file producer maintains an authority file as does LIBLIT (figure 4.2).

```
┌─────────────────────────────────────────────────────────────────┐
│                                                                   │
│  Library Literature                      Data Coverage: 12/84 thru 03/31/90 │
│                    COPYRIGHT the H.W. WILSON Company          READY │
│    WILSONLINE NEIGHBOR MODE                                       │
│                                                                   │
│                                                                   │
│    NUMBER  RECORDS        TERM                                    │
│       3.        1      (AU) CHEN, CHANG-LIN                       │
│       4.       27      (AU) CHEN, CHING-CHIH                      │
│       5.        1      (AU) CHEN, CHIOU-SEN                       │
│                                                                   │
│                                                                   │
│       3.        1      (AU) JACQUESSON, ALAIN                     │
│       4.        8      (AU) JACSO, PETER                          │
│       5.        1      (AU) JADHAV, P.S.                          │
│                                                                   │
│                                                                   │
│       3.        1      (AU) KOEN, C.                              │
│       4.       17      (AU) KOENIG, MICHAEL E. D.                 │
│       5.        1      (AU) KOENNE, WERNER                        │
│                                                                   │
│                                                                   │
│       3.        3      (AU) RAITHEL, FREDERICK J.                 │
│       4.       93      (AU) RAITT, DAVID IAIN                     │
│       5.        1      (AU) RAJ PADMINI                           │
│                                                                   │
│                                                                   │
│                                                                   │
│  USER:  n (au) chen:                                              │
│  F1:HELP   F2:END   F3:Change DATABASE\DISC      F10:Reshow last FIND/NBR │
└─────────────────────────────────────────────────────────────────┘
```

Fig. 4.2. Authority name formats in LIBLIT.

Of course, field-specific indexing and granular record structure may not solve all the ambiguity problems. The mode of indexing also influences the precision of the searches. The database publisher should look at each data element and its potential use as an access point to decide appropriately which indexing mode to use. RES-1 and MAS use word indexing for data in the journal name field. This is a problem with single-word titles that are part of longer titles, even if field-specific searching is available. Searching for articles published in *Life* retrieves articles from the magazines *Soviet Life*, *Family Life*, *Outdoor Life*, and *Boy's Life*. In RGA this is not a problem, because the journal name is phrase indexed, and the query "Life (JN)" limits the results to articles from *Life*. In case of such ambiguity you may search by ISSN in both RES-1 and MAS, but you must know the ISSN. RES-1 offers a much easier alternative of using the intuitive journal codes discussed in "Content and Structure" in chapter 3.

Similarly, limiting a search in LISA to such journal titles as *Online* retrieves articles not only from that magazine but also from *Online Review* and *Online Libraries and Microcomputers*. A precise search by such titles is impossible even if you use field qualification. This problem is aggravated by the fact that LISA offers no prefixed code searching, ISSN browsing, or single-word searching as an alternative.

Other conventions used in producing the dataware may also have a negative effect on the precision of the search. Abstractors of MAS record the date of publication by using only the last two digits of the year. The chronological designation and the pagination of the source serial are recorded in the same field and are lump-indexed. The implication of this is that though you may limit your search term to occur in the source field, you cannot distinguish among 84 as a year and 84 as volume number, issue number, or page number. Figure 4.3, page 168, illustrates how confusing the results of such a search may be. If you want to search for articles published in 1984 about basketball articles of that year you would use "84" in the source field of the template to limit the search to 1984. However, not only those articles will be retrieved about basketball that were published in 1984, but also those where 84 is a page, volume, or issue number. As the display is in reverse chronological order, articles from 1990, 1989, 1988, 1987, 1986, and 1985 would be displayed first.

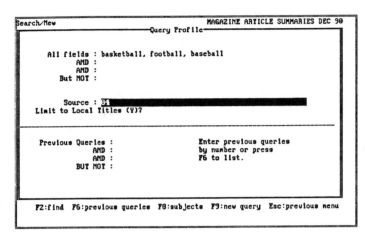

Fig. 4.3. False hits for year search in MAS.

Though it is easy to spot the reason for the false drops, as the term that caused the record to be retrieved is highlighted, there is no perfect alternative to avoid such ambiguity. It would be much better to have a separate index for publication years or to index the year by adding "19" in front of these numbers when generating the access points as OCSI-PAIS does.

Such ambiguity is not a minor inconvenience. By the end of 1990 there were around 10,000 records where the page number, the volume number, or the issue number is within the range of 84 and 90, the claimed period coverage of MAS.

Precision also depends much on the controlled vocabulary of the database and the ability of the software to direct the user to the appropriate subject heading. If there is no such subject heading as "New Mexico" in an abstracting/indexing database of general periodicals or in the full-text database of the *Los Angeles Times*, then even the most powerful software, offering field-specific searching and proximity and positional operators, may not be able to avoid false hits in which the words *new* and *Mexico* are next to each other, as in this sentence: "This was nothing new; Mexico has seen worse rates of inflation."

Reliability of Access Points

The reliability of access points is a criterion by which you may evaluate how reliable searches are using the access points advertised by database publishers. Reliability depends on the presence and the consistency of content and format of data elements used as access points.

Record incompleteness is the most common source of unreliability of access points. If you use haphazardly assigned access points you exclude a large number of otherwise qualifying records just because the data element used as an access point is absent from the record.

Even in otherwise high-quality databases mandatory data elements often used as search criteria may be missing. In Disclosure, searching by the SIC code of scheduled air transportation (4512) retrieves only 19 companies. Searching by the terms "airline*" or "air line*" just in the company name field retrieves an additional three records, as illustrated by figure 4.4.

Ref	Items	Index-term
E1	2	SC = 4493 Marinas
E2	4	SC = 4499 Water Transport Services, nec
E3	71	*SC = 46 TRANSPORTATION BY AIR
E4	1	SC = 460
E5	1	SC = 4600 Transportation by Air
E6	55	SC = 461 AIR TRANSPORTATION, SCHEDULED
E7	32	SC = 4611
E8	27	SC = 4512 Air Transportation, Scheduled
E9	6	SC = 4513 Air Courier Services
E10	6	SC = 452 AIR TRANSPORTATION, NONSCHED.
E11	4	SC = 4521
E12	2	SC = 4522 Air Transportation, Nonsched.
E13	12	SC = 458 AIRPORTS, FLYING FIELDS & SERV.
E14	8	SC = 4581 Airports, Flying Fields & Serv.
E15	3	SC = 4582
E16	1	SC = 4583

```
        S6      71  SC = 46:4522

?S AIRLINE? OR AIR(W)LINE? OR AIRWAY? or AIR(W)WAY?
               193  AIRLINE?
               781  AIR
             6,102  LINE?
                43  AIR(W)LINE?
                12  AIRWAY?
                 0  AIR(W)WAY?
        S7     204  AIRLINE? OR AIR(W)LINE? OR AIRWAY? ...

?S S7/CO
        S8      18  S8/CO

?s S8 NOT S6
        S9       3  S8 NOT S6
```

COMPANY NAME	PRIMARY SIC
AMERICA WEST AIRLINES INC	4511
AMERICAN AIRLINES INC	4511
ATLANTIC SOUTHEAST AIRLINES INC	4512
BRITISH AIRWAYS PLC	NA
CONQUEST AIRLINES CORP	4511
CONTINENTAL AIRLINES INC	4512
DELTA AIR LINES INC	4512
EASTERN AIR LINES INC	4512
KLM ROYAL DUTCH AIRLINES	NA
MESA AIRLINES INC	4511
METRO AIRLINES INC	4511
MIDWAY AIRLINES INC	4512
NORTHWEST AIRLINES INC	6719
PAN AMERICAN WORLD AIRWAYS INC	4512
PEOPLE EXPRESS AIRLINES INC	4511
PRESIDENTIAL AIRWAYS INC	4511
SOUTHWEST AIRLINES CO	4512
STATESWEST AIRLINES INC	4511
TRANS WORLD AIRLINES INC	4512
UNITED AIR LINES INC	4500

Fig. 4.4. Unreliability of code searching in Disclosure.

It is hard to understand how could the SIC code be omitted in such obvious situations. Many other examples in "Dataware Quality" in chapter 3 illustrate how the absence of key data elements may distort the result of searches and make access unreliable. The incompleteness of records may have a detrimental effect on searching if those data elements often used to limit a search are absent in many records.

It is misleading to state that the Directory of Library and Information Professionals (DLIP) can be searched by over 30 access points when in actuality nearly every other record can be searched by only three access points: the name of the person, his/her employer, and address. As was mentioned earlier, the DLIP manual warns that only about 50 percent of the records include the gender of the biographee, but the discouraging incompleteness is indicated only for this data element. This confession is likely to have been made because this field is so obviously of binary value that even a casual user would cry foul when limiting a search by gender and getting suspiciously low hit counts. The same comment could have been added for more than 20 of the 30 fields.

The software could alleviate the problems of incompleteness in the dataware by generating a character string, such as four question marks, "NA", for "not available" (as is the case with Disclosure, shown in figure 3.79), or "undetermined" if publication year is not available (as in LISA). The last is much less effective, however, because the publication year index is not browsable in LISA, and none of the documentation mentions this valuable feature of generating an index entry when the publication year is not available. In Disclosure, the user would be alerted about the lack of data when browsing the appropriate index upon seeing the "NA" code in a numeric index.

Occasionally the good intention to somehow mark the absence of a mandatory data element is ill-implemented. Consider the example of Bowker in the previous chapter, where the value "9999" was used to retrieve those records with an unknown publication date. This was only a partial solution, however, because there are still 72,397 records that have no publication year field present. This means that the "9999" value is not assigned to every record where the publication year field is absent. Even this half-hearted solution helps only those who read the manual because the publication year index cannot be browsed.

The lack of consistency in assigning the appropriate terms and in using the terminology is another common reason for unreliability of access points. It is quite possible that the most essential fields are present in all records, but the index terms are not assigned consistently. Format inconsistencies and inaccuracies in subject headings and classification codes represent a serious problem, as they result in unreliable access points.

If Kampuchea is used in five different subject headings and Cambodia in another five descriptors (as in the authority file of MAS in figure 4.5), the user is likely to miss records.

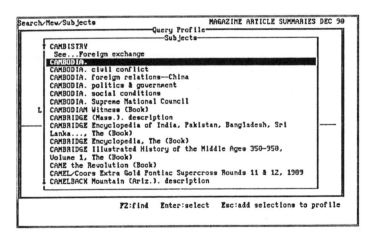

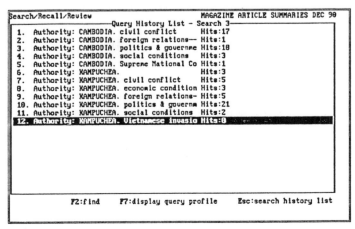

Fig. 4.5. Lack of cross-references in the authority file of MAS.

If this was an intentional change of terminology (which is unavoidable), then a cross-reference should have been provided. The software is capable of handling cross-references, and these are used with many descriptors in MAS, but not consistently. You have to do some spot-checks to reveal such idiosyncrasies in a database. Variously spelled names and terms such as *Beijing* versus *Peking*, *Rumania* versus *Romania*, and *online* versus *on-line* are typical candidates.

Format inconsistency in free-text fields is much more acceptable and quite normal. Subject headings or descriptors are meant to normalize these differences in the source documents, and often they do. No matter how capriciously the primary sources spelled the name Quaddaffi, all three indexing databases of general periodicals consistently used their controlled vocabulary name format. Irrespective of the various format and spellings of the terms *online*, *optical disc*, and *CD-ROM* in the source literature, both LISA and LIBLIT used the appropriate subject headings consistently.

Using different formats in the authority file for the name of the same company or person makes the search results unreliable. Being able to make field-specific browsing of index entries may alleviate this problem, but only if the different spellings are alphabetically near to each other. This is not the case, for example, with the three name formats of the A. C. Nielsen Company found in the descriptor index of MAS (figure 4.6).

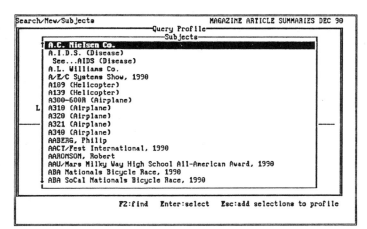 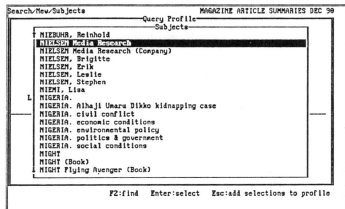

Fig. 4.6. Inconsistent company name descriptor in MAS.

Two of the terms above (A. C. Nielsen and Nielsen Media Research) are dozens of screens apart. It is very likely that the user will miss records, as he or she assumes that any different formats in the authority file would be indicated. Finding one "authority" format without any reference may make the user believe that it is *the* preferred format, and he or she would not look elsewhere. An access point becomes unreliable when these inconsistencies affect a large number of records and do not represent only a few typos. Only intensive use may reveal such problems. A similar problem in RGA was illustrated earlier by the descriptor "wilding." RGA had the same inconsistency with the descriptors "Kampuchea" and "Cambodia" as MAS until the end of 1990 when the descriptors were consolidated.

In another example, shown earlier in figure 3.73, some records about the fire in the London underground had only one or two of the three obviously applicable subject descriptors. This inconsistent assignment of descriptors has the effect that a search by the co-occurence of these two terms (the only feasible search strategy) would miss a great number of records.

Ease of Access

Ease of access is primarily a software criterion, but the dataware component can contribute a lot to it. Apart from a well-designed menu mechanism and an informative help system, the handling of authority files and thesauruses by the software is of key importance for ease of access. This includes the possibility of displaying specific parts of the authority files and the ease with which you may jump back and forth between related terms or look up the textual equivalent of classification codes as shown earlier in figure 3.75.

Access to ERIC records, for example, can be significantly facilitated if the ERIC thesaurus is made available with the database. The CD450 software of OCLC is not able to handle thesauruses. The SPIRS software is capable, as proven by the SPIRS version of MEDLINE and PsycLIT, but this facility is not offered with ERIC. OnDisc Dialog ERIC shows the almost ideal harmony between the software and dataware of a thesaurus. The user may easily navigate in the hierarchical controlled vocabulary to look up and pick broader, narrower, or related index terms. It still could be improved by displaying also the scope notes for the terms and the period when they were in use, when applicable.

Even if a datafile producer uses an authority file it may not be available in the most appropriate format. UMI makes available in its excellent printed documentation the list of controlled subject terms. This is badly needed because the index, though it is browsable, is the simplest possible: single words with no indication of the fields from which they were generated. Searching would be much easier if the thesaurus were browsable from within the search process with appropriate cross-reference guidance.

LISA uses a controlled vocabulary, but the SPIRS software does not make use of it in the form of offering the look-up of cross-references. The lack of the ability to browse in the controlled vocabulary part of the inverted file further aggravates this situation. Controlled vocabulary terms are buried among terms taken from free-text fields.

Wilson does not publish its thesaurus, but you may browse the index, which clearly indicates the field that the terms were taken from and includes single terms, compound terms, and extensively pre-coordinated, subdivided index terms. You may also look up broader, narrower, related, and preferred terms. This feature is available with all the databases using the Wilsondisc software except MLA. The software is clearly capable of thesaurus handling; it is the dataware that does not offer this feature.

Finally, it is possible that the dataware features a controlled vocabulary and it is available on disk, but not in printed form. EBSCO allows browsing of the subject heading list, but no printed version is available. It is a simple, more or less controlled descriptor list of terms with some "see" and "see also" references but not a thesaurus as the EBSCO documentation claims.

In addition to the availability of a cross-referencing mechanism, you may also want to evaluate how straightforward this mechanism is. Blind references that take users down a dead-end are frustrating and confusing. False cross-references are similarly discouraging. In Grolier when you browse the article about Hungary and want to look up the article about John von Neumann, the cross-reference list that pops up and highlights the wrong name does not include his name even though there is an article about him (figure 4.7).

Wilson has not only a good thesaurus, but also a convenient and easy-to-use cross-referencing mechanism. It lets you jump from one term to another or pick a term for searching and alerts you to look up related terms. Occasionally, however, the cross-referencing becomes confusing, as illustrated by figure 4.8.

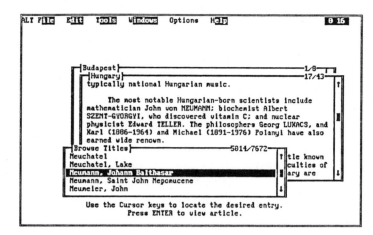

Fig. 4.7. False cross-reference in Grolier.

```
Library Literature                Data Coverage:12/84 thru 03/31/90
            COPYRIGHT the H.W. WILSON Company              READY

PRESS ENTER to SHOW records for HIGHLIGHTED term - PRESS F8 to see related terms
PRESS F7 to have WILSONDISC call computer and SHOW records added AFTER: 03/31/90

     RECORDS  SUBJECT
          1  HASSE, ADELAIDE ROSALIA
          4  HASTINGS LAW LIBRARY
          1  HASTINGS, CORA
          1  HATFIELD POLYTECHNIC/LIBRARY
          3  HATFIELD, FRANCES S.
          2  HATTENDORF, LYNN C.
          2  HATVANY, BELA
          1  HAUPTMAN, ROBERT
          1  HAVENS, SHIRLEY
          4  HAVILAND, VIRGINIA
          *  HAWAII ASSOCIATION OF SCHOOL LIBRARIANS
          3  HAWAII LIBRARY ASSOCIATION
          6  HAWAII STATE LIBRARY SYSTEM


          >>>>>> To BROWSE a NEW term just begin typing <<<<<<
F1 = HELP            ↑ = Move BAR UP      PgUp = Previous 12 terms   ESC = MENU
F3 = DATABASE MENU   ↓ = Move BAR DOWN    PgDn = Next       12 terms
```

```
Library Literature                Data Coverage:12/84 thru 03/31/90
            COPYRIGHT the H.W. WILSON Company              READY

****** There are NO records for this term;  PRESS F8 to see related terms ******

          # Records Term
          ---------------
                   3 HAWAII LIBRARY ASSOCIATION
See also:         * ASSOCIATIONS/HAWAII
                  79 AWARDS, CITATIONS AND PRIZES








     F1 = HELP >>>>>> To BROWSE a NEW term just begin typing <<<<<<
ESC = RESUME BROWSE  ↑ = Move BAR UP      PgUp = Previous 10 terms
F3 = DATABASE MENU   ↓ = Move BAR DOWN    PgDn = Next       10 terms
```

```
Library Literature                Data Coverage:12/84 thru 03/31/90
            COPYRIGHT the H.W. WILSON Company              READY

PRESS ENTER to SHOW records for HIGHLIGHTED term - PRESS F8 to see related terms
PRESS F7 to have WILSONDISC call computer and SHOW records added AFTER: 03/31/90

          # Records Term
          ---------------
                  79 AWARDS, CITATIONS AND PRIZES
See also:          * ADMINISTRATION/AWARDS, CITATIONS AND PRIZES
                   3 ALABAMA LIBRARY ASSOCIATION
                   * AMERICAN ACADEMY AND INSTITUTE OF ARTS AND LETTERS
                  59 AMERICAN ASSOCIATION OF LAW LIBRARIES
                  56 AMERICAN BOOKSELLERS ASSOCIATION
                   9 AMERICAN FILM & VIDEO ASSOCIATION
                   1 AMERICAN INSTITUTE OF GRAPHIC ARTS
                 958 AMERICAN LIBRARY ASSOCIATION
                  13 AMERICAN PRINTING HISTORY ASSOCIATION
                  80 AMERICAN SOCIETY FOR INFORMATION SCIENCE
There are 142 more references


     F1 = HELP >>>>>> To BROWSE a NEW term just begin typing <<<<<<
ESC = RESUME BROWSE  ↑ = Move BAR UP      PgUp = Previous 10 terms
F3 = DATABASE MENU   ↓ = Move BAR DOWN    PgDn = Next       10 terms
```

Fig. 4.8. Cumbersome reference in LIBLIT.

The term *Hawaii Association of School Librarians* is marked with an asterisk, and the message indicates that there are no records for this term. You are advised to see related terms by pressing the F8 key. When you do so, however, the screen displays a list where the first term is not a descriptor either, though it has the "see also" label. The other term, *Awards, citations and prizes*, with 79 postings, is not a related term in the common sense of the word. Only one of the 79 records refers to an article about the award of the Hawaii Association of School Librarians. It is indeed related to the originally entered term, but would a user be willing to scroll through dozens of absolutely irrelevant records?

Only when you look up the related terms of the non-descriptor term is the indeed related term *Associations/Hawaii* displayed, indicating three records with that descriptor.

These glitches in the authority file make searching more difficult instead of facilitating it, because they are likely either to introduce a feeling of insecurity or to incorrectly imply that there are no related subject headings.

Sometimes a search is technically possible, but requires that you go through a cumbersome procedure. This does not apply just to exotic, rarely used searches, but also to the most routine types of searching. If the family name of an author is a common word, a precise search is unreasonably complicated in MAS. You must use the first letter of the first name of the author and his or her family name, change the default proximity of 50 characters to three or four, and use the [ ] character pair to indicate proximity. Otherwise, just entering "George Will" retrieves only those records where he is mentioned in the abstract and not his editorials in *Newsweek*. Truncation of his first name retrieves an excessive amount of false records, and so does the command "G. AND WILL". Using a separate field for the author name in whatever format would make access much easier.

DOCUMENTATION AND USER SUPPORT

Documentation is often the step-child in project developments, and CD-ROM projects are no exceptions. It is considered by many as a necessary evil. It is certainly not the most glamorous job to document the capabilities and features of a CD-ROM database. It also is true that many users never read the documentation, but this is not a good excuse for shortchanging the documentation. Many users need to rely on some authentic source about the database and are willing to dig up something from the documentation to improve the effectiveness of a query or to find an answer about some strange search results.

The principles for documenting any computer system to be used by the public apply equally well to CD-ROM databases. There are several good manuals about documentation techniques.[1,2,3] Although these are for technical writers and they give the set of rules that a document writer should bear in mind, the very same criteria may be used by a librarian to evaluate the documentation of a CD-ROM database.

The documentation may be supplied on the CD-ROM, in print format, or both. The former is called ondisk documentation and the latter is printed documentation. Usually both are needed. The equivalent of errata pages and last-minute documentation is usually supplied in a special file either on the floppy or on the CD-ROM. Always look for files with such names as READ.ME, README.1ST, or READTHIS.DOC for last-minute information about the product.

Sometimes the ondisk documentation is the only source of information about the dataware and the software. It is not too encouraging to realize that the FABS Reference Bible comes only with an ondisk documentation that you have to print out. This is common for $5 shareware programs but hardly acceptable for a product with a price tag of $795. Undoubtedly, there may be databases that are so simple to use that nothing but a help file is needed. This is the case with the Mammals database from the National Geographic Society.

First the general requirements of documentation are discussed, followed by a subjective evaluation of the documentation of some of the databases used in earlier evaluation examples.

Printed Documentation

In this chapter only the printed documentation is discussed. The ondisk documentation is part of the user interface evaluation process discussed in "Interfaces" in chapter 2. It is very important for prompt, on-the-fly cues and guidance but does not compensate for printed documentation that can be consulted off the computer. Comprehensiveness, accuracy, clear structure, good examples, effective typography, and appropriate physical layout all contribute to good documentation.

"The hazards of inadequate documentation are many—it can be misleading, erroneous, and confusing. No documentation in the world can compensate for an inadequate system. It can, however, make problem resolution infinitely easier."[4] The key question is who can solve the problem: the user or the librarian? If the language, style, or organization of the documentation is inadequate for the casual user to consult and find the solution easily, he or she will come to the librarian for guidance too often or simply will give up using the CD-ROM database.

The user manual should include information about the product in general; the commands and procedures of searching, displaying, printing, and downloading information; the coverage of the database; the policy of source selection and exclusion; the content and structure of the records; and a list of error messages and error correction procedures. A separate chapter or manual should provide guidelines for installing and administering the application and troubleshooting. Examples, screen dumps, and samples search protocols should be used for illustration. Unless the controlled vocabulary is voluminous it should also be included in the user manual. If only a few hundred titles are abstracted a title list should be included, indicating the period of coverage for each title.

The organization of the manual should accommodate both novice and experienced users. Well-structured documentation either presents sections on beginning and advanced search techniques or starts with a tutorial about the major steps of a search process and provides a reference section about the details and parameters of the commands.

"The tutorial satisfies those users who would prefer to be led by the hand at first. It is also useful for people who learn better by example than by text."[5] A printed tutorial does not obviate the need for an ondisk tutorial because only the latter can reproduce the dynamism of an interactive search. A table of contents and an index are essential for quick look-ups of information.

It is possible to have a manual for each product incorporating both software and dataware information or to have a general software manual and separate chapters or manuals for each file. The typography used in the manual can very much contribute to the easy understanding of procedures by clearly distinguishing between the fixed part and the user-supplied part of commands and between the system messages and user actions.

A looseleaf layout for a three-ring binder seems to be the best alternative because it makes it easy to keep the manual open next to the terminal and facilitates updating by allowing removal of outdated pages and insertion of new ones. If update pages or leaflets are issued separately they can easily get lost or be overlooked. The documentation and update technology of OCLC, for example, clearly show its experience with large-scale professional documentation. Whenever there is a change in the documentation new replacement pages are sent, the changes are marked on the margin by change bars, and a chronological log of changes is sent with the update pages.

The printed documentation usually should include a quick reference card and a keyboard template along with the user manual. The quick reference card includes the essential commands to use the system along with some examples. It is usually 4 by 11 inches and is to be kept around the CD-ROM workstations. If the database publisher does not offer such a card you may wish to create one. Figure 4.9 illustrates the quick reference cards of Dialog OnDisc and OCLC CD450.

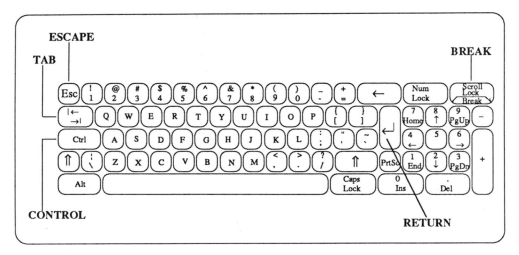

SilverPlatter®

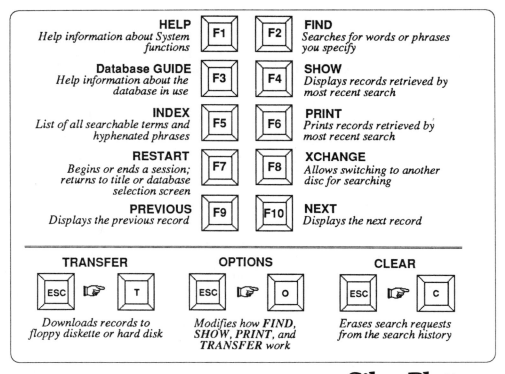

SilverPlatter®

Fig. 4.9. Sample quick-reference cards. Reproduced by permission from SilverPlatter Information.

Quick reference cards can spare the librarian a lot of time, as a good reference card contains enough information and examples to let the users do at least basic searches by themselves. Occasionally the quick card may be a sophisticated piece of art, as is that for Disclosure.

Keyboard templates are essential for CD-ROM products that make heavy use of the function keys on the keyboard and do not provide cues on the screen. It would be impossible to use the InfoTrac or Newsbank databases without keyboard templates, as even the most essential commands require function keys and there is no reference to these on the screens. On the other hand, Dialog OnDisc uses function keys extensively but because it always shows the cues for the function keys available in the given phase of the search, it does not need a keyboard template. The same applies to the EBSCO-CD, KAware, and CD450 software packages. The Bowker databases also have clear function key displays during the search and pulldown menus when function keys are not operational. The names of the groups of menu items (Search, Browse, Format) are orienting enough to open up the appropriate menu list most of the time, so that a keyboard template is not necessary. A weak point in the menu system of UMI databases is that not all of the function keys that are operational and relevant at a given phase of the search are clearly displayed at the bottom of the screen. UMI may have felt that its function key cue displays are not always satisfactory and supplies a good keyboard template.

There might be two problems with keyboard templates. One is that your function key arrangement does not match the one supplied, e.g., you have 12 function keys across the top of the keyboard and you get a template for a 10-function-key vertical arrangement. The other problem is that if you have more than one application using a keyboard template, which template do you put on the top?

Exceptionally, periodically published newsletters are part of the documentation. This must be more than a bragging forum with sweet stories about new users joining the family to be a valuable source of information. SilverPlatter, Bowker, and the Library Corporation have newsletters with tips and tricks.

Printed user manuals show a great variety in quality. The small group of CD-ROM products that was used to demonstrate the methods and results of database evaluation also represents very well the spectrum of user manuals.

At one end is the outstanding and exemplary user manual of UMI's Resource One product, whose table of contents is reproduced in figure 4.10, page 178. The manual is comprehensive, precise, well structured, aesthetically pleasing, inviting to read, and easy to handle and update. Its published policy of selecting journals and articles from journals for abstracting is clear and could be studied by every file producer (see figure 3.19). The field-by-field explanations of conventions deserve the highest score. The list of codes and acronyms used in various fields and the subject heading and journal title lists are well placed and presented. The update format is inappropriate, however. For the book-size manual you get a few letter-size pages listing those journals whose coverage has been retrospectively extended. This is not up to the standard set by this manual in all other respects.

A floppy-based tutorial provides an in vivo demonstration, though it would be better if it were incorporated in the well-structured help menu to let the user invoke it from within the application. The large reference cardboard is adequate if this is the only CD-ROM product used at the workstation, but it is too dominating if other products are also used at the workstation.

MAS has a quality user manual for learning how to use the software, but the information about the dataware is insufficient at best. You can only guess about the record structure from the examples, and nowhere are explained the abstracting and indexing conventions or the journal and item selection criteria. Also, no descriptor list is included. All these are essential for effective searching.

The lists of journals abstracted and indexed are included on a separate promotional sheet. The minuscule typeface makes the sheet difficult to read, let alone to reproduce it here. It is an asset that start and end years of coverage are included with titles that are not currently covered or whose scanning started later than 1984. The latest version of the journal list is more legible, but the period coverage indication is gone.

Table of Contents

Fig. 4.10. Table of contents from the RES-1 manual.

A good tutorial is also part of the login procedure, but cannot be invoked later. There are no quick reference card or keyboard templates but the superb online help and the appropriate display of function key options available in the prevailing context compensate for this. The manual is spiral bound, appropriate for use next to the workstation but not for updating.

H. W. Wilson provides the same *Wilsondisc Guide* no matter which database you subscribe to. It is very much outdated, with no information about RGA, Book Review Digest, or MLA Bibliography. A *Quick Reference Guide* was published in 1990, which, though it indicates the availability of these databases, does not compensate for the other inadequacies of the *Wilsondisc Guide* and makes it necessary to use two manuals, one that is outdated and another that is skimpy.

The lack of database-specific information has its toll. Users do not know the conventions used in the databases. Nowhere is mentioned in the printed documentation the difference between the terms *subject heading* and *descriptor string*, for example. Even the reviewers of the MLA database, who apparently used it extensively, attributed to it features that are nonexistent, and MLA had to set the record straight via a letter to the editor.[6] The online help information sheds some light on record structure and conventions through examples, but it is far from sufficient. The scope and coverage descriptions in the *Wilsondisc Guide* are good and uniformly presented.

The *Wilsondisc Guide* provides appropriate information about the capabilities of the software except for downloading information to disk, which was introduced after the manual went to print. This is somewhat rectified in the *Quick Reference Guide*, where you may find a reference to "redirect printing to disk file." However, it is as much buried in the documentation as in the software.

It should be clearly presented in both documents how and which data elements are searchable in the three modes. Otherwise, the sample searches illustrate well the limitations and advantages of alternate search modes but do not give the slightest clues about the many qualifiers used in the databases in addition to the ones listed in both printed documents.

The spiral-bound *Wilsondisc Guide* prevents its appropriate updating even if there were update information. The stapled layout is appropriate for the *Quick Reference Guide*.

The information about the scope of the database and the selection and exclusion policies is appropriate, but users are absolutely left in the dark regarding the record structure and content. This is aggravated by the lack of explanation of which fields are searched by the three search modes. There is a section entitled "Trouble Shooting," but it is of extremely limited help in solving problems.

No list of journals scanned is available. If you subscribe to the printed equivalent you may find the list of journals, but it does not indicate the period of coverage or those titles not currently indexed. Neither is a printed thesaurus available, though at least it can be conveniently browsed while searching. No quick reference card or keyboard templates are provided. A large reference cardboard is available with some sample searches.

The documentation is very disappointing. It assumes that you subscribe to the online Wilsonline service and have access to the much more detailed manual entitled *Wilsonline Guide and Documentation*. This may not be the case, and the user who has only the CD-ROM version is underinformed and misinformed by the ondisk help file and the Wilsondisc manual. This documentation is below the standards set by H. W. Wilson's outstanding reputation for commitment to libraries and by its time-honored products and services.

SilverPlatter for a long time has not provided any printed documentation for any of the databases using the SPIRS software apart from the SPIRS manual, which deals exclusively with software issues. Since 1990, SilverPlatter has been providing dataware-oriented manuals for some of the databases.

The SPIRS software manual consists of an installation section and a section discussing the features of the software. It includes a good tutorial (which is available on the compact disk and can be used from within the application at any time), followed by a reference chapter with detailed information about each command in alphabetical order and a rather mixed bag of information on how to start the workstation. The section concludes with a reprint of the help screens and a good index. The manual comes in a three-ring binder, which would make it easy to replace individual pages, but SilverPlatter seems to send a complete new edition of the manual whenever the software is upgraded. A good reference card is also available.

The LISA-specific documentation is only available on disk, but the word *documentation* is an overstatement for the mere five to six pages of information. It is not only extremely skimpy, but also erroneous and misleading, as discussed in "Interfaces" in chapter 2. Those who have never used the printed version of LISA may not have the faintest idea about the classification system or the inconsistent indexing conventions discussed in "Accessibility" in this chapter.

The producer of this file, the British Library Association, has prepared a printed guide for the users of LISA but it is available for an extra charge, and there is no reference to it in the ondisk file. The CD-ROM chapter of that guide is outdated but at least gives limited insight into a few conventions, lists the journals abstracted, and includes the controlled vocabulary.

The DLIP manual also represents a negative example of documentation. Its meager user manual comes in a three-ring binder, but that is its only positive feature. The manual is essentially a generic guide to any CD-ROM database using the KAware software with some minor database-specific information sprinkled here and there. It seems to be a sales brochure disguised as a manual. It is very incomplete and occasionally includes misleading information or explanations.

The manual claims, for example, that "proximity searching allows you to limit the number of words found between several designated terms." Later in the documentation it is mentioned that you may use the NEAR operator only between two terms, not several.

The manual is misleading when it explicitly states that "Typing **ORANGES NOT APPLES** will find all documents containing oranges and not apples." The search statement "INFORMATION NOT RETRIEVAL" (to use a more appropriate example for this database) produces the error message "NOT UNAVAILABLE." This is not a double negation, but an indication that the search software was looking for the term "NOT" in the index file and could not find it.[7] In the DLIP database the NOT operator may be used only between sets, not between terms, and set management is not part of the search process but a separate group of functions. Users will find this out sooner or later, but this inaccuracy of the documentation would leave many casual users confused.

Hot-line Services

The documentation itself may be considered by many as a form of user support, but even the best documentation may not be enough for the user to find an answer for an enigmatic search. A hot-line service is the most essential form of user support. Though the casual user is not likely to use it, the librarian certainly would need it to get explanation for some idiosyncrasies and to solve other problems.

Quite often it is not clear who should be consulted with a problem. It is easy when the datafile producer is the same as the database publisher, as in the case of Bowker, PAIS, IAC, UMI, or most of the Wilson databases. Even in this situation, however, UMI offers one number for questions about search techniques and another for questions about database coverage and editorial policies. With many databases, you may not know whether it is a question pertaining to the database or to the software. Of course, this is not a problem if the hot-line is a toll-free number and you are advised to call another number.

To judge the quality of the hot-line service you would have to know if it is a toll-free number, a toll number, or, worse yet, a 900 number. Fortunately almost all of the CD publishers and file producers have toll-free numbers or collect-call services, but given the trend in the computer industry you may expect a decrease in this kind of hot-line service. This service may be very telling about the company's customer liaison policy. It is usually a bad omen if hot-line service is not available, similar to the situation in other industries. Northwest Airlines has a toll-free service for lost luggage inquiries, where some other American airlines do not, and it tells much about Northwest's concern for handling customer complaints.

Another aspect of the hot-line service is when and how it is staffed. The when is easy to answer, unless the publisher chooses to print in the documentation only the toll number, as in the case of DLIP, even if there is a competent 800 service. The how can be answered only by experience. A well-staffed service makes it easy to get through, and even if your question cannot be answered immediately you can expect a call within a few hours. Competence of the hot-line staff varies tremendously. One service representative may draw a blank on the same question that another person answers immediately. If it is a toll-free service this is less critical for you, but if it is a toll number, request a call back, and always get the name of the person with whom you talked.

You certainly will not choose a product by the quality of the hot-line service, but it does not hurt to learn about it during the selection process or the trial period. Make a few calls to get an impression about the competence, the wait and hold times, and how long it takes to get your call returned if needed.

INSTALLATION AND CUSTOMIZATION

When you acquire a CD-ROM product, usually you have to run one or more batch jobs (series of commands with predefined or user-supplied parameters) and modify the system environment. This is the installation process, which accommodates an application in the prevailing environment. Customization is the process when some features of the application are tailor-made by the database administrator, such as the maximum duration of a search session.

Installation

Installation is usually the most dreaded part of introducing new CD-ROM products and services, and it is often the first disappointment for librarians.[8,9] Unfortunately, it is not a one-time process. Each time a new version of the software is released you may have to go through the installation process again. Even if you have all the hardware and software requirements (discussed in chapter 6) you may experience problems during, and most typically after, installation. Regretfully, the installation of a new product not only may be unsuccessful in itself, but also may prevent other, previously problem-free applications from running. Chapter 8 includes a discussion of how to avoid some of the pitfalls inherent in installing a new product. Here the process itself is considered, without the possible side-effects, as if this product would be the only one on your workstation.

This, by the way, is the assumption of many CD-ROM publishers, and it leads to asocial installation behavior and selfish resource allocation conventions in many CD-ROM products. Other very common assumptions of installation procedures are that you have a 5.25-inch floppy drive or that you want to store the CD-ROM software and the related files on drive "C:" on the hard disk, whereas your CD-ROM drive is identified to DOS as device "D:".

Load-and-Go Applications

The best products do not require any installation, but are the "load-and-go" type. They are few and far between. The Computer Library from Ziff-Davis is such a product. You unpack the CD-ROM disk from the package, mount it in the CD-ROM drive, type in from any hard disk the command "L:\CL" (where "L" is the device identifier of the CD-ROM player to DOS), and start searching. The same simplicity applies to the Mammals CD-ROM database from the National Geographic Society. (It is another question that you must make sure that you have the appropriate hardware and systems environment for this application. These are discussed in chapter 6.)

Floppy-less Installation

Short of the above solution, the next best alternative is when the installation software and the search software are stored on the CD-ROM itself. This may spare you the agony of not having a floppy drive compatible with the medium on which the software is delivered. Such incompatibility may be due to either format or density. The delivery of the software on CD-ROM also eliminates the chances of receiving a damaged diskette or file. It is convenient when you do not receive the software on floppy diskette but install the software from the CD-ROM itself. This method is used by, among others, EBSCO, OCLC (but only with the CD450 software, not the CAT-CD450), and CMC ReSearch.

Software Distributed on Dual Floppies

If you must install the software from a floppy an acceptable alternative is to get the software on floppies of both 3.5-inch and 5.25-inch formats and of the lower (720K and 360K) density. The Dialog OnDisc, World Book Information Finder, Wilsondisc, and some other products come with software on dual floppies. If the software is not delivered in dual format, you may still request that the publisher provide it in that format when you order the product. If you are not offered an alternative, you will have to find a place where you can convert the diskette to a format compatible with your workstation. This is inconvenient, and given the less than $1 cost of a floppy, every CD-ROM publisher should deliver the software in both formats and in the lower density.

Flexible Device Destination

Much more serious is the problem when the installation program does not provide an option to specify on which drive you want to install the CD-ROM software. If your C drive is full or for any other reason you do not want to use that drive for your CD-ROM software, you may have difficulties. A related problem is when your CD-ROM drive is not drive D (because you have a second hard disk or a RAM disk) and the installation program does not give you a chance to specify it.

Fortunately, more and more installation programs are prepared for these variations and request either during the process or in the invocation of the installation command that the destination drive for the CD-ROM software and the DOS identifier of the CD-ROM drive both be specified. The latest version of the ProQuest software offers the alternatives shown in figure 4.11.

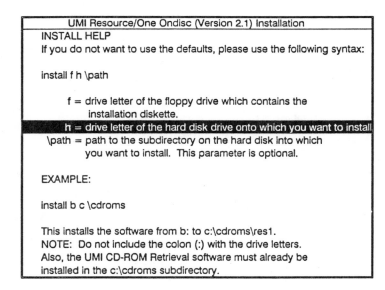

Fig. 4.11. Drive options in ProQuest installation.

If none of these apply, you still may be able to temporarily install the CD-ROM software on drive C and move to another hard disk drive after the installation. However, you may have to tinker with the batch file generated by the installation program to launch this application.

It may happen that the CD-ROM publisher intends to make provisions for you to specify these parameters but fails to do so correctly. The installation program of Compton's Encyclopedia lets you define the destination of your hard disk during installation, but fails to modify its own initiation batch file accordingly. You have to modify the batch file manually after you have installed the CD-ROM software. Figure 4.12 shows the original batch file. The variable "%1" should be replaced by the device identifier you specify in the install command, e.g., it will be the "d" drive if you enter "INSTALL D". In line 6 of the batch file, however, the C drive is referenced, instead of using a variable, which causes the installation to abort with an error message. You must change that line to read "%1:install5.exe".

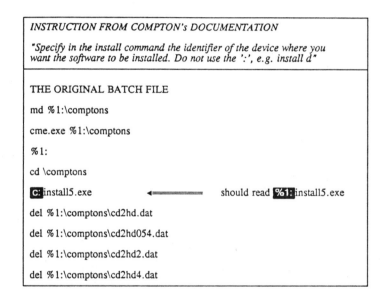

Fig. 4.12. Glitch in the installation batch file of Compton's Encyclopedia.

The worst case is when these parameters can neither be specified by you during the installation process nor changed by you after the installation. Whereas you can modify a batch file as shown above, you may not do so with a program file, which is in binary format and includes these device identifiers within the program. Your only alternative may be to contact the CD-ROM publisher and explain the problem. OCLC, for example, has a special program for the Collection Analysis database that modifies the identifier of the CD-ROM drive within the search program. OCLC sends a diskette with such a program upon request. It would be better if this program were included in the standard package and the documentation referred to this possibility.

As far as you are unable to install a new CD-ROM product it may affect only that application. The real problems start when a new application changes your standard system environment. The newcomer may be able to run in that new environment, but it may prevent other applications from running even though they have operated smoothly thus far. The most common reason for this is that the newcomer application changes your AUTOEXEC.BAT and CONFIG.SYS files (see chapters 6 and 8 for details) during installation.

It may rename the logical name (not the DOS device identifier) of the CD-ROM player from AMDEKCD to MSCD001, for example, and this would be in conflict with the batch jobs of your incumbent CD-ROM applications. More frequently, the newcomer may allocate more buffers (and leave less memory for the programs) by rewriting your CONFIG.SYS file. Your other applications may not tolerate this. The victims of these intruders are usually those applications that require 560 to 570 kilobytes of memory to run and cannot afford to have the usually recommended 20 buffers, but only three to four of them. The Wilsondisc and EBSCO-CD programs are such memory hogs, for example. They may not be able to run after you install another application that assigns 20 or 30 buffers for its own efficiency. How to change such parameters for the sake of peaceful coexistence is discussed in chapter 8.

Customization

Customization is the process when you may change certain retrieval, output, and function options and/or set their default (automatically assumed) values. This is different from the "installation-customization," when you may modify the default location for the software and the identifier of the CD-ROM player. In customizing the application you define the default values of one or more of the following parameters:

- search mode alternatives
- maximum number of items retrieved
- maximum number of items printed/displayed
- destination of output
- format of output
- maximum length of session

- automatic inactivity logoff
- disk changing
- page size, line spacing
- temporary work area
- exiting to DOS

Figure 4.13 shows the customization panel of Wilsondisc, which is among the best products in terms of customization. ProQuest offers similar possibilities, and different customization parameters can be specified for different databases. In Wilsondisc the same customization applies to all the databases. Other products may allow you to customize only a few parameters or none at all.

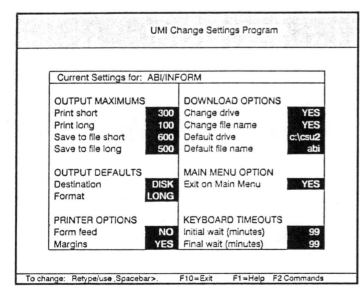
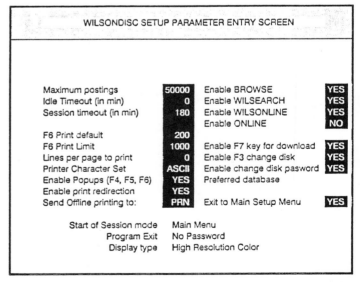

Fig. 4.13. Customization panels in ProQuest and Wilsondisc.

These customization features are important to prevent the misuse or abuse of the system. Limiting the number of records that can be retrieved, printed, or downloaded may prevent unreasonably lengthy queries, mountains of unwanted printouts, or loss of valuable space on the hard disk. Controlling the duration of a search session automatically kicks out patrons who would monopolize the workstation. (It may be annoying, however, if there is no one waiting for the system and the patron is not given a due warning a few minutes before the kick-out.)

Offering only the appropriate menu options or search levels may prevent users from getting into a too advanced search mode. In Wilsondisc you may exclude the Wilsonline mode from the options, thereby sparing frustrations for those who are not familiar with the command language mode of Wilsondisc and sparing for yourself the trouble of escalating telecommunication costs. Prohibiting the downloading of records to the hard disk may spare you the inconvenience of regularly cleaning a hard disk saturated with search results that users did not want to or could not rescue from the hard disk. Preventing users from exiting to DOS, where they can cause serious damage to your files, is absolutely important if the databases are used in public areas. Disabling the disk-replacing functions also spares a lot of troubles.

Sometimes all or many of the above parameters can only be customized during the installation process. This is not practical because you may not wish to go through the installation procedure just because you need to change some default parameters. This applies, for example, to the Bowker databases, which require you to reinstall the application if you wish to modify the user-defined output format or the default destination drive and directory for downloaded output. This latter option can be reset in SPIRS also only if you install the system again. It is much better when the librarian or the system administrator may change the parameters between search sessions.

UMI and Wilson offer this kind of customization, but there is a difference between the implementation methods. Wilson requires a password to access the setup program, whereas UMI stores the customization program in a hidden file. A hidden file is not listed when you display the content of a diskette. The passworded access seems to be better as the hidden file may be too easily unhidden. An appropriately selected password may not be guessed by an ill-willed patron who seeks to tinker with your parameters. Imagine someone making a bad joke by resetting the default value of the maximum number of records retrieved to 1.

Overriding some of these parameters should be possible even during a search. Many of them should require a password (like changing disks), whereas others may be unclassified operations. The best way is when the system administrator or librarian may decide which of the on-the-fly changes should be password protected or made available without any security measures.

CD-ROM products differ very significantly in customization possibilities. Some do not allow any customization; others offer very flexible facilities. In the group of sample databases, UMI, OCLC, and Wilson are by far the most flexible. The display and print format customization are so powerful in the CD450 software from OCLC that even many textual database management software packages used for designing (rather than just searching) databases would pale in comparison.

EBSCO-CD offers fewer customization options (called tailoring). SilverPlatter's customization is limited to specifying the default download destination, the disk-changing facility, the inclusion of the tutorial program, and the setting of vertical margins and line spacing. OCSI lets you define the default display/print format, specify a custom format, and determine the destination of the downloaded records. All of these customization features are available only during installation. The OnDisc and KAware software packages do not offer any customization.

PRICE AND TERMS OF USE

The licensing or purchase price of a commercially available CD-ROM database may range from below $100 to over $20,000. The least expensive product (disregarding free CD-ROM demo products) is probably the database of satellite photos from NASA for $25, and the most expensive are the members of the Lotus One Source product family for between $16,000 and $20,000. Stephen Arnold pointed out that "CD-ROM publishers are pricing either low or high" and demonstrated that nearly 40 percent of the CD-ROM databases were priced below $500 and 35 percent above the $2,000 mark.[10]

There is a clear distinction between prices, however, depending on the type of the databases. Paul Nicholls, who regularly publishes important profiles of the CD-ROM industry, found the following pricing pattern (figure 4.14) during a four-year period.[11]

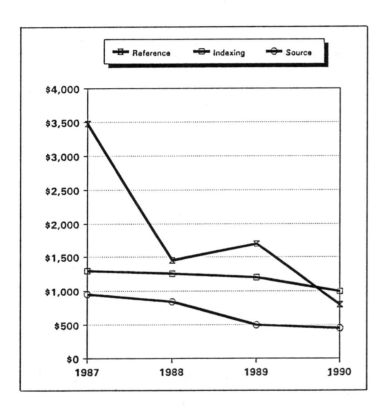

Fig. 4.14. Price pattern by database type.

It is also true, however, that even within comparable categories and subject fields there may be a general periodical index for $399 and another one for almost $2,000. The question is whether the depth and width of coverage, the content and quality of the database, and the update frequency would justify the higher price for the clientele of your library.

The price itself is a very important criterion, but it does not tell you everything because you do not necessarily get what you pay for. The price always has to be considered in light of those capabilities of the software and characteristics of the dataware that are important to you. This means first assessing many of the criteria discussed in the previous chapters and assigning a total score to the product. Then you should take a close look at its price. The unit price per score point would tell you how much you pay for the quality features of the product.

It is easy to rave about the quality of abstracts in RGA without considering its relatively steep price. It is easy to look down at the number of titles abstracted by RES-1 without considering how much more expensive MAS is, with more than twice as many titles scanned but less effective search capabilities and record structure than RES-1. Price certainly also has an effect on your quality expectations. You obviously would be much more tolerant for database quality glitches in a database costing a few hundred dollars than in those with a price tag of several thousand dollars.

This price/performance approach is so important that the producer of the Laserquest database (GRC) does not publish prices or quote them over the telephone. GRC wants potential customers to know the capabilities of Laserquest; it lets users fall in love with the product and then compare its price with competing products such as Bibliofile, Supercat, and Lasercat. This may be an arguable policy, and many users may not even consider a product without knowing its price range, but it illustrates well how important it is to look at the price together with evaluation scores and not as a criterion in itself.

The price of a product depends on the capabilities of the software, the size and scope of the database, content and quality, retrospectivity and currency, and the criteria discussed in chapters 2 and 3, as well as some others, such as the prices of competing products.

Competition is one of the most common price determinants. With the introduction of ERIC on CD-ROM, a healthy price war broke out among Dialog, OCLC, and SilverPlatter and resulted in a very significant price decrease within a few months. This is nothing new, of course. If a car rental company is the only kid in town, it is likely to charge you as much as it thinks you are willing to pay. Airlines start to lower their fares as soon as someone else gets a permit to fly the same route.

Apart from price decreases, such competition may also result in quality improvements. There are many implementations of the GPO datafile, but the one from MARCIVE stands out because of the extensive clean-up job it has done. In looking at the list of the GPO databases implemented by various database publishers (figure 4.15), the only apparent difference apart from price is update frequency; otherwise, you may have the impression that the dataware is the same across the databases. It is not, and you would find this out only after using them or reading about them. MARCIVE has done a comprehensive clean-up project on the datafile as received from the producer, the Government Printing Office. This means that the quality of the MARCIVE dataware is much better than that of the similarly priced, identically updated SilverPlatter version.

Publisher	Update frequency	Price	Notes
Auto-graphics, Inc.	monthly	$1,750	
	bimonthly	$1,100	
IAC	monthly	$2,500	Includes Infotrac workstation
MARCIVE, Inc.	bimonthly	$995	Thoroughly cleaned version
OCLC	bimonthly	$350	Non-members
	bimonthly	$300	Members
SilverPlatter	bimonthly	$950	
H. W. Wilson	annually	$995	Withdrawn; included Index to U.S. Government Periodicals and free online access to monthly updated online version

Fig. 4.15. GPO prices and features.

The printed versions may have some impact on the pricing of the CD-ROM version. A few CD-ROM publishers charge different fees depending on whether you subscribe to their printed versions and, if so, to how many of those. In the Dialog OnDisc family of databases the 20-percent discount applies to the Standard & Poor's, Metadex, and Aerospace Database products. The Institute for Scientific Information has different prices for the Science Citation Index and Social Science Citation Index based on whether you subscribe to the printed version. ISI has a similar policy with their online databases. BIOSIS and PAIS do not have a print subscription-dependent price structure for online users, but do have one for CD-ROM licensees.

On the other hand, subscribing to the CD-ROM version of a database may entitle you to royalty-free searching in the online version of the database. Obviously, this could be offered only by those publishers that also provide online services. You are not entitled to royalty-free searching of the online versions of OnDisc databases from Dialog, the Serials Directory from EBSCO, or the Union Catalog from OCLC even if you subscribe to the CD-ROM version or subset of these databases. On the other hand, Wilson generously offers free online searching in the database that you subscribe to in CD-ROM format and makes access very easy through the Wilsondisc software. You pay only for the telecommunication cost. Considering that the online databases of Wilson are updated twice a week, this a very important perk.

Different packaging of the database by the same publisher also results in different prices. The most common packaging alternative is allowing licensing of backfiles in one- to five-year increments. The smaller the increment, the more flexible your options are to choose the one most appropriate for your requirements. The other packaging alternative, popular with versions of the MEDLINE database, is to offer a subset limited to English-language documents (BRS Colleague), to core journals (EBSCO Core MEDLINE), or to clinical journals (OnDisc MEDLINE Clinical Collection). In cataloging support databases the common packaging alternative is language. You may have the English-only subset of Bibliofile and Supercat or you may subscribe to the foreign language subset, too. Update frequency is the price setting criteria with the MAS database, as illustrated by figure 4.16. Offering subscription options is a good idea and having an academic year option under it is excellent.

Disk(s) in a year	Price	Update frequency	Shipping Dates
1	399	Annual	Any month
4	799	Quarterly	Jan/Apr/Jul/Oct
9	1199	Academic Year	Monthly except Jun/Jul/Aug
12	1599	Monthly	Each month

Note: Price does not include $100 shipping charge in first year

Fig. 4.16. MAS price alternatives by update frequency.

Many publishers offer discounts for schools, public libraries, and other nonprofit organizations, as well as volume discounts. SilverPlatter offers a 50 percent discount on AGRIS for developing countries and an undisclosed discount on the CAB database for member states of the Commonwealth. Meckler had a unique pricing policy until Fall 1991 with its World Currency Monitor. Nonprofit organizations not only receive a 10 percent discount, but also pay according to their combined book and periodical budget. The price is $195 if this budget is less than $100,000, $395 if it is greater than $300,000, and $295 for those in between.

This pricing scheme is used now with a database, one of the revolutionary products of the early 1990s in terms of price. The PhoneDISC USA database, including data from all the white page directories of the U.S.A., is available for libraries having budgets less than $50,000 a year for the incredible price of $198. The West Coast or East Coast editions are available separately for $99 each. Libraries with budgets between $50,000 and $100,000 pay $500 for the national set.

The terms of use to be discussed below may have an impact on pricing, too. Single work-station, multiple local access (networking, shared usage), and remote access may mean different price tags, and it is always database-dependent. Even the same publisher may have different policies within its family of databases. To use a database on a local area network of personal computers there is no surcharge for SilverPlatter's LISA, ERIC, and a few other databases, whereas a surcharge of 60 to 100 percent applies to such databases as PsycLIT and Sociofile. Obviously these pricing differences are based on the assumed amount of usage. If a database can be used from more microcomputers, it is likely to be used more extensively. This is, however, only an assumption, and not an actual usage-based charge.

If a datafile is available from different publishers, the price may vary even if the content is the same. The single-user price of OCSI-PAIS is $1,795 (as of spring of 1991), whereas the SilverPlatter version is $1,995. The difference becomes even more evident when it comes to local area network use. SilverPlatter charges a 50 percent surcharge for two to four users, and a 100 percent surcharge for five to ten users. In the OCSI-PAIS version there is no surcharge for multiple use on a network where the workstations are in the same building.

There is talk about measuring the use of CD-ROM databases with a view to introduce time- or activity-based pricing. Hopefully this will never happen, as it may take away one of the most important advantages of CD-ROM databases: the non-metered, unlimited use. The first product to take use into account is the UMI Business Periodicals Ondisc (BPO), but it only addresses the number of pages printed. This is understandable because BPO produces on CD-ROM the facsimile equivalent of the original journal articles, and UMI itself has to pay royalty for this kind of printing (copying) to the publisher of the original journals. The UMI software keeps track of the number of pages printed from each journal, and you pay a printing fee of 10¢ per page at the end of the year.

The prices mentioned so far are so-called list prices. Occasionally you may get a significant discount if you do not buy from the database publisher but from a mail-order company or in a specialty shop's promotional or sale period. This alternative is discussed in chapter 7.

It is important to understand that with most of the databases you are licensing them. You are a licensee and not an owner. Only a few databases are available for outright purchase, and this may have very important implications as terms of use in your license agreement.

Terms of Use

The terms and conditions of use are important not only in the obvious legal sense of what you may do with the dataware and the software, but also with regard to how you may use the product. This is a unique corollary with CD-ROM databases as information media, but has been present with software since the early days of personal computing.

While there are no special regulations in addition to the standard copyright provisions as to how you may use your printed abstracting/indexing journal, encyclopedia, or dictionary, there are strict provisions for their CD-ROM equivalents. Three conditions deserve special attention in selecting a database: retention policy, multiple local access, and remote access.

The retention policy of many database publishers is often a cold shower for potential customers. Usually you must return each disk to get the next update. There is nothing wrong with this because the next update is cumulated, if you receive a next update. If may happen, however, that after subscribing to a CD-ROM product for three years you have to cancel the subscription. This may mean that you have to return your last disk. If you cannot renew a subscription to a printed publication you do not have to return the back issues. They are yours to keep. It is not necessarily so with the CD-ROM version. This is unacceptable to many libraries and, with a very few exceptions, unheard of with print media.

Many publishers require you to return or destroy the disk when you get the next issue but allow you to keep the last one if you cancel. This seems to be the most acceptable solution, and it is practiced by PAIS, EBSCO, and UMI, among others. Sometimes the license agreement stipulates that you return every disk, but the publisher does not enforce it. This was the case with the Disclosure database. The license agreement spelled out that in case of cancellation you have to return the disk, but a trusted and high-ranking representative of the company is on record (actually on videotape) with the more liberal policy that allows subscribers to keep the last disk.

Wilson has a unique and very generous policy. You may not only keep all your copies, but also may even pass it to other parties within and outside of your organization. This approach should be much appreciated.

Imagine that four libraries team up to subscribe to Library Literature (LIBLIT) by equally splitting the subscription fee. (You may substitute LIBLIT by RGA for a comparison with MAS and RES-1, of course.) Figure 4.17 illustrates how they could rotate the disk fairly and have access to this valuable source. One of the libraries will be nine months behind schedule. This is not good, of course, but is much better than the limited access and inherent inconvenience of the printed version. Furthermore, if you consult the timelag chart in figure 3.88 again, you see that in the competitive LISA database the twice-per-year update and the significant timelag between the date of publication and date of inclusion almost automatically guarantees a nine-month delay.

Library	CALENDAR DATES (92-01...92-12) DISK ISSUE DATES (91-4Q...92-4Q)											
	92-01	92-02	92-03	92-04	92-05	92-06	92-07	92-08	92-09	92-10	92-11	92-12
Hawaii Kai	91-4Q			92-1Q			92-2Q			92-3Q		
Waimanalo				91-4Q			92-1Q			92-2Q		
Kailua							91-4Q			92-1Q		
Kaneohe										91-4Q		

Fig. 4.17. Rotating LIBLIT among four libraries.

By splitting the yearly $1,095 fee of LIBLIT among the four libraries, you have a $270 fee versus the $995 price of LISA, a significant difference. For this fee you get one copy of LISA when you start your subscription and another one six months later, but you have to send back the first disk to SilverPlatter. Of course, the other criteria, such as the availability of good-quality abstracts and the wide geographic and language coverage of LISA, should be considered.

Local Multiple Access

Sharing expensive resources by many workstations is becoming increasingly common. Scanners, laser printers, and high-capacity disks are quite often shared by PCs on a network. This is a reasonable approach (though it can be difficult technically), as these resources are not fully utilized by one workstation. The same applies to CD-ROM databases, which you may wish to share among workstations. Apart from the technical considerations you need to find out if the license agreement allows you to provide multiple access to the database. If it is allowed, you may be charged extra for this option.

Multiple access has been absolutely forbidden with some databases, but more and more publishers realize that it is a requirement for libraries and that it is better to allow it by levying an extra charge. With some databases the multiple access has no extra charge. Figure 4.18 illustrates some examples of different prices for multiple access. This policy may vary among databases published by the same publisher. The figure also illustrates the different policies by two major publishers for the same database. The license fee for network use may also depend on how many users have simultaneous access to the database.

	Single Use	Multiuse	Surcharge %	Number of users
SilverPlatter				
Biological Abstracts on CD 1991	$8,325	$9,825	18%	
Econlit	$1,600	$2,400	50%	
ERIC 1980 to present	$650	no charge	-	
LISA	$995	no charge	-	
MEDLINE (1985 to present)	$1,495	no charge	-	
NTIS	$2,850	$4,275	50%	
PAIS	$1,995	$2,992	50%	2-4 users
	-	$3,990	100%	5-8 users
PsycLIT	$3,995	$5,995	50%	
Sociofile	$1,950	$2,995	54%	
Dialog				
Canadian Business and Current Affairs	$1,450	$2,900	100%	2-10 users
	-	$4,350	200%	11-25 users
ERIC (1980 to present)	$795	$1,203	50%	2-10 users
	-	$1,590	100%	11-25 users
MEDLINE (1984 to present)	$1,895	$2,843	50%	2-10 users
	-	$3,790	100%	17-25 users
NTIS	$2,350	-	-	not available
Thomas Register	$1,495	$2,990	100%	max. 10 users

Fig. 4.18. Multiple access charges.

In a few cases it may happen that though multiple access (networking) would be permitted legally, and there is no charge for it, you are unable to provide multiple access because of the limitation of the random access memory capacity of the PCs or because of some other technical limitation. These issues are discussed in chapter 6.

Remote Access

It was an obvious step that users may wish not only to share expensive resources in the library or in the office, but also to access them from the convenience of their home, dormitory, or distant office through telecommunication lines by dialing in. Remote control software like PC Anywhere or Co-session for dial-in searching requires as many PCs at the local site where the PCs are installed as calls are to be satisfied. This implies that remote access is reasonable during hours when the library is closed and its resources would not be used.

Apart from the technicalities (discussed in chapter 6), you should consider also the legalities when selecting a database. Many publishers that allow for an extra fee or for free local network access would not let you provide access from remote terminals. OCSI-PAIS allows multiple local access without a surcharge but not remote access. SilverPlatter charges an extra fee depending on the number of possible users and does not allow remote access either. Remoteness may be a vague idea, but when asked PAIS clearly defined the limits: the wall of the building where the CD-ROM disk is housed. This means that you may use the CD-ROM on the ground floor from a PC on the fifth floor, but not from the office in the next building.

Some publishers that allow local network access also allow remote access for an additional surcharge. H. W. Wilson has a clear policy and written schedule for local area network and remote dial-in use. The different options are shown in figure 4.19, page 192.

WILSONDISC Network Pricing Policies

Remote access is defined as access via telecomunications lines and modems
or through network hardware and software beyond a single building.

COLLEGE/UNIVERSITY	For a Single Institution defined as a single college or university, students who pay tuition to that institution, and faculty and staff employed by that institution.
1. **Local Area Network** Within a single building	No Additional Charge
2. **Local Area Network** Remote Access	Additional 10% of Annual Fee for each potential remote simultaneous user

ELEMENTARY AND SECONDARY SCHOOL	
1. **Local Area Network** Within a single school	No Additional Charge
2. **Local Area Network** Remote Access for students and faculty of that school	No additional Charge
3. **Local Area Network** Remote Access for additional schools, their students and faculty (same district)	Additional 50% of Annual Fee per person

PUBLIC LIBRARY	
1. **Local Area Network** Within a single building	No Additional Charge
2. **Local Area Network** Remote Access for additional branches	Additional 50% of Annual Fee per branch regardless of the terminals per branch
3. **Local Area Network** Remote Access for general population from home, office, etc.	Additional 10% of Annual Fee for each simultaneous remote user

CORPORATE LIBRARY	
1. **Local Area Network** Within a single building	No Additional Charge
2. **Local Area Network** Remote Access for additional sites or offices	Additional 50% of Annual Fee per branch or site regardless of the number of terminals at branch or site
3. **Local Area Network** Remote Access for users away from the branch or site	Additional 10% of Annual Fee for each simultaneous remote user

Fig. 4.19. Remote multiple access charges. Courtesy of H. W. Wilson Company.

FUTURE CD-ROM DATABASE DEVELOPMENTS

We will see more and more databases that offer the same or almost the same proprietary datafile but that feature different software, as is the case with PAIS datafile. This is a welcomed development because it increases the choices and the competition as it did with public domain files. It may also help in simplifying the occasional end-users' use of CD-ROM databases. This may be the decisive argument for choosing SPIRS-PAIS whether or not you find OCSI-PAIS superior to SPIRS-PAIS if the library subscribes to other databases published by SilverPlatter.

We will see a set of small databases residing in a single CD-ROM disk, not feasible before. Business Software Database, Microcomputer Index, and the Index to Theses (Great Britain and Ireland) now cohabitate on a single CD-ROM disk. You get a password for those databases you wish to use. This kind of sharing will continue to drive down CD-ROM production costs and prices.

More publishers and producers will combine efforts in publishing a database making seemingly strange bedfellows. H. W. Wilson and UMI compete fiercely for the general periodical index market; both of them are datafile producers and database publishers; H. W. Wilson is also a software producer. Still, the two companies teamed up in 1991 to produce the full-text image database Social Science Abstracts that combines the datafile from Wilson with the know-how of UMI so impressively features in the Business Periodicals Ondisc, a full-text image database.

The most important developments, however, are likely to occur in pricing. When IAC announced its Magazine Rack database with a price tag of $89, it seemed to be a typo. After all, this database includes the full text of the 1990 issues of more than 300 magazines (figure 4.20).

Fig. 4.20. Cover sleeve of Magazine Rack. Copyright © 1991 Information Access Company, reproduced with permission.

Abstracting/indexing databases with narrower title coverage and abstracts only (but a longer period of coverage) charge 15 to 20 times more. In the field of general periodicals retrospectivity may be less important than immediate availability of the full text. If the database is also fully searchable, you have a price bonanza.

Products with such killer prices will finally open up the market segment that may be the most important development in the CD-ROM industry: the home and small business market. Lower-priced databases will have mass appeal to users who can couple inexpensive PCs with a superb CD-ROM player priced below $400 (like the Tandy CDR-1000). To have the full text of the 1990 issues of *PC Magazine, PC Computing, PC Sources, CD-ROM Professional, Online, Information Today, RQ, Working Woman, Cosmopolitan, Car and Driver, Good Housekeeping, Changing Times*, etc., will sell this product to tens of thousands of home users in a short period of time justifying the investment in home computing for those who still hesitate.

Similar revolutionary pricing was introduced by PhoneDISC USA, Inc. in the summer of 1991. As mentioned earlier, libraries with yearly budgets less than $50,000 a year can have this database for $198. The print equivalent of this database is 5,000 volumes of white-page directories with 90 million listings costing $60,000 (and about fifty trees a year). In addition, in the print equivalent you could not find all the Jacsó's in the United States who have a listed telephone number in 10 seconds. This is a superb database featuring a software developed by the same person who created the Dialog OnDisc software.

It is also remarkable how considerate this company is in regard to the abuse of this awesome product. Its licensing agreement stipulates, "... in no event shall the PhoneDISC Software and Databases be used to create original lists for use in connection with marketing application, including without limitation, sales prospecting, telemarketing, and direct mail." How libraries (the primary target market) can enforce this policy is a major issue when telemarketing agents and aggressive fundraisers invade the libraries' CD-ROM workstations to download or print names, addresses, and telephone numbers for free. It took me three to four minutes to search and download this information for people living in the Beverly Hills area. You can imagine how valuable this data could be for someone looking for affluent donors. Interestingly, I found the correct, unlisted phone number of a friend that I changed in the sample output for privacy reasons (figure 4.21).

California w/Cross Indexes SPRING		1991	
Enter City:	Enter Street:	House:	Apt:
BEVERLY HILLS, CA	TOWER RD		
BEVERLY HILLS, CA	TOWER RD	1109	
BEVERLY HILLS, CA	TOWER RD	1112	
BEVERLY HILLS, CA	TOWER RD	1113	
BEVERLY HILLS, CA	TOWER RD	1117	
BEVERLY HILLS, CA	TOWER RD	1118	
BEVERLY HILLS, CA	TOWER RD	1121	
BEVERLY HILLS, CA	TOWER RD	1122	
BEVERLY HILLS, CA	TOWER RD	1124	
BEVERLY HILLS, CA	TOWER RD	1125	
BEVERLY HILLS, CA	TOWER RD	1129	
BEVERLY HILLS, CA	TOWER RD	1130	
		1131	
VARI, ALEXANDER		1133	
1117 TOWER RD		1135	
BEVERLY HILLS, CA 90210		1136	
		1140	
* Not from Phone Co. *		1143	
		1144	
213-274-5067	* Residence *	1150	

F1 - Help F4 - ChgIndex F5 - Dial F6 - Region F8 - Print ↓- Next ↑- Prev

Fig. 4.21. Sample search from PhoneDISC USA.

The Supreme Court's unanimous decision in March 1991 (Feist vs. Rand Telephone Services Co.) opened the floodgate for CD-ROM phone directories. They ruled that the printed residential phone directories are not protected by copyright. To put this issue in perspective, until this ruling NYNEX charged $10,000 for a white-page directory on CD-ROM for residential listings in the New York and New England areas only. PhoneDISC USA has set an exemplary model; there will certainly be companies that do not limit the use of the database in the hope of making a fast buck.

Multimedia and timeliness will be the other mass-appeal features in the near future. *Time* magazine and Warner News Media released the Desert Storm database a few weeks after the

Persian Gulf war ended for $39.95. It includes 6,000 screens of information ("record" is not an appropriate unit of measurement in such a database): original dispatches of *Time* correspondents, pool reports, audio recordings, photographs, graphics, and articles from the magazine. We will not have long to wait for the transcripts, photos, video excerpts, and soundbytes of Ted Koppel's "Nightline" programs on CD-ROM either in chronological or thematical collections. Imagine a medley of all the programs about the invasion of Kuwait or the savings and loan scandal for $29.99.

There will be CD-ROM versions of books that cry out for live action, such as "How Things Work" or many of the how-to manuals on car repair or home maintenance. Many public libraries that could not afford CD-ROM technology will be able to acquire CD-ROM versions of hard-to-handle-and-store publications and new products. Imagine the CD-ROM versions of the 20-pound *Motel and Hotel Guide* instantaneously searchable by city, zip code, area code, price range, and facilities or a CD-ROM collection of complaints filed with all the Better Business Bureaus in the United States and you imagine the public library of the future.

REFERENCES

1. John Brockmann. *Writing Better Computer User Documentation*. New York: John Wiley and Sons, 1986.

2. Jonathan Price. *How to Write a Computer Manual: A Handbook of Software Documentation*. Menlo Park, CA: Benjamin/Cummings Publishing Company, 1984.

3. Susan J. Grimm. *How to Write Computer Documentation for Users*. 2nd ed. New York: Van Nostrand Reinhold Company, Inc., 1987.

4. Nancy Wood. "Evaluating Vendor Documentation." *Library Hi-Tech* 28 (July-August 1989): 49-59.

5. Carol Tenopir and Gerald Lundeen. *Managing Your Information*. New York: Neal-Schuman, 1988.

6. Daniel Uchitella. "We Stand Corrected" (letter to the editor). *CD-ROM Professional* 3 (November 1990): 5.

7. Péter Jacsó. "Directory of Library and Information Professionals on CD-ROM." *Laserdisk Professional* 2 (July 1989): 63-73.

8. Karl Beiser. "Why Do CD-ROM Installations Fail?" *CD-ROM EndUser* 1 (February 1990): 17-19.

9. Péter Jacsó. "Singing the CD-ROM Installation Blues." *Electronic Library* 7 (May 1989): 150-52.

10. Stephen Arnold. "CD-ROM Pricing: Bound Down." *Laserdisk Professional* 2 (March 1989): 19-23.

11. Paul Nicholls. *CD-ROM Collection Builder's Toolkit*. Weston, CT: Pemberton Press, 1990.

5

CD-ROM HARDWARE EVALUATION

There are at least a dozen brands and about 50 models of CD-ROM drives currently available on the market. These are often referred to as first-, second-, and third-generation drives, but this classification is far from standard and is more of a marketing tool.

There are indeed many differences between these drives, but there are no criteria by which a product could be unambiguously classified into one of these categories. Differences show up in performance, design, and special features, but may not be as important as the term *generation* can imply. A third-generation CD-ROM drive with 450 milliseconds access time will not necessarily provide twice as fast response time as a first-generation drive with 800 to 900 milliseconds access time.

Much more important may be other factors like the structure of the index file, the free RAM available when a CD-ROM application is run, or the speed of the hard disk and the CPU. These factors are discussed in chapter 6.

The CD-ROM drive itself can be evaluated by the following criteria:

- physical dimension, format, and design
- interface type
- speed

- reliability
- special features
- price

You may wish to use a checklist to evaluate the drives. Appendix 4 presents a possible hardware evaluation form. On this form you might enter yes or no answers and actual performance measures because the criteria are not as complex as with the CD-ROM software, dataware, and database evaluation. The best way to learn about the capabilities of CD-ROM drives is to read at least one of the CD-ROM magazines. Not only do the news items contain important announcements about new hardware, but also there are reviews about the hardware market offerings.[1,2]

PHYSICAL DIMENSION, FORMAT, AND DESIGN

The differences in the physical dimension, format, and design of a CD-ROM drive are quite obvious at first sight. The first commercially available CD-ROM drive, the CM100 from Philips, weighed 11 pounds and measured 12.6 by 4.6 by 10.5 inches. The weight of the currently smallest CD-ROM drive, the NEC CDR-35, is 2.2 pounds and you can hold it in your palm, as shown in figure 5.1.

Fig. 5.1. The NEC CDR-35. (Courtesy of NEC.)

There are more important physical characteristics of CD-ROM drives than their dimension or weight. These are whether a device is:

- front-loading versus top-loading
- external versus internal
- full-height versus half-height
- single versus multiple drive

Only the very first CD-ROM drives were top-loading models. Pioneers seem not to have learned the lesson of the past, that top-loading VCRs for home entertainment were far less popular than front-loading ones. The latter type of CD-ROM drives have the advantage of allowing you to sandwich them in between the base unit and the monitor to spare desk space or to keep things such as manuals on top of them.

The only difference between the external and internal devices is that the former have a case, their own power supply, and cables to the PC and to the wall outlet. The internal drives take their power from the base unit and do not need their own power supply or case. The internal drive seems to be more advantageous, as it takes no extra room and may cost 20 percent less than the external one. Its major disadvantage is that if it fails you have to disassemble the PC to remove the CD-ROM from its device bay to send it for repair. In addition, you may prefer the internal drive but may not have an appropriate bay in your PC to house it and therefore have to opt for the external one.

CD-ROM devices may be also classified by their height. There are full-height (3.25-inch) and half-height (1.6-inch) CD-ROM drives. Most current drives are half-height. Most PCs offer at least one half-height bay that may accommodate such an internal model. Full-height devices are not worthwhile to put in the PC because they may take away the room from three third-height floppy drives.

If an external device malfunctions and you have another, similar configuration, you may just unplug the CD-ROM drive from its current workstation and plug it into the other system for basic testing. If you do not have a twin configuration then you need also to remove the controller card and install it in another PC.

A CD-ROM drive may be a stand-alone unit or a multiple device. Philips first offered a dual drive back in mid-1988, but it was a slow sell. Dual, triple, and quadruple drives currently are gaining some momentum. They cost less than the equivalent number of individual units but carry the threat that if something goes wrong in the common circuitry then all the modules become unaccessible. On the other hand, such units require only a single interface slot for the controller. There are two alternatives that may be appropriate.

The jukebox CD-ROM drive was introduced by Pioneer as the Disc Changer. It is not a multidrive system, but works like a music jukebox. It stores six CD-ROM disks on six disk trays, obviating the need to change disks but working with one at a time. It may have the same problem mentioned above, which may prevent all six CDs from being accessed, but at much less cost.

Another alternative is represented by the daisy-chaining of CD-ROM drives as illustrated by figure 5.2. Note that only the first CD-ROM is attached to the PC directly and all the others are plugged in to the rear of the previous CD-ROM drive. You need only one interface card and one free slot in your PC. A maximum of seven drives may be daisy-chained this way, but only a few brands offer such an option.

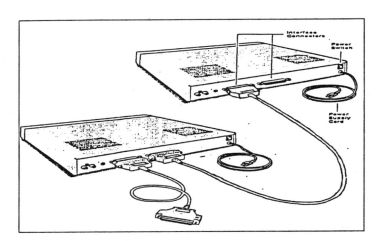

Fig. 5.2. Daisy-chained CD-ROM drives.

The most important criteria may be the brand of the CD-ROM drive. CD-ROM applications support a well-defined set of CD-ROM drives, and often special programs (device drivers) provided with the database are closely related to the physical characteristics of the CD-ROM drive. Though most CD-ROM software can handle any CD-ROM drive that adheres to the international standards, publishers prefer to be on the safe side and list those brands with which they have tested their application. If yours is not among the tested brands you may have a difficult time.

No matter how much more attractive you may find, for example, the Sony brand to the Hitachi, the latter is supported by every CD-ROM application without exception. If you plan to use Bibliofile then the only supported model is Hitachi (and its brand namesake, the Amdek). The reason for this is that the Bibliofile software directly controls the device rather than operating through standard device drivers, which means Toshiba, Denon, Chinon, and JVC models may or may not work. Usually CD-ROM publishers guarantee compatibility only with a few brands and models. More information about the vagaries of the application software and the CD-ROM drives is in chapter 6.

INTERFACE CARD

CD-ROM drives need an interface card, which connects them to the internal bus (pathway) of the PC. The interface card is also called a controller card because it controls the operation of the drive. There are three major characteristics of interface cards:

- type of bus architecture
- size
- transfer width

The three major interface cards are the ISA (Industry Standard Architecture), the MCA (Micro-Channel Architecture), and the SCSI (Small Computer Standard Interface) types. The interface card you buy must match the architecture of your PC. The architecture of your computer may be MCA, ISA, or EISA (Extended Industry Standard Architecture).

All of these may accommodate an SCSI interface card, which is practically an adapter. An ISA interface card will fit into the slot of an ISA or EISA PC, whereas the MCA interface only fits into the slot of a personal computer with the MCA architecture. At present there is no EISA-type CD-ROM interface card, but it certainly will hit the market by the end of 1991. The most important difference between these interface cards is the data transfer speed.

The ISA interface card is the standard interface card for the IBM PC and compatibles, and MCA is the bus architecture of the high-end IBM PS/2 computers and compatibles. Confusingly enough, the low models of the PS/2 family have the ISA bus architecture, yet the MCA interface cards are often advertised and referred to as the PS/2 interface. This is a dangerously imprecise and widely used specification. If you have a PS/2 Model 25 or Model 30 computer and you receive a CD-ROM drive with the PS/2 interface card, it simply will not fit. You need an ISA (also known as the PC XT/AT) interface card.

Quite often you must select a CD-ROM drive by its interface card. While almost every CD-ROM drive has an ISA interface card, only a few have alternatively, and typically for about a hundred dollars more, an MCA interface card. If you have a computer with MCA bus architecture your choices are limited.

The size of the interface card may be full-length or half-length. This is relevant only if you already have a crowded motherboard with lots of interface cards and internal ribbon cables and wires. Otherwise the size of the card does not matter. Most of the cards sold with second- and third-generation CD-ROM drives are the half-length type.

The width of the interface card may be 8-bit, 16-bit, or 32-bit. An ISA interface card may be either 8- or 16-bit, whereas the EISA and MCA interface cards are 32-bit. While the bus architecture of your personal computer defines whether you need an ISA or an MCA interface card, with ISA you also have to know what type of slot is available in your PC. The slots where the interface card will be inserted may be 8- or 16-bit. You may use an 8-bit card in a 16-bit slot, but not vice versa. Most CD-ROM interface cards are the 8-bit type. Data transfer on an 8-bit bus is slower than on a 16-bit or 32-bit bus, but it is not the only factor that affects the overall response time of a CD-ROM application.

If you are absolutely out of space in your PC and cannot accommodate an interface card, there is a solution. A few CD-ROM drives may be connected through the serial port. Every PC has one or two serial ports for devices like modems, mice, and, rarely, printers. If one port is free you may attach a Philips (Laser Magnetic Storage) CM221 or a special version of the NEC CDR-35 through that serial port. This is only a last resort, however, because the transfer rate is dramatically slower than through an interface card.

The daisy-chained drives and the SCSI interface offer a good alternative for those who would like to have more CD-ROM drives attached to their PC. With daisy-chaining you may use one interface card to operate up to four CD-ROM drives of identical brand and model connected to each other. Only the first drive is attached to the PC, and the others are plugged in at the back of the previous drive.

The SCSI interface solution goes one step further because it allows you to use a single interface (and take up a single slot only) but still control seven SCSI-devices. Be careful, because there are two versions of SCSI standards, and implementations of the standard may differ from company to company. If you attempt to share an SCSI interface among devices of different manufacturers you may be in trouble. However, if you have, for example, a NEC printer, a NEC CD-ROM drive, a NEC scanner, and a NEC tape backup system, they are very likely to work from one SCSI card. The SCSI interface is not really a controller but rather an adapter. The control functions are built into the peripheral devices, and the adapter merely provides the interface between your system's bus and each peripheral device.

SPEED

Speed is the most often mentioned characteristics of a CD-ROM drive, and it is often over-rated by users and vendors alike. There are different measures of speed but the most often cited is the average access time. The access time range of CD-ROM drives is between 350 milliseconds and 1,500 milliseconds. To put this into perspective, the average access time of the hard disks available today ranges between 16 and 50 milliseconds and that of the floppy disks is around 120 milliseconds.

CD-ROM drives belong to the group of slow peripherals in the computer world, but their slowness is not as bad as it may seem from the naked numbers above. It is not the speed of the individual components that should interest you, but the performance of the product on your workstation. You may have a lightning fast Hitachi CDR-1700S CD-ROM drive with 350-millisecond access time, but it would not make miracles on a PC with a 4.77 megahertz processor and a 70-millisecond hard disk. To retrieve and display a set of records requires interaction among these components. In a search much of the system time is spent by sorting and comparing record identifiers retrieved from the CD-ROM. This process can be accelerated by a faster hard disk and processor. The access time of the CD-ROM drive comes into play when the records themselves are to be transferred for display.

The structure of the index to the master file, the free hard disk, and RAM capacity may be much more important factors than the speed of the CD-ROM drive. If you run the UMI data-bases with 580 kilobytes of free RAM versus the bare minimum of 450 kilobytes, you will see the difference in response time much more markedly than by replacing your second-generation CD-ROM drive with a faster one. If you can assign a fairly large RAM disk for a SilverPlatter database as a spill-device to store temporary results, it is much more relevant than a 100-millisecond difference in the speed of the CD-ROM drive.

The transfer rate is another speed characteristic of CD-ROM drives. This is the number of bytes transferred per second. CD-ROM drives transfer data at 150 kilobytes per second. Again, to put this into perspective, the transfer rate of an average hard disk is around 600 to 800 kilobytes per second, while that of floppy and tape drives is 60 to 70 and 250 to 300 kilobytes per second respectively. The speed of getting data into memory depends on both the average access time and the transfer rate.

Good layout of the index and the capabilities of the software may have more significant impact on performance than drive speed does. Good indexing and access optimization makes the same search on the same workstation with the same CD-ROM drive much faster in the Dialog OnDisc version of ERIC than in the SPIRS or OCLC versions.

The so-called caching technique may markedly improve the response time as perceived by the user. There are different types of caching techniques. An increasing number of CD-ROM drives come with buffers of 8 to 64 kilobytes of cache memory. This has a much shorter access time than the CD-ROM disk; therefore, if the directory of the disk or part of the index can be stored in this cache memory, the retrieval will be much faster.

The technique used with the EBSCO-CD software is (hard) disk-caching. Whenever data is to be read from the CD-ROM the software fetches more than the user requested. When you ask to display the results of a search EBSCO-CD displays 10 records on the screen but continues to read the CD-ROM and put these records in a temporary file on the hard disk while you are looking at the displayed records, when the system otherwise would have been idle. When you want to look at the next 10 records they are immediately displayed because they were fetched while you were reading the screen. This may explain why you see the hard disk light blinking and hear the hard disk spinning when nothing is changing on the screen. The lack of this technique makes RGA and RES-1 slower in fetching the next group of records.

The negative side of this clever and unadvertised technique is that the software forgets to delete this temporary file when logging out, even though it displays the message "Cleaning up files." This file may be two to three megabytes and may fill up your hard disk to the extent that the next program that requires some free hard disk space will not find any and will abort. In the worst case the program will find enough space to start but will die in the middle of a search, which makes error detection even more difficult.

RELIABILITY

One of the most well known characteristics of CD-ROM technology is the robustness of the medium. But it applies more to the CD-ROM disks than to the drives. In spite of the laser technology the drives still have a number of mechanical components that may malfunction. Even if this happens there are fewer chances for any lasting damage than in the case of hard disk failure, where your data may be lost.

A very common error is caused by the dust or grease from your fingers getting onto the disk and then onto the laser lens and causing read errors. Using traditional CD cleaning gadgets usually solves such a problem. For those who have a serious dust problem with their CD-ROM drive, Karl Beiser describes in detail the steps needed for a "dustectomy."[3]

The most common error on hard disks is caused by the read-write heads crashing, i.e., falling on the disk surface when there is a power failure. In the CD-ROM drive there is nothing to cause similar destruction. On the other hand, it is much more likely that the few mechanical parts, like the open/close button or the disk transport tray, will get damaged. Using a built-in drive (which has no such transport mechanism) can decrease the chances of such malfunctions.

The likelihood of malfunctioning is expressed in hours as the mean time between failure (MTBF). Most manufacturers claim an MTBF between 10 and 15,000 hours. This is not very informative data for the user, who may not know what failures are counted and how the elapsed time is measured.

More important, if your CD-ROM drive fails two or three times in a row within a month, you could not care less what the mean time is, and you do not get back your money just because the product did not meet the reliability claim of the manufacturer. Nothing can be as reassuring for reliability as the announcement made by LMS International to extend its product warranty to 24 months.[4] (The industry standard is 12 months.) Of course, you should also learn the policy of your vendor for repairing and/or replacing an often malfunctioning device and providing a loaner for the repair period.

CAPACITY

Capacity is another confusing feature in product advertisements and reviews. Screaming headlines about CD-ROM drives with 600 + megabyte capacity typically are just sales pitches. As long as the CD-ROM drive can read the industry standard disk formats, the drive has nothing to do with capacity. It is the disk that has capacity, and it depends on the database to what extent the disk is filled. Books in Print or the (text-only) Grolier Encyclopedia are not less valuable because they fill up only one-third of the capacity of a CD-ROM disk.

To add to the confusion, capacity figures ranging from 540 to 660 megabytes are quoted. All depends on how precisely you calculate the kilobyte (1,000 versus 1,024 bytes) and megabyte (1,000,000 versus 1,048,576 bytes) values and whether you refer to the net capacity or the gross capacity (which includes error correction codes), as illustrated by figure 5.3.

CD-ROM sector content		
User data	2048 bytes	(a.k.a. 2K)
Synchronization data	12 bytes	
Address	4 bytes	
Error correction code	288 bytes	
Gross sector capacity	2352 bytes	
Total sector on a CD	270,000	
Total capacity of a CD		
270,000 * 2K	540,000K	540 Mbytes
270,000 * 2,048	552,960,000	553 Mbytes
270,000 * 2,352	635,040,000	635 Mbytes

Fig. 5.3. CD-ROM capacity differences.

SPECIAL FEATURES

Special features may be important for some applications or for the life expectancy of your drive and, in extreme cases, your media. Special features include the following:

- audio capability
- cartridge loading
- vertical mounting
- automatic lens cleaning
- dual-door facility
- daisy-chaining
- dual voltage
- buffering

Audio capabilities were introduced with the second generation of CD-ROM drives. Originally they were meant to let you use your drive as an audio CD instrument while you were not using it for a CD-ROM application. A standard 3.5mm jack was added to the player for the earphone, along with software that provided the same facilities as the various buttons on your traditional audio CD to set the sequence of the program or to jump back and forth. It was meant purely for audio discs and not for sound information on the CD-ROM products.

Later, however, some CD-ROM applications, like the Intelligent Catalog, the Compton's Encyclopedia, and the CD-Guide, included limited amounts of sound data that necessitated audio capabilities on the CD-ROM drive. The existing audio software was not appropriate because the reading of sound data must be interleaved with text and graphical data, and appropriate markers had to be put on the disk if multimedia was recorded. The standard was expanded to cater to these new features and architecture, and the special software (CD-ROM Extensions, discussed in chapter 6) to handle CD-ROM media was also upgraded.

Originally, the CD-ROM disks were simply tossed into the drive or onto a pop-out tray naked. Many of the second- and third-generation CD-ROM drives require you to "dress up" the disks by putting them in a cartridge. First it was a necessity (as vertically mounted drives needed a cartridge to hold the disk and prevent it from skewing), but it proved to be advantageous for extra protection of the disk surface too, irrespective of vertical or horizontal mounting of the drive.

The scarcity of desk space made many users move the PC from its horizontal position on the desk to a vertical position on the floor. You could not do that with an external CD-ROM drive. The footprint of the device was not wide enough for stability and also the disk could not stay put in the tray. Built-in drives and cartridges helped with this problem, and the currently manufactured internal drives may be installed either horizontally or vertically.

Automatic lens cleaning is a welcome option on some of the CD-ROM drives. A common reason for the dreaded "101 CD-ROM Read Error: Abort, Retry, Fail" message is that there is dirt on the lenses. Though you may buy separate lens cleaning gadgets, it is much better when this is taken care of automatically and systematically. The Hitachi CDR 3650 model, for example, cleans the lenses whenever the disk is ejected.

The same concern for dust protection caused Hitachi to pioneer the introduction of the double-door mechanism on CD-ROM drives. This is the same technique used in hospital operating rooms or in computer rooms to reduce the dust in the environment.

Daisy-chaining of CD-ROM drives is discussed above under the interface card options. Though this is a device feature, your CD-ROM drive must have two connecting ports both for the incoming and the outgoing cables. While daisy-chaining is possible with both internal and external devices, you may have difficulty squeezing all the cables into the casing of your PC, so it is most typically used with external devices.

Dual voltage capacity is important only for those who travel with their CD-ROM drive across countries. Typically, CD-ROM drives have their separate European and U.S. versions, and you cannot use the same device on both sides of the Atlantic due to the different voltage and frequency. It is a rather unique feature of the NEC CDR-72 and CDR-82 drives that they are switchable between 110V and 220V as well as 50 and 60 hertz. Dual voltage is not a problem with built-in drives, which get their power from the PC and operate on 9V to 12V. The PC, of course, must be able to operate on dual voltage and frequency.

Buffering is closely related to the speed issue, but because it is still a special feature it is discussed here. The third-generation CD-ROM drives have a special memory area in the drive to store data temporarily for fast access. The buffer stores the data that was transferred to the memory most recently. In a subsequent read operation this buffer is consulted first to find out if the data needed may be there. This can spare a reading of the disk itself, which is a very slow operation compared to reading the content of the buffer. The larger the buffer size, the more data can be stored. There is no reason to go beyond a certain limit, however, because with an extremely large buffer, reading may take longer than the reading of the appropriate sector of the disk. The buffer sizes range from 8K to 64K or even larger.

PRICE

The price of CD-ROM drives varies significantly even within the same league. Single-drive devices with ISA interface and 800 millisecond access time list for between $600 and $900 even though the capabilities are almost identical. The Pioneer jukebox, that has one read mechanism but can accommodate six disks, lists for around $1,400, and a dual drive lists for about $1,100. The same drive may be bought at a 25 to 30 percent discount depending on where you buy it. You need never pay the manufacturer's recommended list price as bundles, discounts, or sales are always available, as is discussed in chapter 7.

There is usually a $100 difference between the internal drives and the external ones. The extra $100 for the external drives is justified by the cost of the case and the power supply. You will have to pay approximately $100 extra also for the MCA interface. Usually, the price quoted for a CD-ROM drive includes not only the device, but also the interface card, the interface cable, and the power cable. A notable exception is the NEC family of CD-ROM drives, where the charge for any interface card is extra. This is somewhat misleading because an interface card is an essential part of this peripheral device.

The best price/performance ratio is undoubtedly offered by the Tandy CDR-1000 drive (figure 5.4). It is available at a breakthrough street price of $399. Tandy throws in for free not only the usual accessories but also software to convert your CD-ROM drive to an audio CD-player if the mood hits you. Other companies charge you $70 to $80 for such a program alone. The Tandy CDR-1000 is the front-loading, drawer type drive and does not require a caddy. The extensive network of Tandy stores and the competent service (at least in Hawaii) may give potential customers peace of mind when it comes to maintenance.

Fig. 5.4. The Tandy CDR-1000. (Courtesy of the Tandy Corporation.)

Philips also announced a lightweight, powerful CD-ROM player at this price, the CM-50 drive. Both the Tandy and Philips drives feature only 800-millisecond access time, but as discussed earlier access time should not be idolized. Other workstation components and search software may have as significant an impact on response time as the average access time. Many users would rather buy three CM-50 drives than the slightly faster IBM internal drive with a street price of $1,250. For the external version IBM charges $1,550. It will be a slow sell.

FUTURE CD-ROM HARDWARE DEVELOPMENTS

The computer industry keeps producing smaller and more powerful PCs and peripherals at a breathtaking pace and at an ever-decreasing price. Notebook-size computers have now the same capabilities of their desktop cousins three years ago. The CD-ROM hardware industry is no exception. The size and weight of CD-ROM players keep decreasing and the performance keeps increasing. With the Tandy CDR-1000 and the Philips CM-50, the price spell finally seems to be broken. The price tag under $400 will appeal to the mass market. Coupled with such affordable databases as Magazine Rack or the PhoneDISC USA, they will continue to make inroads into the mass market of small business and home users.

CD-ROM will become as common a household peripheral as the mouse that became an overnight success with the proliferation of Windows applications. Built-in CD-ROM players will be part of the typical bundle of desktop computer configurations. Multi-media applications will necessitate CD-ROM technology in order to hold the whopping amount of image and audio files.

Multi-drive tower configurations, or jukeboxes, with one or two reading mechanism(s) and several trays to park the temporarily inactive disks will become increasingly popular. Such hardware makes it convenient to use several CD-ROM databases on the same PC in a consecutive fashion and maintain the necessary security precautions in public areas when changing databases.

CD-ROM players will be faster, but they always will lag behind the speed of hard disks that also keep improving speed and capacity. CD-ROM technology will remain unbeatable for delivering and using permanently stored information.

REFERENCES

1. Gelda Scott. "CD-ROM Drives: What's Available and What to Look for When Buying One." *Laserdisk Professional* 2 (January 1989): 13-19.

2. Edward Fox. "Highlights of CD-ROM Hardware." *Laserdisk Professional* 1 (May 1988): 18-27.

3. Karl Beiser. "A Dustectomy." *CD-ROM EndUser* 1 (December 1989): 66-67.

4. "Laser Magnetic Storage International [announces extended warranty period]." *CD-ROM Librarian* 6 (January 1991): 8.

6

CD-ROM APPLICATION REQUIREMENTS

CD-ROM databases, similar to other computer applications, specify their requirements for system software and hardware resources. Some resources are specified exactly (720K floppy diskette); others are defined in terms of minimum and recommended amount of resources (minimum 512K, recommended 640K RAM). Other resources are specified as alternatives, such as an Epson or HP laser printer. Sometimes the reference is generic, e.g., "requires MSCDEX 2.x," which means that version 2.0, 2.1, or 2.2 would be equally good.

Specifications of resource requirements assume that you are familiar with the computer lingo and the meaning of the acronyms and codes. References to "DOS 3.1 or higher," "EGA monitor or better," or "LaserJet II family" are very common and assume that the user knows that there are DOS 3.4, 4.0, and 5.0, VGA and Super VGA monitors, and LaserJet II, LaserJet IIP, and Laser-Jet IID printers. A further difficulty may arise with compatibles. A piece of hardware may not be compatible per se with another device specified, but you may still be able to emulate it with additional software. The Canon LBP-4 is not compatible with the Hewlett-Packard LaserJet family but you may have an extra software program that makes it look like a LaserJet II family printer for the application program. Compatibility is a murky area, and it is best to double-check to make sure your configuration can run a CD-ROM application or to ensure that you may return the product if it does not run on your workstation.

This chapter is a review of the most typical systems software and hardware requirements of CD-ROM databases and an explanation of the implications of such requirements. Networked use of CD-ROM applications implies extra requirements, which are discussed at the end of the chapter.

SYSTEM SOFTWARE REQUIREMENTS

Every CD-ROM product comes with its own retrieval software, but most of them expect a given system environment in which they can operate. In a few cases you get the CD-ROM product lock, stock, and barrel, including all the software and hardware components, but this may not be the best possible deal, as is discussed in chapter 7. This is the case with all the InfoTrac products and with Newsbank. More often you do not get any of the system software components specified as a requirement, but only the application software. This is the case with the Directory of Library and Information Professionals, the Mammals database from National Geographic, and the Frontpage database, among others. Most often you get one or more of the system software components required, and you are offered some others for an extra charge. This is the policy followed by Dialog, Bowker, UMI, and many others, which offer, for example, the MSCDEX software for an extra charge but include the specific device driver programs (discussed below). The commonly needed system software includes the following:

- operating system
- Microsoft CD-ROM Extensions
- device drivers

The application software is always provided by the database publisher. It may include not only the search program itself but also database-specific program and parameter files and utility programs.

Operating System

The operating system is the piece of software that controls the operation of programs, their interaction with peripherals, their use of the processor, and the memory. An operating system is not a special requirement of a CD-ROM application. All programs require an operating system; you cannot use a computer without it. You usually get (or buy for some extra charge) an operating system when you purchase a microcomputer. The CD-ROM applications are special only in regard to the version of the operating system.

Though there are several alternatives of operating systems (DOS, OS/2, UNIX, XENIX), the overwhelming majority of CD-ROM applications require DOS (disk operating system). Here a distinction may be needed. There are two incarnations of DOS: MS-DOS and PC-DOS. Either will do. The differences between MS-DOS and PC-DOS are typically irrelevant for end users. Legally you can have PC-DOS only with true blue IBM computers. All the compatibles use MS-DOS, as it is the one licensed by any manufacturer of PC-compatible machines. Actually, Microsoft (MS) made some modifications of MS-DOS and licensed it exclusively for IBM, which got it registered with a trademark.

Both MS-DOS and PC-DOS have gone through several major improvements since their initial introduction. These improvements are identified by a number commonly referred to as the version number. The version number is important for CD-ROM applications, and you must understand its implications. The version numbers consist of two parts separated by a decimal point (DOS 2.1, 3.2, 4.0). The number before the decimal point identifies major changes and the number after the decimal point (often called the release number) refers to minor, though for CD-ROM users, important changes. Figure 6.1 illustrates the major new features in the different versions of MS-DOS and PC-DOS.

With very few exceptions, all the CD-ROM products meant for the IBM PC and PS/2 families require DOS 3.1 or higher. This means that if you have 3.1, 3.2, 3.3, 4.0, 4.1, or 5.0, you meet the operating system requirement. There is, however, a caveat with DOS 4.x. This long overdue graphical version of the operating system requires so much memory that you may not be able to run some CD-ROM applications. With many CD-ROM applications you will have to reinstall DOS 4.x and get rid of the so-called graphical shell of DOS 4.x (the essence of this version).

Version number	Release date	Major features
1.0	1981	160 K floppy
1.1	1982	320 K floppy
2.0		360 K floppy, 10M hard disk directories, batch commands
3.0	1984	20M hard disk, 1.2 M floppy PATH
3.1	1985	Network support and MSCDEX
3.2	1986	720K floppy, XCOPY, etc.
3.3	1987	1.44 M floppy, FDISK hard disk partitioning (32 M maximum)
4.0	1988	512 M hard disk partition, graphical interface
5.0	1991	windowing, high-loading buffers, TSRs and device drivers, UNFORMAT, UNDELETE

Fig. 6.1. Versions of MS-DOS and PC-DOS.

Your best bet is DOS 3.3, which was released in the spring of 1987 and is an almost completely debugged (error-free) software. It also has many features that make the maintenance of your overall system easier. A few applications may specifically require DOS 3.3 because they use some of these features, like the calling of a batch file (series of commands) from within a batch file.

You will be in a much easier situation if you switch to MS-DOS or PC-DOS version 5.0. It requires significantly less minimum memory than its predecessors and allows the system to use the memory more flexibly. This is important for CD-ROM applications, many of which do not leave any leg-room but for the slimmest DOS, as is discussed in chapter 8.

Microsoft CD-ROM Extensions (MSCDEX.EXE)

The appearance of CD-ROM databases brought along a special problem. One of the advantages of the CD-ROM medium is the whopping storage capacity. DOS, however, could not handle files larger than 32 megabytes (until version 4.0), and all the CD-ROM databases have files much larger than that. Furthermore, the mapping of addresses on CD-ROM was different from that used on magnetic disks (both floppy and hard disks), and DOS could not handle that either.

CD-ROM publishers were quick to write special programs (file managers) to overcome these problems. They also provided patches (modifications) to DOS. Of course, this was an extra burden, because application programs do not have to deal with the physical level of reading data from disks. They just issue a read file-name command and the operating system takes care of finding the file and fetching the data. Not so with CD-ROM files, for which the software had to bypass DOS and do the read operations itself.

Microsoft was working on a special program that would solve this problem independently from the actual layout of data on CD-ROM. This required the standardization of certain procedures and conventions, like the format and content of the file directory on the CD. This was accomplished first by the High Sierra standard and then with its slight modification by the International Standard Organization's standard, whose identifier is 9660.

The special programs written by Microsoft extended the capabilities of DOS to handle the CD-ROM medium, hence the name Microsoft CD-ROM Extensions, or MSCDEX.EXE after the name of the computer program. It was quite obvious that Microsoft would incorporate these extensions in the next edition of DOS as standard facilities. This did not happen with DOS 3.3 or with the release of DOS 4.x. Five to seven years after the release of the first CD-ROM product, Microsoft CD-ROM Extensions are still just that—extensions, rather than built-in features of DOS. This causes a lot of headaches in installing CD-ROM products (discussed in chapter 8) because the user has to deal with and occasionally tame yet another program.

End users had a difficult time getting MSCDEX until the late 1980s because Microsoft did not sell it to end users. Instead, the company licensed it for manufacturers of CD-ROM drives and database publishers for a rather steep up-front fee. They could then bundle MSCDEX with their products for free or for a fee. Many still refused to do so and kept using their own file managers and DOS patches. This was a good solution for the end user, but too often the database publishers were under the belief that users would have MSCDEX from the hardware manufacturer, who in turn thought the same about database publishers, and gave up on maintaining their file managers and DOS patches.[1] SilverPlatter, Bowker, and Gaylord stood fast the longest and did not require that you buy and install another software before installing the CD-ROM database.

Now, only very few products do not require MSCDEX. Bibliofile is one of the holdouts. The only limitations of this policy are that you can run Bibliofile only on Hitachi (and Amdek) CD-ROM drives. This is not too much of a constraint for those investing in a new CD-ROM drive, as these two brands are among the top five in terms of price/performance.

If neither the hardware manufacturer nor the database publisher offered MSCDEX and the product required it, the end user had only one choice: chase down third-party software developers. In the past few years with the consolidation of CD-ROM technology, the MSCDEX software is much more readily available from database publishers and device manufacturers for free or for $25 to $30.

MSCDEX, like most other software, went through changes and has different versions, as discussed in chapter 8. The differences are important. If you do not have the appropriate version you may not be able to run an application. To run any Dialog OnDisc database you must have version 2.0 or higher. To use a CD-ROM database in the DOS 4.x environment you must have version 2.1 or higher. Similar to DOS, the higher numbered versions are backward compatible.

If you receive an MSCDEX software program from the manufacturer of the drive or from the database publisher you may not receive the most recent version. The drive and the MSCDEX software may have been sitting on the dealer's shelf for a long time. An Amdek Laserdek 2000 drive bought in the summer of 1989 still came (free) with MSCDEX 1.0 even though MSCDEX was upgraded in the fall of 1988; of course, this version did not work with the OnDisc ERIC database formatted according to the ISO 9660 standard.

Device Drivers

Device drivers are special programs to control peripheral devices that are not taken care of by DOS. By definition these are device-dependent. Device drivers are nothing new; DOS has built-in routines only for the mainstream peripherals (floppy and hard disks and keyboards, for example). There are device drivers for scanners, mice, ultra-high resolution monitors, and CD-ROM drives. Device drivers are typically provided by the device manufacturers, though software publishers also distribute device drivers with their programs. CD-ROM publishers distribute their own device drivers, too, and this may lead to confusion.

Device drivers have names like PHILIPS.COM, HITACHIA.SYS, and HITACHI.COM. Once loaded they remain in memory until you turn off the system and the contents of RAM are lost. You must load these (through the CONFIG.SYS file) when you boot up the system. You will face, however, the dilemma of which device driver to use—the one received from the manufacturer of the CD-ROM drive or the one sent by the manufacturer? It would be naive to believe that they are the same. In some cases the database publisher may decide for you. SilverPlatter, for example, specifically warns you not to use the device drivers received with your equipment.

One is tempted to think that device drivers are device-dependent and not database-dependent. With a single database you may have luck if you replace your original device driver program by the one received from the database publisher. But what about running several applications on the same PC? Should you reboot your system before changing to another database and include in the CONFIG.SYS file the device driver received from that other database publisher? Hardly acceptable, again. There is no universally valid, good answer to this question. Chapter 8 provides more ideas to solve this dilemma. Suffice it to say here that receiving a device driver with your database is not necessarily a pleasant gift.

CD-ROM Software

You always receive some software as part of your CD-ROM subscription or purchase. It is not necessarily a single program, but often is a suite of programs that provide different functions. Some of them are used only once when installing the program, others are used occasionally to change the parameters of the application or test the drive and the disk, and some are used every time you want to search the database.

The retrieval program, also known as the search software or search engine, is the flagship in the suite of programs. It is the power of this program that is considered by many as the most important component in judging the capabilities of a CD-ROM package. It can be evaluated by many of the criteria discussed in chapter 2.

Database-specific Installation Files

Many CD-ROM publishers offer several datafiles with basically the same software. SilverPlatter and Wilson have the largest number of CD-ROM products, followed by OCLC, Dialog, IAC, UMI, Cambridge Scientific Abstracts, CMC, Lotus, Bowker, and EBSCO. If you subscribe to more than one database of the same publisher the question arises if there is any additional software for the individual databases.

In a few cases you have to install the CD-ROM software only once and it will automatically recognize and handle any database of the family. This applies to the Wilson family. Once you install the Wilsondisc software you may use any Wilson CD-ROM product without any further installation. The same applies to the Dialog family of CD-ROM databases. For most other applications you must also install database-specific control and parameter files. ProQuest, CMC ReSearch, and Compact Cambridge belong to this category. Once you install the ProQuest software of UMI you have to install the database-specific control files of Newspaper Abstracts, Periodical Abstracts, Dissertation Abstracts, and so on. You will have a separate diskette with the database-specific files for all the databases you subscribe to. SilverPlatter also has database-specific installation files, but all of them are on a single diskette. OCLC has database-specific files, but they are delivered on the CD-ROM along with the other software components of the database.

The mode of delivery and the procedures are different, but the essence is the same. With most CD-ROM products from multiple-database publishers you must install database-specific control and parameter files before using a database. As opposed to installing the retrieval software, the installation of the database-specific files usually does not cause any conflict in the established environment. You may, however, face some of the other installation problems discussed in chapter 8.

HARDWARE REQUIREMENTS

The hardware requirements of CD-ROM applications may be quite mundane or sophisticated. What is mundane for a recently purchased personal computer may, of course, be extravagant for a PC you have been using for six to eight years. Often you will have to upgrade your old PC to run certain CD-ROM applications. The adage "more is better" applies to most of the hardware resources requirements, though you may be able to use some CD-ROM applications with less powerful computers at a lower performance. Usually, CD-ROM publishers specify a minimum requirement for hardware components and it does no harm to have a faster, larger, or more powerful component than the minimum specified. The parameters for the following hardware resources are most typically specified:

- random access memory
- floppy disk
- hard disk
- monitor
- CD-ROM drive
- special hardware components

Bill Gates, the CEO of Microsoft, suggested the configuration shown in figure 6.2 as the minimum requirements for CD-ROM applications at the Fifth CD-ROM Conference.[2] Many who consider him to be the godfather of CD-ROM applications may interpret his words as endorsing the 80286 processor as the ideal one for CD-ROM databases. Gates, however, who called these processors "brain-damaged" a short time ago, may not have changed his mind so fast.[3]

CPU	286 processor at least 10 Mhz
RAM	At least 2 Mbytes
Video	VGA
Hard Disk	At least 30 Mbytes
CD-ROM	1 sec access times or faster
System software	DOS, Windows multimedia extensions
Price	Below $2,000

Fig. 6.2. Bill Gates' recommended minimum configuration for CD-ROM computers.

Processor

Though currently there are no minimum requirements by CD-ROM databases for the processor, it is worth discussing. As of now, any processor used in IBM or compatible personal computers would work with CD-ROM databases. Even the simplest Intel 8088 or NEC V-20 processors used in the first IBM PCs and compatibles would suffice. It is likely, however, that there will be applications in the very near future that will require the more powerful Intel 80286 or even 80386 processors. If you are buying a PC for CD-ROM applications (or for any applications) it is definitely worthwhile to invest in a 80386SX processor, which provides the memory-handling capability of the real 80386 processors (often referred to as 80386DX) at the price of the much more limited 80286 processor.

Neither is the speed of the processor specified by any CD-ROM applications as yet, but you have to know that the speed of the processor has a bearing on the overall performance of the application. The faster your processor is, the quicker certain operations will be. Such operations that are processor-intensive (rather than input-output intensive) include Boolean operations and the sort functions. The speed of the processor may range from the venerable 4.77 megahertz of the original IBM PC to the 33 megahertz screamers of the latest personal computers.

Random Access Memory (RAM)

The majority of CD-ROM publications require the user to have a PC with a minimum of 512K RAM, and 640K capacity is strongly recommended. Unfortunately, the specification is often obscure or incorrect, which may confuse the user. All CD-ROM publishers should specify the *free* RAM capacity needed to run their products. Such claims as the Compton's Encyclopedia requires 640K RAM is absurd because in every PC a minimum of 50K to 60K is taken by the operating system, reducing the net capacity to 580K to 590K at best. This implies that no application should require more than that free capacity and should specify its requirements accordingly.

MSCDEX, which is required now for most of the CD-ROM applications takes away an additional chunk of nearly 30K of RAM. You may wish to use some minuscule but very powerful programs that are to stay resident in the memory. These are called terminate-and-stay-resident (TSR) programs and include such gems as a virus-detection program and a screen capture software and may not need more than a few kilobytes of RAM. This accentuates the need for clear and unambiguous specification for RAM requirements of CD-ROM applications. Without this information you will have to experiment with different program mix and system configuration parameters (see chapter 8) to find out what are the tolerable minimum RAM requirements for your applications.

You will be surprised to see how many CD-ROM applications can survive in much less free RAM than the stated minimum requirement. Dialog could run without any apparent glitches in less than 300K free RAM, though the documentation recommends 640K (gross) capacity and requires 512K as a minimum. In certain cases there might be performance degradation when you have less RAM than the required minimum, but you may rather tolerate an occasional higher response time than take off your favorite TSR program. The penalty of too much RAM withdrawal would be an eventual crash of the system when your search results in an extremely large set that indeed would need the specified minimum.

In the group of sample databases, SilverPlatter was very tolerant in case of RAM crams. LISA could be used without any problem in less than 350K of free RAM. UMI was flexible, too. As the free RAM area was decreased below 580K ProQuest allocated temporary storage areas on the hard disk instead of the RAM, and the response time perceivably increased, but the system could survive with 570K of RAM. Wilson could survive—due to its recent "weight loss" upgrade—in less than 520K. MAS insisted on having its 580K as documented in the user guide, and the issue was not negotiable. The DLIP database also insisted on its claimed RAM territory.

Penny-pinching on RAM is not a good idea if you buy a new PC or upgrade an old one. Now that 1 megabyte of RAM costs less than $100, it is worthwhile to have a system with 2-megabyte RAM capacity. Many memory management software programs may relocate certain system programs (such as MSCDEX and device drivers) from the conventional memory, to leave room for the application programs, including CD-ROM retrieval software.

The conventional memory is the first 640K in RAM, and it is of critical importance because many programs cannot recognize memory beyond this boundary and must fit into conventional RAM. Dialog OnDisc was the first CD-ROM application that could directly make use of non-conventional RAM. Many CD-ROM applications will run faster if more free conventional RAM is available simply because they can do, for example, in-memory sort operations in less time if there is more space.

The memory allocation patterns before and after relocating some system programs are illustrated by figures 6.3 and 6.4. Using the Optimize program module of the QRAM software of Quarterdeck, nearly 100K of conventional RAM could be released for application programs by moving MSCDEX, device drivers, and file handlers into extended memory. DOS 5.x is able to do the same trick.

Fig. 6.3. Memory usage before program relocation.

Fig. 6.4. Memory usage after program relocation.

Left screen — Quarterdeck MANIFEST

Menu: System · First Meg · Expanded · Extended · DOS · Hints · Exit
Tabs: Overview Programs Interrupts BIOS Data Timings

Memory Area	Size	Description
0D9F - 0DAB	0.2K	[Available]
0DAC - 0DB2	0.1K	LOADHI
0DB3 - 0F3D	6.2K	SHARE
0F3E - 10A2	5.6K	COMMAND
10A3 - 10E3	1K	COMMAND Environment
10E4 - 10F6	0.3K	LOADRPM Environment
10F7 - 1237	5K	LOADRPM
1238 - 9FFF	567K	[Available]
=== Conventional memory ends at 640K ======		
B000 - B026	0.6K	QRAM
B027 - B035	0.2K	AGMOUSE Environment
B036 - B5E1	22K	MSCDEX
B5E2 - B77B	6.4K	AGMOUSE
B77C - B7FE	2K	[Available]
CC00 - CF17	12K	HITACHIA
CF18 - D030	4.4K	ANSI

F1=Help F2=Print

Right screen — Quarterdeck MANIFEST

Menu: System · First Meg · Expanded · Extended · DOS · Hints · Exit
Tabs: Overview Drivers Files Environment

DOS version 4.00
Kernel: 44K
Drivers: 3.4K
Base Data: 4.4K
Added Data: 0.9K
Total: 53K
FILES=40
FCBS=16,8
BUFFERS=2
LASTDRIVE=K
STACKS=0,0

Memory Area	Size	Description
0070 - 02C6	9.4K	IO
02C7 - 0BAB	35K	MSDOS
0BAC - 0C87	3.4K	Drivers
0C88 - 0D0A	2K	35 FILES
0D0B - 0D1B	0.3K	DOS Data
0D1C - 0D60	1.1K	2 BUFFERS
0D61 - 0D9E	1K	Drive List
====Base data ends at 54K=====		
0F02 - 0F3D	0.9K	16 FCBS

F1=Help F2=Print

Hard Disk

Fewer and fewer CD-ROM applications do not require a hard disk. The space is necessary not only to store the CD-ROM software and its related files, but also to store temporary results that are often transparent, that is, invisible to the users.

Though SilverPlatter databases and a few other databases could still be used on a dual-floppy system, it is extremely inconvenient not to be able to store the programs and the auxiliary files on hard disk, and it is painfully slow to transfer temporary sets to and from floppy diskettes.

CD-ROM applications do not always require their stated minimum hard disk capacity. It depends on the nature of the search. The more space you have on the hard disk, the better are the chances for improved performances. Even those applications that do not install the software on hard disk but run from the CD-ROM may require hard disk space. The Computer Library, for example, is not installed on the hard drive, but requires 500K for temporary results for the work files.

Few applications require more than 2 to 3 megabytes, but there might be exceptional cases. The Collection Analysis CD-ROM product of OCLC/AMIGOS may require a whopping hard disk space due to its unique function. The CD-ROM includes the bibliographic records of well over a hundred academic and research libraries. Users get the bibliographic records of their own collection, however, also on floppy diskettes: the combination of the standard CD-ROM file and the floppy files make up your customized CD-ROM application. In the case of the University of Hawaii Library this floppy-distributed file was 8 megabytes, but a larger library may wind up with a 15- to 20-megabyte file that must be stored on the hard disk.

In some applications you may save considerable space on the hard disk by omitting the installation of optional files, such as tutorial programs. For example, in the case of CD-ROM databases for technical services, which are used by professional or para-professional librarians instead of the public, such a cut-back is feasible. You may save 2 to 3 megabytes if you do not install, or remove after a training time, the tutorial files of the CAT CD450 cataloging support products of OCLC.

Floppy Disk

Floppy disks are mostly needed in CD-ROM applications to distribute the CD-ROM software and database-specific control and parameter files and for downloading search results. The requirements go only as far as to be able to receive the above mentioned distribution files. The best publishers provide these files on both formats (3.5-inch and 5.25-inch) or give you the option to specify which one you require.

Video Monitor and Controller

Until the late 1980s almost all the CD-ROM applications were purely textual databases. The only ones that required graphics monitors and controllers were those that used special characters not available in the extended IBM character set and required an alternative set of graphics symbols for diacritics and special characters used, such as in the ALA character set of the Library of Congress records. The Supercat database from Gaylord is such an example, but even that offered the Hercules video controller and graphic monitor as an option rather than a requirement. Another exception was the Supermap database, which could not be run on anything less than a monitor and a controller card of EGA (enhanced graphics adapter) quality.

From the late 1980s, more and more CD-ROM products included real graphics and images, and you may need graphics display capabilities on your PC to use a product. Though technically the minimum graphics capability, the color graphics adapter (CGA) with a graphic monitor, may suffice, it is the worst possible solution. Their mediocre text quality is appalling, and their color and graphics abilities are poor. If an application does not require graphics it is much better to use a monochrome character-based monitor with a similar controller card. The text is much sharper, and it is a far more important criterion than the possible loss of a hypothetical ergonomic advantage offered by color-coding certain data elements. Dialog OnDisc uses different colors to highlight search terms and sentences in the records when used on a color monitor, but it converts these colors into reverse video and underlining, for example, when a monochrome monitor is used. Sometimes the color combination used by a CD-ROM application is so painful to the eye that downgrading it to a monochrome is a better choice when there is no way to control the background and foreground color combinations of a CD-ROM product.

An acceptable compromise is the enhanced graphics adapter (EGA) and the EGA monitor, but it is much better to go for a video graphics array (VGA) monitor and controller either in monochrome or color for some $150 more. Within the VGA category there are different classes, but even the minimum 640 by 480 picture element resolution is far better than a CGA- or EGA-level resolution. The SVGA (Super VGA) monitors have the finest resolution, but they are worth the investment only if you have graphics applications. Figure 6.5 illustrates the resolution features of the various types of monitors.

The resolution is only one of the factors that have an impact on the sharpness of the images and text on the screen, but it is one of the most important ones. The more picture elements (pixels) that can be manipulated, the sharper the image will be. It is comparable to using a sharper pencil to create smaller and more precisely arranged marks for sophisticated drawings, such as engineering blueprints.

Apart from the obvious superiority of the VGA technology, more and more databases define VGA as the minimum requirement. The Birds of America, the Compton's Encyclopedia, and the Mammals database from the National Geographic Society cannot be used without a VGA monitor and controller. The New

Category	Text mode	Character dots	Graphics resolution	Max. colors
MDA	80*25	9*14	-	1
Hercules	80*25	9*14	720*348	2
CGA	40*25	8*8	320*200	4
	80*25	8*8	640*200	2
EGA	80*25	8*14	640*350	16
	80*43	8*8	640*350	16
VGA	80*25	8*16	320*200	256
	80*50	8*8	640*480	16
SVGA	80*25	10*24	800*600	16
			1024*768	16

Fig. 6.5. Graphics and text resolution of monitors.

Grolier Encyclopedia can be used on a PC without VGA facilities, but you cannot display the images. As graphical user interfaces will dominate in the very near future, even the strictly text-only databases may require VGA capability for their software. Icon-filled menus and other graphical interface dingbats or user interfaces running only under the Microsoft Windows shell will be the norm, like it or not, and they require VGA.

There is an important consideration if you are upgrading your present workstation. If you cannot buy the monitor and the controller at the same time, then get the monitor first because a higher powered controller (VGA) may damage a lower rated monitor (EGA). Of course, you also will enjoy the higher resolution of the monitor until you have the VGA controller card.

CD-ROM Drive

Most documentation for CD-ROM products lists the CD-ROM drives supported, but it may not be an exhaustive list. Unless you have a model of the Hitachi (or Amdek) brand you had better verify with the CD-ROM publisher if your particular brand and model is supported. Philips and Sony are the second best choices in terms of application support.

Theoretically you should be able to run an ISO 9660 or High Sierra-compatible CD-ROM database on any CD-ROM drive advertised as reading these standard disks. If this were true there would be only one generic ISO 9660 and one High Sierra device driver program. The manufacturer of your lesser-known brand may have supplied a device driver program that simulates one of the well-known and widely supported brands. Only its testing with your candidate database can reveal if it really looks like the imitated device for MSCDEX.

Many databases span over several disks. It is very advantageous if you can use two or more CD-ROM drives in such a situation to accommodate and provide access to more than one volume of the disk set simultaneously. Until this is only a recommendation, it poses no problem. When you *must* have two players to use an application this becomes a required minimum. Lasercat, the high-quality cataloging support database from the Western Library Network, is one of the very few CD-ROM databases that cannot be used if you have only one CD-ROM drive.

Special Hardware Requirements

A few CD-ROM databases specify special hardware components. This may be optional or mandatory. If it is optional it means that you may use the product without that feature, but you are locked out of certain functions. In the above example, the Hercules Graphics Adapter is an optional feature for those who want to display the full ALA character set. On the other hand, graphics capability for the Supermap is a mandatory component.

Compton lists an audio synthesizer as a special hardware requirement. You may use the encyclopedia without listening to minuscule excerpts from Martin Luther King's "I Have a Dream" speech, but you may not use it if you do not have a VGA controller and monitor and a mouse. This latter requirement of Compton is certainly unique.

Many other CD-ROM products recommend that you use a mouse as an alternative input device, not as a mandatory one. It is another question that without the mouse your interaction with the database, particularly with one that is non-text oriented, can slow down significantly. This is the case with the Mammals database from *National Geographic*, which works with either the mouse or the keyboard.

Apart from the cost of the special hardware, you have to realize that most hardware devices require a free slot in your computer for the controller card. Even such an increasingly common device as the mouse requires either a free slot (bus-mouse) or a free serial port on your computer (port-mouse). Many computers have only a single serial port. If your serial port is used by some other device, such as an external modem or a scanner, and you do not want to keep plugging and unplugging the cables you will need a free slot inside your computer. Other peripherals, such as a voice synthesizer, can be accommodated only inside your computer in an appropriate slot.

NETWORK REQUIREMENTS

Networking is a complex issue in any kind of PC application. CD-ROM networking is an even more complex issue because the CD-ROM devices are still not considered by many systems software programs to be standard, typical peripherals and therefore are not supported. Even a rudimentary description of the various network architectures, network operating systems, and communications protocols is far beyond the scope of this book. The subject is so complex, even only from the CD-ROM point of view, that a well-done book is dedicated to the topic.[4] The experts on the subject discuss all hardware, software, management, and legal issues of CD-ROM networking and the possible alternatives.

This material only skims the surface, but both the PC and the CD-ROM trade magazines regularly evaluate and compare network hardware and software for CD-ROM.[5,6,7,8]

Many CD-ROM products can be used on networks. Network use means that the same CD-ROM database may be accessed from more than one personal computer. These PCs are interconnected via special network interface cards and cables. To handle the communication among the interconnected PCs additional software is required that must be resident in RAM.

There are two major types of networks: peer-to-peer and server-client. In the former, any PC can use the resources of the other PCs. In the latter, one PC is designated to serve all the client PCs. The resources typically include relatively expensive devices such as laser printers, scanners, or CD-ROM drives.

In the network environment there are extra requirements in addition to those discussed above. In the peer-to-peer network the extra requirement includes the need for a free slot to accommodate the network interface card in each PC and 20K to 25K RAM for the memory resident part of the network software. In the client-server mode these requirements are more stringent for the PC designated as the server. It has to be able to accommodate a network interface card for each PC participating in the network, and it has to run the so-called server-module of the network software, which is much larger (100K to 120K) than the client module of the network software (20K to 30K).

It is imperative in the client-server network that the server machine has as much RAM as possible and as fast a processor as possible. Depending on the number of PCs served, a RAM of 2 to 4 megabytes, and a 80386DX or 80386SX processor running at 20 megahertz are needed for the server PC.

Some network operating systems (such as the most popular Novell Netware) do not recognize CD-ROM drives and need further assistance in the form of additional software to share this device. There are already five layers of software (the CD network software, the basic network software, the MSCDEX program, the disc operating system, and the CD-ROM application software) that compete for residency in the memory. Much better are those network software programs that inherently are cognizant of CD-ROM devices, such as LANtastic or CD-NET.

Apart from knowing the extra requirements, setting up and operating a CD-ROM network require a computer-literate person to take care of all the installation and day-to-day operations vagaries and a much higher budget than CD-ROM applications running on stand-alone PCs. CD-ROM networks offer convenience and better resource utilization, but the extra hardware and software needed even for a peer-to-peer system of four or five PCs may cost well over $1,000. Often you also have to pay hefty surcharges for networked use of a CD-ROM database. Still, installing and managing a CD-ROM network and paying the extra fees may be more cost-effective than buying extra CD-ROM drives and copies of the databases for each PC.

Only a networked configuration can handle simultaneous multiple requests for the same CD-ROM database. The response time may deteriorate noticeably, but it is still better than waiting for hours for the single copy of the database that is being used on another PC. When to switch to a networked CD-ROM service is not an easy question to answer. You have to estimate the use of each database; the hardware, software, and extra royalty costs for network use; and the additional load on your personnel to maintain and trouble-shoot such a complex system. Only when you know the answers to these questions can you decide for or against networking.

REFERENCES

1. Péter Jacsó. "Negotiating Your Way Through the Pitfalls of CD-ROM Installation: A Guide to System Requirements." *Electronic Library* 7 (October 1989): 287-94.

2. Stuart Johnston. "Little Ventured, Little Gained at CD-ROM Show." *InfoWorld* 12 (March 5, 1990): 1, 8.

3. Péter Jacsó. "The Ideal CD-ROM Workstation for the 1990s." In *Proceedings of the 14th International Online Information Meeting, 1990,* pp. 25-32. Oxford, England: Learned Information, Ltd., 1990.

4. Norman Desmarais. *CD-ROM Local Area Networks: A User's Guide.* Westport, CT: Meckler Corporation, 1991.

5. K. Coaldey. "Software Broadens Access to CD-ROM: Evaluations of Three CD-ROM Networking Packages." *PC Week* (January 8, 1990): 23, 28-29, 32.

6. M. K. Thompson and K. Maxwell. "Connectivity: Networking CD-ROMs." *PC Magazine* 9 (February 27, 1990): 237-60.

7. H. McQueen. "Networking CD-ROMs: Implementation Considerations." *Laserdisk Professional* 3 (March 1990): 13-17.

8. M. Ennis. "CD-ROM on LAN." *CD-ROM EndUser* 1 (March 1989): 59-69.

7

SELECTION

Evaluation and comparison procedures are done to select the product most appropriate to your budget and user environment. However, you do not necessarily have to do the whole evaluation from scratch. Instead, you can use the many valuable sources that publish reviews and reports. These include CD-ROM directories and catalogs that list the major features of currently available databases and CD-ROM drives, the promotional materials of CD-ROM database publishers and device manufacturers, and the proceedings of traditional and electronic conferences related to CD-ROM.

These sources, however, are indirect tools of evaluation. Nothing compares to hands-on experience. Hands-on experience may be through the use of either demonstration or complete versions of CD-ROM databases. The results of the direct and indirect evaluations complement each other well.

When you have made your decision, you still have some homework. Shop around to find the best sources for purchasing or subscribing to the product. The time you spend is more than compensated by the significant savings in purchase or subscription costs.

SOURCES OF INFORMATION

Traditional sources of information include scholarly and trade journals, review magazines, monographs, indexes, bibliographies, newsletters, and catalogs. Many of these are also available in online and CD-ROM format. Nicholls[1] and Tenopir[2,3] provide in-depth critical reviews and analyses of most of the sources; the most important CD-ROM directories and catalogs are listed in appendix 5.

These sources vary significantly in terms of coverage, currency, quality, information content, and price. You do not necessarily get what you pay for, and you do not necessarily pay for what you get. The catalog of the Bureau of Electronic Publishing and *CD-ROM EndUser* magazine are free for the asking, but this does not indicate poor quality. The latter, especially, is a gold mine of practical information; it is hoped that the chronic delay in its publication since the second part of 1990 is not a sign of ceasing publication.

The only additions that may be needed to the comprehensive treatment of these sources by Nicholls and Tenopir concern new products, such as the CD-ROM versions of the Meckler[4] and the TFPL[5] directories and the traditional and electronic conferences.

The TFPL directory on CD-ROM debuted in the spring of 1991. The one from Meckler was not available at the time of publication and efforts failed to get samples from the beta-test version. The company maintains that the directory in CD-ROM format will be published by the end of 1991. Gale also announced that a CD-ROM version of the excellent printed publication (Cuadra's Directory of Portable Databases) will be released. Helgerson's Associates first realized that the CD-ROM format may be a natural application for CD-ROM directory information when they released the original Sourcedisk in 1988 and an updated version of it in 1989. Figure 7.1 shows some characteristic data of the CD-ROM version of the TFPL and Meckler CD-ROM directories.

	TFPL (*)	Meckler
Products	1522	1630
Companies	1840	not available
Price	$149	$175

* also includes information about journals, books and shows

Fig. 7.1. CD-ROM directories on CD-ROM.

Another first by Helgerson Associates is the Bibliodisc database introduced in 1991.[6] This CD-ROM database includes the most complete bibliography of publications about CD-ROM technology and applications. Again, this seems to be a very appropriate medium for the subject.

The other sources of information that may be relevant for your evaluation (and later for your optimal use) of CD-ROM products are conferences, both traditional and electronic.

Traditional conferences offer excellent opportunities for meeting and talking with people who use, produce, distribute, and demonstrate CD-ROM databases and CD-ROM drives. Even if you cannot afford the sometimes astronomical conference fees (as high as $1,000), visiting the exhibition halls is affordable and worth every nickel of the $5 to $10 admission charge.

General conferences—such as those of the American Library Association, the Special Libraries Association, the Public Libraries Association, and the Library and Information Technology Associations—and, to a lesser extent, those of the large state library associations have exhibitions featuring a large number of CD-ROM products.

The yearly "National Online Information Meetings" (always held in New York City in early May) and the "International Online Information Meetings" (always held in early December in London) now have separate exhibit areas just for CD-ROM products, and you may see around a hundred CD-ROM databases and a dozen CD-ROM drives demonstrated. These conferences are organized by Learned Information, Inc., and Learned Information, Ltd., respectively, at an affordable fee of $350 to $400.

Meckler's "Computers in Libraries" conference features many CD-ROM sessions and exhibitors, and there is no charge to visit only the exhibition if you apply for a free ticket ahead of time. The conference is usually held in March, and the location alternates between the East Coast and the West Coast.

Online, Inc., has changed the name of its yearly program to "Online/CD-ROM Conference," which reflects the presence of this new medium both in the conference program and in the exhibition halls. The location varies among cities on the East Coast, in the Midwest, and on the West Coast, but the date is usually mid-November.

There are conferences fully devoted to optical information storage and technology, with emphasis on the CD-ROM medium. Microsoft used to organize the "International Conference and Exposition on CD-ROM." Microsoft is still the sponsor, but the organizer and the name of the conference have changed. The date remains mid-March. The venue of the conference is a major city on the West Coast, the organizer is the Cahners Exposition Group, and the title is "International Conference & Exposition on Multimedia and CD-ROM." World Expo Corporation organizes "CD-ROM Expo," usually in October either in the East Coast or the Midwest. These last two conferences are very expensive (around $1,000), and the exhibition-only tickets are not cheap either (around $100), but there is an abundance of CD-ROM related information.

Many of these conferences issue printed conference proceedings and audiotapes of the presentations. Though these may be relevant sources themselves, the major advantage of the conferences is to be there to listen, talk, look, and touch. Exhibitions may be overwhelming, and obviously you should make plans about what you want to see. It is equally important that you do not simply bump into booth after booth, but go prepared with questions.

The best method seems to be to walk around, pick up the promotional materials from those exhibitors who may have something interesting for you, and then retreat and study these materials. Making notes and preparing some sort of questionnaire will help you to get the most information in the shortest time from the exhibitor. Often, you may ask for an appointment for a personal demo, which is much better than standing back in the crowd or having a dozen people breathing down your neck from behind. Going to booths without preparation is often just like tire-kicking in car showrooms. You may use the evaluation forms in appendixes 1-4 as checklists for these booth visits.

A relatively novel and unique type of information source is the large number of electronic conferences (also known as forums or newsgroups) available through national and international networks, such as Bitnet and Internet, often for free. Two electronic conferences are particularly relevant for potential and practicing CD-ROM users.

The Public Access Computer Systems Forum (PACS-L) on Bitnet is hosted by the Information Technology Division of the University of Houston and is described by its moderator (editor), Charles W. Bailey, Jr., in detail elsewhere.[7] Though PACS-L is not devoted exclusively to CD-ROM technology and applications, it has far more items about CD-ROM related issues than the name of the conference may suggest. A quick search about CD-ROM networking issues retrieved well over a hundred items. The subject lines of the items illustrate some typical topics discussed (figure 7.2).

```
002626 90/12/14 09:19  54   NLM CDROM Pricing Changes
002627 90/12/14 09:35  48   Expert Systems - Evaluation and Status
002629 90/12/14 10:26  45   CD-ROM Interfaces
002630 90/12/14 10:27  31   CD-ROM Workshops
002633 90/12/14 10:31  14   RE: LANTASTIC CD-ROM USERS NEEDED
002634 90/12/17 09:09 143   PACS-L Takes a Holiday
002644 91/01/02 09:36 128   Welcome to PACS-L
002659 91/01/03 10:38  19   Le Robert Electronique
002660 91/01/03 10:39  31   Re: What Will Replace CD-ROM?
002662 91/01/03 10:41  53   trouble with Toshiba 3200 CD-ROM drives
002671 91/01/04 09:56  45   CD-Rom access for non-affiliates
002672 91/01/04 09:58  18   Generic CD-ROM Databases
002673 91/01/04 09:58  91   Electronic Information Access = Information Overload?
002674 91/01/06 18:55 159   8th Texas Conference on Library Automation
002676 91/01/06 19:00  95   Summary of CD-ROM LAN responses
002688 91/01/07 20:28  67   CD-ROM Student Instruction
002695 91/01/07 20:39  43   LMSI CD-ROM follow-up
002697 91/01/08 20:17  25   RE: CD-Rom access for non-affiliates
002702 91/01/08 20:25  20   CD-ROM Network comparison to Mainframe Databases
002708 91/01/09 21:10  62   JOB POSTING, HEAD, LOCAL SYSTEMS U OF ROCHESTER
002713 91/01/09 21:19  70   CD-ROM Access for Non-Affiliates
002715 91/01/10 16:53  45   What will replace CD-ROM?
```

Fig. 7.2. Excerpts from PACS-L subject lines.

The full records are short, typically not more than 100 lines, and the content and quality of the items vary significantly, but the messages are often gems. You may subscribe to this conference to receive every item in your mailbox automatically, or you may search the database in a batch mode using Boolean operations. You may also limit your search to a time period. It would be useful if you could limit the automatic receipt of items to those that meet your profile of interest, expressed with a Boolean formula just like when you send a batch mode search to the database.

Do not expect academic treatises on PACS-L. Many of the messages probably would not qualify even as news items or letters to the editor in a magazine. However, they give enough hints for you to follow up and contact the sender of the item for more information. These messages are succinct, deal with down-to-earth issues, give tips and advice, and scoop about the best deals (see figure 7.3). PACS-L is a gold mine of how-to information.

Moreover, you are not limited to passively reading the messages of others, but you may participate in discussions or post a question about technical, administrative, or managerial problems related to CD-ROM. Chances are that within a day or two someone will send you a message directly with a solution to your problem.

From PACS-L@UHUPVM1.BITNET Sun Mar 17 12:54:16 1991
From: "Ka-Neng Au <AU@ZODIAC.BITNET>" <AU@ZODIAC.BITNET>
Subject: where to get diskchanger for $1000

In response to Dan Marmion's question, there are two sources for Pioneer Diskchangers (DRM-600) at less than $1000:

Compact Disk Products $999 (drive and adapter)
Attn: Pete Peters
223 East 85th St New York, NY 10028
212-737-8400, 800-634-2298

CAL-ABCO $990 (drive only)
Attn: Rich Cusolito
500 West Cummings Park, Suite 2100
Woburn, MA 01801, 800-225-4669

We ordered ours from CAL-ABCO after they agreed to match the price from Compact Disk Products. Both vendors also sell a wide variety of drives from other manufacturers.

From PACS-L@UHUPVM1.BITNET Wed Mar 6 15:57:21 1991
From: "Joseph P. Lucia" <JPL3@NS.CC.LEHIGH.EDU>
Subject: Multi-disk CD-ROM Readers

This is a somewhat tardy response to a couple of queries concerning multi-disk CD-ROM readers, in particular the Pioneer DRM-600. At Lehigh, we are currently using two of these devices, with no significant problems.
   The MS-DOS extensions that support this unit seem to be very robust. We're using a bunch of different products on these readers, and we've encountered no serious, unresolvable problems. The search software that we're using with discs on the changers includes Dialog, UMI, Auto-graphics, Readex. [...]
   We have one of these changers on a stand-alone 386 workstation in our Government Documents department, running the GPO Catalog (Autographics), the UN Documents Index, the 1987 Economic Census, and Export/Import stats (in various formats).
   Our second Pioneer changer is actually installed on a LAN (yikes!, you say...), where it houses low-use backfiles of a number of databases for which current years have been mounted in their own single-disk players. [...]
   Of course, I'm not recommending multi-user demands be placed on a changer – under the wrong circumstances, software timeouts resulting from disc swapping might just hang your search software or your LAN.

Fig. 7.3. Sample items from PACS-L.

The other electronic conference is the CDROM-L forum on Internet. This source is much more redundant and fuzzy than PACS-L and shows the lack of appropriate moderation. Though there are valuable postings, too many of the messages seem to be of distant relevance for CD-ROM users (in spite of the more specific name of the conference) and may often remind you of locker-room muscle flexing, as illustrated by figures 7.4 and 7.5, page 222. Even if you have access to both Bitnet and Internet (as many academic, special, and government libraries have), it may be enough to "attend" only the PACS-L conference if you want to avoid information overload. Another forum deals exclusively with network issues; CDROMLAN debuted in June 1991 demonstrating how important this issue has become. There is also a forum dedicated to CD-ROM on CompuServe, the commercial information system available to anyone willing to pay.

```
24-Mar John Stanley         Re:     DAK CD-ROM Package (1504 chars)
29-Mar Mark Toomey          Re: NEC vs. Toshiba CD-ROM (1141 chars)
29-Mar "J. Philip Mill      Denon does NOT support OS/2 (1512 chars)
30-Mar Larry Granroth       NEC CDR-80 and Gateway 2000 3 (1007 chars)
18-Apr UNF Library          CD-ROM Phone Directories (1192 chars)
24-Apr Neil Gould           SCSI / CD-ROM compatibility.. (1171 chars)
24-Apr Ron Bassett          NEC CDR-35 (2585 chars)
27-Apr Christopher Wel      CD-ROM (NEC CDR-35 Consortium (3187 chars)
28-Apr Walter Lewis         Re: Need for an 'unformatter' (1845 chars)
29-Apr Andrew MacRae        Re: Expanded memory and CD-RO (1351 chars)
30-Apr Matthew Seitz        Re: Expanded memory and CD-RO (856 chars)
 3-May Maurizio Lana        cdrom disk presence not recog (1609 chars)
 4-May Kenneth Cheng-L      NEC CDR-36 CD-ROM drive for t (1178 chars)
 7-May Richard Hintz        Re: CDROM disk presence not r (1050 chars)
 7-May "Director of Co      Need "BNB on CD-ROM" utilitie (1290 chars)
 8-May HESTER@KSUVM.BI      SCSI Terminator (967 chars)
 8-May Matthias Winter      Bibliometric access to ISI's  (2361 chars)
20-May LINDELL@CWU.BIT      FTP, MSCDEX, and you (1094 chars)
20-May JBB@L2XA.ACC.VI      Flames, responses and such (1652 chars)
20-May JBB@L2XA.ACC.VI      flames, responses and such (523 chars)
29-May James Jay Morga      MSCDEX AND DOS 4.0 (1334 chars)
```

Fig. 7.4. Subject lines of messages on CDROM-L.

Id: 8461 Date: 31 May 91
Subject: Juvenile flaming about Mini Disc Re: the facts
Summary: Larry vents his spleen at Sony's scam

Also, Larry can't read. Why don't you get your FACTS straight before shooting your mouth off!

*>And MD is a pretty poor excuse for a digital record/playback media. I feel a powerful attack of consumer
nausea coming on.<*
You are a pretty poor excuse for a reviewer.
>How can it be the ultimate when it is not as durable as a compact disk? What a [...] joke.<
No, you are the joke.

Id: 1731 Date: 03 June 91
[...] Stop sending me hate mail! [...]

Id: 5002 Date 03 June 91
[...] Flame me and I will hunt you down and do nasty things to your system (with pleasure!) [...]

Id: 5536 Date: 04 June 91
From: Matthew Seitz <seitz@NETCOM.COM>
Subject: Re: MSCDEX AND DOS 4.0

In article <347330E7C0019D2C@INDYVAX.IUPUI.EDU> [...] writes:
>You need ver 2.3 to work with DOS 4.<
Actually, you need version 2.20 of MSCDEX. There is no version 2.3 available yet. You may be referring to the
Meridian release version number. This number refers to the whole package of MSCDEX and device drivers. It is
not the same as the MSCDEX version number.
*>Since DOS 4 uses a lot of memory I'm more interested in what version will work with DOS 5.0, and when
Microsoft will get around to including the MSCDEX as a part of DOS instead of selling it as extra.<*
So far there is no official word from Microsoft about DOS 5.0 compatibility with MSCDEX 2.20. I have had
some customers report problems with MS-DOS 5.0.
I have a message pending with the product manager for MSCDEX, so I'll let you know. It may be important that
when Windows 3.0 was released, it was not fully compatible with the current release of MSCDEX (2.10). It
was a few months before the compatible 2.20 came out. A similar situation may occur this time.

Id: 7868 Date: 04 June 91
It is very irritating to see over and over again the immature nature of a certain type of person on the net. [...]
Don't send me mail explaining how righteous you are sending flames via news or e-mail, I'll just put it in my
flame-proof /dev/null file.

Id: 8920 Date: 04 June 91
After reading the crap which had been exchanged on this supposed channel for the sharing of ideas and
solutions, I have no other choice but to signoff from the CDROM-L conference. Too bad. It had great potential.

Id: 9043 Date: 04 June 91
If you want to sign off from the list, that's fine. I can understand the impulse since the signal to noise ratio has
been favoring noise lately.
However, please include a subject in your notes like "Signing off" or "Signing off with a flame" so people can
delete before reading. Especially, don't sign off complaining about noise and make the rest of us endure the
noise you yourself generate. [...]
Please send comments, insults, and so on to me privately. Thanks.
Regards,
Richard Hintz opsrjh@uccvma hintz@oz.ucop.edu
University of California
CDROM-L Owner

Fig. 7.5. Excerpts of messages on CDROM-L.

SAMPLE DEMONSTRATION DISKS
AND TRIAL PERIODS

Nothing can help the evaluation of CD-ROM databases as much as hands-on experience with the product. Reading reviews about databases is very important, but if you have not used or seen at least a few CD-ROM databases, the reviews may not be that easy to understand fully. You may not share the same points of reference with the reviewer. The difficulty lies in the fact that an inherently dynamic series of actions has to be described in a static medium. The same applies when you talk with someone about a CD-ROM database.

Conference exhibitions can be extremely valuable if you have the time and energy, go prepared, and meet competent, friendly, and not exhausted product demonstrators. (To the credit of the exhibitors, standing in a booth all day, answering often dull questions, and smiling when someone walks out on you in the middle of your explanation may be more draining than shoveling snow in January in Chicago.)

Using demonstration versions is a very good and inexpensive way to learn about CD-ROM databases. Most of them come on floppy diskette, and database publishers typically distribute these free of charge. You do not even need to have a CD-ROM drive to watch the simulation of a CD-ROM database in the privacy of your office or the semi-privacy of the library.

Floppy-based demonstration diskettes have the significant constraint that they can include only a few records of the real database. Still, even the simplest of the demonstration diskettes, which are not much more than a computer-based slide show, can provide a visual impression of the user interface, the dynamics of navigating in the system, and the other major features of the software. You cannot really do test searches of your own. Usually, the demonstration program tells you what your next step should be and even does it for you.

The CD-ROM Sourcedisc from Helgerson Associates, referred to earlier, combines directory information for nearly 500 CD-ROM databases along with demo versions of 80 of those. If you really would like to know what the most popular software interfaces look like, this is an excellent source for less than $100.

A few demonstration programs come on CD-ROM. These are the real things, the only difference being in the number of records stored on the demonstration CD-ROM. These subsets of the database provide an excellent tool for evaluating not only the software but also the dataware. For example, BIOSIS and the Institute for Scientific Information have such samples for the BIOSIS database and for the Science Citation Index and the Social Science Citation Indexes, respectively.

Dialog offers a superb sample database, Discovery, for those who would like to check the capabilities of the Dialog OnDisc software and get an impression of the quality, content, and structure of the dataware available with the OnDisc software.[8] The $59 price tag is reasonable for a product that has sizable samples of several of the OnDisc databases. The only caveat is that with the several thousand records in the sample databases, the response time may be better than in the full databases. You may still not judge the currency of the database, its subject, or its geographic and language coverage. Some other reservations are voiced by Pitts and Jackson.[9] To evaluate these criteria, you must use the real CD-ROM database; even if you do not commit yourself, you may apply for a trial period to use the real databases of many publishers.

The most reliable and comprehensive evaluation may be done, of course, on the real CD-ROM database. You can do this not only on your existing database to find out details unknown to you, but also on the databases you are considering for purchase or license.

Many CD-ROM publishers offer a 30- to 60-day trial period during which you may test the database. This is nothing new in the publishing industry, which has offered trial subscriptions for a long time with traditional printed publications. But whereas it is easy to sample a magazine in a neighboring library or even at the newsstand, the sampling of a database requires time and preparation.

The criteria presented in this book can be modified and customized to your requirements. Even if there is only one database to be evaluated, a score list with criteria, weights, and grades makes your evaluation systematic and tangible. Use the sample in this book as a checklist against which to test the capabilities of the system. Skip criteria of no interest to you. Call the database publisher to get answers to some evaluation questions, and ask what makes their database better than that of the competition.

These inquiries also give some indication about the customer service you may expect in the long run. After a few calls you will find out how long it takes to get through or to get your call returned and how competent and reliable the hotline staff is.

In the testing process itself, try to involve those who will be using the CD-ROM database. Discuss with them their views and experiences. If you intend to buy or subscribe to a CD-ROM database for public use, try to involve not only the professional and paraprofessional librarians, but also representatives of the patrons. Simply watching their reactions and making informal interviews may be very revealing.

If you have several databases on trial simultaneously, the line to use them may be telling in itself. You may prepare a questionnaire and conduct formal interviews to find out the preferences of patrons. Jaffe describes the result of a test when both librarians and patrons tested the potential products, InfoTrac Magazine Index Plus and Wilson's Reader's Guide Abstracts. Their preferences turned out to be different;[10] the library chose to subscribe to the database preferred by the patrons.

This type of evaluation of the real CD-ROM database is the most convenient when you already have a subscription to the database. The formal evaluation can give you further insights and complement your gut feelings. It may set the stage for the consideration of its replacement by another CD-ROM database with similar scope or by another version of the same database when the time comes to renew your subscription.

SOURCES OF PURCHASE

When you have made the decision which database to select, always shop around, as there may be alternative sources that provide the same CD-ROM database at a significantly different price. This applies mostly to CD-ROM databases you purchase rather than subscribe to.

Database publishers provide CD-ROM databases to independent distributors at a much reduced price. The distributors in turn sell these to end users, passing much of the savings on while still making some profit. Most of these distributors operate as mail-order companies, though EBSCO itself is the producer of two datafiles, the publisher of four databases, and the distributor of hundreds of databases. Faxon and EBSCO as serial jobbers were quick to offer CD-ROM databases along with their traditional publication line, and both regularly produce informative product catalogs. The Egghead retail chain offers good discounts on CD-ROM drives and CD-ROM databases, though their offerings are limited to the Amdek brand of CD-ROM drive and to four or five CD-ROM databases.

A few mail-order companies specialize in CD-ROM. The best known are the Bureau of Electronic Publishing, Compact Disk Products, Updata, and Phethean. Many more mail-order companies, besides other computer and home electronic products and various miscellaneous merchandise, also sell CD-ROM databases. The best known of these types of companies include Micro-warehouse, Software Unlimited, IME, Tigersoftware, and DAK.

You may find good bargains not only for CD-ROM databases but also for CD-ROM drives. Quite often CD-ROM databases are bundled with CD-ROM drives. Both the mail-order companies and the database publishers offer this alternative. Some of the best bargains are available only for a short period of time.

IME, for example, advertised the Bookshelf database for $59 for a few weeks in the summer of 1991. This CD-ROM database has a list price of $295 and was offered at the same time by other mail-order companies for $220 to $240. In spite of the outdatedness of some of the component files in this database, the $59 price tag was difficult to resist. After most of the outdated copies of Bookshelf were probably sold, Microsoft announced an updated version in June 1991. The trick is that you need to have Windows in order to run it. It is an excellent multimedia product including sound and pictures for a reasonable list price of $195.

Tigersoftware had a close-out sale in the spring of 1991, and the miniature NEC CDR-35 was sold for $399, including the interface card. At the same time other mail-order companies charged around $600 for it. Software Unlimited offered the New Gorlier Encyclopedia for $265, when DAK (a good discounter itself otherwise) charged $395 for this CD-ROM database, the same as its list price.

The bundles made by database publishers usually are less attractive than those offered by mail-order companies. However, many databases are not available from anyone except the publisher. You may wish to buy the database and CD-ROM drive as a package from the publisher, but the price is very likely to be higher than the total of the separate prices you would pay for a CD-ROM drive from a mail-order company and the database from the publisher.

You also may buy a complete CD-ROM workstation package, which includes not only the CD-ROM database and the CD-ROM drive but also the personal computer. The Library Corporation, IAC, and Newsbank favor this approach. The subscription price quoted by these publishers for their CD-ROM database includes the lease of the hardware components.

These bundles do not necessarily represent the best deal for you. But remember that the best deal is not always a simple comparison of price tags. Primarily, it helps the database publishers to trace down errors on a system whose every component they know very well. Of course, you may expect better customer service in this case. It is also a safe way to eliminate possible incompatibilities among databases, CD-ROM drives, and personal computers. Another advantage is the plug-and-play approach. You unpack the box, plug in the cables, and off you go. No hassles with finding an appropriate slot for an interface card or with installing the drive and then the application. By the time you get the workstation, everything is in place except the power cord.

On the other hand, the PC and the player may not be among the top 10 in their price/performance category. They may have been sitting in the warehouse for quite some time. This doesn't mean they are lemons, but just that they may not represent the cutting edge of technology. Publisher-bundled systems often come with a customized keyboard, which is convenient when you do not want to use other CD-ROM databases on the same PC. Keyboard templates offer more flexibility because you can easily remove or replace them in case of using databases from more than one CD-ROM publisher. However, in public areas the keyboard templates disappear faster than free goodies at exhibition booths.

If you wish to use other CD-ROM databases, you also will have to tinker with the AUTOEXEC.BAT file (discussed in the next chapter), because bundled configurations—understandably enough—launch you automatically into their own database after you turn on the system, without giving you the option to choose other applications.

A better way to have such bundles may be to buy a PC with a CD-ROM drive from a computer manufacturer or a mail-order company rather than from a database publisher. The Headstart family of personal computers and the Sun Moon Star computers now come with built-in CD-ROM drives and usually with databases and some popular software bundled. Others also offer complete packages. Some samples are presented in figure 7.6, page 226. You may not need or use all the software packages in the bundle, but even if you just let them collect dust the bundle very well may be worth the price.

HARDWARE COMPONENTS	HEADSTART 300CD	TIGERSOFT Sun Moon Star
Processor		
Type	Intel 286	Intel 286
Speed	12 Mhz	12 Mhz
RAM		
Built-in	1 Mbyte	1 Mbyte
Maximum	4 Mbytes	4 Mbytes
Hard disk		
Capacity	40 Mbytes	40 Mbytes
Access time	28 msec	28 msec
Video		
Display size	14"	14"
Resolution	640*480	640*480
Dot pitch	0.31	0.31
Free bays		
5.25"	0	1
3.50"	0	0
Free slots		
8-bits	0	3
16-bits	2	2
Floppy disk	1.44	1.2
Serial port	1	1
Paralell port	1	1
Mouse	yes	yes
Built-in modem	yes	no
Warranty	12 months	36 months
Built-in CD		
Brand	Sony	Hitachi
Model	531	3600
Access time	500 msec	800 msec
Warranty	12 months	18 months

SOFTWARE AND DATABASE COMPONENTS	HEADSTART 300CD	TIGERSOFT Sun Moon Star
Free CD databases		
Grolier	■	■
PC Globe	■	
World/US Atlas		■
CD Audio Guide	■	■
Hotline Exec	■	■
MS Bookshelf	■	■
MS Small Bus. Cons.	■	■
MS Stat Pack	■	■
CD Game Pack	■	■
Free PC software		
DOS 4.01	■	■
Quattro 1	■	
Q & A 3.0	■	
Publish-It!	■	
Deluxe Paint	■	
Mavis Bacon Typing	■	
Backup Pro	■	
Twist and Shout	■	
Word for Word	■	
DS Optimize	■	
DS Recover	■	
Prodigy	■	
FLASHlink	■	
First Choice		■
GEM3 Desktop		■
GEM3 Draw Plus		■
Check-it		■

Headstart 300CD: $1,795

Sun Moon Star: $1,899

Fig. 7.6. Complete hardware-software-database packages.

Though some caution is recommended with brands that are absolutely unknown and have not been reviewed in the professional trade magazines, the track record of the company and the warranty may be reassuring enough. Posting a question on one of the newsgroups described above will also bring you some feedback from current users of such systems. The fact that DAK has been in business for over 25 years and offers a 30-day money-back guarantee plus 12-month onsite service and toll-free service for a no-name computer (BSR) seems to be reassuring. The price for its CD-ROM computer, software, and database bundle cannot be beat. On the other hand, you will learn from reading the news in the above-mentioned electronic conferences that attempts to reach the toll-free help desk can wear your patience thin.

Carefully consider your situation to make the best decision. What kind of local help is likely to be available? How comfortable do you feel with buying from a mail-order company versus from a local dealer? How important is the 20 to 30 percent savings? Do you really need all those bundled software packages and databases? Price alternatives should be considered always with a view to these questions.

REFERENCES

1. Paul Nicholls. *CD-ROM Collection Builder's Toolkit*. Weston, CT: Pemberton Press, 1990.

2. Carol Tenopir. "The Database Press." *Library Journal* 114 (March 1, 1989): 56-57.

3. Carol Tenopir. "Collection Development." *Library Journal* 115 (September 1, 1990): 194-97.

4. *CD-ROMs in Print* [CD-ROM edition]. Westport, CT: Meckler, 1991.

5. *The CD-ROM Directory 1991 On Disc*. London: TFPL Publishing, 1991.

6. *CD-ROM Sourcedisk*. Falls Church, VA: Helgerson Associates, 1988, 1990.

7. Charles W. Bailey, Jr. "The Public Access Computer Systems Forum: A Computer Conference on BITNET." *Library Software Review* 9 (March-April 1990): 71-74.

8. Péter Jacsó. "Dialog Discovery CD-ROM Database from an Educator's Perspective." *Laserdisk Professional* 3 (May 1990): 66-72.

9. Roberta Pitts and Kathy Jackson. "Do Demo Discs Deliver?" *CD-ROM Professional* 3 (November 1990): 98-100.

10. John J. Jaffe. "For Undergrads: INFOTRAC Magazine Index Plus or WILSONDISC with Readers' Guide and Humanities Index?" *American Libraries* 19 (October 1988): 759-61.

CHAPTER

8

INSTALLATION PROCEDURES

Installation was discussed briefly in chapter 4, but only from the point of view of the ease of installation as a product evaluation criteria. In this chapter the most typical files and procedures of installation are discussed, which can help in trouble-shooting if something goes wrong during or after the installation of a CD-ROM product.

In the non-networked environment the creation and/or modification of three files is at the center of every installation process. These are the CONFIG.SYS, the AUTOEXEC.BAT, and the application startup file. The procedures are usually automated to a large extent and are straight-forward if this is the first and only CD-ROM application on a workstation. They may, however, induce conflict if there are other applications that have been using the CONFIG.SYS and AUTOEXEC.BAT files set to their requirements.

You may have been using your PC for a long time without ever hearing about these system files. They are not mandatory files in general, but you cannot use CD-ROM databases without these files. The reason for that is that both files are needed to start the running of special programs—the MSCDEX program and the device driver—when you boot up the system. The application startup file is optional and simply facilitates the activation of a particular CD-ROM application.

When you buy your CD-ROM drive you may get an installation program along with the MSCDEX program and the device driver. Executing the installation program makes the CD-ROM drive known to the DOS operating system. The installation program typically creates the AUTOEXEC.BAT and the CONFIG.SYS files and a directory to store the above-mentioned programs. If you already have these files it may modify them. Only one CONFIG.SYS or AUTOEXEC.BAT file can be active. If either of them is changed you must reboot the system for these changes to take effect.

CREATION/MODIFICATION OF CONFIG.SYS AND AUTOEXEC.BAT

Most installation software received from the manufacturer of the CD-ROM drive automatically generates the CONFIG.SYS and AUTOEXEC.BAT files. The names of the subdirectory, the device driver, and the identifier of the device will be different, but the process is the same whether you install an Amdek, a Hitachi, a Philips, or a Sony drive. Figure 8.1 illustrates the steps of the typical installation procedure.

This is a very smooth operation even for an absolute novice. You would not need to know anything about the installation process, let alone the system files, if the CD-ROM applications did not change them at will or require you to edit them. It is much easier to check these system files once you learn their content.

```
┌──────── AMDEK CD ROM INSTALLATION ──────────2.51─┐
│                                                   │
│                                                   │
│   The CD ROM utilities on this disk will automatically install the │
│   software needed to run the Amdek CD ROM drive.  You must specify │
│   whether installation should occur on a hard drive or diskette │
│   drive.   The installation procedure will create or modify your │
│   AUTOEXEC.BAT and CONFIG.SYS files.  You must then re-boot the │
│   system so that the files are recognized. │
│                                                   │
│   Default answers have been provided which will install the software │
│   for typical configurations.  By pressing 'Enter' you are accepting │
│   the default answer.  Feel free to change the default if your │
│   configuration is different.   You may press the 'Esc' key at any │
│   time to quit -- your files will not be changed. │
│                                                   │
│   Please indicate the type of drive onto which you will be installing │
│   the software.  Answer H for hard (fixed) drive, D for diskette │
│   (floppy) drive, or Q to quit this program. │
│                                                   │
│   INSTALL TO HARD DRIVE, DISKETTE DRIVE, OR QUIT? ► H │
│    Copyright (c) Amdek Corporation, 1987, 1988. All rights reserved. │
└───────────────────────────────────────────────────┘

┌──────── AMDEK CD ROM INSTALLATION ──────────2.51─┐
│                                                   │
│   What is the letter of the drive that contains the Amdek CD ROM │
│   Utilities diskette?  Example: 'A' is your first diskette drive. │
│                                                   │
│   SOURCE DISKETTE (A:,B:) ► A_ │
└───────────────────────────────────────────────────┘

┌──────── AMDEK CD ROM INSTALLATION ──────────2.51─┐
│                                                   │
│   What is the letter of the destination disk drive and the pathname │
│   where the files should be placed?  Example: 'C:\CDROM\' will │
│   place the files on the hard disk drive (C:) in a subdirectory │
│   called \CDROM. │
│                                                   │
│   DESTINATION AND PATH ► C:\CDROM_____ │
└───────────────────────────────────────────────────┘

┌──────── AMDEK CD ROM INSTALLATION ──────────2.51─┐
│   The Utilities diskette should be in the source drive listed above. │
│                                                   │
│   Is the above information correct? (Y,N) ► Y │
└───────────────────────────────────────────────────┘

┌──────── AMDEK CD ROM INSTALLATION ──────────2.51─┐
│                                                   │
│   INSTALLATION COMPLETE │
│                                                   │
│   Installation has been succesfully completed. The system will now │
│   recognize the Amdek CD ROM drive when booting. │
│                                                   │
│                                                   │
│   Press CTRL ALT DEL keys simultaneously to reboot. │
└───────────────────────────────────────────────────┘
```

Fig. 8.1. The installation process.

The CONFIG.SYS File

The CONFIG.SYS file sets important parameters of your system and specifies the actual configuration of the system. You need to learn about four important commands in the CONFIG.SYS file: DEVICE = , BUFFERS = , FILES = , and LASTDRIVE = .

The DEVICE = command specifies the device driver that provides the communication bridge between the device and the operating system or, in the case of CD-ROM drives, between the device and the MSCDEX program. There are no separate device drivers for floppy and hard disk drives because these are already built into the operating system. There are, however, separate device drivers for relatively new peripheral devices like mice, scanners, and CD-ROM drives.

Typically, the device drivers are produced by the manufacturer of the mouse or the CD-ROM drive, but this is not always so. Sometimes the database publisher supplies one or more device drivers, and this may lead to conflict. The name of the device drivers alludes to the brand of the device and it may have a SYS or COM extension, e.g., AMDEK.SYS or HITACHI.COM. The format of the command needed to activate the device driver is the following:

DEVICE = drive:\pathname\filename /D:device name /N:drives /P:address

where

drive is the drive identifier where the device driver program is located

pathname is the subdirectory that contains the device driver program

filename is the name of the device driver program

/D:device name tells MSCDEX the name to identify the CD-ROM drive

/N:drives specifies the number of CD-ROM drives connected to the system through a single interface board

/P:address specifies the I/O address of the CD-ROM interface card

The sample DEVICE command below specifies the following for DOS: (1) the name of the device driver is AMDEK.SYS, (2) it is stored on drive C: in the subdirectory named "CDROM," (3) there are two drives, (4) the interface card is at the address of (hexadecimal) 200, and (5) the logical name of the device for MSCDEX is AMDEKCD.

DEVICE = C:\CDROM\AMDEK.SYS /D:AMDEKCD /N:2 /P:200

You do not have to specify the drive and pathname if the device driver is in a subdirectory that is included in your path automatically (via the PATH command in the AUTOEXEC.BAT file). The number of the devices must be specified only if there is more than one, and the address, only if it is not hexadecimal 300. The device name and the file-name are always mandatory, and the device name must be consistent with the one used in the AUTOEXEC.BAT file and in the application startup file, if there is any. The address of the interface card should only be changed if there is an address conflict with some other device. You may have to change the address not only here but also on the interface card by setting a jumper.

The BUFFER = command specifies the number of buffers to be set aside in RAM for speeding the input/output operation from and to the hard disk. (Buffers can be set aside also for the CD-ROM but it can only be specified as a parameter for the MSCDEX program—see below.) Each buffer takes 512 bytes away from RAM; a BUFFERS = 20 command reduces the available RAM by 10K.

As the name implies, a buffer is a temporary area where the processor sends and receives data. While the buffer is being loaded or unloaded the processor is free to do something else and does not have to wait for the relatively slow hard disk. When the buffer is ready, i.e., when it is emptied or filled by a read or write operation, the processor gets a signal to load new data into it or fetch data from it for processing or display.

Buffering can speed applications but take away precious RAM storage. Some level of buffering is considered to be so important that even if you do not specify the BUFFERS command, DOS will set aside two to four buffers depending on the hardware configuration and the version number of DOS. You cannot fool DOS by assigning a zero value or one that is smaller than the prevailing default value. DOS will override the command if you try this.

Though there is no universal optimal number of buffers, most CD-ROM applications instruct you to specify BUFFERS = 20 in the CONFIG.SYS file. This may be efficient for most programs but may reserve too much space for a few memory hogs. Not accidentally, EBSCO advises you to specify BUFFERS = 10; otherwise, you will not be able to run any of the EBSCO products because the software requires 580K net RAM capacity.

You may further reduce the number of buffers if you want to save some RAM for your favorite memory-resident program (such as a menuing program or a virus protection program). Reducing the number of buffers may slightly reduce the performance of the CD-ROM application, but it is an acceptable trade-off for those who must run memory resident programs.[1]

The FILES = command specifies how many files may be open simultaneously. Each open file must have a file handle; DOS makes available as many file handles as specified in the FILE command. File handles are like the pegs in a coat closet. If there is no free peg you may still put two coats on one peg, but if all the file handles are busy when a file is to be opened, the application that tried to open a new file will abort. A file handle takes 48 bytes. This is such a minuscule amount of RAM that it simply is not worth it to cut back on the value (typically FILES = 20) recommended by the CD-ROM publisher. On the contrary, it may be safer to increase the number of this value, because the CD-ROM applications think only about their own requirement when specifying this value, whereas it applies to *all* the files simultaneously open in the system. If an application specifies more than 20, heed that advice as a bare minimum. EBSCO products, for example, require that you specify 40 file handles, but it does no harm to specify 50 to make sure that files of other applications that are active when the EBSCO software is loaded will get their own file handles.

The LASTDRIVE = command specifies for DOS the last drive designator it should recognize. In the simplest configuration there are three or four drives. Drives A: and B: are always the floppy drives. The first (or only) hard disk is always C:, even if there is no second floppy drive. The CD-ROM drive would be drive D: in such a situation, and the LASTDRIVE = D command would suffice. However, you may wish later to assign a RAM disk or create a new logical hard disk on your physical hard drive, and then the LASTDRIVE = D specification would not be enough. Though you "waste" 1K or 2K by doing so, you can assign value Z as a parameter and then forget about this parameter, even if you add to your configuration a new floppy drive, hard disk, or optical drive every month. Note that no colon follows the drive letter with the LASTDRIVE command.

Use the LASTDRIVE command as the first in your CONFIG.SYS file and the DEVICE command as the last one. The reason for this is that DOS has to know right at the beginning which drive identifiers are valid, and you may not install drivers after the one for the CD-ROM drive. Figure 8.2, page 232, shows the content of a simple CONFIG.SYS file before and after the installation of a CD-ROM device.

```
                         BEFORE
 BREAK=ON
 BUFFERS=25,8
 FCBS=20,8
 FILES=20
 LASTDRIVE=E
 SHELL=C:\DOS4\COMMAND.COM /P /E:256
 DEVICE=C:\DOS4\ANSI.SYS /X
 INSTALL=C:\DOS4\FASTOPEN.EXE C:=(150,150)
 DEVICE=C:\MOUSE.SYS

                      AFTER

 BREAK=ON
 BUFFERS=25,8
 FCBS=20,8
 FILES=30
 LASTDRIVE=Z
 SHELL=C:\DOS4\COMMAND.COM /P /E:1024
 DEVICE=C:\DOS4\ANSI.SYS /X
 INSTALL=C:\DOS4\FASTOPEN.EXE C:=(150,150)
 DEVICE=C:\MOUSE.SYS
 DEVICE=C:\CDROM\AMDEK.SYS /D:AMDEKCD /N:2 /P:200
```

Fig. 8.2. CONFIG.SYS file before and after the installation of a
CD-ROM device.

The AUTOEXEC.BAT File

This file includes a number of commands that are automatically executed whenever you turn on your system. It may include commands to clear the screen, to set the path where DOS should look for programs, to specify the content of the prompt used by DOS to indicate that it is your turn to enter a command, or to load a program automatically when the system is booted. Only this last command is mandatory for CD-ROM applications. You may find the details about the other commands in any DOS manual.

The command that loads the MSCDEX program has the following syntax:

drive:\pathname\MSCDEX.EXE /D:device name /M:buffers /V /E /L:drive identifier

where

drive is the drive identifier where the MSCDEX program is located

pathname is the subdirectory that contains the MSCDEX program

/D:device name tells MSCDEX the name to identify the CD-ROM drive

/M:buffers specifies how many buffers will be allocated to MSCDEX when it is loaded

/V instructs MSCDEX to display detailed information about memory allocation when loaded

/E instructs MSCDEX to use expanded memory instead of the conventional memory

/L:drive identifier determines the drive identifier to be used for DOS to identify the CD-ROM drive

The sample command below

1. specifies that the MSCDEX program is on drive C:

2. is in the subdirectory "CDROM,"

3. identifies the drive for MSCDEX by the device name AMDEKCD,

4. asks that six buffers be allocated for MSCDEX,

5. which is to be installed in the expanded memory region of RAM, and

6. assigns the DOS drive identifier K: to the CD-ROM drive.

C:\CDROM\MSCDEX.EXE /D:AMDEKCD /M:6 /E /L:K

The drive and the path do not need to be explicitly identified if the subdirectory is included in the PATH statement in the AUTOEXEC.BAT file already or if the MSCDEX program is in the root directory instead of a subdirectory.

The device name must be identical to the name specified in the CONFIG.SYS file. If you do not assign buffers for MSCDEX it automatically reserves four to eight buffers (depending on the version of the program). Each buffer takes 2K of RAM, so you may need to reduce the number of CD-ROM buffers if you have such memory hogs as EBSCO-CD or Compton's Encyclopedia. On the other hand, the more buffers you have the less access to the CD-ROM drive is required and the faster your application will be. If you assign fewer buffers than the default value, MSCDEX will override your decision. Specifying /M:4 seems to be a good compromise for both performance and memory strain, and it is the minimum in version 2.1 of MSCDEX. Its default would be /M:8.

The optional /V parameter has the effect of displaying some information about the nitty-gritty of memory allocation for MSCDEX itself. This is not very informative data for the user, so there is no reason to specify it in the command.

The /E parameter can be extremely useful if you have expanded memory in your system. This is the area between 640K and 1 megabyte, so you need a minimum of 1 megabyte RAM and also either a 286 processor with a special memory manager software that makes that region of RAM an expanded memory or a 386DX, 386SX, or 486 processor, all of which have enough built-in flexibility for such memory handling. If you have these prerequisites and use the /E parameter, MSCDEX and its buffers will be loaded in the otherwise under-used region. This memory is also often called high memory, and the process to load programs and device drivers and to assign buffers here is called high loading. By high loading you may save a lot of space in the conventional (below 640K) region of your RAM for your CD-ROM search software and other memory-resident programs without sacrificing speed.

The process of creating or modifying these two files not only is simple and transparent to the user, but also takes only a few minutes. The problems start only when you install your first CD-ROM application and you want to follow all of its installation instructions and recommendations.

Your first CD-ROM application may wish to overwrite both these files, to use its own device drivers, and to automatically invoke its search program whenever you turn on the system. This may not be acceptable to you. Some CD-ROM products have installation procedures that shoot themselves into the system, whereas others advise you that they have changed these files. The better ones may have made a copy of your most recent CONFIG.SYS and AUTOEXEC.BAT files (typically under the names CONFIG.BAK and AUTOEXEC.BAK), and some ask permission before the modification or let you do the changes manually. In any of these cases you must understand the implications of the changes, as you may have to deny some changes or modify the changes after the installation. This is even more likely to occur when you install your second and third or more CD-ROM applications.

For example, the MAS database of EBSCO modifies the original CONFIG.SYS file by setting the parameters to BUFFERS = 10 and FILES = 40 when installed. If later you install another database, it is likely to overwrite these parameters to BUFFERS = 20 and FILES = 20. You will then not be able to run MAS anymore due to lack of enough RAM space.

Another database may have changed your AUTOEXEC.BAT file during installation to make sure that its search program is automatically invoked when the system is booted and also may have positioned itself at the beginning of the PATH, i.e., cut in the queue. This not only is very asocial, but may also have the effect that there is no room left in the tiny RAM area that is set aside to store this information. This happens when you see such messages as "Not enough space for environment variable" when you boot your system. Another source of conflict may be the application startup file.

APPLICATION STARTUP FILE

```
rem Start-up batch file for Compact Cambridge
c:
cd \cd-real\csa
cc /d:AMDEKCD /me
c:
cd \jacso\cd-bats
```

```
rem Start-up batch file for Grolier Encyclopedia
cd c:\cd-real\elecenc
EEPGM -cAMDEKCD
cd\
cd \jacso\cd-bats
```

```
rem Start-up batch file for 1989 version of PAIS
echo off
cls
cd \cd-real\pais89
SET VCDROM = AMDEKCD
ps > ps.log
cd \jacso\cd-bats
cls
```

```
rem Start-up batch file for Compton's Encyclopedia
CD e:\COMPTONS
E:JOS_TSR0.EXE E: E: e:\COMPTONS -S -DI
JMI.EXE
c:
cd \jacso\cd-bats
```

```
rem Start-up batch file for mas
echo off
C:
cd \
path > oldpath.bat
path C:\MAS
cd \MAS
eeisrch -b %1 %2 %3 %4
cd \
rem to flush the junk left by mas
del c:\cdrom.buf
oldpath
c:
cd \jacso\cd-bats
```

Fig. 8.3. Application startup files.

Application startup files are usually a convenience for users. These batch files include commands to clear the screen, switch to the appropriate subdirectory, activate the search program, and provide parameters as needed. Figure 8.3 illustrates the content of some application startup files.

You simply type the file-name and these commands are executed. There may be problems, however. If this batch file uses a device name to identify the CD-ROM drive it must be the same as the one used in the CONFIG.SYS and the AUTOEXEC.BAT files. In figure 8.3, the Grolier and Cambridge startup files are the ones that include device names. Such applications take care of this problem when first installed by modifying the CONFIG.SYS and AUTOEXEC.BAT files to their hearts' content, but the installation of a new application may overwrite the special device names, and the application startup file then will be in conflict with the newly modified CONFIG.SYS and AUTOEXEC.BAT files.

How can you resolve such conflicts? Should you have a CONFIG.xxx and AUTOEXEC.xxx pair for each of your applications? It would be very inconvenient, because you have to overwrite the active AUTOEXEC.BAT and CONFIG.SYS files with these files and then reboot the system whenever you want to switch from one product family to another. Even if you automate the copying and rebooting processes it may not be appropriate on a public access workstation and provides a good excuse for patrons to fool around with your system.

It is much better to experiment with different settings that would satisfy all your applications even at the expense of some performance degradation in one or two of them. You need to find out the minimum free RAM requirement of your largest application, which product insists on a specific device name, and for which products device names are negotiable and set your one and only CONFIG.SYS and AUTOEXEC.BAT pair accordingly. Also change those application startup files that expect *some* device name as a parameter for their program. In the previous example Grolier was flexible in choosing any device name, but for some applications you must use the MSCDOOx filename, where *x* may be any number, but the first six characters are mandatory.

A typical boot-up process is shown by figure 8.4.

```
HIMEM: DOS XMS Driver, Version 2.60 - 04/05/90
XMS Specification Version 2.0
Copyright 1988-1990 Microsoft Corp.

Installed A20 handler number 1
64K High Memory Area is available.

QRAM 1.00
Copyright (c) 1989-1990 by Quarterdeck Office Systems
Serial number: 101-D1-3167-002476
Registered to: Jacso Peter

     High RAM created: 176K (B000-B7FF,CC00-EFFF)

** Hitachi CD-ROM device driver 'HITACHIA.SYS' Version 2.10 **
 (C) Copyright HITACHI,LTD. 1987-89.
  Device Name:    MSCD001
  Number of drives: 1

FASTOPEN installed

C>SET CDPATHD=E
MS-DOS Version 4.01
****      NYUGI, MSCDEX IS LOOOOOOOOOADING     **********
MSCDEX Version 2.10
Copyright (C) Microsoft Corp. 1986, 1987, 1988, 1989. All rights reserved.

     Drive E: = Driver AMDEKCD unit 0
```

Fig. 8.4. Typical boot-up process.

System Software Supplied by the CD-ROM Publisher

A very few CD-ROM publishers deliver not only their retrieval software and device drivers, but also the MSCDEX program. This may be convenient, unless their MSCDEX version is earlier than yours. If the date stamp of your file is higher than the one on the distribution diskette, you may have to overwrite the publisher's version of MSCDEX after the installation of this new application is over.

Occasionally, the database publisher also supplies you the core of DOS (disk operating system). It consists of three files: COMMAND.COM, IBMBIO.SYS, and IBMDOS.SYS (for MS-DOS the last two files are IO.SYS and MSDOS.SYS). These are the system files without which your system would not start working. You have these files already on your hard disk, or on a so-called startup diskette, if you have ever used your computer. The SYS files are hidden, so you may not see them when displaying the directory of the floppy diskette you received from the CD-ROM database publisher, but they may cause problems as discussed in the following section.

There is nothing wrong in booting your system from a floppy that includes the core of DOS if your workstation is dedicated to a single application that you start in the morning and leave running until the library or office is closed. But if you must use several CD-ROM databases on the same workstation (an increasingly common situation) then this prerequisite is hardly acceptable. You would have to reboot your system every time you wanted to change to another CD-ROM database.

You may install such application software to the hard disk; just make sure that you do not simply copy the content of the floppy to the hard disk as it may play havoc with your other existing applications. If you have a more recent version of DOS (or MSCDEX) than the one(s) on the floppy, the application will overwrite your more current version along with some other files that you used to start your system. Make sure that you have a copy of your system files on a floppy.

The following section introduces some tips and tricks that may help you in trouble-shooting and in making compromises when you use several databases on the same workstation. CD-ROM publishers are beginning to realize that their product may not be the only one used on a workstation, and they are attempting to make the installation and use of their product more considerate and less antisocial.

TIPS AND TRICKS

1. *Have a copy of CONFIG.SYS and AUTOEXEC.BAT files.* There is hardly anything more annoying than when your new application not only refuses to work, but also prevents incumbent and problem-free products from running due to changes in the CONFIG.SYS and AUTOEXEC.BAT files. *Before* you set out to install a new application, make a copy to a floppy diskette of your latest CONFIG.SYS and AUTOEXEC.BAT files that worked correctly. The simplest way is to copy them by replacing the file extension with a mnemonic as follows:

COPY AUTOEXEC.BAT AUTOEXEC.OK

COPY CONFIG.SYS CONFIG.OK

Using a simple text editor you may add remarks to remind you that applications ran without any problems with this pair of files. Thereafter you may let your new product start the installation procedure and rewrite these files. This way you are not interfering with the new application, and you see what it is going to do without inflicting any harm on incumbent applications. Following the installation print out both the current and the last correct pair of files. You will need these for comparison.

If the installation of a new application messed up these two files you can simply restore your original ones by issuing the following two commands. (If the mess is such that you cannot even boot your system from the hard disk then you need to boot from your back-up boot diskette.)

RENAME AUTOEXEC.OK *.BAT

RENAME CONFIG.OK *.SYS

2. *Test your new and old applications.* After you install your new application it is obvious that you test it by running it. Chances are that it will run, as the latest coming application has the power to rearrange your system environment as it pleases. A modest installation program, however, may just have appended some commands to your existing ones, and these may not have been appropriate. This is most likely the case when a newly installed application does not find enough space on the hard disk or in the memory. Check all your other applications to find out if you can start them up and use them as before. If you encounter some problems here, it is very likely that the new application caused the problem.

3. *Check your AUTOEXEC.BAT file.* Compare the printouts of the current AUTO-EXEC.BAT and the AUTOEXEC.OK files to find out where changes were made. Check very thoroughly, as every minor change may have importance. Increasing the buffer value parameter, for example, may take away too much RAM from your incumbent application. The change of the device name in the MSCDEX command may be in conflict with such names in the application startup files. A similar problem may be caused by using a DOS device identifier in the /L parameter of the MSCDEX command that is different from the one in the startup files of other applications.

Reset the modified parameters one by one to their original values and test all the applications again. If you reset the device name you must do so also in the CONFIG.SYS file and probably in the startup file of the application currently being installed.

If the installation program added a new directory to the beginning of your PATH statement, this may have kicked off another one at the end of the line, resulting in the "Bad command or file name" message. The list of the directories to be consulted by DOS when looking for a program name is stored as an environment variable, and its length is limited. You may need to enlarge this environment space (see your DOS manual) so that all the directories listed in the PATH statement can be stored.

4. *Check your CONFIG.SYS file.* Do the same thorough comparison between the CONFIG.SYS and CONFIG.OK files as recommended above. Check the value in the parameter of the BUFFER command. If it is higher than it was before set it back to its previous value. Check the FILES command. If its value is lower than or the same as it was, increase its value by 5 or 10. Check the device name parameter. It should always be the same as in the counterpart AUTO-EXEC.BAT file.

5. *Check the startup file of the new application.* If the installation software of your new application has offered you a choice to specify the drive and the subdirectory where you want to store the program and the parameter files, it is supposed to reflect these changes also in the automatically generated startup file. It was shown earlier that this may have been done by the CD-ROM publisher only half-heartedly, as in the case of the Compton's Encyclopedia. These glitches typically are corrected immediately when the publisher learns about them.

Check if the reference in the startup file to the drive and the subdirectory matches your choice. There may be more than one line that refers to the path to the software. Check if the software has indeed been installed where you requested, and then change every such reference according to your choice.

6. *Check your free RAM space.* A new application may require more RAM than your standard environment offers. If you have terminate-and-stay-resident programs automatically invoked from your AUTOEXEC.BAT file you may have to remove their automatic activation. Just add the letters "REM" in front of those commands to make them a remark instead of a command, and then you may easily restore them later if they prove not to be the culprit.

You may check the available RAM of your system by using the CHKDSK DOS command. In spite of its name, it advises you not only about the free disk space, but also about free RAM. If the free RAM area is still not enough, try to reduce the number of buffers both in the BUFFERS command and in the /M parameter to make more RAM available than in your standard environment. If all else fails and you still need some more RAM, include in your AUTOEXEC.BAT file the following command: STACKS=0,0. This under-documented command of DOS can release an additional 6K of RAM, which is automatically reserved to improve the speed of some internal operations.

7. *Check your free hard disk space*. Most CD-ROM programs clean up after themselves when you quit from them, by deleting all their temporary work files, which are not needed anymore. It may happen, however, that if you could not exit the application normally because of a power failure or the freezing of the system, these temporary files are still there occupying a lot of space on your hard disk. Some programs forget to clean up after themselves even if they have the chance and claim to do so. EBSCO gives you the message "Please wait, deleting files ..." when you quit, but it leaves a file of nearly 2 to 3 megabytes with the name CDROM.BUF on your hard disk, which not only is absolutely useless but also may prevent other applications from running due to lack of free disk space. Delete such files without hesitation. You may automate this procedure if you include the appropriate statement in the batch file (see figure 8.3) that launches the application.[2]

On other occasions a user may have left a few megabytes of downloaded records on your hard disk. Try to copy them or (at least temporarily) squeeze them with some special file compressors. It is also possible that your new application required so much space for installation that what is left free is not enough for other applications. Temporarily remove one of the least used files or directories.

8. *Have a simple boot diskette*. All the changes in the AUTOEXEC.BAT and CONFIG.SYS files take effect only after you reboot the system. These changes are delicate even if they seem to be minor. A typo not only may prevent the execution of the commands in these files but also may hang your system. But you cannot correct the error because you cannot get into the system, a "catch-22" situation. Always have a boot diskette that you may use if your modified CONFIG.SYS or AUTOEXEC.BAT files on the hard disk freeze your system. Never experiment with these files on your boot diskette.

9. *Check the version of MSCDEX*. It may happen that your version of MSCDEX lets your existing applications run happily, but the most recently acquired CD-ROM database requires a higher version than you have. It is also possible that your current version of MSCDEX was overwritten by an earlier one, or an earlier version was copied in a directory and the path in your AUTOEXEC.BAT file specifies this directory to call MSCDEX. Check if you have more versions of MSCDEX on your hard disk, and then verify if the AUTOEXEC.BAT file invokes the one with the most recent date stamp. Because the name of this file is the same irrespective of the version, you may have multiple MSCDEX programs only in different subdirectories; otherwise, the later installed MSCDEX program would overwrite the former one.

When MSCDEX is loaded it displays its version number, but the introductory screen with this information may disappear so fast that you cannot read it. Also, this may depend on the MSCDEX version itself. Just as the first edition of a printed publication does not explicitly indicate that it is the first edition, MSCDEX 1.x does not display the version number.

Your best bet to learn the version number of your MSCDEX program is to look at the date stamp of the file. Though the date stamp of your MSCDEX.EXE file in a directory display is indirectly indicative of the version you have, it is not straightforward because the same version may have been produced at a different time. Unfortunately, different distributors of MSCDEX may assign different version and release numbers to virtually identical MSCDEX programs. As a ballpark estimate, however, here are some dates for orientation:

Version 1.0	before 1988
Version 2.0	in 1988
Version 2.1	in 1989
Version 2.2	in 1991

10. *Test your hardware*. The above tips may help in pinpointing or solving problems encountered during or after the installation of a new product. Sometimes, however, problems seem to come out of the blue, and you do not know what may have triggered the problem. In such situations your hardware may need testing. It is possible that your connecting cables or interface cards are loose or that dust on the lenses or on the disk are preventing you from using your CD-ROM drive.

The easiest way to do a physical check-up on your hardware is to try to use another database to see if it is working. If another disk is readable, then wipe off the disk that was unreadable. Use a lint-free cloth and wipe across the tracks rather than in a circular fashion. Do not forget that you have to clean the down side of the disk, not the one with the label. If there are visible scratches on your disk you cannot repair it. The publisher is likely to replace it. Ask for a return merchandise authorization (RMA) number before returning the disk, and print the RMA on the package. This applies also to returning the CD-ROM drive if that is necessary.

If cleaning of the disk does not help, you may check the connection by making a directory of the disk in the CD-ROM drive. If you have MSCDEX loaded, then the DIR command of DOS will display the name of the files, their date, and their size on the CD. It will also tell you if it is not a disk in the High Sierra or ISO 9660 format. In either case it proves that the physical connections are okay.

If this test fails, check the selector switch at the back of the CD. Someone may have playfully turned it off. The manual of your CD-ROM drive tells you how this switch should be set, if it is available. If this does not help, check your cables to see if they are connected firmly. If the error persists, open the cover of your PC to see if the interface card sits firmly in the slot. Always disconnect the power before doing this and ground yourself by touching something metal before you reach for the interface card, as static electricity may harm it.

Removing dust from the lenses is not a simple task and is better left to experienced technicians. You may prevent the dusting of your lenses by buying a drive with automatic lens cleaning or, short of that, by using special cleaner disks such as the CD-ROM LC-1 from AudioSource. It has a built-in brush that the manufacturer claims safely sweeps the lenses in a few seconds.

11. *Use the application's own testing programs*. Some CD-ROM publishers include with their software one or more utility programs to test the hardware and software environment. OCLC has a nice suite of test programs in the system administration module of the CD450 software.

Wilson also provides a test program, and in addition to displaying diagnostics messages it will store some debugging information in a special file. You will have to use this program if you contact Wilson about a problem.

Other programs automatically display diagnostic information whenever you start the application. The startup procedure of IAC and Bowker databases shows a step-by-step diagnosis that may help to pinpoint where the problem lies.

12. *Use a product-independent testing software*. Your application may not have adequate testing procedures built into the startup process or one that you may activate separately. In this case you may consider buying a product-independent CD-ROM testing software package, such as CD Diagnostics from American Helix. It has a rather steep price of $70, but it is able to test features of the CD-ROM drive and the disk that product-specific testers cannot. CD Diagnostics checks the physical connections, the legibility of the disk, the compatibility of the drive, and its performance (access time, transfer rate, etc.).

13. *Call customer service*. If all the above efforts fail, call the customer service department of the device manufacturer or the CD-ROM publisher. The latter seems to be a much better

source for help. It is difficult to reach someone at the device manufacturer who is competent in the long-distance diagnosis of the problem. The dealer where you bought the drive may be appropriate for a loaner or for handling the return and replacement transaction, but is unlikely to be of help with application-oriented problems.

On the other hand, database publishers have accumulated lots of experience from desperate user calls and can guide you through some testing and draw your attention to some of the possible problems mentioned above. Bowker, for example, includes a lot of valuable and clearly explained advice for trouble-shooting in its newsletter and its user manuals and provides information about newly discovered glitches and incompatibility problems that could not make it into the manual.

In any case, have your computer next to you when you make the call because you will be requested to use it during the diagnosis. It helps a lot to have a printout of your AUTO-EXEC.BAT, CONFIG.SYS, and application startup files and to know the parameters of your configuration (drive identifiers, free RAM, hard disk space, type of monitor and video controller, brand and model number of CD-ROM drive, its interface card, and so on).

You may use the documentation received with your hardware to collect some of this information. Other data may be found using DOS; the CHKDSK command will tell you about your free RAM and hard disk space. Special PC diagnosis programs for $80 to $100 (Norton Utilities, PC Tools Deluxe, System Sleuth, Manifest) can provide excellent diagnostic information about the technical details of your configuration, the use of RAM, and so forth. CD-ROM drives and disks, however, cannot be tested with generic PC diagnostic programs. You need a special software package such as those discussed above. These utility programs very well may be worth the investment by reducing the downtime of your CD-ROM workstation and your agony in trouble-shooting.

These possible problems should not discourage you from CD-ROM technology. The same problems prevailed in the early days of PC applications in general. The more widespread the use of CD-ROM applications becomes, the wider the help resources will be. The very popular "Tips and Tricks" columns of *PC Magazine*, *PC Computing*, and *PC World* will cover more and more CD-ROM related information. Two excellent magazines of the CD-ROM industry (*CD-ROM Professional* and *CD-ROM Librarian*) have regular advisory columns where CD-ROM experts share their knowledge and experience with users, in addition to feature articles about installation anomalies. Back issues of *CD-ROM EndUser* also includes articles about installation and technical management problems of CD-ROM databases.

Electronic bulletin boards provide an appropriate forum for exchanging ideas and solving problems related to CD-ROM. You may post your problem on the bulletin board and someone is likely to provide an answer very soon. The promptness of these facilities is valuable in times of distress.

The more sophisticated CD-ROM applications become, the more important it is that you be able to evaluate and compare their capabilities as well as their requirements for resources and that you be able to optimize the installation and manage the eventual conflicts between CD-ROM applications and the system environment.

REFERENCES

1. Péter Jacsó. "Of Buffers and Cards." *CD-ROM EndUser* 1 (October 1989): 36-38.

2. Lee Lyttle. Personal communication, March 1991.

1

SOFTWARE
EVALUATION FORM

CRITERIA	WEIGHT	GRADE	SCORE	NOTES
INTERFACE				
Type of interface				
Level of interface				
Style of interface				
Help and tutorials				
Ergonomics				
Navigation ease				
SEARCH FEATURES				
Index browsing				
Cross-references				
Thesaurus browsing				
Posting information				
Term selection from index/thesaurus				
Lateral searching				
Hyperlink searching				
Truncation				
Masking				
Boolean operations				
Field qualification				
Proximity operations				
Positional operations				
Arithmetic operations				
Range searching				
Implicit operations				

SOFTWARE EVALUATION FORM (continued)

CRITERIA	WEIGHT	GRADE	SCORE	NOTES
SET HANDLING				
Number of sets				
Size of sets				
Domain specification				
Predefined sets				
Query log display				
Query modification				
Query re-execution				
Query saving				
Query listing and review				
SDI services				
Note taking				
Statistical information gathering				

CRITERIA	WEIGHT	GRADE	SCORE	NOTES
OUTPUT FEATURES				
Status display				
Automatic short-entry list				
Marking items for inclusion				
Built-in alternative formats				
User-defined alternative formats				
Specification of record layout				
Navigation within records				
Navigation between records				
Format switching and retention				
Marking items for output				
Sort options				
Downloading				

2

DATAWARE
EVALUATION FORM

CRITERIA	WEIGHT	GRADE	SCORE	NOTES
SCOPE				
Sources				
Document types				
Comprehensiveness				
Period coverage				
Language coverage				
Geographic coverage				
CONTENT				
Data elements				
Value-added information				
Number of index terms				
Length of item, abstract				
Title augmentation				
Citation style				
Informativeness				
Record structure				
QUALITY				
Authenticity, accuracy				
Controlled vocabulary				
Thesaurus				
Consistency				
Completeness				
Currency				

CRITERIA	WEIGHT	GRADE	SCORE	NOTES
ACCESSIBILITY				
Choice of access points				
Precision of access				
Reliability of access				
Ease of access				
Implicit access points				
DOCUMENTATION/USER SUPPORT				
User manual				
Accuracy				
Completeness				
Usability				
Reference card				
Keyboard template				
Vendor hot-line				
INSTALLATION				
Software delivery				
Destination drive				
Installation etiquette				
Startup job				
Set limiting				
Save limit				
Print limit				
Session time				
Inactivity logoff				
DOS-exit prevention				
Disk change				
TERMS				
Price alternatives				
Update frequency				
Local network use				
Remote access use				
Return policy				
Free online use				

4

HARDWARE EVALUATION FORM

CRITERIA	☑ or Value	WEIGHT	GRADE	SCORE	NOTES
FORMAT					
Front-loading					
Top-loading					
Internal					
External					
Full-height					
Half-height					
DRIVE					
Single					
Dual					
Triple					
Quadruple					
Daisy-chainable					
Jukebox					
INTERFACE CARD					
ISA					
MCA					
SCSI					
EISA					
Full-length					
Half-length					
8-bit					
16-bit					
SPEED					
Average latency					
Average seek					
Average access					
Transfer rate					
Cache memory					
OTHER					
MTBF					
Warranty					
Audio capability					
Vertical mounting					
Horizontal mounting					
Auto lens cleaning					
Dual door					

5

CD-ROM DIRECTORIES
AND CATALOGS

DIRECTORIES

ISBN/ISSN	TITLE		PUBLISHER	FREQUENCY / YEAR	PRICE
1-870889-17-7	The CD-ROM Directory 1991	in print	TFPL	1990	$89.95
	The CD-ROM Directory 1991	on disk	TFPL	1990	$149.95
1048-406x	CD-ROM Shoppers Guide		Helgerson Associates	1990	$12.95
0-929314-01-8	CD-ROM Sourcebook		Helgerson Associates	1990	$795.00
	CD-ROM Sourcedisc	on disk	Diversified Data Resources, Inc.	1989	$89.95
0-88736-587-6	CD-ROMs in Print, 1991	in print	Meckler	1991	$49.50
0-88736-732-1	CD-ROMs in Print, 1991	on disk	Meckler	1991	$175.00
0-8103-2944-1	Computer Readable Databases		Gale Research	1990	$165.00
0-444-01522-1	Directory of Portable Databases		Cuadra-Elsevier	1990	$85.00

CATALOGS

ISBN/ISSN	TITLE		PUBLISHER	FREQUENCY / YEAR	PRICE
0897-6139	Access Faxon		The Faxon Company	twice	$24.00
	Bureau of Electronic Publishing		The Bureau of Electronic Publishing	2-3 times	free
	CD-ROM Bibliodisc		Helgerson Associates		$99.00
	CD-ROM Catalogue & Reference		Future Office System, Ltd.	quarterly	free
	CD-ROM Handbook		EBSCO Industries, Inc.	irregular	free
	CD-ROM Inc. Catalog		CD-ROM, Inc.	irregular	free
	Updata CD-ROM Catalog		Updata Publications, Inc.	irregular	free

INDEX

Numeric data, 137
Numeric indexes, 135

OCLC-CD. *See* CD-450
OCLC-ERIC. *See* CD-450 ERIC
OCSI
  cross-references, 35
  installation, 185
  output, 61, 62, 67
  producer, 1, 4, 6, 7
  query handling, 57, 58
  records, 68, 73, 74
  searching, 52, 54
  set building, 55
  wildcarding, 41
OCSI-PAIS. *See also* PAIS
  accuracy, 136
  interface, 16(fig.)
  output, 68(fig.), 73(fig.), 74, 76
  pricing, 189
  producer, 4-6
  record structure, 129-30, 153
OnDisc ERIC. *See also* ERIC
  access points, 172, 200
  coverage, 100(fig.)
  searching, 43(fig.), 48(fig.)
One Source/Corporate, 84
Online/CD-ROM Conference, 219
Online Computer Systems, Inc. *See* OCSI
Operating systems, 207-8
OS/2. *See* Operating systems
Outline format, 65
Output, 60-81. *See also* Downloading
Overlapping window menus, 16
Oxford Textbook of Medicine, 88

PACS-L forum, 220-21
PAIS. *See also* OCSI-PAIS; SPIRS-PAIS
  coverage, 92, 109, 111
  format, 64-65
  indexing, 139, 142
  interface, 11
  output, 73, 129, 153
  pricing, 188
  retention policy, 190
  searching, 44
  terms of use, 191
  user aids, 180
Parsing, 28, 78. *See also* Indexing
PATH statement, 237
PC Anywhere, 191
PC-DOS. *See* Operating systems
PCX format, 77
Pediatrics database, 88
Period of coverage, 97-100. *See also* Retrospective
  coverage
Phethean, 224

Philips CD-ROM players, 215
  CM-50, 205
  CM100, 196
  CM221, 199
PhoneDISC USA, 113, 188, 194, 205
Phrase indexing, 30, 32
Physician Data Query, 88
Pioneer Disc Changer, 198, 204
Plug and play systems, 225
Pluralization, 41, 52
PolTox database, 160
Popup window menus, 16
Positional operators, 47-49, 53. *See also* Proximity
  operators
Postings
  double, 30
  field, 32
  record, 32
  term, 32
Precision, 45, 48-49, 165-68. *See also* Accuracy;
  False drops
Precoordinated descriptors, 48-49
Predefined sets, 56-57
Prefix qualification, 43-44
Prefixed indexing, 31
Pricing, 161, 186-89, 191-95, 204
Processors, 211-12. *See also* NEC
Producers (of datafiles and software), 5(fig.)
Programmer Library, 109
ProQuest. *See also* UMI
  indexing, 40(fig.), 43-44
  installation, 182, 184, 210, 212
  interface, 16(fig.)
  output, 21, 61, 62, 69, 74
  searching, 37, 40-42, 44-48, 51, 52, 53(fig.),
    55-58
  user aids, 17
Proximity operators, 45-48, 53. *See also* Positional
  operators
PsycLIT, 92(fig.), 158
Public Access Computer Systems forum. *See* PACS-L
  forum
Public Affairs Information Services, Inc. *See* PAIS
Public domain datafiles, 6
Public Libraries Association, 219
Publication date fields, 164-65, 168
Publisher indexes, 139
Publishers (of databases), 5(fig.)
Pull mode searching, 37
Pull-down window menus, 16
Punctuation marks, 52

Query. *See also* Searching
  logs, 57
  modification, 36-53, 57-58
  reexecution, 58
  saving, 58-59
  set building, 54-57
Quick reference cards, 175-76